But Will You Love Me Tomorrow?

ALSO BY EMILY SIEU LIEBOWITZ

National Park

But Will You Love Me Tomorrow?

AN ORAL HISTORY OF THE '60s GIRL GROUPS

LAURA FLAM and
EMILY SIEU LIEBOWITZ

hachette
BOOKS
New York

Hachette Books
Hachette Book Group
1290 Avenue of the Americas
New York, NY 10104
HachetteBooks.com
Twitter.com/HachetteBooks
Instagram.com/HachetteBooks

First Edition: September 2023

Published by Hachette Books, an imprint of Hachette Book Group, Inc. The Hachette Books name and logo are trademarks of the Hachette Book Group.

Library of Congress Cataloging-in-Publication Data
Names: Flam, Laura, compiler. | Liebowitz, Emily Sieu, compiler.
Title: But will you love me tomorrow?: an oral history of the '60s girl groups / [compiled by] Laura Flam and Emily Sieu Liebowitz.
Description: First edition. | New York, NY: Hachette Books, 2023. | Includes index.
Identifiers: LCCN 2023002123 | ISBN 9780306829772 (hardcover) | ISBN 9780306829789 (trade paperback) | ISBN 9780306829796 (ebook)
Subjects: LCSH: Girl groups (Musical groups)—History—20th century. | Popular music—1961–1970—History and criticism. | Women singers. | African American women singers. | Music and race—United States—History—20th century. | LCGFT: Oral histories.
Classification: LCC ML82 .B89 2023 | DDC 782.42164082—dc23/eng/20230124
LC record available at https://lccn.loc.gov/2023002123

ISBNs: 9780306829772 (hardcover); 9780306829796 (ebook)

Printed in the United States of America

LSC-C

Printing 1, 2023

Contents

PART 7
Motown Outgrows Detroit: 1967–Present

PART 8
Coming Back Together and Saying Goodbye: 1970–Present

For the women of the girl groups

Introduction

The songs sung by the girl groups need no introduction. Watch a movie, walk into a supermarket, or turn on the radio, and you will encounter one of their records. Maybe your heart leaps, maybe you crack a smile, and for three minutes, you recall the more tender parts of life. But what's the group's name? Who sings this song?

The girl group sound is a genre of rock and roll that got its start in the mid-fifties and carried on until the mid-sixties. This oral history presents an account of the people who sang, wrote, created, and popularized this generation-defining genre.

Just as now, when you hear "Chapel of Love," "He's a Rebel," or "Will You Love Me Tomorrow" and the groups are nameless, so, too, in their heyday were they treated as interchangeable and faceless—beautiful girls, to be switched around and replaced at the whims of managers, record producers, and songwriters.

The singers who voiced this music were just girls—some as young as twelve—and they had no expectation that their first forays into the music industry would propel them into the rest of their lives. The very youthfulness and innocence essential to the girl group sound also left these young women particularly vulnerable to be used, as women often are, to serve the purposes of the powerful.

When people discuss the song "Will You Love Me Tomorrow," from which we derived the title of this book, the women who sang it—Shirley Alston Reeves and her group The Shirelles—are rarely spoken of. Instead, we applaud the songwriters, such as Carole King and Gerry Goffin, and the producers, such as Luther Dixon. Granted, King and Goffin and Dixon are significant talents—but Shirley's performance, marked by its deftly applied vocal wavering, echoed the openness and rawness of the subject. The Shirelles voiced a song that became an anthem for a generation and for a nation coming into its own adulthood.

And yet The Shirelles, and maybe even the girl group sound itself, are at risk of erasure from the canon of pop music history. Maybe if they had lived in another era, the women of the girl groups would have been valued differently. But many of the young girls who started these groups were considered fleeting investments by the music industry that gave them remarkably shortened careers, and by a society that expected them to retire in order to have children and work closer to home.

Even when remembered, the genre as a whole is often dismissed. Some think of the songs as silly, frivolous—the first genre of popular music made to appeal to teenage girls. Many of those who have seen success post–girl groups have chosen to distance themselves from their early starts in this genre. When this music has been written about, the women appear in the shadows of producers like Phil Spector and Berry Gordy, who are frequent subjects of new books and documentaries. In many of those accounts, even the most famous women of the sound, such as Diana Ross or Ronnie Spector, are caricatures—vehicles used by men for their grander achievements. The women of the girl group sound don't often come up in conversations about feminism, but their influence in culture and music continues through to today. The women of the girl groups should be celebrated, their contributions acknowledged.

Hundreds of notable girl groups recorded during the girl group era, and we wish we could cover every one. If you are interested in an encyclopedia of the groups, please check out our friend John Clemente's project, *Girl Groups: Fabulous Females Who Rocked the World*, an incredible and meticulous listing of groups of the era.

A few things to keep in mind while reading this book: This is an oral history based on over a hundred interviews that we did between 2019 and 2022. Only in rare cases when someone was unavailable have we used interviews from other sources. The individuals in this book are recalling their own personal histories and people remember things differently; each speaker represents only their own perspective. We are humbled by the stories entrusted to us, and we have not included stories that were passed along in confidence or secondhand accounts of events that are not public knowledge. When needed for clarification, interviews have been edited. We did not translate dollar amounts to today's value; any number represents the financial value at the time and as the speaker remembers it.

This oral history is a compilation of the stories we have access to and people shared only what they felt comfortable disclosing. It is constructed from what was told to us as the people we are, by the people who lived it, and it represents only a small portion of those people's lives. This book recounts the memories of many Black women, who took the time to teach us about the important role they played desegregating pop music and culture—the girl group sound was once described to us as the "sweetness" brought in to make rock and roll more palatable to a white middle-class audience. We would like to stress to the reader that *every* voice is an individual person with a larger story and encourage everyone to read the available autobiographies of the figures involved. We want to acknowledge our own perspectives and limitations—we are two women of Jewish descent, one white and one white and Vietnamese.

We have been attending doo-wop shows for years and wrote this book not only because we love this music but also because we think this history is important and necessary. We hope others will lend their own skill and perspective to another telling of this history, because it, like the women, is an infinite source of knowledge and inspiration.

PART 1

The Beginnings of the Girl Group Sound

The 1950s

CHAPTER 1

Singing on the Corner and Growing Up with Music in the Air

The Chantels and The Bobbettes

EMMA POUGHT, The Bobbettes: They would run us out of the hallways, because we were always in there trying to get the echo. One time a man gave us six cents. He gave us the six cents to get out of the hallway—we were making so much noise.

BROOKS ARTHUR, sound engineer: Different doo-wop groups singing on different corners, street corners—all that stuff that you hear, it was actually true.

JEFF BARRY, songwriter: Doo-wop is what you made when you didn't have money for instruments.

MELANIE MINTZ, writer: My friends in Brooklyn were standing on the street corner making harmony—I mean, *literally*. Now, they were all boys because none of us girls were interested. We didn't necessarily think we had a voice.

EMMA POUGHT, The Bobbettes: We lived in the projects and what it was is that we had little boyfriends and they were called The Ss—the letter *S*. And for a while, we called ourselves The Bs, but it was only because we all lived in the same area. Then, we named ourselves The Harlem Queens.

TRUDY McCARTNEY, The Clickettes: I was in my own world, because they were on the street corner and I was upstairs at my window looking out and harmonizing with them. It was mostly guys. On my block, I had The Chords that sang "Sh-Boom."

BARBARA ENGLISH, The Clickettes: My aunt would make me sing for all of her friends at their card parties. She would stand me in the corner and make me sing a song, then she'd take up a collection and buy me a dress the next day or something. I would sing a spiritual song at the top of my lungs and with my eyes closed, [*singing*] "*Lord make a way somehow*." And she would go, "Sing, baby, sing!"

JEAN BOULDIN, The Clickettes: On Eighth Avenue you could always hear some group on the corner—guys doing doo-wops and things like that. There was always music around, always music in my house.

ARLENE SMITH, The Chantels: I really didn't think about it. I had been listening to Shirley Gunter and Etta James and a lot of West Coast people. My peers were getting together and singing, but I never really wanted to sing girl songs and I never wanted that typical girl sound . . . my thing wasn't cutesy. I wanted to go up there—and I was competitive. I'd go to these musical centers and I'd hear these guys, they were just throwing down—singing and the harmonies were so rich and full. That's the sound that I wanted.

LOIS POWELL, The Chantels: It was Arlene's idea, and I think that was based on the fact that we lived in an area of the Bronx where a lot of the guys, like the guys who came before us . . . it was a couple of Bronx groups that . . . The guys who did "Sh-Boom," originally, they were The Chords. I had a lot of boy cousins and one of them sang in a group on the corner where our church was, and we would stand there and listen to them.

ARLENE SMITH, The Chantels: My thing was, "The guys are not the only ones that can do this," and I thought that we could be every bit as good as the guy groups.

LOIS POWELL, The Chantels: And then we decided they shouldn't have carte blanche with this. We can sing. We know we can sing because we're in the choir. And out of that was Arlene's idea—that if these guys could do that, then so can we. That's when she started to form this group.

BOBBY JAY, disc jockey: The Chantels opened the door for all the subsequent female groups. Every group that followed them wanted to be The Chantels. They opened the floodgates.

LOIS POWELL, The Chantels: Oh, it was actually a good experience for me to grow up in the Bronx in the fifties. Everybody between the block that I lived on and the church that I went to—actually, the church where The Chantels got formed—knew me. Most of the neighbors had children who took piano lessons at my house because my aunt was a piano teacher. So, most of the adults knew me, and it was like a family thing. You know, they knew us, we knew them, it was very safe, and we knew that eyes were on us between home and where we had to go.

And then, when I was twelve, I moved out of the neighborhood and had experienced my first—what they call blockbusting. My mother had bought a house, and the house . . . the block was fully integrated when we got there, and by the time—maybe a year and a half to two years—and it was totally a Black block. So, that was very shocking to me because I had never experienced anything like that. And it kinda put a damper on things for me. But while we were there, the people who were there weren't very nice—they were gracious, but they ran. I don't know what that was about, but they did run away from the neighborhood.

When I was in elementary school, all of the Black kids, we were in the majority. There were maybe two or three actually white kids in my class of forty-four and maybe about three Hispanics. Then when I got to high school, there was me and maybe three other girls, and the rest were all white. So, that was totally different.

That was the point where I realized that Black people weren't the only ones discriminated against. The German girls hated the Italian girls, they didn't like the Irish girls. I'm thinking, like, *Really?* I had no clue. It was like, "Oh, she's German. Don't be her friend." And, "Oh, she's Italian. They're terrible," and all this stuff, and I'm just thinking, *Wow, I thought they just hated us.*

SONIA GORING WILSON, The Chantels: We attended Catholic church and school and we were influenced by the Gregorian chant.

LOIS POWELL, The Chantels: I had stayed in my church choir, and at that point, Arlene Smith was beginning to form the group that would become The Chantels. In that group we knew harmonies and we knew how jazz singers kind of put across their songs. And so because of that, and because we had that firm background in the Catholic Church . . . ask us to sing something gospel—we can't do it. Because that's not who we are and that's not how we came up singing. But combined with all of the other things that we knew, we kind of kept the sweetness of the choir, and that's why we sing the way we do.

JUDY CRAIG, The Chiffons: What was so great about them was they almost sang opera. Their range was *way* up there.

LOIS POWELL, The Chantels: People say we sound like angels.

GLORIA JONES, The Blossoms: The Chantels sang high—I mean *really high*. 'Cause we sang one of their songs one night and I thought my nose was going to bleed.

LOIS POWELL, The Chantels: It was Jackie and Sonia who called me and said, "We're thinking about a name for the group and I don't know." They wanted something unique and we liked the name of a school that they played in basketball, Saint Frances de Chantal. We liked their name and they couldn't figure out what to do with it, and then I said, "Well, it's French and it's a nice flair." I know *chanteuse* in French is "singer" and "to sing" is *chanter*. And we played around with that, and then somebody said, "Oh, well Saint Frances de Chantal . . . Chantel . . . Chantel." And then they said, "*Oh, Chantel!*" Somebody said it and it sounded right. And so we said, "Okay, we'll be The Chantels."

We started going around and doing talent shows in the public high schools. We would win. And then, after church, we'd go into the city just to roller-skate or do something. But we would always sing on the train. The subway was different than what it is today—they would have that little alcove where people could stand in between cars. A lot of times that's where we'd stand and sing. And then people would come and go and they would, you know, peep their heads to look in, see where the sound was coming from. So we built audiences that way.

*

JOEY DEE, Joey Dee and the Starliters: I say The Bobbettes were probably the first ones, you know, "Mr. Lee."

ARLENE SMITH, The Chantels: We and The Bobbettes came out at the same time. We were like a day away from each other.

ARTIE RIPP, music executive: The Bobbettes were completely different. Remember, if you listen to "Mr. Lee," it's an up-tempo dance record. The Chantels didn't make up-tempo dance records, really. They made records about heartache, love lost. The Bobbettes didn't do that.

EMMA POUGHT, The Bobbettes: It was in 1956. At the time, two of us were in elementary school, that was Jannie and Reather. Jannie is my sister. Laura, Helen, and myself were in junior high school. We started writing little songs and rhyming things, just playing around, singing on the corners and in the hallways.

Our manager's name was Mr. Dailey, James Arthur Dailey, and he got interested because we were so young. Everybody wanted us because we was young, you know what I'm saying? Just kids playing around. We ended up going to a show called *Star Time*, and we performed on there twice. The second time we performed our manager got a phone call from Atlantic Records. So we ended up going down for an interview with Jerry Wexler and Ahmet Ertegun—they were the head kids of Atlantic Records. And we went down there and we thought it was just having fun, really; we had never thought of it as a job, *never*.

They told us, "Well, what do you girls do and what you interested in?" And we sang three songs that were actual songs, because we wrote songs every day. None of us are musicians—never trained—we would write those songs and sing them a cappella.

They were interested; they said, "What else do you have?" And we said, "Well, we got this gimmick that we do . . . we made up a joke about a teacher." That teacher was Reather and Jannie's teacher in elementary school, his name was Mr. Lee.

REATHER DIXON, The Bobbettes: He had these thick horn-rimmed glasses; we said he was four-eyed.

EMMA POUGHT, The Bobbettes: And Mr. Lee was what you call a very strict teacher. He wasn't a bad teacher—he was a good teacher, but it was that he didn't take any mess, you know what I'm saying? This is the original words, "I met my teacher / his name is Mr. Lee / he's the four-eyedest teacher / that you ever did see."

We sang that little part, and then Ahmet Ertegun, he was very, very excited. He said, "Oh, that's cute. That's cute. Well, you know what you do? Take that little verse, that little thing that you have, and you go home and you write a song about it." And he said, "This time, make him your lover boy." And we started laughing because we were just kids then. What lover boy? Nobody want to write a lover boy song about our teacher. We went and we sat down and played around and we started, "I met my sweetie / his name is Mr. Lee / the handsomest sweetie / you ever did see."

We were rehearsing it down at Mr. Dailey's house and we were singing it, [*singing*] "*A-one, two, three.*" Mr. Dailey had parrots in his house, big birds, and one of them could talk—one of them just made a lot of noise all the time. And we didn't like the birds, either. We was singing that song and we got to that part, [*singing*] "*One, two, three, look at Mr. Lee,*" and that bird shouted, "Hey!" Oh God, [*laughing*] and Reather, being the clown, she kept on doing it. So, the guy that was working with us, training with us, said, "Oh, keep that in there! Keep that in there." When we got down to Atlantic, and we got to that song and sang that, they were overwhelmed with that one for some reason. We had a lot of songs that were, to me, much better than "Mr. Lee," but they liked that because it was commercial.

LAURA WEBB, The Bobbettes: It was Ahmet and Jerry who believed in us. He's the one who really pushed us to write our own material.

Because we had no musical training, we wrote what was in our hearts. Sometimes in the studio, we had to hum to the musicians so they would understand how we thought a certain part of the arrangement should be.

EMMA POUGHT, The Bobbettes: We did the double vocal on it because at that time our voices was not strong enough for what they actually wanted for that particular song. So, what we used to do, we had to look at each other. Reather would stand in front of me, we'd sing looking at each other's lips. I hated that. We had to do it that way onstage and everything, she's spitting on me and I'm spitting on her, because when you singing you spitting—saliva is coming out of your mouth.

*

ARLENE SMITH, The Chantels: Frankie Lymon was a major influence. I guess I identified with the sound and he was just thirteen. To me, that was just amazing. Prior to that, I was listening to Tony Bennett and Nat King Cole. All of these people were adults. Here was this kid who made a record. I wasn't much older.

LOIS POWELL, The Chantels: We went to the city because we wanted to go to some show.

JACKIE LANDRY, The Chantels: We were all dressed alike, white blouses with aqua skirts and bucks, we had taken the train downtown.

ARLENE SMITH, The Chantels: [DJ] Alan Freed mentioned that Frankie lived on 160-something Street on the West Side. We got a little group together and we went around the block. I guess we were stalking him, but we were looking to see if we could see him or his family. We met some people that were related to him, and then they mentioned that Richard Barrett was his manager, and he was with The Valentines.

LOIS POWELL, The Chantels: I saw three of The Valentines. They were still in their uniforms because they were on that show, and so I told the girls, "Ooh, there's The Valentines!"

RICHARD BARRETT, producer: They saw me and said, "Hey, The Valentines!" And they came running down the stairs. They said, "We sing."

LOIS POWELL, The Chantels: So, I don't even know if Renée, who was the youngest in the group, knew who The Valentines were, but I did. I had an older cousin who listened to their music on the Black stations—I wasn't allowed to in my house. I could only listen to either classical or [the radio show] *Make Believe Ballroom*. So, on the sly, I would listen to these other things on my little radio in my room.

ARLENE SMITH, The Chantels: So we surrounded Richard. "We have a group, we want you to hear what we sound like, and blah, blah, blah."

LOIS POWELL, The Chantels: "Are you all sisters? How come you're dressed alike?" and we said, "Well, because we sing." And so, he said, "Yeah, well, sing something."

ARLENE SMITH, The Chantels: So we wound up singing "The Plea" a cappella for him. And he just stood there with his mouth open.

RENÉE MINUS WHITE, The Chantels: And we hit "He's Gone" in pitch and in harmony. It was a good song written by Arlene Smith that started with the group singing, "*Gone, gone, gone, gone.*"

RICHARD BARRETT, producer: The girls were cute and everything, but when they started singing . . . WOW! I heard this sound that I was accustomed to in church, this angelic sound. They were all Catholic girls and I thought that it would be really good to put a sound like that in rock and roll.

LOIS POWELL, The Chantels: He said, "Yeah, I think I could do something for you all," and we said, "Mm-hmm . . . sure." And, he said, "Well, I didn't lie to Frankie Lymon," so we said, "No . . ." We knew that he discovered Frankie.

RENÉE MINUS WHITE, The Chantels: On the spot, Barrett offered to be our manager and exchanged telephone numbers with Arlene,

Jackie, and Lois. Mr. Barrett told us he would make us stars. We all walked away on cloud nine for the rest of the day.

LOIS POWELL, The Chantels: He took Arlene's phone number and her address. He said that he would call. And it seemed like months went by that we didn't hear from him—it wasn't, but that's what it seemed like to us. He did call, and we had a meeting at Arlene's house. He said that he would rehearse us, and then he would take us to George Goldner.

ARLENE SMITH, The Chantels: And we sang "The Plea" for George Goldner, and George Goldner had a contract right in his drawer and pulled it out. I mean, we wouldn't sign it unless our parents got involved with it.

RENÉE MINUS WHITE, The Chantels: "He's Gone" was one of our first recordings, then of course "Maybe."

ARLENE SMITH, The Chantels: The song was given to me on a 78 demonstration record. It just rambled *on and on and on and on and on and on*. I didn't care for what was written. It was like a gospel song. I wrote the whole centerpiece. It was a collaboration. Richard added that beautiful piano thing and that instrumentation to it.

JEFF BARRY, songwriter: "Maybe if I cried every night." Well, geez, give me a break . . . that was great.

ARLENE SMITH, The Chantels: I had a tendency to lean toward all the songs that had some kind of heartbreak or some kind of sadness . . . there was always a beauty in the sadness.

EMMA POUGHT, The Bobbettes: At that time, you didn't have the technology you have now, where you can splice records and punch it in and punch it out, you know what I'm saying? You couldn't do that. You had to sing the song all the way through—every recording was all the way through. And then what they would do is they would pick the best take, as they call it. We sang "Mr. Lee" twenty-three times, and that was in 1956. I'll never forget it because it was the worst night. We got home at, like, two o'clock in the morning.

LOIS POWELL, The Chantels: Now, the story with "Maybe" is that when we were in the studio we had fifty-two takes before our manager said, "Okay, that's the record."

By that time, Arlene was in tears because it was, "Nope, that's not what I want," . . . "Nope, I don't like that sound," . . . "Nope, sing it," . . . "I want to hear it," . . . or a guitar string broke, or somebody coughed, or somebody . . . whatever the reason we did fifty-two takes for that song. By that time I didn't care if I never sang that song ever again. But a lot of people say, "How did you find . . . how at that age could you sing a song of such angst and such?"

ARLENE SMITH, The Chantels: I was singing about the kind of love I didn't know. . . . I loved my parents.

*

EMMA POUGHT, The Bobbettes: Six months later, which is in June of '57, the reason I can't forget it is because I graduated from junior high school, and it was a Friday. I begged my mother for a pair of high-heel shoes. At the time we were so young, you didn't wear them. I'm on 125th Street and I'm walking down—I had gone there to take a picture for my graduation and there was a record store there called Bobby's Record Shack, right on Eighth Avenue and 125th. What he used to do is he used to play new records over the loudspeaker. I didn't even know that record was out because I forgot all about it. So I'm walking down the street and all of a sudden I hear this song. I said, "Yeah, that sounds like that music that we made." And then I heard my voice—"*One, two, three*," that's me saying that—you know, that "*One, two, three*" loud as hell, excuse my language. So I stopped and I said, "Oh God, that's us!" I remember taking the shoes off because it was hurting so bad. I put the shoes in my hand, and I was running for the bus. I got the bus and got back to my house.

I'm ready to tell my mother, "I heard the record! I heard the record!" But when I got in the house, by that time, other people had heard the record because there was a DJ called Dr. Jive (his name was

Tommy Smalls) and he was playing it. They said The Bobbettes . . . by that time we had changed our name to The Bobbettes because they didn't want The Harlem Queens, they didn't want that. Anyway, I was really upset because I said, "Damn, I'm trying to tell you about the record and everybody already know about the record." But let me tell you, that was on, I graduated on a Friday, but next Friday we were in the Apollo Theater. That's how fast it went.

REATHER DIXON, The Bobbettes: I remember when Mr. Lee heard the finished song of "Mr. Lee" for the first time. He was ecstatic.

EMMA POUGHT, The Bobbettes: But they always say the wrong thing—the way they say, "Oh, they hated him." That's not true—we didn't hate him.

REATHER DIXON, The Bobbettes: He called Jannie and me out of our class to make sure it was the same song we had sung for him a couple of months before—when it was derogatory about him. He said he just wanted to make sure it was the same song, because he thought someone had stolen our song.

EMMA POUGHT, The Bobbettes: Oh, he was elated. He bought cases of the record and was giving it out. And we went back to the school and did a benefit for him. He was there and they had the DJ from 1010 WINS, Murray the K. He came and Mr. Lee took a lot of pictures as evidence.

CHAPTER 2

Learning the Show Business Ropes

The Clickettes and The Hearts

BARBARA ENGLISH, The Clickettes: I had lyrics and, you know, ideas when I met The Clickettes. I composed my first little jingle or song when I was about four and a half . . . it was a thing. 1957 when we moved to New York, that's when I really got into music. I had maybe two or three songs that I had penned, you know, but my first, I wrote "A Lover's Prayer."

SYLVIA HAMMOND, The Clickettes: Before I met Barbara, Trudy and I, we were in Yorkville Vocational High School.

BARBARA ENGLISH, The Clickettes: And in Yorkville Vocational there was 999 groups. No matter where you went, there was a group of girls—three to six—singing somewhere. There was music in the bathrooms, music from period to period—you go walking up the stairwell and there's a group singing.

SYLVIA HAMMOND, The Clickettes: I was just singing with people in the hallway until I met Trudy. I'd come up and hear somebody just singing lead and whatnot, and I'd just join in.

TRUDY McCARTNEY, The Clickettes: We'd sing in the hallways. I'm seeing it now . . . we would sing on the stairway, we'd go up on the stairway, going back to our classes. We'd harmonize these beautiful harmonies.

BARBARA ENGLISH, The Clickettes: There was a group standing on the stoop during recess and they were singing. I went to them and said, "You know, I have this song that I wrote, I want you to help me find the background for it." It was Sylvia's group—I don't remember the name—and they said, "Okay, well, sing it." And I started with my "Lover's Prayer" song and Sylvia said, "Okay, I think we've got a group."

I had that plan, you know, it was kind of sneaky of me. [*laughing*] Both of them quit the group they were with and started one with me because of my, I guess, my voice and the song. That was the beginning of The Clickettes. Well, that means we only had three. So we said, "We need another girl in the group." You know, we rehearsed all the time in the bathrooms at school, right? "So my sister sings," Trudy said. "And she's in the Bronx." And we got together with Charlotte and *bam!* We were The Bouquets. Trudy and Charlotte knew The Chantels. They grew up together in the same neighborhood.

TRUDY McCARTNEY, The Clickettes: My sister's best friend was in The Chantels. So The Chantels' Jackie Landry, we all grew up—in fact, her brother was my first boyfriend.

BARBARA ENGLISH, The Clickettes: The Chantels were huge at the time, and so was Little Anthony and the Imperials, Richard Barrett had just, you know, finished with The Teenagers, with Frankie Lymon.

We were in the elevator—I don't know if you're familiar with the Ed Sullivan building? Well, you know, it would be full of hopefuls, and we were going up the elevator—we would ride the elevator up and down to sing, hoping we'd run into a manager. We were searching, hoping to be discovered and we were singing on the elevator and Richard Barrett heard us. The elevators were old elevators then—they were the ones with those wire doors, those metal doors, and you could peep through. He ran out of the room, out of the rehearsal room, and asked us to come in.

We sang for him and that's when he decided he's going to try to do something with us. So he decided to give us to his road manager, Gordon King. He gave us to him, and he didn't know what he was doing.

There were many, many record labels and publishers in 1650 Broadway at the time, and he would go up and he would stay up there for hours. Gordon would leave us in the lobby, you know, waiting. So hence his demise, because that's where Zell saw us waiting for him on a very cold, cold evening, huddled in that lobby.

SYLVIA HAMMOND, The Clickettes: We were just singing and harmonizing a little bit in the lobby where the people was going in and out of that building. And that's how Zell Sanders came along and asked if we were a group.

BARBARA ENGLISH, The Clickettes: Zell came down from one of the offices and she said, "Oh, you look like a group."

"Yes, ma'am, yes, we are."

She said, "Can you hum for me? Come into the station wagon." People had station wagons then. "Come and take a ride with me and hum for me a little bit." So she put us all in this station wagon and drove a couple of blocks around and we started to sing and that's how we became property of Zell. Somehow she bought the demo from Gordon King and then signed us. I don't even think we ever signed a contract. That's how we met Zell Sanders and that's how we lost Gordon King.

Our success and our venture was like a flash. We were one day on the bus on First Avenue going to school, the next day it seemed that we were on the Apollo stage. When we met Zell, we called ourselves The Bouquets, which I thought was so cute; still do. So she decided to put us on her daughter Johnnie Louise's Dice Records. Because dice clicked when you threw them, she decided to call us The Clickettes. Everybody was an "ette" at that time. [*laughing*] It's a trend—Ikettes, Bobbettes, Wilsonettes—Wilsonettes were the background singers for Jackie Wilson. You see? You follow a trend? So we became The Clickettes.

LOUISE MURRAY, The Hearts, The Jaynetts: Zell was taking us to different places. And then all of a sudden, when she started making money with us—that's when she changed her name to Ms. Sanders.

TRUDY McCARTNEY, The Clickettes: Zell was like . . . she was a correction officer. So she was . . . that's just honest [*laughing*] . . . and then she was big and tall and masculine, you know.

REX GARVIN, The Hearts: She was a store detective and she used to carry this gun around. She was a big woman and very threatening.

JEAN BOULDIN, The Clickettes: Zell, she was like a drill sergeant. She was very strict as far as, you know, performing, and she whipped us in shape. She would make sure that we dressed nicely, that our diction was perfect. Always a thing about not eating your words when you sing.

LOUISE MURRAY, The Hearts, The Jaynetts: If you're late, she'd charge you. If you're late, and I was always late because I didn't want to go. Listen, when we sang, we had to really be in formation. Formation was her thing. Make sure you're in formation. But Ms. Sanders, she was a security guard. She was so strict, I thought she was a policewoman. And she was always bouncing when we'd sing, *boom, boom!* And she was heavy and *boom, boom, boom!*

TRUDY McCARTNEY, The Clickettes: She would make us pay, like, fines. If you were late—a fine; if your slip was hanging—a fine. No pins in the clothes, of course. I don't know where that came from, but somebody must have had some pins somewhere because that was brought up.

My parents did a lot for the group. You know, my mother used to make our outfits. I have pictures when we were at the Apollo. We wore those dresses, white dresses. And then she made us green net overskirts to go over it. They used to have overskirts back in the day. That was our little outfit.

BARBARA ENGLISH, The Clickettes: A white PK Simplicity pattern dress and a little green fishnet. The first show we would wear the tutu, the second show we wouldn't wear the tutu. We had no clothes and Zell wasn't doing right at the time.

LOUISE MURRAY, The Hearts, The Jaynetts: We did the Apollo for a week, that's when I really didn't like the clothes. The original Hearts' costumes had that little star on the side. I wanted that star off of there so bad, and I couldn't take it off because it was made onto the dress, with argyle socks on . . . oh my goodness . . . funny-looking argyle socks—it was those socks! [*laughing*] And I would always complain about the clothes, and the dresses, and skirts and blouses, I never liked to dress like that. I was too fresh. I was too grown. I was with a man. I was too grown. When I was fourteen, the guy was twenty-four. I wanted to dress the way *I* wanted to dress. I'm telling you, with mini clothes. That's how I was. That's how I liked to dress. So I guess I was getting on her nerves about that, I don't know.

TRUDY McCARTNEY, The Clickettes: Our first recording was coming out. We had a big party. We were walking from my house to the party and somebody threw some eggs down. Egg went all over this outfit that my mother just finished making for us to go to this party and we had to go back home. My mother had to wash it and iron it. Oh, you know, she got it together, though. We went back to the party, I said, "What—were they waiting for us?" *And* the dresses were white.

*

LOUISE MURRAY, The Hearts, The Jaynetts: All of us, The Hearts, the *original* Hearts, we all sat there and wrote "Lonely Nights." We aren't listed as writers for that song . . . nope, nope. Zell is. She took over everything, *everything*. People say, "How much did you make?" And I was too embarrassed to tell people how much I made. So I said, "Oh, she's cheating us. She's a thief." Most of the promoters around then were thieves in those days, and they still are. After we did "Lonely Nights," that's when she bought the house. And I said, *Oh, that's our money. That's our house, really.*

And then after that, she put me out the group because I wouldn't listen and I wouldn't come to rehearsal. So she put me out. We were together about almost two years. So the girls, they said, "Well, if Louise is not in the group, we're not going to sing." That's how we broke up. I've never seen those girls again in life. I tried to find those girls for the longest years, and I've never found them. Oh, I loved those girls. Oh, we had so much fun. So much fun.

CHAPTER 3

Living the Girl Group Dream

The Shirelles

SHIRLEY ALSTON REEVES, The Shirelles: Beverly and myself were neighbors and good friends. She wanted to start a little group because, back then, everybody was doing their little street corner harmony. The two of us tried it and it was just going to be the two of us, but we couldn't get the harmony. We needed a couple of other voices, so we said, "Let's ask our other friend." Her name was Addie—she hated her name, so we ended up nicknaming her Micki. She used to make these little noises onstage all the time, so we called her Mickey Mouse. Doris would do the heavy stuff—her father was a preacher, but he finally agreed to let her sing. It just came together.

BEVERLY LEE, The Shirelles: We all knew each other one way or another since we were young. In grade school, I went to Sunday school with Micki, and later on with Shirley—church. But we all officially met in junior high school. When we got to Passaic High, we were fooling around in gym, two of us one day, and a teacher passed by and said, "There's going to be a show, do this show or fail gym." Quite naturally we opted to do the show.

SHIRLEY ALSTON REEVES, The Shirelles: Of course, we had never been on any stage anywhere. We said, "Okay, we'll do it." Everybody started getting crazy toward the time. "What are we going to wear?" We decided to buy some black skirts and we bought some white nylon blouses; they had the tuxedo pleats in the front and little rhinestone buttons. Before we got there, we decided we wanted to sing something that we made up—our own stuff—we didn't want to do anyone's material. We got together and were sitting around deciding what to write a song about. I said, "Everybody just pick a day in the week and sing a line." Someone said, "Like what?" I said, [*singing*] "*I met him on a Sunday*." Then Micki continued, [*singing*] "*And I missed him on Monday*." Each girl started something. We wrote it down and put the "do-ron, do-ron's" to it.

BEVERLY LEE, The Shirelles: We wrote "I Met Him on a Sunday," at my apartment at the time, 11 Aspen Place in Passaic, New Jersey. Well, we each took a line, we started out with a hand clap, and then, [*singing*] "*Do-ronde ronde ronde pa pa, Do-ronde ronde ronde pa pa, Do-ron de ronde ronde pa pa doo ooo oo*." That was in harmony. Not saying who was going to do what, one started [*singing*] "*I met him on a Sunday*," the next [*singing*] "*I missed him on Monday*," next [*singing*] "*Well, I found him on a Tuesday*," I said [*singing*] "*I dated him on a Wednesday*," then [*singing*] "*I kissed him on a Thursday*," and [*singing*] "*He didn't come Friday*," and [*singing*] "*When he showed up Saturday*," and [*singing*] "*I said bye, bye, baby*," then [*singing*] "*do-ronde doo day*." . . . But it was all a front about your first date and your first kiss.

SHIRLEY ALSTON REEVES, The Shirelles: We sang that song and took our little bows, and did they thunder! We got a standing ovation. We were like "What?! You're kidding!" We were so tickled.

BEVERLY LEE, The Shirelles: The kids went *berserk*! We didn't know at the time there was a classmate by the name of Mary Jane Greenberg in the auditorium. Then she approached us daily . . . could her mother listen to our song? Her mother had a record company. . . . We didn't know what she was talking about, we knew nothing about show business.

SHIRLEY ALSTON REEVES, The Shirelles: When Mary Jane Greenberg came running up there and asked us to sing for her mom, we said, "Wow! What's going on? Your mom owns a record company? What's the name of the record company?" She said, "Tiara." Our faces went blank—no one ever heard of Tiara. She had one male artist on her label, his name was Lou Conetta. I never forgot him, because that was it. We met him, we saw him, and then our record hit the charts and we didn't see him anymore. She focused on our group.

FLORENCE GREENBERG, music executive: The Shirelles were my daughter's classmates at Passaic High School here in New Jersey. The girls would sing at all the class plays. Mary Jane used to bother them and tell them, "My mother is going into the record business, and she'd love to hear you sing."

SHIRLEY ALSTON REEVES, The Shirelles: She kept telling us to come sing for her mom, and we would dodge this girl—we would go a different way home from school.

BEVERLY LEE, The Shirelles: We got tired of her chasing us. We would separate sometimes, say, "Here comes Mary Jane!"

SHIRLEY ALSTON REEVES, The Shirelles: One day I said, "Look, let's go and see what it's all about. The girl keeps coming after us. It's not nice. Let's just see. It can't hurt." We agreed and made a date and went to her mom's house. As we rode up there, we said, "Hmm, nice neighborhood." When we got to the house, we said, "Hmm, nice house." I can remember the house because I always thought of a gingerbread house and the way it looked, but this was a big gingerbread house.

We sang in the middle of the living room. One of the girls said, "You start it." . . . "No, you start it." We were embarrassed to be standing there singing in front of the woman and her son. Her son was a music major, and his name was Stanley Greenberg. He was blind. That's who she wanted us for. She wanted us for a project for him to work on.

STANLEY GREENBERG, producer: Well, my mother, um, she believed for a blind child, music would be an ideal career.

ARTIE RIPP, music executive: Stanley was a kindhearted, talented young man. And he was the motive of why she went into the music business. Because Stanley was talented and she wanted Stanley to be something other than a blind young man.

SHIRLEY ALSTON REEVES, The Shirelles: She owned a very small company that wasn't as big as a dressing room. It was small. He listened to us sing. Then he started to pick out the notes. He'd play it on the piano and we'd sing. He was very excited; he thought it was great. She actually wanted to sign us up. We had to go home and tell our parents. My auntie that raised me said, "No, I don't think so. You have to finish school. I don't want you to be out there. It's a tough world." She was telling me all of the right things, as far as she knew. She held out, and I started crying, "Everybody's going to hate me. They're all going to hate me because you're the last holdout." Florence wouldn't take the group if I wouldn't sign. She finally agreed and I signed.

BEVERLY LEE, The Shirelles: We got together and we decided to tell them, "You're the only one who didn't sign." And that's how we got our contract signed.

FLORENCE GREENBERG, music executive: So they came and they sang for me, and then I cut their first record, "I Met Him on a Sunday," in 1958.

STANLEY GREENBERG, producer: "I Met Him on a Sunday" sort of took off locally, then came into New York, and was sort of a hit in the area.

BEVERLY LEE, The Shirelles: First time we heard "I Met Him on a Sunday" we were in school. We heard it in the classroom along with our classmates. Florence had arranged for the principal to play it over the intercom, so we all heard it at the same time.

JERRY BLAVAT, disc jockey: She loved everybody. She was your Jewish mother. Bubbale, Mamaleh, you know? She wasn't a small woman and you embraced her as someone that you could love.

BEVERLY LEE, The Shirelles: She was very warm, like a mother, motherly. We were teenagers, you know, so she just was like a mom.

RENEE PAPPAS, music executive: She was this little housewife from New Jersey.

ARTIE KAPLAN, session musician: I have [the] sense she came to work sometimes with her housedress on. I don't know if that's a rumor or not, but that's the way I pictured it—not business clothes, just a plain old housedress.

STANLEY GREENBERG, producer: Well, she was . . . she didn't stay a housewife for very long.

CHAPTER 4

Origins of the Girl Group Sound

The Radio, Rock and Roll, and The Chordettes

JEFF BARRY, songwriter: Well, I mean, actually there were girl groups when I was growing up, The Andrews Sisters, The Chordettes.

MARGIE LATZKO OSBORN, The Chordettes: In 1946, The Chordettes were founded by Jinny in Sheboygan, Wisconsin. She's the founder of the group, whom I had replaced in 1953. I didn't know The Chordettes at all until I was invited to sing with them.

The Chordettes knew this barbershopper, Bob Hagar, and my mother liked the barbershop harmony, so we had a quartet and we sang with quite a few barbershoppers. So, when Jinny was pregnant, they called Bob, and they were doing a club date in Pittsburgh and said they needed a replacement for Jinny. Could he recommend somebody? He recommended me.

I was an airline stewardess at the time. He called me on a Wednesday. Right then and there, said, "How would you like to sing with The Chordettes?" I said, "You've got to be kidding!" Because I knew who they were. He said, "No, they're looking for a replacement." So I said, "Do you think I can sing that high?" He said, "When can you get to Pittsburgh?"

MELANIE MINTZ, writer: If you want to talk about the first girl groups, The Andrew Sisters, The McGuire Sisters, Rosemary Clooney and her sisters, The DeMarco Sisters. They were sisters, *really*, and they had a synergy of vocals. So that's what "girl group" was then.

ALLAN PEPPER, nightclub owner: They would sing with the big bands.

MARGIE LATZKO, The Chordettes: Before I joined The Chordettes, they were on Arthur Godfrey's show. They had just left the show and started doing pop records. Mostly, you hear men singing barbershop harmony, but The Chordettes started singing . . . were the first female group that made it well known because of coming on the *Godfrey Show* and then crossing over into pop stuff. So it got a lot of women, I think, interested in singing harmony.

RON DANTE, musician: I grew up a child of the fifties, and there were sweet girl groups in the fifties.

MARGIE LATZKO, The Chordettes: I met with them at their hotel, and we talked for a while and then they asked me to sight-read an arrangement of a song side by side, which my future husband had arranged because he was their arranger and coach.

I sang with them, and then went out to a room and talked a little bit and came back, and they said, "We'd like to have you sing with us. When can you join us?" I packed my worldly belongings and, not knowing where I was going to live or what money I was going to make or anything, I just said to my mom, I said, "I'm joining The Chordettes. Goodbye."

JEFF BARRY, songwriter: Adults were writing songs for adults because, before 1950 . . . before the fifties, kids were not a market in the financial sense—the kids didn't have money. Then in the fifties, it was peacetime, and Eisenhower was president. Things were good, and kids literally had a buck. They started to get an allowance, but kids . . . nobody was catering musically to kids.

MARGIE LATZKO, The Chordettes: "Mr. Sandman" was the second recording that we made; that was 1954. When we were handed the arrangement, we had to start sight-reading those bell chords. But bell chords is what we used to do in our a cappella singing. So it wasn't anything new to us. It's just that I was surprised to see it in a pop recording.

And I said, "My gosh, are we supposed to sing this?" And it was something that was different and caught people's attention.

JEFF BARRY, songwriter: I mean, *really*. "Mr. Sandman" was not written by teenagers, and I would bet the farm on that.

MARGIE LATZKO, The Chordettes: We sang for President Eisenhower and it was so wonderful. We had a receiving line afterwards and he came down the receiving line and shook hands with me and he said, "I like that song 'Mr. Sandman,' all except the part of, 'Wavy hair like Liberace,'" [*laughing*] because Eisenhower was bald.

JEFF BARRY, songwriter: Songs like "How Much Is That Doggy in the Window?," to me, it's adults trying to get into the youth market. So, "Oh, kids like puppies. Let's write a song about puppies."

MARGIE LATZKO, The Chordettes: I describe our music as listening music. It's not a hard rock, a hard rhythm kind of thing that people out there are dancing to. It's listening music. I understand why young people like some of the music—if they want to dance—that certainly has a rhythm background.

So I was with them until the end of '56, and when I left, Jinny came and she recorded "Lollipop." Jinny came back and replaced me again. I replaced her, and she replaced me. [*laughing*] And they retired in 1962.

*

ARLENE SMITH, The Chantels: The radio was big. People don't understand that television wasn't all that. A lot of people didn't have TVs—they were just coming in. My next-door neighbor had a son who had one of the first televisions in the building. Everybody would go over to this lady's house like it was the movies. Basically, we listened to the radio.

RENEE PAPPAS, music executive: There came a time, right after World War II, where there were Black radio stations to play Black music. But once you had a transistor radio, you could listen to it if Mom and Dad were listening to, I don't know, whoever . . . Bing Crosby or somebody. Once transistor radios came into fashion, and kids could have their own music—rather than being tied to whatever the parents had—they started listening to the Black radio stations.

ALLAN PEPPER, nightclub owner: So then, along that trajectory comes Alan Freed in the mid-fifties. In Cleveland, he did a show called *The Moondog Show*. And he coins this expression, "rock and roll," which had been called "rhythm and blues." At that point, if you wanted to find an R & B record, they were in a section—it wasn't R & B.

JAY SIEGEL, The Tokens: They used to call them race records at that time.

RENEE PAPPAS, music executive: Suddenly, they found that white kids were buying the records, and it changed the whole dynamic. Until that time, they were all Black artists, and that was their audience—that's who they were selling to. So things changed because of the transistor radio . . . the whole kind of synthesis that became rock and roll—between R & B and country music, and that whole thing.

ALLAN PEPPER, nightclub owner: In other words, businesspeople, the people of that time, saw there's a lot of money to be made from this market. Alan Freed was progenitor—he started it.

RICHARD GOTTEHRER, songwriter: Alan Freed was a disc jockey that came out of Cleveland. And he would play, you know, what today we call R & B music, but it was basically Black blues artists and doo-wop groups. These people come out of gospel, which is also rooted in the spiritual side of the blues.

BILLY VERA, musician: One morning a kid at Our Lady of Mount Carmel, the school I went to, he said, "Hey, man, did you hear rock and roll last night?" "What's that?" "Alan Freed, man! What's the matter? You stupid or something!? 1010 WINS on the radio dial, seven o'clock at night." I went home that night not wanting to be left out of it.

BOBBY JAY, disc jockey: Even in Cleveland, he was playing Black music for white kids and he was vilified for it. He had an ability to recognize hit music, hit songs. And he never played, what we called, covers. He would only play the originals, and the originals were by Black artists. He didn't play "I'll Be Home" by Pat Boone; he played it by The Flamingos. So you know, the kids just knew that they liked the songs. However, if they started listening to Alan on WINS, that's when they became aware of those Black artists.

JAY SIEGEL, The Tokens: A lot of the white stations wouldn't play that music. They would play Pat Boone singing "Tutti Frutti," not Little Richard, and Pat Boone singing "Tutti Frutti" could make you . . . uh, nauseous, you know? Don't tell Pat I said that, okay?

ALLAN PEPPER, nightclub owner: Then he came to New York. It wasn't a matter of whether he favored Black artists—those were the people that were creating the music.

CAROLE KING, songwriter: It was this interest in another . . . another culture that we were not close to and we became close to it through the music.

JERRY BLAVAT, disc jockey: Music, music! And radio always was an important part of my loneliness, you know? Our music was *our* music. It was new, it was different, it was exciting, and it was followed by teenagers, not by our parents, all right? No different than when the bobby-soxers were doing the bobby-sox things, you know? Now it was rock and roll. Listen, rock and roll was basically gospel, rhythm and blues, all wrapped in with a big beat. That's what it was.

ARTIE RIPP, music executive: Well, let me give you a line: Alan Freed opened up this gusher. Okay—that was the bloodless revolution that circled the earth. The Iron Curtain couldn't stop it. Bamboo Curtain couldn't stop it. Nothing could stop rock and roll music getting into and engaging the young people in those countries. Even though they have walls up, somehow, someway, somebody got a copy of the record from some place, or a pirate station could pick it up in England, or so on. Rock and roll was the thing that revolutionized—changed—this thinking. The sociological thing that nothing else ever did. And it was without a bullet. No one got killed.

ALLAN PEPPER, nightclub owner: So taste is starting to shift. And so then somebody like Alan Freed says, "What the hell?" He's looking to make a buck. "We'll do a live show." And holy shit!

JERRY BLAVAT, disc jockey: You get Little Richard, Frankie Lymon's Teenagers, you get LaVern Baker, you get Chuck Berry. For ninety-nine cents you see the movie and you see all these rock-and-roll stars.

BROOKS ARTHUR, sound engineer: The Brooklyn Paramount was the place.

ALLAN PEPPER, nightclub owner: They were generally a movie and then the show.

BARBARA ENGLISH, The Clickettes: Kids would come there, they'd stay there all day to see you from eleven o'clock in the morning until the last show, over and over again—two movies, serials, newsreels, and The Clickettes, and then whoever. They were big shows back in the day. You know, you'd have people from Ray Charles, ten to twelve acts on this stage and a movie, and a newsreel, and cartoons for twenty-five cents.

ALLAN PEPPER, nightclub owner: If you went to see a lot of these shows, it was a very ritualized thing—you got up at a certain time, you went with your clique of friends—I was crazy and I would stand in line for hours. Because you're with a community of people, we were all young kids. We all felt that we were all part of the same nation.

LA LA BROOKS, The Crystals: We stayed up all night waiting for daylight to come so we could go to this concert. It was crowded as *heck*. We told each other, "When the doors open, we'll run real quick to go to the front," and we did. We was pushing, and I was always a skinny little girl, so I could go through people. I could go through them, go underneath their legs, and get in there. My sister was a big girl—she couldn't move as fast as I could, and my niece was a big girl—so I was gone, and I saved the seats for them. I put my hands up, "No, no, don't come, I need my sister and my niece." . . . Brenda Lee, The Cleftones, Frankie Lymon and the Teenagers, Little Anthony and the Imperials.

MELANIE MINTZ, writer: I went once at four in the morning with my best girlfriend. The movie came on at 10:00 a.m., that's when they opened the doors, and then the show came on at twelve. And then there was a break, which is when I learned I didn't have to get up at four o'clock in the morning. If you came when the twelve o'clock show broke and everybody left, you get the same seats that you got at 4:00 a.m. That's what my brother did. *Chief Crazy Horse* . . . I remember it well. I saw it twice on one of the shows—you had to sit through a movie if you wanted to see another show.

BIBS ALLBUT, The Angels: Jiggs and I went to the Alan Freed show and I saw Jo Ann Campbell and I had an epiphany—that's what I wanted to do.

JIGGS ALLBUT, The Angels: Once we got there, there was no way we were gonna leave. We stayed there all day long, just all day long. I remember in between sets some of the singers went over to a restaurant to eat, and I remember running through the back door in the kitchen and trying to get their autographs while they were eating. And it was so much fun and so thrilling, so thrilling we didn't eat all day, and at night we got back onto the platform at Port Authority to get on the bus and I fainted. I never fainted in my life, before or since.

ALLAN PEPPER, nightclub owner: Nothing is in a vacuum. Everything is working to create something. Think of when you first saw *American Idol*, because that's this whole thing in a nutshell—it's the star-making machinery. In other words, songs are introduced, there's a way of reinforcing them. These kids go to these shows, they buy the programs, they start becoming fans, they start to know the names of each person, they start to buy other stuff.

And so you have a business—a huge business that was never there before. So the music business is now turning into another thing. With me, I always bought the program—no matter what show, I bought them. I'd come home and I'd take the pictures out and the way other people have ball players on their wall, I had all these Black musicians' faces on my wall. So the kids sitting there watching wanted to be like them. So then you'd have kids singing in the hall, you heard them singing, like trying to find an echo.

LA LA BROOKS, The Crystals: I remember sitting there at eleven years old with my hand on that bar and looking at them perform, and said to myself in a strong thought, *One day I'm going to be up there.* That's all I said—as a kid. The next thing you know, when I'm thirteen, I got in The Crystals.

CHAPTER 5

Teenagers in Love

The Sound Behind the New Business of Pop

RICHARD GOTTEHRER, songwriter: That general area from 49th Street up to 53rd, around Broadway and Seventh Avenue in Manhattan, is generally defined as the Brill Building—a term to indicate that period of development of music. Traditional songwriters had been writing and creating great music for decades in that area. Prior to it being called the Brill Building, it was Tin Pan Alley, where publishers would exist.

ALLAN PEPPER, nightclub owner: It's like that whole notion with the onion, with stuff having to be peeled back layer after layer after layer. So you have to take a step back and see what the social conditions were like—what the business was like. And also, if you kind of think in terms of music, before rock and roll, we were talking about Tin Pan Alley.

RICHARD GOTTEHRER, songwriter: Before the radio there had been a big market for sheet music. People would buy sheet music of a song that was a hit, and they would learn to play it *themselves* on the piano—sheet music was the valuable element. And little by little that became less and less significant.

BARBARA ROSE, ex-wife of Jerry Leiber: A lot of the money came in publishing music.

ALLAN PEPPER, nightclub owner: So the publishers realized it, holy shit.

ARTIE RIPP, music executive: White kids *and* Black kids are buying music. That was an astonishing awareness.

ALLAN PEPPER, nightclub owner: Well, there were a lot of young guys at that time trying to get into the business. They were all hustlers. A lot of them were young Jewish guys. They would've gone to their father's garment business if they weren't pulled by the music business. These were young guys that figured out something and got in there and did it.

JAY SIEGEL, The Tokens: Well, growing up in Brooklyn and Brighton Beach, there was music all around—especially in high school. There was a lot of music that came out of Brooklyn, a lot of famous people. In Neil Sedaka's graduating class was Harvey Keitel, and before that at Lincoln High School with Lou Gossett, Arthur Miller, who wrote *Death of a Salesman*, all came out of Lincoln High School. Carol Klein, who became Carole King, came out of Madison High School in Brooklyn, New York. On every street corner, four or five guys would get together and start to sing. And, you know, that's how we attracted all the girls.

NEIL SEDAKA, singer/songwriter: All of the people who were born in Brooklyn—Streisand, Neil Diamond lived across the street . . . there was something in the egg creams.

BROOKS ARTHUR, sound engineer: It was the water or it was the knishes, maybe.

NEIL SEDAKA, singer/songwriter: And I think also the Jewish kids . . . the parents pushed for culture. You had to either learn the piano or violin . . . and I think that was one of the things that gave us ammunition to do and go on further.

I lived in the same building as Howard Greenfield. I was thirteen and he was sixteen years old. I was a Juilliard scholarship student studying the piano. I was a child prodigy, and his mother heard me through the walls playing Chopin or something. She met me up in the Catskill Mountains—it was the Kenmore Lake Hotel, and I was there with my parents. She said, "Oh, I'm Ella Greenfield, and I live in 3260 Coney Island Avenue. My son, Howie, is a poet, and I'd like for you two to get together." October 11, 1952, I'll never forget the date. He rang my bell and I'll never forget it—I said, "I don't know how to write songs," and he convinced me. We wrote a song every day that year. Kids in school, in amateur shows, started to sing Sedaka/Greenfield songs. The songs got better and better, and we signed to Aldon in 1958.

RENEE PAPPAS, music executive: The idea that a singer would sing his own compositions really doesn't come in until maybe the late sixties, early seventies. So, the song search was always a big thing.

ALLAN PEPPER, nightclub owner: You had people who worked in the studios—producers and songwriters. And you had conglomerates of songwriters, at the Brill Building and 1650 Broadway.

JEFF BARRY, songwriter: The Brill Building, to me, is those brass doors and the long black-and-white tile marble foyer leading from those brass doors straight back to the elevators.

RON DANTE, musician: It was full of people. I mean, there were people singing in the hallways to audition. If you went to the little luncheonette on the side of the main entrance, there were people—managers were trying to manage groups. . . . You know, people were trying to get deals.

BARBARA ENGLISH, The Clickettes: It was a very, *very* busy building and many, many groups, many managers. Groups that were already being managed and on their way to being produced, and those who just hung out in the hallway trying to be discovered.

TONI WINE, session singer: Everyone was there, girl groups, guy groups, writers, singers, producers, label owners.

BILLY VERA, musician: There was a crazy guy named Larry that used to stand out in front. If you'd walk by there, he'd give you the Bronx cheer and he'd curse at you—but if he didn't curse at you, that meant you were a nobody.

RON DANTE, musician: The Brill Building was across the street from another music building, 1650 Broadway. There was almost a competition between the two buildings.

JAY SIEGEL, The Tokens: The Brill Building gets all the press for some reason. All the fabulous, tremendous songwriters were in 1650 Broadway, *not* in the Brill Building.

RON DANTE, musician: I mean, I still visited the Brill Building across the street many times with my guitar trying to get a deal, trying to get somebody to listen to my songs.

TONI WINE, session singer: I'll tell you why, because it's a real thorn in my side. Nothing to take away from the Brill Building—the fabulous Brill Building. The lobby is gorgeous; it's a momentous building and time in all of our lives. But the reality is, the rock and roll and the R & B worlds were all housed at 1650 Broadway. Your contemporary *Billboard, Cashbox, Record World* people were all housed at 1650 Broadway. Maybe because it's easy to say "the Brill Building." It does have a magic to it to say "the Brill Building," alliteration *B-B*, and it's longer and you gotta remember the number to 1650 Broadway. 1650 didn't have a name of the building; we were just 1650 Broadway.

RON DANTE, musician: That's where Don Kirshner's office was. It was called Aldon Music—Al and Don—they were the owners, Al Nevins and Don Kirshner.

JERRY WEXLER, founder, Atlantic Records: Somehow Donnie [Don Kirshner] and Al did it. You could say, "Sure, they had great songwriters," but they had the format. Look, these kids were running around with songs—anybody could have picked them up. Anybody that had the vision. It was Al and Donnie that had the vision to put them under contract and give them a weekly stipend.

RICHARD GOTTEHRER, songwriter: If they signed the song or took an option on it, it then became the job of the publisher to get a recording artist to record it. They had connections with the larger record companies, and they would submit it to A&R [artists and repertoire] divisions.

MELANIE MINTZ, writer: It was an opportunity to write. They needed a champion and somebody needed to hear that they had talent. Otherwise, they were like a thousand other kids trying to write songs and doing things and not getting anywhere.

RICHARD GOTTEHRER, songwriter: There was Neil Sedaka and Howie Greenfield, Barry Mann and Cynthia Weil, and of course, Carole King and Gerry Goffin. Now this is among others, but these people had a significant part in establishing what became commercial pop music in the late fifties into the early sixties.

NEIL SEDAKA, singer/songwriter: Howie and I were the first at 1650 to be signed to Aldon Music. I went to school with Mort Shuman, who was a great writer with Doc Pomus. He suggested that we go to a new publishing firm in 1650 called Aldon Music and they had just opened up, about a week. We knocked at the door and Don Kirshner opened it, and I said, "Well, we were referred by Mort Shuman." And he said, "Well, can you come back after lunch?" They were discussing how they were going to pay the rent for the office, because they weren't sure what the hell was going on at the time.

ARTIE KAPLAN, musician: Anybody could show up at any time of the day or night, and there were three rooms with a piano and an ashtray available to them to write. That's how this thing began. You could come in and write all day at Donnie's place.

NEIL SEDAKA, singer/songwriter: We had five days a week from ten in the morning till five in the afternoon, like a regular job.

TONY POWERS, songwriter: It beat a job . . . but it was a job. We came in and punched a clock every day, in a way.

RICHARD GOTTEHRER, songwriter: They're the ones that set up that factory system, and it was in 1650 Broadway. There'd be little cubicle rooms, they would sign writers, and these writers would be given a room and then they would go out and make the connections—meaning Kirshner and Aldon would make the connections with songwriters and artists. He'd call the writers into the office and there'd be competitions between the various writing teams.

TONI WINE, session singer: Donnie would say, "Hey, this one's coming up." So, everybody would go into their little cubicles and try to write songs and hope that after they made demos, their songs would be played. Then, with any luck, their songs would get picked and cut.

TONY POWERS, songwriter: We were kids hanging out and we swapped stories and swapped leads, "Hey, so-and-so is looking for a song" . . . "so-and-so is a good publisher" . . . "maybe they're close to this artist, maybe they'll get it to them."

NEIL SEDAKA, singer/songwriter: And the competition was good . . . was good competition. We all were on our toes.

JAY SIEGEL, The Tokens: But everybody wanted to get the next hit record. It was very competitive, actually, *very* competitive. But it was fun too—all super talented people, super talented people, all young, all kids.

NEIL SEDAKA, singer/songwriter: Teenagers writing for teenage markets. You can write a song, make a demo, and in a few weeks, it was out on the radio and then a few weeks, it was on the charts and billboards. It was one of those crazy times.

RICHARD GOTTEHRER, songwriter: They were particularly interested in young kids, like us. I say kids, I mean, I started going down there when I was sixteen because we were "in tune with what was going on," in terms of the songs.

NEIL SEDAKA, singer/songwriter: I was dating Carole King for a short time when we were teenagers. I brought her up to Aldon Music and I wrote a song, "Oh! Carol," for her, as you might know.

MELANIE MINTZ, writer: You talk about Carole and Gerry and . . . how old do you think they were when they were writing the songs?

They started writing about their lives because they were young, they were falling in love.

ALLAN PEPPER, nightclub owner: And meanwhile, these guys own half of the song for fronting the money.

MELANIE MINTZ, writer: And the songwriters had no idea the copyrights would be worth that kind of money. They really . . . once they found out, they got greedier. But at the time it was kind of fair. "I'll put up all the money, I'll give you the office, here's a piano, you go to the studio, we'll do all that, but we share publishing fifty-fifty." That's not unreasonable. You were going to share with them if they were right about your talent.

ALLAN PEPPER, nightclub owner: And I don't think at that particular time the writers felt like they were getting ripped off. They didn't; they felt fortunate.

BROOKS ARTHUR, sound engineer: I wasn't signed for much money at Aldon Music, twenty-five dollars or something a week, or fifty dollars a month . . . something like that. But how did Donnie Kirshner influence me? He just kept on preaching hits. Hits. Hits. You've got to write hits. You got to write songs that the people love universally.

TONI WINE, session singer: He could marry any song to any artist. If he heard it, he would say, "I think this would be great for so-and-so. . . . I think this sucks." He was called "The Man with the Golden Ear" for very proper reasons.

RON DANTE, musician: I mean, he was the king of the music business in New York City. Don Kirshner was the greatest inspiration for songwriters, ever. When he believed in you, you believed in yourself.

BROOKS ARTHUR, sound engineer: Donnie taught me one thing, short and sweet. Don't waste time and money on the ethereal stuff. We love the charts, we want to stay on the charts.

CHAPTER 6

The Brill Building's Own Girl Group

The Cookies

MARGARET ROSS, The Cookies: Well, we always dressed alike onstage, but not when it came to street clothes . . . then we all saw these dresses. They were black turtleneck, kind of clingish a little bit. And leopard coats, a leopard jacket, and we had leopard booties.

We went to do a recording session and we were walking down the street. We had gotten out of the cab, but we had to go someplace before we went to the studio, and when we were coming across Broadway, this one guy—I just want to make you laugh—this one guy fell on his knees. We were waiting for the light and he said, "Oh my God, put a chain around my neck and lead me a dog life." And we fell out laughing. He said, "Look at what you got on, you look so good." He said it so loud and we're standing there and people are waiting to cross the street. And everybody fell out, and they started clapping at us, and, "Oh yes, you girls look fabulous. They must be a group. They must be a group." We said, "Yeah, we are," [*laughing*] and they clapped.

Oh yeah. Oh yeah. We knew we were cute. We knew we were cute. We knew we looked good, so when we looked good, we walked down the street with our heads up like, *We're somebody* once in a while.

BROOKS ARTHUR, sound engineer: They were all very fastidious. They were all, "Is my makeup on straight? Is the lipstick good? Does this dress look good on me? Does this pair of slacks look good on me?" Or the converse would be they walk into the control room and they get blasted by their groupmates saying, "How could you wear that kind of a dress when we're doing photos today?" yada, yada, yada. So we'd have all of that kind of stuff going on. It was, in a word, thrilling. Thrilling.

TONI WINE, session singer: They were all fabulous. Everyone in The Cookies, to me, were lead singers. Every one of them. Margaret, Earl-Jean, all of them.

MARGARET ROSS, The Cookies: We went to the Brill Building that particular day, and we had to do a recording. We went inside and Al and Don Kirshner and Carole King, all of them were . . . everybody fell out. "Oh my God, look at you girls! You look so fabulous!"

So, Al said, "Now, that's the look." Him and Don Kirshner were our managers and Al couldn't get over how we looked. He said, "You know what, from now on, I want you girls to dress alike. I want my girls, my Cookies, to look like this."

*

MARGARET ROSS, The Cookies: I came to New York from North Carolina. I think I was about between twelve and fourteen. I came to visit my mother's sister who lived here in New York, and I ended up staying because my mother passed away at a very early age. So I stayed. She raised me.

I had no idea that I had a cousin named Dorothy Jones that was singing, you know, was a Cookie. She was the one that was the founder of the group and I had no idea that I had a family that was in show business. My cousin Dorothy was the sound of The Cookies, and they all lived in Coney Island, where I am still right now.

They had a contract with Atlantic Records—they made some recordings, they did a lot of background. They were doing background for other artists that was a part of Atlantic Records.

BOBBY JAY, disc jockey: Ray Charles said, "Hey, I like them." And he says, "I want them girls to sing with me." And The Cookies became The Raelettes.

MARGARET ROSS, The Cookies: Neil Sedaka called Dorothy and said he needed background singers. She said, "Well, I don't have anybody because Ethel and Margie are with Ray Charles. They became

Raelettes." He changed the name, you know. He couldn't keep The Cookies.

NEIL SEDAKA, singer/songwriter: I heard them on a demo or someone's record. I loved the sound.

MARGARET ROSS, The Cookies: So Dorothy didn't have anybody, so Neil said, "Well, can you get anybody?" She said, "Well, I have a cousin named Margaret. She's still in high school. Maybe Ethel's sister, Earl-Jean?" So he said, "Test them out, and let's see what we can do. Maybe we got another set of Cookies." And that's what happened. That's how I got in.

NEIL SEDAKA, singer/songwriter: The Cookies were on almost all of my hits from 1958 to 1963. They were on "Little Devil" and "Breaking Up Is Hard to Do" and "Stairway to Heaven" and "Next Door to an Angel." I must tell you, my first hit as a songwriter, Howie Greenfield and I—not a hit but the first record—was called "Passing Time," and it was on Atlantic with The Cookies. I was thrilled, over the moon. I had dreamt all my life of seeing my name on a 45 RPM as a writer, and I'll never forget, I got a call from Jerry Wexler saying, "I have good news and bad news. Your song 'Passing Time,' you're going to make money, but it's become the B-side of the record." The hit side was called "In Paradise," which I think made Top 10 in R & B, and every time "In Paradise" came on the New York radio station, I envisioned my song "Passing Time" scraping underneath, not being heard.

TONI WINE, session singer: They sang background on just about every record that came out of Aldon Music.

MARGARET ROSS, The Cookies: That was my big break. I was in Abraham Lincoln High School, and I would have to go after school. They would be waiting for me in a cab to go back and forth to the city to do background singing—a record for Carole King and Gerry Goffin and Neil, and whoever else needed background to be done at Aldon.

NEIL SEDAKA, singer/songwriter: I used to pick them up. I lived in Brighton. I picked them up in Coney Island in my car on the way to RCA Victor Records on East 24th Street, and I taught them the harmony in the car as we were riding to the studio, and by the time we got into the studio, they were such quick learners that they nailed it on the session.

I had come up with the riff the night before the session of "Breaking Up Is Hard to Do," [*singing*] "*Down doobie doo down down,*" and I said, "Hmm, this is an interesting riff. Let me start the record with it, and then let me continue the riff and double it with a guitar under the major part of the record." So, I called up the arranger, and he wrote it the night before into the arrangement and I would give out lead sheets, but of course, not to The Cookies because their ears were so good. I don't even know if they read music. They were a good change from "the readers." The Cookies were natural singers.

DARLENE LOVE, The Blossoms: Everybody was really just starting to use backup singers. It was usually just, as we called [them], "the readers"—white singers. They did all the background for everybody.

NEIL SEDAKA, singer/songwriter: "The readers" were very legitimate background singers that could read music, and sometimes they were very square sounding.

MARGARET ROSS, The Cookies: Neil showed us the background, [*singing*] "*Don't take your love, down doobie doo down down,*" you know, he wanted us to do that part. And then [*singing*] "*Breaking up is hard to do.*" And we learned the song right in the taxi. Yeah, that's right, we sure did. . . . We sure did, we learned it right in the taxi. Only took us about a few minutes to put it together, and once we got in the studio, naturally that's how it came out. It came out good.

NEIL SEDAKA, singer/songwriter: I rehearsed with them in the car, going to the studio, and then a few takes over and over in the studio. Did you get to interview Carole? She forgot about her past or just doesn't want to remember it, but I still have great respect for her. I don't think any of our teams in the Brill Building were as successful as Carole and Gerry. I think she's a genius.

MARGARET ROSS, The Cookies: I was in high school and we had to do a recording session with Neil. We had to be in the studio at a certain time, and I had one class left. Do you know what I had to do? I played hooky. I snuck out and didn't go to that class. It was on a Friday. The cab was waiting for me downstairs with Dorothy and Earl-Jean in it.

Monday when I came back to school, they came to the class and said, "You're wanted in the principal's office. Somebody saw you when you snuck out, and we want to know what's going on, because you don't do that. That's not like you, Margaret."

I started crying. I said, "Are you going to tell my aunt?" So after I got myself together, I said to them, "Well, I can't lie to you, but I had to go to the city, because I'm a background singer." And I said that we had to do a background for Neil Sedaka.

So the person stood up and said, "A background singer for Neil Sedaka? How come you didn't come in the office and say something? We know Neil. He graduated from here." They said, "The next time you have to do something like that, just let us know. And why are we just finding out that you're with a group called The Cookies?"

CHAPTER 7

Tonight's the Night

Taking the Show on the Road

REATHER DIXON TURNER, The Bobbettes: In 1957, we were five busy little girls. The times I remember most are the tours, where all we did was what was called then, and is still called, one-night stands.

EMMA POUGHT, The Bobbettes: We ended up going on this tour, which was about two weeks after we came out of the Apollo. We didn't know anything about that. They have to set up a chaperone. You had to have correspondence learning because the board of education is after you, so we went to a school called the Professional Children's School.

REATHER DIXON TURNER, The Bobbettes: When we were home we'd attend, and when we were working, we'd do our schoolwork and mail it in.

EMMA POUGHT, The Bobbettes: So we went out on that road. And let me tell you, that is a life that I wouldn't put on anybody, especially a child. And by there being five of us, we gave our chaperone, that lady, a hard way to go. I'm telling you, *she had a time* controlling all the five girls.

REATHER DIXON TURNER, The Bobbettes: It was fun on the bus, we'd talk and laugh and pull pranks on one another.

EMMA POUGHT, The Bobbettes: They were trying to take Frankie Lymon and separate him from his group, right? In other words, he was going to become a star without his Teenagers. And so one night, we were in a hotel—all of us. We had stopped and, being that we were so young, we couldn't go nowhere. So we were in our rooms and our chaperone had gone out with the other people to the party. So Frankie was supposed to be in the hotel in his room, because he was underaged too. So we heard somebody knocking on the door. It's Frankie Lymon. "It's Frankie, open the door!"

We opened the door and let him in. He looked like he was high, because he'd been dabbling with drugs for as long as I can remember. He came in, and he said, "You guys don't know anything about sex, do you?" We're looking at him, and saying, "Now what is he talking about? What's wrong with him?" We could tell something was wrong with him. So he said, "I'm going to teach you guys how to do this." He was very explicit about what he was going to do, right?

So we jumped him. We jumped that man. He was a boy like us, he was young. We jumped on him, and threw him across the bed, and stripped his clothes off, took all his clothes off, all of them. Then what we did, we took his pants and tied knots in the legs, so he couldn't get them back on fast. Then we threw him out in the hall, and that was a big hotel. And you could hear the maid, "Oh my God, oh my gosh!" She's running, and he was out there trying to untie his pants.

*

LOIS POWELL, The Chantels: The record hit in October. At that point, the record company was pulling all of the girls out of their regular schools and putting them in Professional Children's School. The nuns at my high school said, "Absolutely not." My mother said, "Absolutely not." So, I got pulled off the road. The girls got new pictures taken without me—I was devastated. The girls had stories about some of the trips that they had made, and it didn't include me. So that was a little difficult.

JACKIE LANDRY, The Chantels: Lois's mother stuck to her guns, and I remember she cried, but I wrote her letters to let her know what we were doing. I remember being upset because I was homesick.

ERNIE MARTINELLI, manager, The Chiffons: The Chantels were the first girl group. They were girls. They were pains in the ass. They fought with each other, they got mad at each other. No two girls agreed on the same thing, at the same time, at the same place. They had no idea other than their corner in the Bronx what their lives were supposed to be like. Everything was new to them. Everything.

EMMA POUGHT, The Bobbettes: If I hadn't been in one, I wouldn't want to get in one. I'd tell you the truth because you know yourself how we are, women. "I don't like that color. It doesn't look good on me. I'm not wearing that. I don't like that wig." We argued about everything. "I'm too fat for that, I'm too skinny for this"—that kind of thing. When you go shopping, you have to get something that looks good on everybody. It was rough.

RENÉE MINUS WHITE, The Chantels: On the road, Richard Barrett was responsible for us. The Chantels were his life. We were always locked in our dressing rooms, and no girl was left alone. We traveled to the restrooms and everywhere backstage in teams.

EMMA POUGHT, The Bobbettes: We've known The Chantels since the beginning of time. They were with Richard Barrett. Richard Barrett was with them and we had the old man as our manager, and they had a young guy 'cause he used to be with The Valentines. Everybody used to say, "Oh, that's them girls that got that big record. And they got that old man as a manager." I think we must've been the worst dressed girl group out there, *the worst*, because he used to make our clothes. He was making them out of the worst material, it was the worst style.

We was in New York and we was at the theater. So that night we said, "We're not going onstage no more with these ugly damn outfits." So what we did was we tore all those outfits up, all of them. And then we got in the hotel, and we called him and told him that somebody broke into the theater and had destroyed some of the people's clothes in the dressing rooms. And, honey, he had a fit. We were laughing so hard. And he came and he had to buy us new outfits.

LOIS POWELL, The Chantels: Our mothers had said to Richard, "Nothing better happen to our daughters. And make sure they're safe." Sometimes he took it overboard and literally would lock us in our dressing rooms.

GLORIA JONES, The Blossoms: Oh my God . . . they couldn't come from backstage. They couldn't associate with the other singers. And I know Arlene was telling me that all the time. She didn't know how to act around people because he kept them so locked up . . . like the only time you would see them would be when they were onstage because he wouldn't let them mingle.

ARTIE RIPP, music executive: He wasn't just in The Valentines, he was a great creative force—a great visionary, a wonderful, insane personality—and a great control freak. Richard was a genius. And had an . . . almost a pimp personality with how it was with the control of these young girls. If you didn't control them, you could be involved with all sorts of stuff. He didn't want to have to deal with boyfriends who now were talking for his artists. So he understood what he had to do to be able to come up with hits and what he had to do to make sure that he can control the group. That was not an easy trick.

Well, just think of a guy controlling: "No, you can't do this. You are going to do this, okay? I don't want to hear any more about that, okay? Here's what you got to do." It was a lot of stern parental-gymnastic-coach type of control. And at the same time, inspiring the girls to be commercial, to be smart, to be classy, and so on. I mean, what he did behind closed doors, who knows?

BEVERLY LEE, The Shirelles: We did a show with The Chantels. We decided to switch up tops one time—like girls do with your best friend. Their manager got very upset; he didn't understand girlhood. I guess he wanted them to be unique.

BARBARA ENGLISH, The Clickettes: It was almost as if they were brainwashed. I mean, they had no freedom—he's trying to protect his investment there. Richard was pretty strict on The Chantels because they were girls. You know . . . the boy groups, men are men, but with the girl groups . . .

JEAN BOULDIN, The Clickettes: We were not allowed to mingle with the other artists a lot. Sometimes we'd run down to the backstage and look to see who was performing, but as far as Zell, she kept us under lock and key.

BARBARA ENGLISH, The Clickettes: Zell Sanders was similar in the way that she commanded us to be on time, you know, the rules and regulations. No pins in your bras and your crinolines had to be clean—and *no boys*. I mean, Trudy found a way to meet somebody, but, you know, I wasn't interested. . . . Trudy would find a way. [*laughing*]

*

BEVERLY LEE, The Shirelles: Our first tour was with The Coasters and The Drifters. The Shirelles were called the female Drifters because there were a lot of similarities in our arrangements. But the guys were like big brothers to us—they were all very protective of us. They knew we knew nothing about show business. With some of them, it was new for them too. We all basically had on-the-job training.

SHIRLEY ALSTON REEVES, The Shirelles: We used to tour all the time. I remember when we first went out on tour, we didn't know what to expect. We dressed up; those slips were killing us. Florence Greenberg got on the bus and told the bus driver, "Make sure my girls sit in the front of the bus. We don't want them back there with the male groups. I want them to know where they are so they can get out of there if anything goes wrong."

BEVERLY LEE, The Shirelles: Crinoline was something that you put on your skirt to make it poof out in those days. And if you wanted it really poofy, you'd put some starch in it. When you sat in it too long, you would start itching. We were going south, and I'll never forget Ruth Brown's face when she saw us. She took us aside and said, "Go get you some jeans, be comfortable. Get a pillow—this is how you travel on the road."

Etta James and LaVern Baker were on the show too. LaVern Baker would do our hair sometimes. We didn't know at the time, but Florence had asked Ruth Brown to look after us on the tour. Etta told us if somebody wanted to take us out, "Say that the others have to go too," because we were too young.

SHIRLEY ALSTON REEVES, The Shirelles: Etta James was the first one who taught me and the girls how to handle our money on the road, how to spend our money, how to buy our food. We weren't making a lot of money. We had a number one record, but weren't making anything, hardly. She always told us, "Remember, don't go anywhere alone. Always stick together. If somebody invites you out, fine. Say, 'We'll be happy to come.'" That's the way it always was. If we went to any parties, we went together. If things started looking shaky, we'd leave.

We were on the road all the time. We never paid any attention to anything else. We would do thirty one-nighters. We'd come home and be home for about a week or two weeks, and we'd be back out again on another bus tour. It was rough, but we had the most fun. We used to sing ourselves to sleep. It was just something that you had to be there.

EMMA POUGHT, The Bobbettes: I remember LaVern Baker was the one that, like, hipped us to what was actually going on, because we had the biggest record of everybody and we didn't understand it. We didn't know how much money was being made, we didn't know anything, because Mr. Dailey was in charge of everything and our parents were not educated people. You know what I'm saying? They knew nothing about getting a lawyer to check things and they knew nothing about that.

I always gave LaVern Baker credit for showing us a lot of things. She told us that our parents need to ask questions and get a lawyer because when we were talking about how much money the manager was taking, she was saying that he must be crazy. He must be crazy because he was taking a large amount of money.

REATHER DIXON TURNER, The Bobbettes: We were like everyone's little sisters and were well taken care of. We'd be working with one headliner, such as Clyde McPhatter, and when we left that show to go to another, he'd tell the next headliner, such as Sam Cooke or Jackie Wilson, to take care of his little girls. And they would.

EMMA POUGHT, The Bobbettes: We started out very young, very young. When Jannie and Reather went on tour, they were twelve years old. And I was fourteen, and I turned fifteen while I was on tour.

We saw a lot of things out there, and they used to say, "All you've got to remember is, whatever you see on the road, stays on the road, do not repeat it," and we didn't. You got used to that, after a while. You got used to seeing people being dogged, and on drugs, you saw it all.

Oh God, even though they were married, they had all these women, and I'm seeing them crying, and whatnot, because at the end of the tour, they didn't have no money. None at all. Now you got to go home to a family, you done messed up all your money out there in the street, you know what I'm saying?

I remember, we were in Juarez, Mexico, the doctor had to come up on the bus. We didn't know what it was for. But what they did was they stretched a blanket over the back of the bus, so we couldn't see. But what he came for is because they were contracting venereal diseases. A doctor would actually come up on the bus with a black bag and give them shots and stuff like that because they would sleep with so many prostitutes.

*

BARBARA ENGLISH, The Clickettes: We were regionals—we went from Washington or Virginia to Connecticut to Syracuse, New York, to Pittsburgh. We were like tristate superstars, you know, because Zell was limited. She would deliver records up on the back of a truck by herself . . . distribution to the record store at 4:00 a.m., 5:00 a.m.

How did we all fit in that car? They didn't have bucket seats and there was . . . you can put three people in the front, three people in the front, Zell driving, three people in the back seat, the stuff in the trunk, plus the cooking plate, because she had a tendency to be cheap and cook in the hotel rooms, not go out—not order or go out.

JEAN BOULDIN, The Clickettes: I remember her cooking in the room with one of those little hot plates.

BARBARA ENGLISH, The Clickettes: Sometimes chicken wings, which she would take the large part—which I call the hips; you know, the drumstick—and give us the arm and the fingers. [*laughing*] So we didn't see the other part of that chicken wing ever.

I mean if she had money, she would have been dangerous, because she did all of this as a trailblazer and first woman. Which people . . . nobody writes about her, but she was a bad B, to tell you the truth—to be able to do what she did when there was nobody . . . this was new. There was nobody doing what Zell was doing at the time—not a female—so she did the best she could.

She was a security guard, the warden, everybody—the cook. We had no chaperone; she was the chaperone. Zell was the doorkeeper. We didn't need a chaperone.

JEAN BOULDIN, The Clickettes: Now that I think about it, I have to laugh.

BARBARA ENGLISH, The Clickettes: In fact, Zell pretended we were The Shirelles. They were asking for The Shirelles, and they were hot with "Will You Love Me Tomorrow." It was a Connecticut show, I'll never forget. And these people . . . they booed, because they knew we weren't The Shirelles.

JEAN BOULDIN, The Clickettes: Zell introduced us, then Barbara said, "She didn't say The Clickettes, she said The Shirelles." The stage was really small and we had some toe-out shoes and somebody was touching my toes and counting my toes . . . oh God. [*laughing*] That's how small the stage was.

BARBARA ENGLISH, The Clickettes: I mean, how could you do that? This is showing you the character of that person. I remember them picking at my toes on the stage, but it was a horrible situation. To tell you the truth, it was in Connecticut and, you know, you're always walking around afraid of racial bias in some of these places. . . . Believe me, it wasn't easy to go work places, always thinking that you're discriminated against. They would show you hostility, even though they're loving your music.

*

LOIS POWELL, The Chantels: Finally, I graduated. And then, we went on a six-week tour of the South. Was that an eye-opener! We would see these things in the newspaper and we actually were living them now in these six weeks that we were below the Mason-Dixon Line. Colored bathrooms . . . we couldn't eat at the lunch counters. We couldn't try on clothes in the stores. It was horrible.

EMMA POUGHT, The Bobbettes: Jackleg promoters that run off with the money, you do the program and don't get paid, a lot of stuff . . . and the traveling in the South . . . I don't even want to talk about that.

BEVERLY LEE, The Shirelles: I'll never forget when we went to check in to hotels, we went on one side of the town, where some of the Black people had rooms they would rent out to the performers.

EMMA POUGHT, The Bobbettes: Dion and the Belmonts, they were allowed to get off the bus and go into the big-time hotels. But we had to be taken into the town, I guess you would call it the deploy area, whatever, but they were rooms in houses and some people, they made their living renting those rooms. And we would end up staying in places like that.

SHIRLEY ALSTON REEVES, The Shirelles: When we walked in, we had on makeup because we'd just come offstage. It was a Dick Clark tour. He wanted us to stay in a Holiday Inn with the rest of the people. The man said, "I don't care who they are. They're not coming in here." Clark said, "Don't worry. We're going to leave extra early tomorrow. We'll drive in and pick you up. Just be ready."

You talk about *ready*. We were standing there with our bags and were ready to get out of that place. It's a shame that you had to do that. When we came in there, we were like fresh meat. These guys started looking at you like, "Oh man!" They were probably thinking that we were ladies of the evening. I didn't want to go to sleep. I was tired because we had been on the road all day. Everybody was hugging us when we got back on the bus.

EMMA POUGHT, The Bobbettes: We even stayed in an undertaker's house one time . . . a funeral home, yeah. He rented it upstairs and we didn't know it until the morning. We were so tired when they checked in, we went up and we went to sleep and we were milling around the next morning, we started down the steps and we see these coffins. So I'm pretty sure there was dead people in that building. We saw it and we started coming down those steps like horses, we was running to get out of there.

SHIRLEY ALSTON REEVES, The Shirelles: We once were in Lubbock, Texas, and the guy that used to travel with us all the time, Ronnie, sat up against the door. There was nowhere for Black people to stay, there were no hotels—this was sort of like a flophouse. . . . People were out in the hallway gambling and doing all kinds of stuff. We were scared and we all stayed in one room and slept in one bed. There were no king-size beds back then, and we slept across the bed. Ronnie sat up in the room with us and sat against the door. He put a chair up against the door. He said, "If they come in here, they're going to have to come through me." And he was tough.

EMMA POUGHT, The Bobbettes: Oh God, you couldn't eat; we had to eat sardines and stuff like that because they wouldn't sell you no food at the counter.

LOIS POWELL, The Chantels: And you know, we were from New York, we were young and silly. Sometimes we attempted to challenge, you know, "Well, we're from New York, and we can sit here if we want to," and the native people grabbing us and saying, "You're going to get you killed, and you're going to get us killed. You're going to leave, we still have to live here. You have to follow the rules." And we were just, you know, incensed that we had to do this, but we did—we had to.

EMMA POUGHT, The Bobbettes: Women have to buy little things, and we went to get bobby pins and stuff like that, it was in a Woolworth's in Georgia. And our chaperone took us there. Each one of us had a fifty-dollar bill. And the lady looked at us and she wanted to know where in the hell they got fifty dollars each. So she said, "Oh, you must have picked a lot of cotton." I'm telling you, some of the things we went through, you don't know humiliating really, really.

LOIS POWELL, The Chantels: It was bittersweet, doing the tour. In some of the states that we sang in, we would sing in the main auditorium for white audiences and then in the basement of the theater for Black audiences. They were equally as packed, but they wouldn't mix them in the same theater, so we had to do two separate shows.

BEVERLY LEE, The Shirelles: In Selma, we went to this college. There was a demand for The Shirelles. They had no idea who we were—that we were Black—but they wanted us to come and perform. When we got there, they were surprised, but since we were there they let us perform. We integrated that college. It was the first time somebody Black had worked there. Quite naturally, some ignorant person called us the N-word—but we did get a letter of apology. Now I look at it to a certain degree, we were like guinea pigs. If you wanted a door open, send The Shirelles.

LOIS POWELL, The Chantels: It was crazy, the audience loved us. We couldn't get it, you know, how do you clap and love what the Black people are . . . It was so hard to wrap our heads around the fact that people applauded us, and they loved us, and they wanted autographs, but they didn't want to sit next to us. They didn't want us to go to their schools. They didn't want us to eat in their restaurants. We couldn't live in their neighborhoods. But they would come see us and clap and be swaying to the songs that we were singing. It was just, for me—and I can only speak for myself—it was just mind-blowing. I just couldn't understand that. What was the logic in all of that?

EMMA POUGHT, The Bobbettes: I had never in my life seen a water fountain that's marked Colored, white. We saw some terrible things, really terrible. I saw the Ku Klux Klan, all of them came up on our bus—I saw them in Tennessee. The older people on the bus were telling us, "You girls be quiet! *Shut up!* Don't make no *noise*." I remember the buses being stopped, and we didn't know what it was for, but they said, "All right now, everybody be quiet." They said, "Let's save the kids" because Frankie—I'm a little young too at that time. I think we were the two youngest people on that tour—but the Klan actually came up on the bus and he came up on the bus to ask them where they were going.

BEVERLY LEE, The Shirelles: We were down at South of the Border in South Carolina—there's a spot where people stop and get a little something to eat, or knickknacks, or whatever. We come out of there and got in the car, and a car to the right of us, a window rolled down—just enough for a gun to come out—you could see the gun pointing at us. We got out of Dodge. We were from Jersey, but we knew what that meant.

WHOOPI GOLDBERG, entertainer: The evolution of the girl group is really wonderful when you look at it. You see all these groups, it's just like, "Damn, y'all left home, got on a bus and toured the world. *You toured the world?* You came out of the projects where everyone, you know, I'm sure said, 'No, not you guys,'" and then they did it.

CHAPTER 8

Here Today, Gone Tomorrow

ARTIE RIPP, music executive: Payola was the means to be able to get the edge on your competition. The guys who had the money in their pocket and were ready to spend the money to influence the general manager, the program director, the disc jockey, the record librarian, the person controlling the charts. George Goldner had that down to a science. He was the number one lobbyist.

LOIS POWELL, The Chantels: We didn't know how it all worked. Because we would hear conversations or bits and pieces of conversations, we kind of knew that there was this payola going on. We knew something would go down in terms of people getting record play and that kind of thing. We didn't know how involved it was, and then again, even if we voiced something about it, people would shush us up and say, "Oh, you don't know what you're talking about. This is not for kids." That kind of thing.

ARTIE RIPP, music executive: I began to learn everything I could about the record and music business. One day I concluded, it'll take me a hundred years to learn all the aspects of the business—creatively, business-wise. Maybe there's a guy who does all of this stuff—owns the record company, picks the artists, picks the songs, produces the records, and owns the artists and the recordings—and one of those guys happened to be George Goldner. So I pursued him until finally he sat me down, and he says, "What do you want?"

I said, "I want to work for you. You're the greatest. And I think I'm the greatest and I need you. I think I can help you have more hits."

So I went to work for him. And at that point in time, he had The Bobbettes, he had The Chantels, he had The Flamingos, he had Little Anthony and the Imperials, he had The Dubs.

But George had to deal with the fact that you had to go get your money from the distributors, you had to pay the artists, you had to pay the overhead. You had to sell records, and there were guys who were bootlegging the records. So you manufactured a thousand, they manufactured a thousand. You sold the thousand and the stores got two thousand.

BROOKS ARTHUR, sound engineer: Goldner had a different kind of power going for him, and that is, he was very plugged into radio stations. He knew a lot of DJs and knew a lot of programmers. And he would take records, throw them in his trunk, and deliver them across the country—in person. And buy the guys a lunch or a dinner and treat them to a small gift of appreciation. I mean literally a gift—I don't mean cash or nothing like that. I never saw that. But he had power at the radio stations and program directors and the jocks themselves.

ARTIE RIPP, music executive: He was an eight-dimensional movie. He was an impeccable dresser—all custom-made clothes.

BROOKS ARTHUR, sound engineer: Great-looking guy, really great-looking guy. Looked great in a cardigan sweater, and in a suit, and in a Lincoln Continental—he always had all three.

JOEY DEE, Joey Dee and the Starliters: And he'd have two radios on, listening to the ball games and horse racing.

BROOKS ARTHUR, sound engineer: George Goldner was like . . . uh . . . respectfully, he was the good side—the nice side of . . . of a Damon Runyon character.

BOB FELDMAN, songwriter: A Damon Runyon character's a guy who doesn't really shave, who's got a cigar in his mouth, and he's a wiseguy. Talks like this, like a *New Yawker*, like Brooklynese. That was this kind of guy, *tawlked like this*, had a cigar out of the side of his mouth. Twelve-day beard. A wiseguy, he knew everything. *You know whadda mean, sista?*

ARTIE RIPP, music executive: I went on the road with George, and we went from city to city. He did not like flying, so it was a car trip. Drive to Pittsburgh, drive to Cleveland, drive to Detroit, Philadelphia, and so on. It was always an adventure. I used to wake up in the morning and say, "Wow, I think I'll get a shrimp cocktail and a filet mignon for breakfast." When it was, "Gee, I can't even afford a hamburger, but on the boss's tab, I'm good."

We pulled into a city and he would rent out the whole hotel floor. We put call girls into those rooms and then I would bring disc jockeys, program directors, Black and white, from all the stations that were important in that town and bring them in for a good time. And we'd be able to get close to the guys, have some wine, have some . . . and be able to joke with them. "Oh my God. She was unbelievable." I said, "The redhead will kill you." So there were great, what I'll call, comic scenes that were terrific and they were bonding moments between myself and the disc jockeys.

I still delivered great records, great songs, great artists that George had come up with. I remember one of the competing record company promotion guys saying to me, "There's no way for us to follow you and George into a town. Nothing tops what you guys do." They could talk about, "Oh my God, that party that George Goldner threw, my God, I died after the third girl."

AUTHORS' NOTE: In 1959, payola investigations began, carried out by a White House subcommittee. In early 1960, President Eisenhower called it an issue of "public morality," and the Federal Communications Commission (FCC) created a new law, making involvement in payola a criminal act.

BOBBY JAY, disc jockey: The payola scandal was because the powers that be in Washington and other places were upset with people like Alan Freed, who were exposing young, nubile, white girls to these Black singers—*we got to get rid of this stuff.*

STANLEY GREENBERG, producer: Payola had something to do with everything that went on in the record business. But if you ask me any more questions about payola, I'm afraid I'll end the conversation.

RICHARD GOTTEHRER, songwriter: You see Alan Freed's name on some songs. I don't know that he wrote the songs, but he played them on the radio. There's a price for everything and I can't be critical of . . . you have to live in the time and realize what the time is. Looking back on it, it sounds like highway robbery, but if you were there in the moment, and you were them, and you wanted to get where you wanted to be going to, there was a price. We all pay the price from time to time. He might not have written it, he might have laid out the arrangement with them, or he might have just said, "Well, the deal is I participate in the songwriting." We can criticize all of that all we want, but that's the price you pay for getting to where you want it to go. It's like anything in life.

ARTIE RIPP, music executive: And it goes back to Judas selling out Jesus. Payola wasn't a brand-new thing. Bribery was not something new. What was new was somebody going against the established white culture that was there and now proudly and enthusiastically presenting Black artists, Black music, Black culture, rock and roll, garrison belts, chains, kick people's ass, gang wars, and so on. It was a whole 'nother world from an American point of view.

Alan Freed was the scapegoat for the white people in power, because he was introducing white teenagers to Black people, and Black music that was infecting them. And all of a sudden, the senators, the congressmen now saw their daughters, their granddaughters, etc., now responding to this "animal" music, to this "sex-focused" music, to this music that wasn't Rosemary Clooney and Frank Sinatra. This was young kids singing to young kids.

BOBBY JAY, disc jockey: And it was unfortunate, very unfortunate, because it destroyed a lot of careers. Alan got swept up in it, other people in New York—Peter Tripp; Tommy Smalls, Dr. Jive—and they thought that was going to be it—*let's get rid of these people.*

ARTIE RIPP, music executive: And so, you had Alan Freed, and you had Dick Clark. Dick Clark was the perfect white guy. And his show, basically, white people. If you turned on to Alan Freed, his TV show, his damn show, they were Black kids *and* white kids.

BOB FELDMAN, songwriter: Dick Clark had layers in front of him, okay? He was never caught up in that scandal, but he was the *king* of payola.

MELANIE MINTZ, writer: But he also, he had ABC behind him, so you don't mess with them, you're not just talking to his lawyer. Because that . . . remember *Bandstand* was a huge, *huge* moneymaker. Dick Clark had the biggest show on television.

BOBBY JAY, disc jockey: But Dick was so astute, they had nothing in his name, they couldn't pin anything on him. So, he got away with it. He survived and became a mogul, Dick Clark Productions.

BOBBY JAY, disc jockey: Alan was being fired everywhere, he couldn't get a job, he couldn't stay employed. He began to drink and died of uremic poisoning. He virtually drank himself to death.

JOEY DEE, Joey Dee and the Starliters: The poor guy died in I think it was forty or early forties, a brokenhearted man. And he created the expression "rock and roll."

*

BARBARA ENGLISH, The Clickettes: By 1960, our whole career, you know, the whole span, had been over. We'd had all our little hits in the span of eighteen months. That's the way the business was during that time. Superstars in the doo-wop era weren't around for more than a few years. It's amazing. . . .

I haven't received a royalty to this day. What Zell had done is she . . . I remember signing a BMI [Broadcast Music, Inc.] card out. She would use, would show my name on the promotional copies, and the printed copies—the *actual* copies, sale copies—would not have my name; my name wouldn't appear at all, did not appear.

JEAN BOULDIN, The Clickettes: All the songs that we did, Barbara English wrote all those songs, but Barbara never got credit. Barbara, she never got any royalties from anything. It was under Zell's name or her daughter's name. You write a good song and somebody else takes it and puts their name on it, which wasn't fair.

BARBARA ENGLISH, The Clickettes: My life was such a misery growing up. My mom was sick all the time. I was the woman of the house. I was just happy to sing, to get away. I wasn't . . . I didn't know that you were supposed to get paid for what you did, you know what I'm saying? I didn't realize what Zell had done until after our records, you know, were being played like crazy.

BMI had no record. I mean, I have never gotten a dime for mechanical royalties. And then when I looked at the . . . "Because of My Best Friend," which was our biggest record, it was registered, of course, but all of the royalties were paid to the publishing company. As a matter of fact, *our families* paid for our first recording. They gave her fifty dollars each. I'll never forget and fifty dollars was tearing me up . . . come on . . . I don't even want to talk—fifty dollars was hard, hard to get then.

EMMA POUGHT, The Bobbettes: Everything we did, we wrote at that time; we wrote a lot of songs, but the only thing good about that is that Ahmet Ertegun and Jerry Wexler put our names on our songs and we have copyrights. I have copyrights for everything that I did that I wrote. They had to even create a publishing company because we wrote so many songs, but we would write songs almost every day. And at the beginning, the only thing we wrote about was little boys.

It is very unusual. I got a check the other day. But anyway, I give them credit for that because I hear so many other people out there that they never got credit for a writer's role.

BILLY VERA, musician: So, your career was like a year, or maybe sixteen months or eighteen months long, at that. We couldn't work nightclubs in the fifties because we were underage. All we could work was these theater shows, where half the time you were expected to kick back some of your money to the disc jockey for the privilege of being on the show. And you know, it's like a year and a half, and then either you're back to school or bagging groceries at the supermarket.

BARBARA ENGLISH, The Clickettes: I tell you, I didn't know whether I was supposed to be paid or not. But you're not thinking about it when you don't have anything. It's not like today that you got something on paper. *She* told us what we were making.

TRUDY McCARTNEY, The Clickettes: With our little money that she was cheating us out of . . . because I know when we sang at the Apollo, that we made much, much more than we got.

LOUISE MURRAY, The Hearts, The Jaynetts: We were just so glad to be singing. That was it. We didn't even care if we got paid at first. Then after we did the Apollo for a whole week and get no money, I said, "Oh my God." I got disgusted with it, really disgusted. Zell was something else, something else.

JEAN BOULDIN, The Clickettes: We thought we were in good hands, that's what we thought. I think that maybe, maybe she got a little bit lost because of her being a lady.

BARBARA ENGLISH, The Clickettes: That ideology, that thing that says you need to be with a white manager, a white company in order to make it . . . I think that's why—because we were dealing with Zell and she was Black—we weren't going anywhere. Everybody just seemed to be rising and getting the breaks with these big record labels, record companies, managers doing, they, you know, they were white.

SYLVIA HAMMOND, The Clickettes: I enjoyed it myself, really. I hated that it ended, but that was it.

BARBARA ENGLISH, The Clickettes: We wanted to stay The Clickettes, but Zell got whiff of that and she said uh-uh, you can't use the name. I didn't even know that she could do that. Of course, she owned the name, um, copyrighted the name or, or we recorded on her label with a name and The Clickettes automatically—that's her property.

✳

LOIS POWELL, The Chantels: After school, around 1959, the record company called us in, told us that they were going out of business. We said, "Well, you have our money that you had in savings for us." And they said, "Well, there is no money." But we knew that when you did a show, the union man was in the wings waiting for his compensation and then the manager collected the check or cash that went in his pocket and supposedly it went down to Gone Records, and they put it in this account for us so we could get a twenty-dollar-a-week allowance.

So, they robbed us. They used our money. We would get twenty-dollars-a-week allowance from the record company, but based on the money that we made from either doing shows or recording, we knew that they had a substantial amount of money, but they used it.

Years later, we found out that George Goldner, who was the head of the record company, was a compulsive gambler and had embezzled lots and lots and lots of money. And so, he lost his whole company.

ARLENE SMITH, The Chantels: There was a standing joke that if you wanted to see The Chantels' money, go to the racetrack.

ARTIE RIPP, music executive: He was a rare, rare genius and a wonderful, crazy man. And unfortunately, a habitual gambler. He had three great successes as a record label owner. And he lost all of them because he lost money to bookies, and he had to sell what he had. He started out with Tico Records, and he had great artists on Tico. He helped to initiate the presence of real Latin music in the United States and was a great dancer, loved to go to Palladium. Then he created Gee Records, Rama Records. And then lost those companies. Morris Levy bought those labels from him, and then he went and created Gone and End Records. And again, a tremendous success.

JOEY DEE, Joey Dee and the Starliters: I had Morris Levy as the owner of my record company, Roulette Records. And he was not very fair or honest, but he was controlled by the Mob, the Genovese family.

RENÉE MINUS WHITE, The Chantels: When George Goldner called us downtown for our last meeting with him and Gerry Roth, his accountant, we were shocked to hear they had run out of money and could no longer afford to keep the group under contract in 1959. It was also the day Arlene Smith revealed to us she wanted a solo career. We were devastated. It was too much news for one afternoon.

LOIS POWELL, The Chantels: Arlene was always a pretty strong personality. I mean, she kind of knew what she wanted. She left the group in 1959 when the company folded. We were all kind of like scattered. We didn't know what was up.

ARTIE RIPP, music executive: Now, Arlene Smith said, "Hey, I'm what this thing's all about. It's my voice. And I don't want to be part of the Richard Barrett show anymore, so I'm going to go off on my own." Okay, go see how that works out.

LOIS POWELL, The Chantels: Once that happened, my mother said, "Well, you're not going to sit around here and wait for something to happen for your singing group. You're going to either go to school or go to work." So, then I chose school.

ARTIE RIPP, music executive: It was unfortunate for the artists and for George. What happened was that he blew it all again, and Morris Levy wound up with Gone and End Records. I worked for George through the deaths of Gone and End Records. And at that point, he says, "Well, Morris bought the company, and you're going to come and you're going to work for Morris." I said, "Never. I will never work for him."

LOIS POWELL, The Chantels: The other girls were kind of at loose ends and then Richard got them back together and found somebody else to sing with them.

RENÉE MINUS WHITE, The Chantels: My thinking is that the public fell so in love with all five of us and our sound together. Whether it was Arlene Smith as a single artist, or the four Chantels as a group, things for both entities were never the same after the split in 1959.

JOEY DEE, Joey Dee and the Starliters: Goldner was a great guy and an honest guy, and it's a shame that he had that difficulty with gambling and he lost everything. Morris took everything over.

ARTIE RIPP, music executive: I didn't want to work for the Mob. And as nice as Morris Levy was and as charming as Morris Levy could be, at the end of the day, he was involved with gangsters.

DEE DEE KENNIEBREW, The Crystals: Once Prohibition . . . once they can't sell illegal alcohol, guess where they went? Into the music business. Same guys.

EMMA POUGHT, The Bobbettes: I think that's what turned me against it . . . too many crooks, and people running off with your money, especially when you were children, because you don't know what's going on.

ARTIE RIPP, music executive: Who owned the jukeboxes? Who owned the vending machines? The Mob. So, how did you get around it? You couldn't. I mean, certainly rock and roll coming along and people actually getting managers and there being legitimate booking agents and legitimate managers. But if you really wanted to move mountains, you had to be with somebody who was connected. They were wise, smart, and they could be appreciative. But it was not something I wanted to work for.

EMMA POUGHT, The Bobbettes: We got tired of singing "Mr. Lee." They always wanted us to come up with more gimmick songs. I really, really got to the point where I was just sick of them. It's like being typecast. The only thing they want you to do is keep singing this thing. I stopped singing it onstage. Reather started singing it by herself, didn't need me to sing it no more. And I never liked to be singing it anyway. But the thing is that we said, "You know what? We going to write something and maybe if we kill it, that sucker, they'll stop bothering us about that." So we sat down and we wrote "I Shot Mr. Lee."

After when we graduated, I went to work. Even though we still sang, I still got a job, you know what I'm saying? Because even though you have that record, a lot of people thought you were rich, but you wasn't. All those songs, what it was is that the company is making all the money and you're not making any.

CHAPTER 9

Breaking the Record Industry's Vinyl Ceiling

STANLEY GREENBERG, producer: The Shirelles surprised everybody when "I Met Him on a Sunday" turned out to be a hit.

FLORENCE GREENBERG, music executive: My first record company was called Tiara Records. I had Tiara for about a minute. It wasn't a real functioning label, because I sold it to Decca. Then when Decca paid me $4,000 for The Shirelles hit, I decided to go into business for myself.

MARVIN SCHLACHTER, music executive: I met Florence Greenberg at a radio station. She was promoting The Shirelles' record "I Met Him on a Sunday," on Decca. Ultimately, they dropped The Shirelles, and Florence spoke to me and asked me if I would like to start a company with her and use The Shirelles as the first artist. And I said, "Why not?" And that's how we started Scepter Records.

FLORENCE GREENBERG, music executive: Decca wasn't crazy about the girls and said they were a one-hit act. They gave The Shirelles back to me. That's when I started Scepter Records. By this time, I had rented a little space in 1674 Broadway, a one-room office, divided in two—a waiting room and my office.

SHIRLEY ALSTON REEVES, The Shirelles: It didn't click. They said that we were a one-hit wonder. That's what Decca told Florence. She took us back. She had accumulated a little money from them. Not that she didn't already have money, but she didn't want to use her money.

FLORENCE GREENBERG, music executive: I picked the name Scepter and Tiara for my labels by looking at a picture of a throne and a queen. And thinking of all the things a queen possessed: a scepter, a tiara, a mace, a royal chair.

BEVERLY LEE, The Shirelles: We just finally got the publishing a couple years ago for "I Met Him on a Sunday." That was a big plus for us.

STANLEY GREENBERG, producer: Then the next record of The Shirelles, which I also did, was called "Dedicated to the One I Love." That was another hit that launched Scepter Records.

FLORENCE GREENBERG, music executive: The Shirelles heard a record that hadn't been successful called "Dedicated to the One I Love" and fell in love with the sound of it. They wanted to record the song, so we cut it at Beltone Studios in Manhattan. My son, Stanley, who was still in school, coproduced it with me. Well, it was a flop when it was first released in 1959. I think promotion had a lot to do with it. If you just play a record in your backyard, nothing is going to happen.

The early Shirelles records always broke R & B first, then they would cross over to pop. I used to go to Washington, DC, and sit in the window with the DJ at Waxie Maxie's record store. Sometimes they would broadcast live from the store window while the kids would dance in the street. Sometimes I'd sit with him all night. And that could break a record.

ARTIE RIPP, music executive: Ah, Florence Greenberg. Florence Greenberg's office, Scepter Records, was down the hall from George Goldner's office. Same floor, 1650 Broadway. Florence was brilliant, Florence was dominating, and Florence was controlling. She was a visionary. She had balls bigger than any man in the room and she knew she needed them. Otherwise, she was going to get run over, and they'll put her behind the desk and say, "Hey, honey, get me a cup of coffee."

JOEY DEE, Joey Dee and the Starliters: It was a more macho era, the late fifties. Girls weren't given the honor and the respect for their talent and their musicality—except Florence Greenberg. I can't think of another person who was in charge of a record company that was female.

ARTIE RIPP, music executive: So Florence Greenberg was extraordinary. There ain't been another Florence Greenberg. She took care of the girls. And she picked hit songs.

JOEY DEE, Joey Dee and the Starliters: She loved the music, and she really cared for the acts and the artists, and that shows. Maybe we should have had more women involved.

FLORENCE GREENBERG, music executive: I was still in my same office. I did a lot of promotion myself, and I hired a promotion man by the name of Wally Roker. One day we were in the elevator, and Wally said hello to Luther Dixon and introduced him to me. Luther had just had a hit called "Sixteen Candles," by The Crests, so I said to him, "Would you be interested in listening to The Shirelles to see if you could work with them, and give them a song?" He said, "Of course." And that's how we began our association.

BILLY VERA, musician: Stanley helped with the records in the beginning until they met Luther Dixon, who became their main producer.

FLORENCE GREENBERG, music executive: I knew after a few meetings I wanted to work closely with Luther, and we became partners. "Tonight's the Night" was the first record Luther produced for The Shirelles. Soon after that we moved into the 1650 Broadway building.

STANLEY GREENBERG, producer: When Luther came in to Scepter, we were not there together, because I wasn't supposed to be cognizant of his relationship with her. I wasn't allowed to see it, though everyone in the world knew about it.

STEVE GUARNORI, author of *Scepter Wand Forever!*: Pretty soon after starting Scepter, Florence was away with Luther Dixon having an affair with him. It wouldn't have been easy for her, dating a Black man back then. And of course, she had young adult children that were caught in the middle of that as well. Wally Roker, who's dead now, unfortunately, but he told me that the kids were camped outside his house one day, saying, "Where's Mom gone?" and all this kind of stuff. "We know she's with that Luther Dixon," and da da da. And he was like, "Don't ask me nothing, nothing to do with me."

BROOKS ARTHUR, sound engineer: He is a wonderful man, Stanley. Stanley Greenberg was in the control room most of the time, lending a hand, lending an ear, and pitching in as if he didn't have any handicaps at all. What he didn't see, he heard.

STEVE TYRELL, producer: Stanley kind of built Scepter, he and Luther Dixon. He always wanted to drive my car and I said, "Are you nuts, man?" And he said, "Yeah, I can do it." Because his vision, the way he described it to me, would be like you were looking through a shower . . . you could see shadows and stuff, but you couldn't really make anything out. So he could see light and stuff. He got behind the wheel and we drove down Second Avenue. I had to tell him, "Hey, Stanley, slow down." That was one of the highlights of my life, that I made it through alive.

*

MELANIE MINTZ, writer: "Tonight's the Night"—are you going to give up your virginity? You're not going to give up your virginity? The next song is "Will You Love Me Tomorrow." Did you give up your virginity, or didn't you? But we were all living through it.

LUTHER DIXON, producer: Donnie [Don Kirshner] brought Carole King to me and asked if I could help the young lady. Donnie managed Bobby Darin—Bobby and I were great friends, and he recorded a song of mine called "Irresistible You." And so because of my friendship with Bobby and Donnie, I agreed to work with Carole. The second song she brought me was "Will You Love Me Tomorrow."

STANLEY GREENBERG, producer: "Will You Love Me Tomorrow" is written by Carole King and Gerry Goffin, and Carole produced the strings. Well, actually she produced the whole record.

GERRY GOFFIN, songwriter: Carole was out playing mahjong at her mother's, and I was at a Marine Corps Reserves meeting. When I came home, there was a note that said, "Donnie needs a lyric for The Shirelles." She wrote the melody and left it for me on a huge Norelco two-track tape recorder. I heard it and I thought, *This is something different*, and I was inspired by it. It just came out of me. We were struggling, so it was like God was watching over us. And I wrote the opening lyrics in about five minutes.

CAROLE KING, songwriter: This all sounds really crass and monetary and everything, but Gerry was the family provider, he was more concerned about making sure we had enough money because he *was* a family provider. I was just there, like, "What are we . . . what am I needed to do here?" You know, "Oh, we need to write a song. Oh, okay. The baby's crying. I'm gonna take care of the baby." I was eighteen years old, and a mom, which was obscene, but I was out of high school. I graduated high school at sixteen. So I wasn't a high school mom.

FLORENCE GREENBERG, music executive: Carole came up to our office and wrote most of "Will You Love Me Tomorrow" there on our piano. I remember giving her baby a bottle while Carole was writing the song.

STANLEY GREENBERG, producer: Carole went everywhere with her baby. When they came to rehearsal at Scepter, Florence held the baby while Carole played the piano.

ARTIE KAPLAN, session musician: She went out to 48th Street and Broadway and bought a book about how to write for strings. The next day, she showed up with a chart of strings and asked me to hire the players. That's pretty good when you stop to think of how many people went to Juilliard and were looking for jobs to write strings for songwriters, and here's Carole King, a maestro in one day.

GERRY GOFFIN, songwriter: Carole originally wanted violas, but she couldn't get them, so she wrote for two cellos and four violins and made it sound like a string quartet. I was so proud of her.

CAROLE KING, songwriter: Gerry Goffin's determination to succeed in the early sixties had driven me harder than I might have driven myself. Not only did we write more songs in service of the pressure he felt to provide for his family, but we wrote better songs because of his insistence on excellence.

SHIRLEY ALSTON REEVES, The Shirelles: Carole King, who I love, has an odd way of singing a little bit. It's not so much an odd way, but back then, to me, it was more like a country sound. People would come and sing their songs that they wrote for you. She played very bold and she sounded like she did when she recorded it. When she played it, I said, "Uh-uh." Florence looked at me and I waited until she finished. I said, "It's not a Shirelles song." "What do you mean 'It's not a Shirelles song'?" "It's a good song," I said. "It's a beautiful song, but that's country music. We don't do country."

BILLY VERA, musician: Shirley didn't want to record that because she said it sounded like a country song. But they talked them into doing it. And, of course, that became their biggest, most memorable song.

STANLEY GREENBERG, producer: I wouldn't go as far as not wanting to record it. I think they thought it wasn't a hit record for four African American women because it was too white. I'd be very careful how I wrote that.

BEVERLY LEE, The Shirelles: Carole King did the demo and it was totally different. It was raw and it was really twangy, and we didn't like it. We said, "We're not singing that," and he said, "Yes, you are." We went into the studio—it was a whole different ballgame.

SHIRLEY ALSTON REEVES, The Shirelles: When I got to the studio and I heard the music, I just thought it was so pretty.

BEVERLY LEE, The Shirelles: It blew my mind when I went in and saw this room filled with so many musicians. There was a big orchestra in there. When they started playing the arrangement, it was lush with strings and cellos—you name it. I said, "Oh wow"; it just blew my mind. I'll never forget it. As a matter of fact, we were told that Carole didn't like the way one of the guys was playing kettledrums. Carole King is playing kettledrums on that record. Listen—she was a hands-on woman. This was between The Shirelles and Carole King. This was girl power.

MELANIE MINTZ, writer: "Will You Love Me Tomorrow" was put on a list by the Catholic Church and banned in Catholic countries because of what it suggested, that you were going to have sex and you weren't married.

AUTHORS' NOTE: "Will You Love Me Tomorrow" was released in 1960, the same year the Food and Drug Administration (FDA) approved the birth control pill.

BEVERLY LEE, The Shirelles: It was time for women to come forth. Men had always been dominant. We had a voice, and we had a message that we could convey. We conveyed it very well. A female has the right to ask a question: "Will you still love me tomorrow—after you've had my most prized possession?" Guys don't . . . they tend not to like a woman who can think for herself. So she's saying, "Hey, I'm taking control of this situation."

SHIRLEY ALSTON REEVES, The Shirelles: They didn't let me live it down at the company. Whenever we'd record anything, they would say, "Shirley, which one of these songs do you like?" I'd pick one, and they'd say, "Which one of these songs don't you like?" I'd tell them what I didn't like, and that's the one they said they were going to put out. We laughed and had a lot of fun with that.

AUTHORS' NOTE: In January 1961, "Will You Love Me Tomorrow" became the first number one song by a Black girl group.

MARVIN SCHLACHTER, music executive: We believed we had a hit record, we didn't know how big it was going to be.

STANLEY GREENBERG, producer: Of course I knew it, I sold two million copies before the first one came out. [*laughing*] We thought a lot of records were hit records until they weren't.

BILLY VERA, musician: Shirley had a warmth in her voice that people responded to. They heard it.

GREIL MARCUS, music writer: I once played "Will You Still Love Me Tomorrow" eight hours straight and the song just kept getting better.

AUTHORS' NOTE: This song's title is often cited incorrectly. The accurate title is "Will You Love Me Tomorrow."

MARVIN SCHLACHTER, music executive: And lo and behold, we had a gold record and Carole King's first gold record also.

DON KIRSHNER, music executive: I grabbed Carole and we got a limo, and we drove up to Queens where Gerry was working. When we went inside, he was mixing all these potions. I told him, "Gerry, you don't have to do this anymore. Your song is number one. You're going to be one of the greatest songwriting teams in history."

CAROLE KING, songwriter: But all of a sudden, he could quit his day job. And that was momentous.

GERRY GOFFIN, songwriter: When Don said that, it felt like a big load was lifted off of us. He told us we'd each earn ten grand on the song—enough for us to get credit cards.

BEVERLY LEE, The Shirelles: When it became a million seller, we were told that Carole had the melody to "Will You Love Me Tomorrow" play her doorbell.

BROOKS ARTHUR, sound engineer: Yes, sure. Absolutely. [*singing*] *Da, da, dee, da, da—da, daaaa, da.* In South Orange, New Jersey. Sure. Absolutely.

PART 2

The Sound on the Street

1960–1963

CHAPTER 10

The Foundation of the Wall of Sound

The Crystals

DEE DEE KENNIEBREW, The Crystals: My mom worked at a junior high school. There was a guy there who lived in the neighborhood and he was in his fifties at the time. He used to come to the school—the after-school centers—and they would let him use the music room because he was trying to put together groups to put into the music business. And his name was Benny Wells. I guess he wanted to do a girl group. So he asked my mom if she knew any kids around there that sang. She said, "Well, I have a daughter at home," and he liked my voice.

Benny heard that his niece had won a talent show at her high school. Her name was Barbara Alston, and Barbara Alston brought in the girls. So that was the four of us. We had a great time. We were learning harmonies and all that sort of stuff. I was fourteen, not quite fifteen at the time.

MYRNA GIRAUD, The Crystals: Barbara, Mary, and I, with some other girls, all were part of the choir at William H. Maxwell High School in Brooklyn. Practicing for the choir contest is what led to Barbara's uncle hearing us, because in those days, my stepmother was a bit of an ogre and she wouldn't let us practice in the house, so we practiced in the hallways of Mary's apartment building. And we had the whole hallway, all the floors to ourselves, and Barbara's uncle brought in Dee Dee and Patsy Wright.

DEE DEE KENNIEBREW, The Crystals: He took us to the Brill Building. So he brought us over to a company there that had a panel, of course, and producers and songwriters would come in and out.

MYRNA GIRAUD, The Crystals: We were actually in the Brill Building rehearsing "There's No Other (Like My Baby)," and we had a different tempo on it. Phil Spector heard us and he just barged in. He barged in and took over. He said, "Try it like this," and he changed the tempo. Really, literally he just took over.

DEE DEE KENNIEBREW, The Crystals: He said, "Ooh, I like that." He said, "Are you all signed to somebody else?" And we said, "No, we're not." He said, "Do you want to record?" "Well, of course," Benny piped right up. 'Cause of course that's what he was looking for.

So he said, "Well, could you sing that song a little bit slower? Sing it slow." So we did it. And he said, "Okay, I want to take you all over. I want to record you all." And he said his name was Phil Spector. We knew nothing about him at the time, because he was new to basically . . . he wasn't new like *we* were, he had been hanging around the music business for a while.

DARLENE LOVE, The Blossoms: Phil Spector was making a name for himself in New York. He was hanging out with Ben E. King, and he was in the writing stable that they had in New York.

MIKE STOLLER, songwriter: Lester Sill was working with him. I know he called and spoke to Jerry and he said, "I got this kid and he's very talented and he wants to come to New York and apprentice with you guys." So we sent him a check to get an airline ticket and he came to New York.

JERRY LEIBER, songwriter: Phil Spector arrived on our dime. He came directly from the airport to our office and asked if he could sleep on the couch. What could we say? It didn't matter that he forgot to thank me for the ticket or that he was an annoying presence. I had the feeling he was smart.

MELANIE MINTZ, writer: He was sleeping on Leiber and Stoller's office couch. So he was seeing what Leiber and Stoller were doing with their songs.

MIKE STOLLER, songwriter: And we were doing, at that time, maybe two, three record sessions a week. And we used three or four guitar players and so he became the fourth or fifth, and we had all the guitars doing something a little bit differently. Later on, he apparently used multiple instruments like we were and that became, as far as I know, what he called "the Wall of Sound."

JERRY LEIBER, songwriter: Once he couldn't stand sleeping in our office anymore, I let him live in my house. At our sessions, he watched us like a hawk—the instrumentation we used, the multiple percussionists playing the baião rhythm pattern, our method of mixing, the whole schmear.

BOB FELDMAN, songwriter: If they did a Mount Rushmore of songwriters, the first two up there would be Leiber and Stoller, okay? It's two nice Jewish boys who wrote the best R & B and blues that you ever heard.

MIKE STOLLER, songwriter: My first exposure to boogie-woogie was at summer camp when I was seven. I heard a Black teenager playing on an upright piano in the barn, which was our recreation hall. That was around 1940. I was mesmerized by it. I loved it. I tried to make my fingers move the way I saw his fingers moving and I got to be fairly adept by the time I was around eight.

Well, that summer camp I went to for many years in the summer for two weeks or four weeks, whatever my folks could afford, and it was an interracial summer camp—totally interracial. Some of the counselors were Black, some were white, and the campers were mixed. The camp was partially run by the Harlem Y and the IWO, International Workers Order—it was very left-wing. But we had a Paul Robeson recreation hall that was named for him because he used to come up and sing to us. Woody Guthrie also came up and sang to us.

I asked my father to buy me some boogie-woogie records so I could listen to them and he bought an album which had two 78 RPM records in it. Later, of course, I could buy my own at the five-and-ten-cent store, at Woolworth's. I would buy anything that said *boogie-woogie* on it or that had it in the title. And usually there was a blues vocal on the other side. A 78 RPM single had two sides, so I became somewhat familiar with the poetry of blues.

ARTIE BUTLER, musician: Everybody's influenced by people before them, even the generation that . . . Tchaikovsky was influenced, Rachmaninoff was influenced, Leiber and Stoller were influenced. When you grow up and you become an artist in your own right, you don't know it, but you take things that are tucked away way down inside your psyche, that you don't even know how it influences your artistic endeavors. You're influenced by your mother, your father, your dog, your school, the girl that turned you down, the guy that turned you down, whatever—you draw on it. You don't even know, but it comes through.

MIKE STOLLER, songwriter: I was sixteen and went to Los Angeles City College. I met a fellow there who was a pretty good piano player, I think probably better—yeah, I'm sure—much better than I. He had a gig; it paid three dollars. He got a better gig that paid five, so he gave me the three-dollar gig and I played with a pickup band.

The drummer took my name and phone number and I thought I was going to get some more three-dollar gigs, but instead he gave my phone number to his schoolmate at Fairfax High School whose name was Jerome Leiber.

And I got a phone call from Jerry and he wanted to make sure I was the right person. Was I Mike Stoller? Could I write music? And then he said, "How would you like to write songs with me? I write lyrics." And I said no, because I assumed he was going to be writing some kind of songs that I didn't really like to listen to. But he was very persistent and he eventually came to visit me in downtown LA where I lived with my folks, and he showed me his notebook of lyrics, and I said, "Well, these are twelve-bar blues. I like the blues." He said, "They are? Well then, I guess that's what I write." So we went to the piano, I started playing a little bit, and he started singing along, and we shook hands and said, "We'll be partners." And we were for sixty-one years.

ULA HEDWIG, background singer: Leiber and Stoller wrote "Hound Dog."

MIKE STOLLER, songwriter: On the way into the studio, Jerry said to me, he said, "You know, she [Big Mama Thornton] ought to *growl* it." I said, "Yeah, you tell her." He said, "No, you tell her."

BROOKS ARTHUR, sound engineer: Jerry was very visceral. He would really rather have it raw, and even with some mistakes, than have a recording or a sound on a record overproduced.

MIKE STOLLER, songwriter: She said, "Don't be telling me how to sing the blues." However, the idea stuck and from the very first take she was growling and it was perfect. It was really perfect. And Johnny Otis, who was running the session . . . the band wasn't happening in rehearsal, and we said, "Hey, John, you better get out there and play the drums." He said, "Well, who's going to run the session?" And we said, "Well, we'll run it." He said, "You kids?"

BROOKS ARTHUR, sound engineer: Mike, he'd want those notes to be right and the harmonies to be right and the modulations to be right. So it was a marriage made in heaven, so to speak. One had eighty-eight keys and one had twenty-six letters in the alphabet.

MIKE STOLLER, songwriter: We ultimately started making records, producing them. We were given, later on, by Atlantic Records—when we asked for credit for making the records—they gave us the title "producer." We thought "director" would have been more appropriate because "producer" sounded like we were paying for it, but it stuck and it then became the nature of the record business, independent production.

It was a title that Ahmet [Ertegun] and Jerry came up with, mostly because we were now recording some songs with their artists that we hadn't written. Because at first, Jerry Wexler said, "How many times do you want to see your name on the record label?" Because our names were on as writers on songs. So we said, "But we're making these records. How about a credit for that?" And so finally they said, "Well, all right." And they finally agreed and they came up with the title "Produced by."

CHARLIE THOMAS, The Drifters: Jerry and Mike, they were *the* producers.

MIKE STOLLER, songwriter: I was twenty-two and I went to Europe for three months. I came back from Europe and I decided to come back as I assumed my grandparents had come to America, on a ship. And it was a beautiful ship, actually, called the *Andrea Doria*, and I was on it and it sank. It was in a collision with a Swedish ship, the *Stockholm*. It was dramatic because I thought I was going to die. The ship was angled, listed, and I had no idea there were any other ships around. I was picked up from a broken lifeboat on a freighter.

Jerry was at that dock when I came in with dry clothes. I came down the gangplank from this freighter, and he said, "Mike, we're rich! We got a smash hit!" I said, "You're kidding?" He said, "'Hound Dog'!" I said, "Big Mama Thornton?" He said, "No, some white kid named Elvis Presley."

BILLY VERA, musician: I mean, those records that Leiber and Stoller did with The Drifters and Ben E. King, I mean, they're some of the most magnificent recordings of all time.

MIKE STOLLER, songwriter: During the rehearsal of the song "There Goes My Baby," which we worked on with Ben E. King and The Drifters, I started playing something on a piano, a counter line, and Jerry said, "That sounds like violins." I said, "Well, why not? Let's do it." So we did the session with . . . it was a cello and four violins and the rhythm section, everything all at the same time in the studio. I mean, strings were always used frequently for performance, for singers, but it just hadn't been done in the rhythm and blues field. It gave us . . . the success of it, the impetus to use other colors, other instruments, and to try different kinds of musical effects.

CAROLE KING, songwriter: They were definitely always that one step ahead that we always looked at and said, "Look at that, we should go that way." They were really trailblazers.

ARTIE BUTLER, musician: I'll tell you, for me, personally, I look at them as a pair of Houdinis, because they knew every trick in the book about making records.

MIKE STOLLER, songwriter: We were fascinated by the rhythm, the Brazilian rhythm and the baião. And so we started to use the baião rhythm and others . . . basically on the drum. But the famous *boom, boom-boom . . . boom, boom-boom*—that was picked up by everybody else, by Burt Bacharach, who was a good friend, and certainly by Phil Spector. So that became, that rhythm really held together—even a ballad—it really held it together. Well, actually, I first heard it on the soundtrack of the film *Anna*, the Italian film, and they had a Brazilian group in the film playing, and it knocked me out. Then a record came out, and I loved it. So we started using that and adding the triangle, we used a lot of different percussion instruments. A lot of them were playing the same basic *boom, boom-boom* rhythm. But then we used other instruments and eventually the musical instrument rental service used to get calls from other people asking for the "Leiber and Stoller kit," which was a collection of rhythm instruments that we used on a lot of records.

*

DEE DEE KENNIEBREW, The Crystals: We wound up going to the studio in May, and in fact the girls were having their prom, because they were graduating high school that year. They were seventeen and I was fifteen at the time. The girls came in their prom dresses because in those days nobody went to spend a night out after the prom.

BARBARA ALSTON, The Crystals: My date for the prom was my neighbor friend, Douglas, who escorted both me and Myrna to the prom.

MYRNA GIRAUD, The Crystals: My stepmother would never have allowed me to have "a boyfriend" that she was aware of, so we decided it was best if we did it this way, and I went without a date, and he escorted us both.

BARBARA ALSTON, The Crystals: Benny came to pick us up for the recording session later that evening. Our date, Douglas, had to go to the session with us because we didn't have time to take him home. So he was stuck with all us girls and was grinning from ear to ear because of it.

MYRNA GIRAUD, The Crystals: We left our prom early, Barb, Mary, and I in yellow prom dresses, and went to record.

JEFF BARRY, songwriter: I could see him trying to get them to skip their prom, because the fact that on the day of their prom, he had them come in the studio. . . . It's ridiculous, ridiculous. It's a power play, period.

DEE DEE KENNIEBREW, The Crystals: They came straight to the studio, which was about ten o'clock that evening. We did the two songs: "There's No Other (Like My Baby)" and "Oh Yeah, Maybe Baby."

BARBARA ALSTON, The Crystals: Benny made plans to take us away as a gift for completing the record the same night. He just wanted to show us a good time at a motel in Delaware that was owned by a friend of his. We had to take Douglas along with us there, too, because we never found time to take him home from the prom. The motel was beautiful, everything was free, and they treated us like royalty. We ate ourselves silly and had a marvelous time overall. Benny said, "This is just a taste of what is to come."

DEE DEE KENNIEBREW, The Crystals: Didn't hear any more from Phil for a while. Well, one day I come in from school—this is in early October—and I put on the radio, like most kids did when they come home from school, and I hear "There's No Other (Like My Baby)." I was shocked because I don't know what we expected, I guess . . . not a lot, and it was on the radio.

BARBARA ALSTON, The Crystals: We were so glad someone had taken a professional interest in us that we never considered the ramifications of agreements of any kind at that time. Phil was very meticulous and the cost for getting us together to record was never an issue for him and now I understand why. He knew eventually we would be responsible for the bills. We just didn't know that at that time and even if when he did ask us if we have any questions, we didn't know what to ask because we didn't know what we didn't know—right, wrong, or indifferent. And no one was telling us what we didn't know.

DEE DEE KENNIEBREW, The Crystals: This guy [Phil] was living in a studio apartment. We were the only act that he had. Philles Records did not even exist before The Crystals. His first record was with us. It was a hit. The second one, it was with us. When we started with him, he really didn't have all that money and power.

We ran up and down the East Coast from New York to Delaware doing shows for the likes of Jerry Blavat, Hy Lit—all the disc jockeys that were popular at that time playing music. We were doing these free shows. We didn't even have costumes. We didn't have pictures. We didn't have anything. We didn't know what to expect. So anyway, we just bought some white shirts and black skirts and we would go run and do these hops and sometimes we do as many as three a night all the way down to DC. That was the first time I'd ever been out of state. So, sure enough, the record got a lot of airplay.

MYRNA GIRAUD, The Crystals: Phil was a sweet, sweet guy, but he was weird. He ate a lot of grapes, he did a lot of crazy things. We were on a trip to DC for a radio interview and Barbara and Dee Dee and Patsy were in the back, Mary and I were in the front, and Phil was driving. We prayed the entire trip because Phil played with all the buttons—even the windshield wipers—and we're on the road, on a freeway to DC, and he's playing, the wipers are going—we're holding on to each other and saying, "Oh my God." He was like a big child. Phil's anger and his craziness was usually directed at himself; rarely was it directed at us.

DEE DEE KENNIEBREW, The Crystals: Then we started getting calls, but not only for the free hops to go around for promotion—we were getting calls to get paid to do shows. And remember we didn't have choreography, we didn't have pictures, we didn't have anything. Phil Spector did nothing but do the recording—he was not our manager. Our manager was this guy, Benny Wells, and he had no money. So the parents, my mother and Barbara's mother, had to kick in money. We were just brand-new, like thrown in the water and told to swim.

MYRNA GIRAUD, The Crystals: But the second song, "Uptown," which I loved—that was different, because I was married then and expecting my first child.

DEE DEE KENNIEBREW, The Crystals: Myrna decided she was going to leave home and the only way a girl left home in those days was to get pregnant, get married, and get out of the house, so she left.

MYRNA GIRAUD, The Crystals: I really would have kept on singing, but my husband was from the Caribbean and old-fashioned and he didn't think I should be singing, traipsing, and I think he was a tad bit jealous of the fact that we traveled with and met celebrities and this kind of stuff. It was a different life than he was used to. I went along with the whole thing, because I did want to take care of my baby.

DEE DEE KENNIEBREW, The Crystals: And that only left us with four. We thought we needed a fifth girl. So, Benny asked my mom again if she knew any girls that sang. Anyway, she said, "Well, there is a kid around here that really has a strong, good voice." She said, "I'll bring her in. You can see if you like her."

MYRNA GIRAUD, The Crystals: I remember that particular session, because that's when we met La La, they brought La La Brooks in, she was going to take my place once I left.

LA LA BROOKS, The Crystals: I went to a school, PS 73, where there were after-school programs. Mrs. Henry, which I didn't know was Dee Dee Kenniebrew's mother, she said to me, "Was that you with that big voice in a little girl's body?" And I said, "Yeah, yeah." And she said, "Would you like to join a group?" And I said, "Yeah, but you have to ask my mother." So my mother said yes, and I was twelve, and by the time I turned thirteen, I was doing my first tour.

DEE DEE KENNIEBREW, The Crystals: The girls said, "We can't have a kid in here." By then they had graduated high school. I was the youngest, I was just a sophomore still in high school, but this girl was, like, in junior high. So that was like *no, no, no*. But I begged Benny, "Oh please, let's keep her." She had a very strong voice and she and I were both still in school. And I wanted to have somebody, like, my size, so I begged him to keep La La Brooks. The girls said, "She doesn't even sing harmony that good." I said, "Just put her on the lead note in the background, she'll be okay. She'll learn," which she did.

LA LA BROOKS, The Crystals: Dee Dee was fifteen. She was only two years older than me, so her and I was like sisters. I was like the baby of all of them. All the rest were eighteen, so I had to listen. Hated that.

BARBARA ALSTON, The Crystals: Our first vehicle was a white Chevy station wagon with our names printed on both sides.

LA LA BROOKS, The Crystals: When the driver, Arthur, would pick us up, the kids would be there. "Are those The Crystals? They're The Crystals!" You know, one time we got this limousine, though we didn't have far to go, and they brought it in our neighborhood, and the kids are poor—they wanted to get in. I let them sit in it, all the kids sit in it, a black limousine. "C'mon, y'all can sit in it." They were happy, but it wasn't that great.

BARBARA ALSTON, The Crystals: We experienced seeing a lot of things we really didn't want to see. In hotels, guys would leave their door open and would be having sex with many girls at one time. Behind stage in some of the dressing rooms, groupies would be servicing entertainers before or after their performance. We saw many young girls giving guys blow jobs even before we knew what a blow job was.

LA LA BROOKS, The Crystals: Sam Cooke took The Crystals underneath his wings and he'd always want us to work with him on his tours.

DEE DEE KENNIEBREW, The Crystals: Although I was crazy about him, I would never do, I would never go all the way with anybody at that age. "No, no, no, I'm not going to do that. No, I can't do that." . . . So even though I would say I was crazy about Sam Cooke—I would even ride in his limo and he would jab me around, you know, but he never really forced me to do anything. And like I said, I was only seventeen—I hadn't even graduated high school yet, but I was flattered. He was one of a kind, I'll tell you that. I wasn't a fool. I knew he had a wife and a daughter named Linda. Mm-hmm.

LA LA BROOKS, The Crystals: I was with Dionne Warwick on a Sam Cooke tour and we go to this restaurant and I see the white people on one side sitting and I see the stools available, so I went to sit on a stool, but Dionne told me to get up. And I'm a *kid*, I stand up because I'm going to listen to her. Dionne said, "Let's go back in the back." I'm trying to figure out, what the heck are we going in the back for? We want to order a sandwich. She said, "What do you want?" I said, "Tuna fish." I'm trying to figure out what are we back there for? Dionne's not saying anything because she knows—she's older and she's trying to keep the peace.

We go back there and it's a hole in the door. So now Dionne knows the protocol, the woman's going to bring the menu. She brings the menu down . . . and now I'm upset. I said, "What are we going to do here?" to the lady. She said with the Southern accent, "Stand there and shut up." And I just swung the menu back, she went to hand it, and I said, "Don't tell me to shut up." The menu must have hit her chest or something. Next thing I know, Dionne got me by my shoulder and we're running—I don't know what I'm running for. We get back to the theater and she tells Sam Cooke and all of them, and they put me in the basement.

They hid me because they would have hung me—they still was hanging Black people.

So I'm in the basement and I'm listening to the man—you know the men with the big boots on and the big hats. I don't know what they are, but they're different type of police—sheriffs. I hear him say—because I'm in the basement, so there's an echo—he said, "Where's that nigger gal that came down to the restaurant and smacked the white woman in the face?" That was hanging material. So I didn't say anything, I stayed quiet. They say, "We know nothing about it." He said, "Let me tell y'all niggers something. Y'all doing the show here?" He said, "Y'all niggers, after y'all do that show, y'all going to haul asses out of here." Now we was supposed to stay in that town. . . .

BARBARA ALSTON, The Crystals: Sam wasn't too pleased to hear about the incident, but he understood how young La La was and how she might have felt. He talked with her and she understood not to let anything like that happen again, because it could have put all of our lives in danger. He told La La, "If you want to make a point, I'll show you how to do it the right way."

LA LA BROOKS, The Crystals: Okay, 'cause this is the same town that, when we was doing the show with Sam Cooke, there was a stage in the middle where we sang to white people on one side and Black people on the other.

BARBARA ALSTON, The Crystals: The place we were supposed to perform had a two-sided stage. On one side, the whites sat in theater-type chairs, and on the other side, the Blacks stood up in a basketball gymnasium. We were instructed not to sing to the Black audience. Sam sang one song to the whites and the rest to Blacks. . . . I can't remember exactly how he pulled it off.

LA LA BROOKS, The Crystals: Phil put me in the back because my voice was so big. I didn't know how to blend as well. My voice was big, I wasn't a background singer, I was more of a lead vocalist.

DEE DEE KENNIEBREW, The Crystals: La La at that time, having the stronger voice, was biting to be the lead singer. Barbara, who had never wanted to be the lead singer, was shy. Anyway, although she was the voice that was on all of the hits at that point, La La wanted to be the lead singer. She said if she couldn't be the lead singer, she would have to leave. It caused a lot of tension in the group.

LA LA BROOKS, The Crystals: But Dee Dee lies and says Phil never liked my voice as well. Hell, if he didn't like my voice . . . I made the biggest hits you guys could have imagined and that's not true. If she says it, it's not true. But he didn't know that I could sing because I'm a kid and Barbara started off with him . . . and at that time Phil wanted that soft sound until he went to California.

CHAPTER 11

Behind the Scenes with the Original Background Singers

The Blossoms

FANITA JAMES, The Blossoms: It started in junior high school. I was in the choir and I met the twins, Annette and Nanette Williams. And then we moved on to Fremont High School and met Gloria Jones and she joined.

GLORIA JONES, The Blossoms: Fanita, Annette, Nanette, and myself . . . we would just go on down the hallway singing and going into the bathroom singing, and the sound was just *good*. And all the people start telling us how good we sounded.

We got on the bus after school and we started singing and the people just loved it on the bus. Okay, it's daytime—three o'clock—when we get out of school, the bus driver took us from one end of the city to the other end and we're singing, and we looked up and it was dark outside, and we knew we had better be in our houses before the streetlights came on. The sun was going down, I said, "Oh my God—we got to get off this bus and we have to walk!" I was the first one to get off and you talk about running home before those lights came on. My dad was standing outside looking for me. I said, "Daddy, you wouldn't believe what happened." Fanita and them had to go a longer way to run. She was telling me, "Run, Wormy, run!"

That's everybody's nickname for me, Wormy—that comes from "Glow-Worm," the song by the Mills Brothers. So they first started calling me Glow-Worm, then it went into Worm, then it ended up Wormy. Darlene to this day will call me Wormy.

And we still didn't think about putting a group together. Somebody in a kind of well-known group, he heard us singing, and he said, "Let me take you to this guy who's our lead singer," which was Richard Berry . . . he would sing the lead, and we would just make up a background. And we really didn't have a lead singer. Fanita was the closest thing, but she sang real sweet—our group sounded sweet. You know, in fact, we'd go somewhere to sing and people would be surprised. They had heard us, then we walked in and they didn't think we were Black. And they would look at us like, "The Dreamers?" And we'd say yes. You know what I mean? Because we didn't have the typical sound, I guess you'd say. Our first song with Richard was "Bye Bye Baby," and we sounded like little chirping birds, I swear to you.

And we still didn't think about a girl group. I think Shirley Gunter and The Queens, they were out at this time, and we didn't have a sound like them. You know, it's still, I hate to say it like this, but they had the Black sound; we had the white sound. And by us having the white sound . . . got us in a lot of doors before they saw us, you know what I'm saying? Because it was still the Black and the white thing, I mean, that's the way it was.

FANITA JAMES, The Blossoms: And from there the word got around about our harmony and he started calling us for background. And we got really busy, and we were just so blessed. Then Nanette dropped out, one of the twins, and we needed a lead singer. So a girlfriend of mine at Fremont High School told me about a girl at Saint Paul's Baptist Church that could really sing. And I said, "Oh my," and come to find out it was Darlene, her name was Darlene Wright. And I know you've heard of Darlene Love.

DARLENE LOVE, The Blossoms: I was singing in a big church in Los Angeles. I mean, it was over five hundred people. And one of the girls that was in the choir was getting ready to get married, and she wanted to know if I would sing at her wedding. I didn't know The Blossoms yet, but they were in her wedding party. So when they heard me sing at the wedding, they asked me if I would sing with their group, and

I said, "Let me ask my mom and dad first," because I was not singing secular music yet. I was just singing gospel music. So my mom and dad actually met their parents and met their manager, and they figured it was okay. That was in '57.

FANITA JAMES, The Blossoms: So it was hard to get her, but she came and it was a lucky thing because she became our lead singer. And we went from the pretty jazz harmony/pop harmony to rock and roll—to hit that church quality in her voice. And we got a contract with Capitol Records and the man there thought we looked like a bouquet of flowers because we were different colors of brown, and he called us The Blossoms. That's where the name came from, because we looked like blossoming flowers.

DARLENE LOVE, The Blossoms: We had to go to Hollywood to rehearse with our manager, and Gloria Jones is the only one that had a car. We'd all jump in her car to drive to Hollywood, which was about a thirty-five, forty-minute drive. Gasoline was only twenty-two cents a gallon, and we'd get in her car, and everybody would give her a quarter, and we'd fill up the tank with a dollar.

Somebody asked our manager, "Did you know any girl groups that could do background singing?" Our first recording session was with Capitol Records. We were all very nervous and very scared because we didn't know whether we could do it or not, you know. But that was back in the days when everything was done at one time. All the music was there—the musicians, all the singers. And well, almost the only person that was away from us, that was in a booth, was actually the lead singer. That's how I came up. Little by little, by the time we got to the sixties, they started separating everybody. They put the music on it first, and then the background singers, and then the lead singer, and it went from there.

We were recording for Capitol Records at the time. The only problem with them, they didn't know what to do with us. They didn't know what kind of material to give to us to sing. We didn't sound like The McGuire Sisters or The King Sisters, who were on, you know, *The Perry Como Show*, those kinds of shows that were going on at the time. So they found it really, really hard.

FANITA JAMES, The Blossoms: They were all Caucasian white girls. We started that thing on the West Coast. They wanted a more . . . because rock and roll was coming in, and they wanted a more rock-and-roll style.

DARLENE LOVE, The Blossoms: We were already a group. It made our sound much better than "the readers," because we were used to singing with one another and used to doing our own harmony.

GLORIA JONES, The Blossoms: There was a difference between us and the white singers, but we could do what the white singers . . . we called the white singers "the readers." They would come into the studio, pick up the music, and start singing that. Give them the key, and they'd sing that music. We started to *let's go in here and pick up this music like we know . . . like we're reading this music*, and we played it out, played it off.

But it wasn't hard to me or to any of them. It's almost like we felt each other. That's why people thought we read music. They thought we read music, but we didn't.

DARLENE LOVE, The Blossoms: One of our major singers that we actually started doing background for was Sam Cooke.

GLORIA JONES, The Blossoms: Oh, oh my God. Don't start. Sam Cooke—he's still my favorite singer. He was . . . oh my God . . . that's . . . don't even start. But anyway, I heard him on the radio one night being interviewed. So, you know, I'm brave and I didn't care, I said, "I'm going to talk to Sam Cooke tonight." Didn't know him—none of us knew him. So I . . . what did I do? I called up there and I dedicated a song to him from The Dreamers. So on the radio, he said, "Well, tell Gloria to call me back."

Oh, that's all I needed. *Call you back?* I started dialing that sucker. And he came back, you know, he's flirty anyway, but that was okay. He asked me did we want to do some background work with him? We went down to the office and he showed us some songs and, you know, he was really paying attention to . . . you know, he'd be talking to us and looking in the mirror at himself. We sat there and said, "Oh my God, oh my God," you know, and Darlene and I, we couldn't stand to see him sing and he would always catch his bottom lip and he would *lay you out!* He thought that was the funniest thing. We didn't think it was funny. We were in love.

Oh, that bottom lip! You just don't understand. Oh my God. And we went in and we did "Everybody Loves to Cha-Cha-Cha," and I can't even remember what else we did with Sam. Hell, I can remember, we were just looking at him, he was so sexy and stayed there for a long time at the session because we were . . . he was flirty.

Our parents were with us most of the time. I know we were backstage, so Sam came and grabbed me and I don't know what he thought, but I had a big wooden purse. He never forgot me either because I hit him across his head. Oh my God, you would not believe—and I would never have said that I would have done that to Sam Cooke, but I did. And after that we were good friends. He would always bring his car over so I could drive it—go around high school, pick up Darlene, because Darlene was still in high school. It was a convertible Cadillac, green.

Now, when we first got in the car, you know how you move the seat so you can drive, right? Something broke. And a liquor smell came all over the car. None of us drank or anything back then. He had put the bottle up under the seat.

"Oh my God," I said. "How am I going to explain this to anybody?" But we were all in the car, you know, and we were kind of like Goody-Two-shoes, you know what I'm saying? Like, if you smell weed, we all would get hung in the door, trying to get out of the door. You know, we'd always say, "Suppose we'd go to jail? What would our mothers say?"

FANITA JAMES, The Blossoms: We were working a lot. I couldn't believe the money we made. We had to join the unions, which was really something.

GLORIA JONES, The Blossoms: We were the first Black background singers out there—females, so very first.

DARLENE LOVE, The Blossoms: We didn't even realize till much later that we were actually the first Black background singers that started doing sessions. We weren't known as background singers at the time. They called them session singers. So it was something that the new record producers wanted, rather than just that block harmony that the white singers were doing.

By the time I got out of high school, it was becoming a real job. You know, we would just, we got to the place where we had to turn down sessions. But our singing just went crazy. By the time the sixties came along, we were already well known as the background group doing recording sessions.

*

DARLENE LOVE, The Blossoms: We were working with a gentleman named Lester Sill, and we did not know that was Phil Spector's partner. He was just another record producer that we were, you know, trying to get hits with.

He pulled me to the side one day, and he said, "My partner's coming to town. He's looking for a singer that can do a recording for him." I said, "Well, okay." I had never recorded a solo yet for anybody, and he said, "He would like to meet you." We actually met at Gold Star, at the recording studio. Lester introduced us, Phil said, "Well, I have a song I want to do, and I want to kind of do it in a hurry because I want to get it out soon."

So he started playing it for me on the piano, and he actually sang it to me a few times. Then I started singing it back, and I learned the melody of the song. And he said, "Well, this is the record. I want to put it out, but I want to put it out under the name of The Crystals." So, at that point I didn't care. I didn't even think about it. It was a session. But when he told me he wanted me to sing lead, I said, "Well, I can't sing lead for regular scale. I have to charge you over scale." He said he didn't mind. He asked how much did I want? I said, "Well, let's make it triple scale." So I figured, *Hey, that's a whole lot of money right now for one session.*

FANITA JAMES, The Blossoms: He paid us $1,500, and at that time we thought we were rich. $1,500 each.

MELANIE MINTZ, writer: So now then you take someone like Darlene . . . now she did really well. Some of these other girls didn't have the smarts to say, "Give me triple scale."

DARLENE LOVE, The Blossoms: Jack Nitzsche, at that time, was Phil Spector's arranger—and it was amazing. All the session players that we'd worked with for the last five or six years were all the people that Phil Spector used. So we knew everybody, knew one another, because it's the same people that went from session to session to session all day long, all week. And they had never seen Phil before. So here we were all in the same place. *Who is this nut? Where did he come from?*

And I think I was probably the only one that knew Phil Spector had on a toupee. Nobody was really paying any attention to it. And he would always look at me, "What's wrong? Is something wrong?" I said no. And he goes, "Well, you're looking at my hair." I said, "No, I'm not looking at your hair." I said, "I love every person's hair." But if you can imagine this little guy that weighed about 125 pounds in a suit with his hair very neatly coiffed and, you know, a tie, and these boots with a heel—I don't know if that's the way they were dressing in New York, but I doubt it, because I had friends in New York who were record producers, and they didn't look anything like Phil. But he wanted to be different, and he was.

LA LA BROOKS, The Crystals: I liked the way he dressed. I liked those little high-heel boots he wore or the shirt that he wore that was white, that had puffy sleeves, and his hair was sort of like The Beatles. So I liked the funky look. He has a little swag, you know? You could tell he was articulate with the way he dressed, because the next day I would go to the studio and he looked fabulous too.

DARLENE LOVE, The Blossoms: I learned the song. He said I should be ready to record this song in the next couple of days after I learned it, and we went into the recording studio. It was amazing to me how fast we did it with the musicians, with the girls, you know. It was like three or four hours and he said we were done with the record. He said they were going to put it out. He had plans to put it out next week. And I went, "Wow! Okay."

Well, anyway, we found out later that another girl in California had already recorded "He's a Rebel," and he wanted to put *his* version out before she got a chance to put hers out. Well, Phil put his record out within a week. It was out and on the radio. Before they even knew the record was out in New York, it had started already climbing the charts. And within a month, that record was in the Top 10. And within a week after that, it was the number one record. And by the time they put her version—Vikki Carr is who it was—before she put her version out, the record was almost . . . it was in the Top 10. And therefore, her record didn't have a chance because now all the disc jockeys were playing my version. So they just forgot all about her, her version.

DEE DEE KENNIEBREW, The Crystals: What had happened was we had started rehearsing the song, and we had to go on the road, you know. We were always on the road.

LA LA BROOKS, The Crystals: We were on the road and we were going to a gig and our driver would always put on the radio.

DEE DEE KENNIEBREW, The Crystals: All of a sudden we hear, "The Crystals' latest record," and they start playing "He's a Rebel."

LA LA BROOKS, The Crystals: I mean, nobody could be more shocked than we were because we were confused trying to figure out . . . *what the?* We thought somebody stole our name.

DEE DEE KENNIEBREW, The Crystals: We're like, "We didn't even get to the studio to do . . . who the hell is this?"

LA LA BROOKS, The Crystals: And we figured it out. We called Joe Scandore, our manager, he got in touch with Phil.

DEE DEE KENNIEBREW, The Crystals: You know, we were shocked. But you know what he told us? "I own your name. I have you for another . . ." I think it was about another five years more. "Your name belongs to me, and I can do anything with it I want." We were so stupid we didn't know that wasn't even true. If we had read the contract. . . . I have the contracts now.

FANITA JAMES, The Blossoms: It was number one on the charts for like six weeks, and he put The Crystals' name on there, and it was us.

Darlene Love sang lead and we sang background. The word got out that The Blossoms actually did it in the industry. It wasn't our fault—they should have blamed Phil; we didn't know.

DARLENE LOVE, The Blossoms: And the disc jockey would say, "Well, now we understand that's not The Crystals singing that song. It's somebody in California named Darlene Love."

LA LA BROOKS, The Crystals: We didn't know her from a can of paint. We didn't know who the hell she was.

DARLENE LOVE, The Blossoms: That's how my name got around because I wasn't working during that time as a solo artist. Murray the K found out that it wasn't the "real" Crystals singing that song, but it was me.

LA LA BROOKS, The Crystals: Told on the radio, when it became a hit, point-blank—these are not The Crystals. We were devastated. The proof is in the pudding—there couldn't be no more proof in that pudding!

DARLENE LOVE, The Blossoms: So, little by little, it got around. It was kind of frustrating for The Crystals for a while. It didn't bother me as much. I knew what I was doing. People would try . . . disc jockeys, and press would try to come to me and make a big thing about it, but I didn't go along with them. I said, "Hey, I made big bucks off of that record. I didn't care whose name was on it." [*laughing*]

BARBARA ALSTON, The Crystals: The release of "He's a Rebel" was a total embarrassment to us. And everywhere we went, people seemed to know someone else recorded the damn song other than us. Phil Spector put us in a position of having to lie in order to save face.

DARLENE LOVE, The Blossoms: I think I dealt with it better than The Crystals. [*laughing*] Because they had to lip-sync to my version, the version that was the hit. They didn't go in and do a whole 'nother record and put it out. But I saw them on a television show where they were actually singing The Blossoms' version of "He's a Rebel," with me on the lead. So they were having a hard time, especially with disc jockeys that was doing shows.

LA LA BROOKS, The Crystals: Every time we'd go on the road, Barbara couldn't do the lead because her voice wasn't as strong. I did "He's a Rebel," and I sang the hell out of it. They didn't even know—they didn't miss Darlene, because I could sing like that—and that "No, no, no," I killed that, because I came from church—so I know how to come from church on it. So it was fabulous anytime we'd do it onstage.

DARLENE LOVE, The Blossoms: It . . . uh . . . do you know we never became friends? [*laughing*] I used to tell them all the time, "I don't know why y'all mad at me. It's Phil Spector you should be mad at." I had nothing to do with it. It was a gig for me that I got paid very well for. And that was it.

GLORIA JONES, The Blossoms: Dee Dee from The Crystals is one of my . . . I mean, when I tell you my *best friend*, she's one of them. And then, Darlene is my *bestie, bestie*. And because of "He's a Rebel," this thing between The Crystals and our group . . . it was hard. You know what I'm saying? Because Dee Dee would say that they did the song, and we did the song. And she's my friend, but she and I never ever talked about it and . . . she has her own story. She said Phil came back to New York and recorded them on the song. But I know on the hit record who it is, and she does too . . . but I think it just got to the point where it was just a rivalry there.

FANITA JAMES, The Blossoms: I want to cry when I think about it.

LA LA BROOKS, The Crystals: How dare Phil? How dare he be so ruthless? But he didn't give a damn, it was all about Phil. He didn't think about the repercussions, what's going to happen to us, and how hurt we were by it—people gossiping.

DARLENE LOVE, The Blossoms: The biggest reason why Phil Spector couldn't use The Crystals is because their parents would not let them fly to California. Their mom wasn't letting them fly to no California to do no record with Phil Spector.

FANITA JAMES, The Blossoms: Oh yeah, I did hear that. Maybe he couldn't . . . maybe he didn't want them. I don't know why they didn't want to come out here to record.

MELANIE MINTZ, writer: When they were going to do a record with The Chantels, they did it around Arlene Smith's schedule because she was the voice of The Chantels. Same thing with Supremes and all, but La La wasn't . . . she wasn't considered like The Crystals couldn't exist without her. She was considered part of these four or five girls. Which was why when La La wasn't there, it wasn't like they said they couldn't . . .

JERRY BLAVAT, disc jockey: They only knew the record and the name of the group. They didn't know who was in the group, and that's the situation.

JEFF BARRY, songwriter: It was all very modular, really. It was, as I said—the songs were interchangeable. Any artist could do it.

CHAPTER 12

The New York Hustle

The Ronettes

BILLY VERA, musician: If you weren't there, you cannot understand the impact of the Twist. It was like what the Charleston was in the 1920s. It defined the pre-Beatles sixties.

BILLY JOEL, musician: There was a lot of dancing going on in those days. And it seems like every other week there was a new dance—the Twist, the Watusi, the Hully Gully, the Swim, the Frug, the Jerk. Just a lot, a lot, of dance crazes.

JERRY BLAVAT, disc jockey: The Twist was a dance which was created by the kids, and as Chubby Checker says, it's like being in the shower and you've got the towel and you're wiping your back to get the water off your back or your tush—that's the Twist.

JOEY DEE, Joey Dee and the Starliters (the Peppermint Lounge's house band): We were doing a version of the Twist that we saw at Ben's Cotton Club in Newark, New Jersey. We started dancing and then a couple of the kids in the audience would get up and actually try to mimic what we were doing. And the thing is . . . it became super popular with our audience. And then we had some people come into the Peppermint Lounge and see these kids dancing—*What the heck are they doing?*

JERRY BLAVAT, disc jockey: It was the newest dancing creation, the newest club.

BILLY VERA, musician: The Peppermint Lounge was literally a hooker-and-sailor joint before the Twist came along.

JOEY DEE, Joey Dee and the Starliters: It was a dump, really. You walked in the front door, there was an L-shaped room. It was a long bar, maybe sixty feet long on the right-hand side, and a paneled wall on the left-hand side. Then there was a stage the size of a postage stamp. And then to the left—the L part of it—there would be a little dance floor and tables and chairs.

It had a fire capacity of like 237 people, and they used to put 600 people in there. There was a wrought iron railing around the stage.

BILLY VERA, musician: And the phenomenon of the Twist, I mean every little hooker-and-sailor joint in Times Square was suddenly a Twist lounge.

JERRY BLAVAT, disc jockey: We're talking about this phenomenon where Zsa Zsa Gabor is dancing, Cary Grant is dancing.

JOEY DEE, Joey Dee and the Starliters: Well, you can't get any bigger. Marilyn Monroe was there. Jackie Kennedy was there. John Wayne was there. Nat King Cole was there. I mean—anybody who was anybody was in the Peppermint Lounge dancing this phenomenon. These major stars are doing this new dance—old people! Jackie O. was learning the Twist!

BILLY VERA, musician: Suddenly, you had the swells from the Upper East Side in their gowns and tuxedos coming to do the Twist. [*laughing*]

NEDRA TALLEY-ROSS, The Ronettes: The Peppermint Lounge was on 45th Street off Broadway, and we went down dressed alike—which we always did. There were lines with the ropes, and so the bouncer-type guy, at the front there, he's like making a way, he's going to other people, "Move, come on, come on, come through." We're like, "Is he talking to us?" [*laughing*] They thought that *we* were the people that were going to perform because we were all dressed alike.

RONNIE SPECTOR, The Ronettes: Our mother said, "You gotta put stuff here and have a cigarette in your hand to look older, to get in even."

JOEY DEE, Joey Dee and the Starliters: They came into the Peppermint Lounge, I would say in November, maybe December, of 1961. The place was already super famous and they got in because of their looks—the doorman at the front thought they were dancers and part of the show, so he let them in. They were all dressed up, but they were only like fifteen or sixteen years old at the time—Ronnie, Estelle, and Nedra, two sisters and a cousin.

NEDRA TALLEY-ROSS, The Ronettes: And we went in, we were like, "Okay, we're in the door. What are we doing now?"

RONNIE SPECTOR, The Ronettes: The management was waiting for another girl group, we never found out what group. He says, "Girls, you're late!" I said, "Don't say anything!" . . . I told the girls, "Don't say a word." And they took us in there and they said, "Get up onstage, hurry up!"

JOEY DEE, Joey Dee and the Starliters: So they came up to the stage on my break and they said, "Can we sing with you?" I say, "Can you dance?" And they said, "Oh yeah, we can dance." So I said, "Yeah, in the next set, I want you to come up on one of the songs that we do."

NEDRA TALLEY-ROSS, The Ronettes: Joey Dee and them were performing—they were like, "Come on up!" And they were singing, so we went up, we did a few steps and then it was like, *Okay, try the railing, see if we can dance on the railing,* and we did it.

JOEY DEE, Joey Dee and the Starliters: The song happened to be "What'd I Say." So we were in the middle of it and Dave Brigati, one of the Starliters, handed Ronnie the mic, the girls got around it, and they tore the house down.

NEDRA TALLEY-ROSS, The Ronettes: We gave it all we had because we were like, *We got in here, let's just show them what we're working with!*

RONNIE SPECTOR, The Ronettes: They hired us that night. They gave us ten dollars per girl per night.

JOEY DEE, Joey Dee and the Starliters: I said, "Would you like to work for me?" And they said, "We would love to, but you have to come to our house and talk to our parents about it and get their approval." So I took a ride up to Harlem the next day, and I met the parents. They checked me out and they said, "You sure you're going to take care of our girls, right?" And I said, "Of course." They said, "No hanky-panky." I said, "Nope." And they said, "Well, just to make sure—guarantee that—we're going to send their Aunt Helen with them as a chaperone." So Aunt Helen became the chaperone.

RONNIE SPECTOR, The Ronettes: I'm still in school and my mother was a little upset because she said, "Now how are you going to get your homework done?" And I said, "Don't worry, I'll get my homework!"

*

NEDRA TALLEY-ROSS, The Ronettes: People will say, "Oh, if you're Black, you must've been raised singing in the church." We were not, we were singing for our family and making money. [*laughing*] We were raised with Sidney Poitier as a friend of the family, and my grandmother was like, "They were just here two weeks ago, and now they're on TV." That's when she said, "Do something with your daughter."

RONNIE SPECTOR, The Ronettes: Weekends at my grandma's house were the best. That's when all my aunts and uncles would come over, and there would be nothing but food and singing the whole time.

NEDRA TALLEY-ROSS, The Ronettes: Ronnie and Estelle are my first cousins. My Aunt BeBe, Beatrice, is Ronnie and Estelle's mother, my mother is her younger sister, Susie Talley. My grandmother and grandfather had fourteen kids and everybody went to Mama's house. Mama was the core of who we were and our base was 477 West 140th Street—that's where our family home was. That's where our grandmother had lived, which was Sugar Hill. I mean, people know "Sugarhill Gang" and stuff like that, but it was called Sugar Hill because it was a high point in Manhattan and we lived on the seventh floor. When you opened the windows on the west side, there was a breeze from the

Hudson and on the right side was the East River, which was where Yankee Stadium was. You could hear the balls hit. And Ronnie and Estelle at one point lived on 152nd. It was tough, but we loved where we lived.

RONNIE SPECTOR, The Ronettes: I had, like, seven girl cousins.

NEDRA TALLEY-ROSS, The Ronettes: It was really just our family. There were so many of us that we didn't need to really have friends over.

RONNIE SPECTOR, The Ronettes: My uncles would be harmonizing like the Mills Brothers in one corner, while three aunts worked up an Andrew Sisters number in the other. Another aunt would be throwing her leg up in ballet movements in the kitchen while someone else practiced an accordion in the bedroom.

NEDRA TALLEY-ROSS, The Ronettes: One would get up and do this thing, and one would sing, and one would recite something, and do different . . . tap dance, stand on your head, whatever you wanted to do—you just had to do something. And my family was so supportive of you, they would make you think you were really good, [*laughing*] and then they'd give us money. So we started getting paid at five, you know? "Give her a quarter"—you could buy a lot of candy back then with a quarter.

RONNIE SPECTOR, The Ronettes: By the time I was eight, I was already working up whole numbers for our family's little weekend shows.

NEDRA TALLEY-ROSS, The Ronettes: You know, we were very influenced by The McGuire Sisters and The Andrews Sisters, all those things. Because being family, you tend to have a family sound. . . . Ronnie did "Jambalaya." There was a song, "Jambalaya, coffee, pie, fillet, gumbo." She would scream it.

RONNIE SPECTOR, The Ronettes: I sang, with no idea what the words meant or even had them right.

NEDRA TALLEY-ROSS, The Ronettes: Ronnie was honestly my breath growing up—my life. If I could be with Ronnie, I was okay. We were such close cousins. We shared the toilet together. How many people can say they sat on the toilet butt to butt, cheek to cheek—that's how we did it. Because if she went, I needed to go. I loved Ronnie so much.

My mother would say, "Ronnie took every bottle Nedra had." [*laughing*] She's two and a half years older than me. So, it started early days. It's like, *Oh, Nedra's got a bottle, let me pull it out of her mouth.*

RONNIE SPECTOR, The Ronettes: The cousin who I was closest to was my Aunt SuSu's daughter, Nedra. . . . Her father was a Spanish man, which made her a half-breed like me. Even though she was two years younger, we were inseparable.

NEDRA TALLEY-ROSS, The Ronettes: Ronnie and I were just having fun, but Estelle was very book smart, she was easy to get along with. She was soft-spoken, but if you listen to some of the interviews, when they would ask her name, when she was saying, "Estelle" [*whispering*], it was like she lost her breath getting the whole "Estelle" out. Ronnie was more . . . Ronnie used to be in the middle. . . . Ronnie needed to be in the middle.

NEDRA TALLEY-ROSS, The Ronettes: Aunt BeBe worked at a little donut shop, sort of attached to the side of the Apollo Theater.

RONNIE SPECTOR, The Ronettes: She said, "I'm going to put you at the Apollo. And then we'll see how good you are."

NEDRA TALLEY-ROSS, The Ronettes: We did amateur night at the Apollo . . . and won. Ronnie, Estelle . . . it ended up being the three of us with my cousin Ira, but he got stage fright. He didn't have his belt, he forgot his belt, so he was like, "I can't go onstage, I don't have my belt."

RONNIE SPECTOR, The Ronettes: That was my key—I knew I was good.

NEDRA TALLEY-ROSS, The Ronettes: That was the beginning, and my mom had no fear of going downtown, knocking on doors, and saying, "There are these three pretty young girls, they can sing, and we'd like something to happen with them." And they were saying, "You know what? Boy groups are good, girls will want to get married. They'll want to have children." So a lot of people said, "No, it's not going to work." She worked *hard* for us to be who we were—and my mother could turn heads—that's part of why she got in doors too.

My Aunt BeBe, which is Ronnie and Estelle's mother, she was tiny—she was only about five-foot-three, but she was very quiet. We came from such a big family, there were so many of us, and that volume could get very high, so Aunt BeBe didn't really try and compete in the conversation. My mom didn't play. She held the other girls tight too.

RONNIE SPECTOR, The Ronettes: The three of us were determined, especially me.

NEDRA TALLEY-ROSS, The Ronettes: We started doing the Brooklyn Fox with Murray the K. We did it on our breaks. And that would be on Labor Day, Christmas, and Easter. And we would do these big rock-and-roll shows. We didn't have a hit, but Murray the K was like, "These are my dancing girls." You know da, da, da. . . . It would say on the poster on the marquee "And Others." So we used to all laugh and go, "We're 'And Others.'"

DARLENE LOVE, The Blossoms: That's where I first met them and we became friends with everybody that was on the show. 'Cause we were together from, like, ten o'clock in the morning to ten o'clock at night for twelve days. We got to meet The Shirelles on that show too.

NEDRA TALLEY-ROSS, The Ronettes: We did our own dance routines. I'd say, I was probably, for me—I'm not boasting—was more the dancer. I just loved to dance. Ronnie would say, "Come on, Ned, you pick up the dancing!" Estelle, you know, didn't ruffle her hair. Her hair came offstage looking exactly the same. I was sweating—my bangs were going up my face, my hair getting curlier and curlier . . .

BILLY VERA, musician: I remember seeing The Ronettes there and, of course, they were *the* sex symbols for kids my age—three gorgeous girls with the big hair piled up way high on their head, tight dresses, and the sexy dance moves.

NEDRA TALLEY-ROSS, The Ronettes: Our heels and our makeup was for the audience to see us way off. So our eye makeup was exaggerated, our hair was exaggerated because it was like, *See me in the balcony*. You had to project your voice, but you had to project your look too. So that's how we performed and went onstage going, *Try and see us, try and remember us, and hopefully you'll see a look that you like that you'll try for school*. [*laughing*] So that's sort of the early days of The Ronettes.

PAUL SHAFFER, musician: Of course The Ronettes were . . . had an image. They were the "bad girls" of rock and roll, and they were dressed with high bouffant hair and tight dresses, and, you know—they were a teenage fantasy, the way they were marketed.

NEDRA TALLEY-ROSS, The Ronettes: Estelle loved fashion—she went to the Fashion Institute of Technology. So she was the one going, "Well, let's wear this and wear that." She liked Brigitte Bardot and had a picture in her room. . . . Estelle was always very soft-spoken, but she was so sophisticated.

RONNIE SPECTOR, The Ronettes: A lot of Puerto Rican girls in my neighborhood, they wore the eyeliner, and the Black girls had the tight dresses on and the street look and everything.

LA LA BROOKS, The Crystals: They were original with that. And the bouffant hair. Everything was very original.

NEDRA TALLEY-ROSS, The Ronettes: You had to find something to make you stand out from the other girl groups. So then all of a sudden—because of how we dressed—we brought attention to ourselves. It's so easy for New Yorkers not to see you, because they're just on their way. But if you're coming in threes, looking alike, you know.

RONNIE SPECTOR, The Ronettes: My mother always told us to look for a gimmick that would make us stand out from all the other groups.

NEDRA TALLEY-ROSS, The Ronettes: My mother was a cosmetologist, so she believed in the teasing and doing the buns and all that. But we always did that—we had extremely long and thick hair. So I did the beehives, the buns, *and* had hair left over to pull down the side and all that.

RONNIE SPECTOR, The Ronettes: My mother is Cherokee Indian and Black, and my father's Irish.

NEDRA TALLEY-ROSS, The Ronettes: My grandmother was dark, she had a very cute shape and all those things, and her husband was the Indian affair. She understood what being dark meant. She knew that there was a difference—if you're dark, things are not going to be at your door so very easy. With having all the kids that they did, they had a variety from redheads, to freckles, to this, to that, and my mother just happened to be one of the darkest kids that was born.

RONNIE SPECTOR, The Ronettes: Being half-breeds, we were born different, so we figured the thing that set us apart from the other groups was our look.

NEDRA TALLEY-ROSS, The Ronettes: We wore high collars with Asian-looking tops. We did slits in our dresses because they were tight, but we danced, so you needed room for your knees to move. If you're going to wear something form-fitting, you had to have the place where your knee went out. We didn't do the flare little dresses with bows—that's not who we were. We were New Yorkers. And I think when people saw that, they said, "Yeah, this is sort of it. This is New York." Nobody was doing that—the girls were all flare, fifties with the crinolines underneath. It's like, *What's a crinoline?*

I think we got the bad girl image because we would do the shake and we had fringe dresses, so the fringe would really accent your hips.

RONNIE SPECTOR, The Ronettes: So when we turned our backs to the audience and shook . . . the crowd would go nuts.

NEDRA TALLEY-ROSS, The Ronettes: We were special to the family. We felt the security of all of our family. You could only walk a few blocks without running into an aunt, an uncle, cousins, and all of that. We did the Apollo Theater. And when we did it, I mean, we went with not one dad or aunt or uncle—we went with multiple people to protect us. The aunts would take turns traveling with us and the uncles were there as the chaperones.

LA LA BROOKS, The Crystals: It was like *The Partridge Family*. I mean so many people of family in a dressing room. It was like, "Oh my God." It was crazy—uncles, cousins. They took everybody in—and those halls had echoes at the Apollo—the halls was lit up.

NEDRA TALLEY-ROSS, The Ronettes: But it was like, "We can do this, we've got the strength of each other." Because we were a trio, you know, and family. And we knew our family was someplace in that building supporting us and rooting us on. And we had a big, big following of different parts of the people in the community.

BILLY VERA, musician: Estelle was the great beauty of the three. I mean, she was like, you know, a folk model. She was just a breathtakingly beautiful woman.

NEDRA TALLEY-ROSS, The Ronettes: So the whole thing about us being sex symbols, I didn't think about us being sex symbols at all—we were sexy, but not being overtly. So yeah, there was a lot of guys that wanted to be with us and then there was a lot of girls that wanted to look like us.

LA LA BROOKS, The Crystals: Ronnie would say, "La La, I'm ready to go," and she was, like, lifting up her dress.

NEDRA TALLEY-ROSS, The Ronettes: After a while, we were known for that. Ronnie got a little bit wild. She was always the one to say, "Okay, I can go a few steps, hike my skirt a little higher," or whatever. How many times did I say, "Get the dress down. Pull it further down."

LA LA BROOKS, The Crystals: I was shocked. I was like, "Oh my God, Ronnie." And she took it with a grain of salt, because she wanted the attention. Ronnie loves attention—she'd sing to a pineapple.

NEDRA TALLEY-ROSS, The Ronettes: And when we wanted to change the name, everybody pitched in on what they thought the name could be. My mother's maiden name was Mobley and she was like, "Moblettes . . . that doesn't sound good." Everybody was yelling to give their opinion. And then Ronnie—you gotta understand Ronnie's personality—Ronnie did need to be that person that was very out front. So the name came from "RO," for Ronnie, "NE," Nedra, and "ES," for Estelle. We put it together, *Ronettes*.

But when we got down to just the three of us, we were very, very, very, very close. We always held each other's hands before we went onstage. Just this feeling of, "Okay, let's squeeze hands, say a little prayer, go out there and hit it. I've got high-heel shoes on. I got my hair tall, and we're going to go out and we're going to do the best show we could do."

Anyway, life was good, and things just came our way. Colpix Records, I was fifteen—first contract. Signing a contract, you know, to be with a major company . . . that was major for us. When we had stuff pressed, we could start doing sock hops. You were legitimate when you had a record with a label on it.

RONNIE SPECTOR, The Ronettes: We were the most popular girl group ever for bar mitzvahs—people wanted The Ronettes.

NEDRA TALLEY-ROSS, The Ronettes: Honi Coles was a friend of ours—he's the Black guy in *Dirty Dancing*—but he really did those clubs, the country clubs, back in the day—and we performed there in real life. It was a couple of places, predominantly Jewish, that we played—Grossinger's was a big country-club type thing right in upstate New York, which I didn't think about, because when you're a New Yorker, there's nowhere else except New York.

Patrick Swayze was not there, saddens me, but Honi Coles did our choreography for the clubs. Laurels was another—Laurels and Grossinger's. We felt very accepted there. We would go up there and get spoiled, because they would bring you a white tablecloth, blueberries and cream. They put you up in your own little cabin and you were eating good . . . getting paid for not doing that many shows.

*

RONNIE SPECTOR, The Ronettes: One day Estelle called Philles Records, which was run by Phil Spector. He was probably the hottest producer in America, but he answered the phone himself.

NEDRA TALLEY-ROSS, The Ronettes: The big lie. No, it didn't happen that way. He came to the Brooklyn Fox Theatre, and came backstage and said, basically, "You know, you're very good, you got a look."

DARLENE LOVE, The Blossoms: Ronnie had told me when we first met her at the Brooklyn Fox, she was going to marry Phil Spector, and I was like, "Child, you don't want to marry him. He already married."

NEDRA TALLEY-ROSS, The Ronettes: I think from the beginning with Phil he had eyes for Ronnie. She was eighteen, so she wasn't illegal.

RONNIE SPECTOR, The Ronettes: We met Phil at a place called Mira Sound in New York on 57th Street. And the first night we walked in it was just him sitting at the piano and he looked at me and I looked at him—like eye contact. And he says, "Well, sing me some songs." And I said, "Well, all I know is, like, Frankie Lymon and Little Anthony." And he said, "Well, let me hear it." And I started [*singing*] "*Why do birds sing so gay*" . . . and Phil said, "That's the voice I've been looking for!"

ELLIE GREENWICH, songwriter: Phil always had a mad wild crush on Ronnie and thought she was an exceptional-looking girl, which she was, and had a very strange and unique sound.

NEDRA TALLEY-ROSS, The Ronettes: He did the audition in the apartment building that he lived in. He had the office there and lived down the hall from it. So we went there and just went to the piano. You know, I even heard . . . Ronnie said he heard a voice and he said, "Oh my God, this is the voice I've been waiting for!" It didn't happen that way.

RONNIE SPECTOR, The Ronettes: Phil knew if he approached Colpix and offered to buy out our contract, they'd never let us go, thinking that if Phil Spector wanted us, we must be better than they thought. . . .

NEDRA TALLEY-ROSS, The Ronettes: We had a contract with Colpix. And so it was like, okay, we got a contract. What? How do we get out of this, you know?

RONNIE SPECTOR, The Ronettes: My mother prepared a whole story about how the three of us wanted to leave the business and go back to school. She told them that Nedra and Estelle wanted to go to secretarial school and that I planned on going into nursing. It sounded right, since that's probably what we would have done if Phil hadn't come along when he did.

NEDRA TALLEY-ROSS, The Ronettes: By the time we got around to Phil, I was seventeen, so Mommy had to sign for me. So then all of a sudden we had pictures being done professionally, and you begin to open some doors that way, because those things are very expensive to do, especially if you're going to get somebody that's been with the top stars.

RONNIE SPECTOR, The Ronettes: The story worked, and Colpix let us out of our contract within a week. Phil finally signed us in March of 1963.

CHAPTER 13

They've Got the Power

The Exciters

MIKE STOLLER, songwriter: Well . . . we had an office—Jerry [Leiber] and I started an office for our record productions and our music publishing company, Trio Music, in the Brill Building, around 1961. I remember Ellie coming into the office—we had a room with a piano in it.

ELLIE GREENWICH, songwriter: So I just sat there playing the piano, and in walks this guy and says, "Hi, Carole"—he was expecting to see Carole King and listen to some of *her* material.

LAURA WEINER, Ellie Greenwich's sister: So they said, "Hi, Carole," and my sister said, "No, I'm not Carole, I'm Ellie."

ULA HEDWIG, background singer: Well, her Long Island accent, she had a *very* heavy Long Island accent.

ELLIE GREENWICH, songwriter: When he saw I wasn't Carole, he asked who I was and I told him, and I played him some songs, and he said they were "interesting," and that I should come up whenever I felt like it, to write or whatever. He said his name was Jerry Leiber and he introduced me to his partner, Mike Stoller.

LAURA WEINER, Ellie Greenwich's sister: Then they hired her. That's how she got started at the Brill Building.

VICKI WICKHAM, manager, Labelle: She was one of those people that everything would happen to. Meaning, she'd walk outside in . . . I don't know . . . a white suit or a dress or something, and there would be one puddle in the street. A car would come by, and the puddle would go over her.

ELLIE GREENWICH, songwriter: I didn't know who they were, and then when I got home I saw their name on one of my records, and then another, and another. All of these great records by The Coasters and Drifters, and Leiber and Stoller and Carole King. I couldn't believe it. I just started running around the house screaming.

VICKI WICKHAM, manager, Labelle: She had the best sense of humor—she knew everybody. She loved, *loved* music. I mean, it was her life.

JERRY LEIBER, songwriter: Ellie was a good singer who made demos of her songs that rivaled the released versions.

BROOKS ARTHUR, sound engineer: She was not unlike Carole King. She'd go out and do all three parts, you know, and knock them down. Bass—she'd knock down the tenor, the alto, and the bass part, or the soprano part—she'd knock it down in fifteen minutes. So it's her same vocal chops, it takes on a sound of its own and a world of its own. She was indeed the girl groups wrapped up in one.

MIKE STOLLER, songwriter: We had a record deal before we started Red Bird, at United Artists. And a deal had been made, for some reason, we paid for the recording sessions and they would reimburse us. And this had worked fairly well. We did Jay and the Americans and the group The Exciters, a wonderful singer named Brenda—very exciting. We did produce their big hit "Tell Him."

LILLIAN WALKER-MOSS, The Exciters: Leiber and Stoller in the sixties were the *know-all and be-all* of hits.

BRENDA REID, The Exciters: We went to United Artists and they loved us. They gave us "Tell Him" and said to go home and learn it.

We didn't like it, but we didn't want to tell them that, of course. We got it and we were like, "Oh wow, thank you. We love it! We love it!"

LILLIAN WALKER-MOSS, The Exciters: That's the other thing that impressed them because not one of us was taller than five-foot-three. You know, these little girls—we're not women then, you know, we're like little teenagers. We walk in the door—*teeny, teeny* little girls walk in the door—and we open our mouths and it blows everybody away. That was Leiber and Stoller's reaction when we went to our first audition.

BRENDA REID, The Exciters: They said that they wanted us to take the record home and learn it. On the way out the door, they said, "By the way, we want you, Brenda, to do the lead." "Who me? I'm not the lead singer." And they said, "Well, we want you to learn it, we want you to be the lead." Now I'm thinking, *Oh my God, Lillian started the group. She's the lead singer. They startin' trouble already.* [*laughing*]

LILLIAN WALKER-MOSS, The Exciters: I like my voice, but she's way *way* . . . she's up there with the big, you know, with the big people.

*

LILLIAN WALKER-MOSS, The Exciters: It was the first day of school and they had given us, in junior high school, these index cards with our homeroom on it. And I'm walking down the street, getting ready to go inside the school. Brenda's mother just walks up to me, she said, "Do you happen to know where this classroom is?" And she shows me the index card. And I said, "No, I'm new. But that's the same room that I'm going to."

BRENDA REID, The Exciters: My mom said, "Oh, that's wonderful!" And my mother grabbed her by the hand and said, "Come on, let's go!"

LILLIAN WALKER-MOSS, The Exciters: Brenda was on the other side. I hadn't even *seen* her yet. So I looked around and I said, *Oh, that's the girl that lives a couple of blocks from me.* Brenda lived, I would say, maybe two or three very short blocks from me. And I had to pass her house every day to get to Sylvia's house.

SYLVIA WILLIAMS, The Exciters: I met them when I moved to Jamaica, Queens . . . met them at school.

BRENDA REID, The Exciters: I met Sylvia first. She lived not far from me to the right, like about two, three blocks, and Lillian lived two, three blocks to the left. I was in the middle, in the corner house.

LILLIAN WALKER-MOSS, The Exciters: And so I sat in front of her. The very first day she tapped me and she said, "I like your hair." This is such a coincidence too. I thought I invented this hairstyle with, like you took your bangs and you fluff them up with a ponytail. Brenda had the same style. I thought *I* invented it. And she thought *she* invented it, because nobody else—nobody had that on TV, or where we lived.

BRENDA REID, The Exciters: So every morning at school, I get there a little early—her and I and we go to the ladies' room, and we primp and I do her hair and she said, "Spray it with hairspray." And you know, it was like *a lot* of cute.

LILLIAN WALKER-MOSS, The Exciters: And we kept saying, "Oh, I do the same thing!" And that's how we came to be friends.

BRENDA REID, The Exciters: It was like each day was something new to look forward to . . . in my mom's basement I used to put up sheets to make, like, a stage—the sheets were the curtains. And I had a jukebox in the corner that lit up when you plugged it in, so that was my stage light. And I would pretend to be onstage and Lillian said, "Oh my God, I do the same thing!"

She said, "Oh, I can't believe it, so do I! You know, I know I'm gonna be a star, because that's all I think about." She said, "I'm gonna be on that stage, and I'm going to be a star."

LILLIAN WALKER-MOSS, The Exciters: I was thirteen, and I had seen The Shirelles. They were all dressed up in beautiful dresses, and makeup, and hair—and all of it. The people went wild when they came out and started singing. And I remember sitting there saying, *One of these days, I'm going to be up there just like them, and I'm going to be beautiful like them, and I'm going to have a beautiful dress on, and* *sing. And me and my girls—everybody's gonna go crazy, clapping and screaming—just like them.* And I kept that image in my mind forever.

BRENDA REID, The Exciters: So she said, "You know, me and Sylvia are starting a group." She said, "We want you to be a part of the group. Let's start rehearsals tomorrow. I'm gonna let Sylvia know." So she said, "Okay, I'm gonna go. Bye." I'm not trying to make fun of her. But her personality is engraved in my heart.

LILLIAN WALKER-MOSS, The Exciters: At first we all could sing, but we didn't know that much about harmony. So we would do a lot of unison singing and very little harmony singing and then we met The Masters, Herbie from The Exciters. He was one of The Masters, and another man, Dickie.

BRENDA REID, The Exciters: Our group was The Masterettes because Herbie's group was The Masters. So they said, "You could be our sister group and call yourself The Masterettes."

LILLIAN WALKER-MOSS, The Exciters: So they heard us singing and they said, "Oh, you guys is good, but where's the harmony?" So they said, "Okay, we're going to take you under our wing." And they took us under their wing and they taught us how to *really* sing and do harmony, how to perform on shows. They used to take us to their shows. And Herbie wrote most of the songs so that we would have our own original songs.

BRENDA REID, The Exciters: He said, "The first thing I want you guys to understand is you need to create your own sound. Because everybody else that's already making records and recording, they have their original sound, and the record company don't need another sound like that—they need something new." And I'm saying, *Now that makes a lot of sense to me*. I said, *So this is somebody we could trust.* And from that day on he was coming by rehearsing and writing new songs for us to sing.

LILLIAN WALKER-MOSS, The Exciters: So one day out of a clear blue sky, they told us we were ready.

BRENDA REID, The Exciters: Now I'm scared that Lillian might feel a little offended, you know? Because it was her world that she invited me into, and she has such a powerful voice. She still does. And she was doing most of the leads. So when we got into the elevator, I said, "Lillian, I hope you won't be upset that they chose me." She said, "Are you kidding me? I don't care about you singing that song, girl. We need a hit record now! I don't care nothing about that—you better go home and learn that song!"

But I don't know if I can even do a good job. But them being producers—and major producers—they knew what they wanted to hear. So when we got on the train, we were like, "I don't like the song," but Herbie said, "Calm down. I'm gonna take the record home and learn it, and I'm gonna teach it to you guys."

LILLIAN WALKER-MOSS, The Exciters: Brenda had the flu, but you know, they say the show must go on . . . we never let anything stop us. The girl was about to pass out—I'm serious—if you saw how she looked when we did that session, it's every bit true. We said, "Brenda, maybe you need to stop." "No, no, no, I can do it."

BRENDA REID, The Exciters: "*I know something about love*"—like *I* know something?! What did I know? I didn't know. And I'm thankful for it, because that's what got us on the map. It's a powerful message for young ladies, you know, to go out and assert themselves with a young man.

LILLIAN WALKER-MOSS, The Exciters: She could barely breathe, but she got it out somehow. And then they told us that we had to change our name from The Masterettes. And you know, the minute we had opened our mouths at the audition, Leiber and Stoller said, "These are little girls with big voices. They sound so *exciting*." So then, you know, they said, "Oh, that's it. We're gonna call you guys The Exciters." Because our backgrounds, our backgrounds are very aggressive too. That's our style—that aggressive singing. Girls back in the days, girls sang sweetly, they didn't sing very aggressively, like we do, you know.

But Leiber and Stoller *forbid* us to go to musical training because then, they said, "they're just going to teach you guys how to sing, how to sing sweet. And that's not what we want. The Exciters have that raw street"—this is their exact words—"The Exciters have that *raw street* sound."

BRENDA REID, The Exciters: And we were just happy—*Pinch me, this is not real.*

ELLIE GREENWICH, songwriter: Brenda had one of the best female voices I've ever heard. As far as I was concerned, she could do no wrong—she would only add to the song, make it greater.

BRENDA REID, The Exciters: Our friend Sylvia had quit the group and the replacement for her quit the group . . . so we were afraid they wasn't going to want us if there was only three girls.

LILLIAN WALKER-MOSS, The Exciters: She left, because one thing . . . she was going to get saved religiously. And the other thing was that she and Dickie were getting married.

SYLVIA WILLIAMS, The Exciters: I made the decision to marry Dickie. I remember my mother asked me, she was very frank, she said, "Are you pregnant?" I said, "No, of course not!" And I was, like, shocked that she would ask me that, because I *wanted* to get married. But my real reason for wanting to get married was that I wanted to get out of the house. Because I felt like leaving that control would make me free. What I did was jump out of the frying pan into the fire. *Hello!* That's what actually happened.

BRENDA REID, The Exciters: So Herbie said, "I'll just sing her part," because he knew how to play a song on the piano. And turns out that they *loved* the fact that Herbie was a guy with three girls.

SYLVIA WILLIAMS, The Exciters: Of course, as the girls went on to become The Exciters . . . excel, and so forth. Of course, they got many, many, many, many, many fans. And at first at one point in my life, I said, "Oh, I should be going on with them." But that wasn't God's plan for my life. It just wasn't. And I'm not mad, I'm not angry, I'm not sad, I'm not disappointed. I'm very happy. I'm grateful for the five minutes of fame.

BRENDA REID, The Exciters: Herbie and I eventually got together, you know, and we joined a union and had four children together. . . . So, that's where the song came from, "He's Got the Power," because he did, yeah . . . the power of love.

ELLIE GREENWICH, songwriter: It was done at Bell Sound and I sat up in this little observation booth watching and listening. My father was there with me because I still lived at home on Long Island and he would wait to drive me home. They cut about five tunes and it was about four or five in the morning when they finally finished. Then they sat there and listened to them, and about five thirty in the morning Leiber and Stoller turned to each other and said, "The single is gonna be 'He's Got the Power.'" I couldn't believe it.

MELANIE MINTZ, writer: This was pre-Jeff. She wrote that with Tony Powers—that good-looking guy.

ELLIE GREENWICH, songwriter: At the time I was writing with a guy named Tony Powers before I was writing with Jeff, and I was not yet signed to Leiber and Stoller, but I was on what they call a first refusal basis, where I could use their offices as long as whatever I wrote they heard first and had first choice whether they wanted it or not.

TONY POWERS, songwriter: Jerry and Mike had the big piano in their big room and we played it for them and they liked it—I just wasn't so sure—and I still am not so sure, but that arrangement, maybe the song itself . . . sounds so Jewish. I'm Jewish, by the way. That song—it's got that [*singing*] "*da da da DAA da da da*"—it's got that Yiddish kind of melody—it sounds like it should be played at a bar mitzvah to me—but hey, listen, it was a good song and Brenda's a hell of a singer.

ELLIE GREENWICH, songwriter: They called me and told me that there was a guy coming up to the office who was cutting The Paris Sisters and did I have something for him. I said, "Sure." And I went to the office that day, and I'm there, I'm nervous and I'm playing my tune. . . . This person comes walking in with ruffles, and he's wandering around the room making noises, looking in the mirror. I mean, he was an eccentric human being—very lovable once you get to know him and work with him.

But initially, it's sort of like, *What is . . . ?* This was rude to the point of I kept stopping, saying, "Do you want to hear my song or not?" And by the fourth time of him wandering around and making noises, not listening, I got annoyed and I slammed on the piano. I said, "Forget it! I mean, forget it!" You don't tell Phil Spector forget it. And he went storming out of the office. And Leiber and Stoller came running and, like, *What did you do?* I said, "Who was that?!" That was the most humiliating thing. I'm singing my heart and I'm scared to death—and this guy—he didn't even listen to me.

That was the first meeting with Phil Spector. Then I played Leiber and Stoller, shortly thereafter, a song called "(Today I Met) The Boy I'm Gonna Marry," which they didn't like. After three times of playing . . . they said, "Nah, take it wherever you want." And I brought it to a publisher named Aaron Schroeder. Aaron says, "I love it. I want it. I think I know someone perfect to cut the song." And two weeks later he calls me, he goes, "We have a meeting. I want you to go to 62nd Street and meet with Phil Spector." I said, "Does he know who's going to meet with him?"

And Phil had . . . whatever . . . he didn't connect it with being at Leiber and Stoller. We had a two o'clock appointment. I got there at two o'clock, he showed up at six. I waited the four hours, *seething*. He walked in and he took one look at me and I went, "Hmm." We started off *so wrong*. And we had it out. I said, "If I didn't want this record, I would never have sat here, but I want this record. I think this will be a great song. Don't you ever be late again. Don't you make those voices! You listening to me?" And he was so taken with me, that I was, like—I was hysterically . . . I was so upset. But, you know, I sort of tongue-in-cheeked because I didn't want to get too serious. We hit it off so perfectly. And that was the beginning of our working relationship. We worked together all the time. And I then was married to Jeff Barry, so I brought Jeff in. Then we just—three of us really hit it off, and just wrote a bunch of songs together.

MIKE STOLLER, songwriter: Jeff came in and he had been offered a very lucrative position somewhere as a staff writer and we couldn't offer him that at the time.

JEFF BARRY, songwriter: I declined and made a deal with Leiber and Stoller.

MIKE STOLLER, songwriter: But he decided to come with us because he felt he could learn more.

JERRY LEIBER, songwriter: Jeff learned a lot when he became one of our writers. But we also benefited greatly from his songwriting sense that was so in tune with teens.

JEFF BARRY, songwriter: Ellie and I met when we were little kids—when I was four, and she was three. Her cousin married my cousin, and we met at that wedding, supposedly. And then later—and then fade out, fade in—when I had had a couple of hits and had some kind of a name, and she was graduating from Hofstra College as a music major—she wanted to do music—and so my cousins—the two that got married when Ellie and I met—put us together. They said, "You got to meet Ellie. I think you guys would be great together." So that's how that happened.

JERRY LEIBER, songwriter: The two of them were a terrific team. They wrote with an elegant simplicity and lack of self-consciousness.

LAURA WEINER, Ellie Greenwich's sister: It was a nice wedding. It was very nice. At the time, everything was typical. You went to a place, you had the smorgasbord, then you had the ceremony, then you had the dinner. It was nice. It was held at Leonard's in Great Neck—and at that time it had a really good reputation. In fact, Toni Wine was in the wedding party. It was beautiful, actually. It didn't last long, but however it lasted, it was. That was their marriage.

JEFF BARRY, songwriter: It was all very exciting and very . . . no time—there was just no time for anything but what we were doing. It was literally twenty-four hours a day sometimes. I remember one stretch there, I didn't shave for three days. We were in the studio and it was crazy.

ELLIE GREENWICH, songwriter: It was nerve-racking and tense, but they were healthy tensions. Decisions were made relatively quickly, sometimes right on the spot. Then the record would come out and within three weeks you'd know if you had something.

MIKE STOLLER, songwriter: They started writing and they were . . . by this time, Phil had already started his Philles label, which was originally started with Phil and Lester Sill—"Phil" and "Les." But somehow Lester got moved out by Phil. I don't know how or what, but at any rate . . . he loved what they were writing—I'm talking about Jeff and Ellie. And so we made a deal with them on publishing if he wrote with them, the songs were credited to Barry–Greenwich–Spector, which meant once again we had to deal with Phil. It wasn't easy, but we managed.

CHAPTER 14

The Center of the Square

Phil Spector

DARLENE LOVE, The Blossoms: Phil Spector knew about Gold Star. A lot of record producers stopped using the big studios because, back in those days, they didn't record just with a little band—they had full orchestras with everything. And Phil didn't need all that space that they had at Columbia or RCA Victor or Capitol. So they started using a smaller space, which was Gold Star. It was cheaper and they didn't need all that room anymore.

FANITA JAMES, The Blossoms: That was Phil's favorite spot. He had the Wall of Sound. He created a whole new sound for the music industry.

DARLENE LOVE, The Blossoms: The one thing that Phil Spector started doing was overdubbing. Plus, he found out that Gold Star had an echo chamber—which was unheard of. He wanted the sound to feed into all the different microphones that were open, with only what they call "mono"—which means you have three tracks to put everything on. But he could do it. He found a way to do it, and he did it. He was just amazing, he really was. Man, we had a lot of hits in that room . . . everybody got famous in that building—the engineers, everybody—the parking lot attendants. [*laughing*]

ALLAN PEPPER, nightclub owner: Everyone who worked with him wanted to be on background singing. Cher, who was Sonny's girlfriend, she was there—not only singing background but doing the tambourine.

GLORIA JONES, The Blossoms: He was looking for that certain something that he wanted to hear. And when he heard it—Phil heard it—he knew what it was. And to me, it was like we were doing the same thing, over and over and over again.

DARLENE LOVE, The Blossoms: Most sessions that The Blossoms were doing back in those days, record producers would ask us, "What do you hear? Is it *oohs* here? Is it *aahs* here? Is words here?" Phil would tell you, "Okay, I want you to do this here, this here, this here." So that was actually great because we didn't have to think about anything. He knew exactly what he wanted.

GLORIA JONES, The Blossoms: He wasn't my favorite people. I shouldn't say that, but he wasn't. I thought he was brilliant—I think he's the only one who knows how to record Darlene—absolutely, unequivocally.

DARLENE LOVE, The Blossoms: Black singers were having hits, you know, and he was fascinated with that sound. I think that's the biggest reason he was so fascinated with girl singers, because of his connection with gospel music. Which most famous gospel singers were female. And I think that's what made him fascinated with trying to make girl groups popular. He knew or heard all the gospel singers, so he wanted a rock-and-roll girl group. Because it was the girl groups that got Phil Spector started.

GLORIA JONES, The Blossoms: Phil would show her exactly how to sing, and at the end of the song, he'd let her go—let her just do what she wanted to do. I think they were good for each other. But he was almost like a kid who had been bullied in his childhood, and he was trying to grow up and bully the other folk.

DEE DEE KENNIEBREW, The Crystals: After his father committed suicide, the mother moved the family to California. And one of the guys who was a student at the same school said he remembers that Phil came onstage, in high school, in a talent show. And he had his guitar, and he sang a song. When he got finished singing, he said nobody clapped—nobody. You know how humiliating that had to be? Not one—that had to be so humiliating. I guess in the back of his mind, he said, "I'll show them all one day."

GLORIA JONES, The Blossoms: I don't like bullies. I really don't, so no, he wasn't one of my favorite people. Nope, absolutely not, but he knew what he was doing, I'll give him that. I didn't trust him, and I didn't have to trust him. Just pay me for my little background work I'm doing, that's fine. We went into the studio a lot of times and nobody ever knew when it came out to the public what name was going to be on the record.

DARLENE LOVE, The Blossoms: With "He's a Rebel," it was great hearing myself on the radio because I would tell my family and friends, "Y'all know that's me, right? You know that's me, right?" Some of them believed it and some didn't. But it wasn't bothering me, it was like I knew what I was doing, and I did it and got paid for it. That was the end of it, I thought. That was going to be my first and last gig with Phil Spector. But, you know, then he signed me on his record company, and I said, "Well, this man knows how to make his records. I need to be with him." He was the first producer I ever knew that said, "This is going to be a hit and I know it's going to be a hit." And it was a hit.

FANITA JAMES, The Blossoms: Her name was Darlene Wright. So that's the stage name she took. Phil Spector gave her that name.

DARLENE LOVE, The Blossoms: I wouldn't let him change my first name, but I didn't mind him changing my last name to Love. There was a gospel singer, her name was Dorothy Love Coates—big-time gospel singer all over the country. He asked me one day, did I like the name Love? And I went, "Why not?" Who knew it was going to be around fifty years later, and it would make me famous? And after a few years, I legalized it. Because I could see him coming back years later saying, "I gave you that name and you can't use it."

GLORIA JONES, The Blossoms: Phil had promised Darlene she'd have hers, and every time a record came out . . .

DARLENE LOVE, The Blossoms: So, when "He's Sure the Boy I Love" came out, I thought that was going to be my first release—up until the day I heard it on the radio. Now, that really just floored me because I couldn't understand . . . you changed my name, and his whole excuse for doing that was because my voice was on "He's a Rebel," and he wanted to keep that same sound when he put out The Crystals' second record. That was like another slap in the face. It was a big record—it was a Top 10 record, and, you know, it wasn't mine. I really did get upset at Phil about that, and I didn't think I'd ever really see him again. At that time, I didn't really want to work with him anymore. *Hey,* I say, *listen. I could have less trouble just being a background singer.* Don't have to go through all of this madness, you know? I had my children, I was married. So, that's part of the business I don't need, I don't want.

GLORIA JONES, The Blossoms: Phil was like a little sissy. He had little bodyguards around him because he was small anyway. I can't even tell you what song we had recorded for him . . . so I tell my husband to take me up to the studio—Phil was at the studio—to go pick up my money. We walked in the studio and he started running. I guess because he saw my husband. He was a fool. He was a little chicken to me.

DARLENE LOVE, The Blossoms: I came to a session one time as a background singer. But when I got there, I saw all the guys coming out of the session, like somebody was chasing them. I said, "What the heck is going on?" "Phil is in the recording studio with a gun and he's waving it around. He's talking about shooting and carrying on." I said, "Well, listen, I'm going home." [*laughing*] I was on time, but I went back home because I am not going into a studio with nobody with no guns—*you're crazy, because I ain't going in there.* So I went back home. And after I had been home about an hour, I get this phone call from his secretary, wanting to know where I was. I said, "Well, I'm at home." She said, "Well, Phil is looking for you. He's acting crazy. He can't believe you're not here." I said, "Well, you want to put him on the phone?" But he wouldn't talk to me on the phone. So he had his secretary call me back and say everything is okay—I don't have the gun.

I said, "Okay, well, I'll be there in an hour or so." And I came to the studio and he was a very calm person. They looked at him like, *That's not where he was an hour ago*, but now she's coming to the room and he's very calm and very civil and acting like he got the sense. But I just . . . with everything else that he was doing to me with the record, I wasn't going to give him control over the other part of my life.

When I came to the studio, Phil knew I'm here to work, and . . . and all that other stuff, I ain't going to be dealing with all that. And then when I get through, I'm going home.

GLORIA JONES, The Blossoms: You ought to see how she used to talk to Phil Spector. [*laughing*] She would tell him, "If you don't do so-and-so, I'm not singing a note." I said, "Well, hell, here goes the money. Okay, here we go . . ." [*laughing*]

DARLENE LOVE, The Blossoms: We found out that, uh . . . there's a button you push, and you can talk to the producer, and you guys can talk back and forth. And when they're back in the room getting ready to record, we're talking and we're laughing—before they get ready to push the button—to say, "Okay, we're getting ready to start." But Phil left that button on *all the time*. So he knew everything we were saying. *Everything* we said about him—the whole bit. When I found out that he was doing that, I said, "I'm glad he heard what we were saying and what we thought about it." [*laughing*]

He couldn't control me. That was the biggest thing. He could not control me, okay? Before I met Phil Spector, I was already a famous background singer and I was making a wonderful living, so I didn't need him. I was a background singer. Ronnie needed him as a solo artist, The Crystals needed him—they all needed Phil as a record producer. I did not.

When I did record under the name of Darlene Love, my records weren't as big as The Crystals. I mean . . . sure, "Wait Til' My Bobby Gets Home" and "(Today I Met) The Boy I'm Gonna Marry."

MELANIE MINTZ, writer: They did the demo on Monday. She lived in Long Island and used to drive into the city. Thursday she's coming into the city, and she's pulling up to the toll booth, and the song comes on the radio—she had no idea. She said she almost crashed smack into the booth because she started screaming, "Oh my God, it's my song!"

DARLENE LOVE, The Blossoms: Which I love today, "(Today I Met) The Boy I'm Gonna Marry," but it didn't reach . . . they were Top 20 records. But they didn't go any further than that . . . and I think it's because the disc jockeys—they had so much control back in those days with payola and all of that kind of carrying on—that . . . they didn't want another Darlene Love record that sounded like The Crystals. So, I suffered in that respect.

LA LA BROOKS, The Crystals: The Crystals wanted a record out so bad. After he messed up with Darlene . . . I think they just wanted to have their own girl—their own Crystal—which I was, to do the record.

DARLENE LOVE, The Blossoms: I was doing so many great songs that I thought was great, but Phil Spector didn't think were great. You know, those albums that they shove and put on the shelves. What I fought against for a while is . . . I am *not* a member of The Crystals—I *never was* a member of The Crystals.

DEE DEE KENNIEBREW, The Crystals: My mom had to go take La La to California to put a vocal on her recordings, because her mother didn't go anywhere with them—none of the mothers participated—only mine, basically. And my mother wasn't getting a penny. A lot of times she had to put money in just to help us. But who picked them up at the airport? Come on, Mom . . . Sam Cooke picked up La La and Mommy.

DARLENE LOVE, The Blossoms: Matter of fact, I don't think The Crystals ever came from New York. La La came to California when we were doing the Christmas album, but I didn't know any of The Crystals. Nobody knew The Crystals. They never came to California to record.

LA LA BROOKS, The Crystals: They had too many background singers in LA to bring The Crystals out. Phil's not going to spend all the money to get the girls out to California when he had The Blossoms out there. Dee Dee, Barbara, and them didn't know Darlene from a can of paint—I'm the only one from The Crystals that saw The Blossoms.

DARLENE LOVE, The Blossoms: "Da Doo Ron Ron," it started out to be mine. I got pissed at Phil, and I said—that was during that time where I said, "No more! I'm just not doing any of your songs because you're a liar." We did the background and everything for it. Everything but the lead because I said, "Phil, I'm leaving." I left the session.

LA LA BROOKS, The Crystals: I recorded "Da Doo Ron Ron" and "Then He Kissed Me" when I was fifteen. I had never been kissed. I didn't think anything, I just did it. You got forty people . . . twenty, thirty people in the studio. It's so much going on—I don't think you can process so much—it's, like, overwhelming as a child. You've got two kettledrums, two drummers, you got violins, two piano players. It's like, *ack*, you know? Phil's yelling, "No! Do it over again! No!"

I never paid attention to the lyrics. I didn't connect as well with the lyrics, because I was so worried about making sure I'm so on point music-wise.

MELANIE MINTZ, writer: They couldn't think of a lyric, so they wrote, "*Da Doo Run Run Run, Da Doo Run Run.*" That was just to fill in—they didn't think that was going to be the record.

JEFF BARRY, songwriter: Phil was never, like, what you might call gracious or considerate of people, and he was never trying to be a host.

LA LA BROOKS, The Crystals: When I was in California, he talked to me more and I could see . . . see a different personality. He was gentle with me, maybe because I was a kid. He had to come in a few times—in the studio—to coach me with certain things. When I was doing "Then He Kissed Me," Phil would turn down the lights and just have, like, a little bulb over the lyrics—but that was "Then He Kissed Me." "Da Doo Ron Ron," he'd brighten up the studio—so he would give me certain type of images to pull things out of me—to be happy or to be more mellow. So he worked with me like that, because I was a kid.

JEFF BARRY, songwriter: When he knew he had the take, he would keep going just because once he stopped and said, "Okay, that's the take," technically the curtain comes down. The show is over. Everybody goes home. It was about him putting on a show while he was making the records . . . and thoroughly enjoying the attention. That was his stage, that was his show.

BROOKS ARTHUR, sound engineer: Jerry and Mike always put the artists first and kept that as the center of the square. Phil Spector *was* the center of the square. It's a completely different philosophy.

DARLENE LOVE, The Blossoms: Madness . . . madness . . . always said, it's like going to a circus and you see the circus man standing there in his tall hat with a whip in his hand. That's the way Phil Spector was, you know?

ELLIE GREENWICH, songwriter: I think he instinctively felt certain things in music and was unafraid to go after them at any cost—be it his reputation, the studio bills, the equipment blowing up—I mean, if he heard something, he went for it. He had an insatiable personality. He just could not get *enough* onto a record.

JEFF BARRY, songwriter: And the other thing was, he would play it so loud in the control room my teeth would rattle.

DARLENE LOVE, The Blossoms: I had never been in a recording session that the playback was so loud. I said, "By the time I get to twenty, I ain't going to be able to hear."

LA LA BROOKS, The Crystals: Them reels used to be turned up—the reel of the sound—the reels used to drive me crazy. When you spin it back and put it on again, and again, and again.

NEDRA TALLEY-ROSS, The Ronettes: Because after a while the sound was so big in your head, that you're sort of crazy.

DARLENE LOVE, The Blossoms: After he had a tape, he would go in and play it down real low, lay his head on the table and listen to it the way he said it sounds coming out of a radio. That's how he made his records.

JEFF BARRY, songwriter: He was never a friend. I never really liked hanging out with him. He was kind of caustic and a definite genius. I mean . . . in his narrow—fairly narrow—musical scope, I mean that—that's genius right there. Just developing his own sound and style, which is obviously part of history.

LA LA BROOKS, The Crystals: So in his mind he didn't give a damn about nobody—Darlene, Ronnie, Crystals—he thought *he* was the Wall of Sound.

JEFF BARRY, songwriter: The vocals, interestingly enough . . . even though his ego and all of that was apparent, he didn't bury the lead vocals. In the mix, you can hear every word.

RON DANTE, musician: I always thought that the first sound that anybody hears sung to them is usually their mom's voice. And I think the girl groups . . . there's something so familiar about it. And of course the harmonies were a little different than the guy harmonies. They were higher, so they stuck out. You could take a really raucous music track, and put a girl group on top of it singing, and it would cut through.

Because girl voices, they float on top of the track—so you got the feel of the track, which moved you and you loved it. The girls stuck out. Especially on those little AM radios in the early sixties. You needed something like that to cut through and it did.

DARLENE LOVE, The Blossoms: Nobody really knew The Blossoms was doing The Ronettes' background, or The Crystals' background, or the Righteous Brothers' background, or Tina Turner's background. We were just background singers. It's amazing because that's what they were doing in Detroit, at Motown. The Blossoms did most of the background singing for everybody. The only group that came here actually to record were The Ronettes.

LA LA BROOKS, The Crystals: Then Ronnie got with Phil and Phil started paying The Ronettes attention and forgetting about us. He wasn't thinking with his head, you know what I'm saying?

✳

JEFF BARRY, songwriter: I would always be looking for something to tap on, you know, to make a rhythm while we were writing. And we were in his office and he had this rolling metal file cabinet—it was very short and you could roll it around from desk to desk. I don't know what the real purpose of it was, but the top of it sounded like a snare drum and the side of it had, like, a deeper sound—like a tip drum. So I would tap it, but I came out of the Leiber and Stoller—Jerry Leiber and Mike Stoller—camp. And they introduced me to that rhythm which is called a baião. It goes: *boom, boom-boom . . . boom, boom-boom.* And they used that in so many of their records, like "Spanish Harlem." So I was playing that on the metal . . . the metal file cabinet, and it ended up in the record.

BILLY JOEL, musician: I loved it. I love Ronnie's voice. She has this big, slow vibrato. It's almost like—it's almost like—it's *sweaty*. You can just imagine the performance of this song, [*singing*] "*Be my baby, be my little baby.*" It's almost an exaggerated vibrato, but it works—it's good and greasy.

CHER, singer: I was seventeen when I met Ronnie. I can still remember the day Phillip brought her down to Gold Star Studios for the first time. I'd never seen anybody like her. She had this big hair, these huge eyes, and no hips. I remember thinking that she seemed really, really teeny. And that voice! Well, nobody sounded like her, did they? She really was one of a kind.

NEDRA TALLEY-ROSS, The Ronettes: I had problems from the beginning with the thing with Phil. Because I could see that Phil was favoring us . . . but he had his eyes on Ronnie.

ELLIE GREENWICH, songwriter: Phil had an office on the main floor of a building and he had his apartment upstairs. And very often, like, he would be upstairs in this one room, listening, with the speakers blasting—like, conducting Wagner, I mean it was his idol.

NEDRA TALLEY-ROSS, The Ronettes: But I was like, "He's married . . . he is, you know, he's married." His wife used to stick her head out the door down the hall and I felt so bad for her. Within his office in that building, he had another apartment where we would rehearse. I told Ronnie, I said, "Ronnie, you know it's not right. *You know*." Our grandmother would always say, "God don't like ugly." It would be ugly for you to . . .

RONNIE SPECTOR, The Ronettes: I fell in love with his coolness. He was very cool. Always had one hand in his pocket. And he had a cute butt. I loved his tush, he had the cutest tush. The way he handled the band—here's a guy, twenty-four years old, yet he's telling married men with children what to do? That turned me on so much. I fell in love with that power.

NEDRA TALLEY-ROSS, The Ronettes: With Ronnie, I knew what she liked. When you're that close to somebody . . . you're doing . . . girls talk—they do nothing else but talk.

ELLIE GREENWICH, songwriter: He fell in love with her and thought he could really make her into this monumental star, and I think a lot of his other acts did suffer. All of a sudden everything was geared for Ronnie and The Ronettes.

NEDRA TALLEY-ROSS, The Ronettes: She wasn't saying she was dating him. It was just favoritism that was coming, favoritism—so I knew it couldn't be that . . . because Ronnie and I knew each other so well, I said, "There's no way that *this* is who you're falling in love with. He looks nothing like the boys we've dated, and he's married. *You cannot*."

RONNIE SPECTOR, The Ronettes: I was at Phil's penthouse upstairs. And Jeff Barry and Ellie Greenwich, who wrote it with him, were there. And my ex said, "Go in the back room. We don't want anybody to know you're here."

NEDRA TALLEY-ROSS, The Ronettes: She was like, "I don't remember him being married." You know you do. You knew it. You knew her name. And she was down the hall, looking to see who was what.

And then I heard . . . in some book they said she said that she thought *I* was with Phil. I was like "No, no. No, no, no. That's a no-no-no." I said, "Ronnie, you really want to invent something. You will invent anything."

LA LA BROOKS, The Crystals: He was still married to Annette.

NEDRA TALLEY-ROSS, The Ronettes: I didn't know Annette that well because he wasn't having her come down when we were rehearsing.

RONNIE SPECTOR, The Ronettes: We went out to get sandwiches in his limousine and soon he was taking me for candlelit dinners. When I rehearsed songs at his penthouse, he'd keep me later and later. Things just got hotter and hotter. He was infatuated with my voice, my body, everything. It was mutual.

NEDRA TALLEY-ROSS, The Ronettes: We had Mirasound Studios in New York, but the big deal was when we would go to California. That's, you know, that's our first cross-country flight.

DARLENE LOVE, The Blossoms: We were a few years older than The Ronettes. And they were very well chaperoned by Ronnie's mother. But when they first came to California, we fell in love with them because they were so nice, you know, and so easygoing. Ronnie was the loud one, it was me and her. I don't think anybody really wanted success like Ronnie did. The other two, Estelle and Nedra, they weren't really that interested in having all that fame. But Ronnie was the one, so she was the one that was the most outspoken one. The one that was always out in the front. Nedra and Estelle were laid-back. We hung with them because they were like us.

RONNIE SPECTOR, The Ronettes: In the studio, I had to hide in the ladies' room so the musicians could get their work done—I was very pretty and they'd keep looking at me. While I was in there, I came up with all those "*Oh oh ohs*," inspired by my old Frankie Lymon records. It took three days to record my vocals, take after take. The recording captures the full spectrum of my emotions: everything from nervousness to excitement. When I came in with [*singing*] *"The night we met I knew I needed you so,"* the band went nuts. . . . After that, I wasn't allowed in the studio. There may have been a little jealousy thing going on. I had to stay in the hotel while Phil finished the record.

NEDRA TALLEY-ROSS, The Ronettes: So even for Ronnie, I said, "You're just being weak about this guy. It's the money—it's not letting you see what is so obvious." I said, "Ronnie, one thing you can't do, you can't lie to me about what you like in a guy." He was little and thin of hair, weak of chin—all these things. He was very weak-chinned. Yeah, you know, and if he talked too much, he would drool a little bit. I'd say, "Oh shit, how would you kiss him?"

CHER, singer: I'd just left home and moved in with Sonny (Bono), and he still worked for Phil Spector in those days, so everyone just thought of me as Sonny's girlfriend. At first I was a little envious of Ronnie, because even though she was only a year or two older than I was, she'd already been on tour and everything. But I was happy for her too.

NEDRA TALLEY-ROSS, The Ronettes: He brought back some certain tracks to Mira Sound, for the ones we didn't fly out for. Hear it. Hear it. Play it, play it, play it. Then you were finishing up stuff out at Gold Star, so you're between the two places—and then you got Ronnie alone again.

RONNIE SPECTOR, The Ronettes: I rehearsed in New York with The Ronettes, then I had to go to California on my own to sing the lead.

CHER, singer: That was around the time I started my own singing career. In fact, "Be My Baby" was the first record I ever sang on. I'd been dying to sing since the first day I walked into Gold Star, but I never had the nerve to tell anyone except Sonny. Then one day Darlene Love and one of the other background singers didn't show up, and Phillip looked at me and said, "Sonny tells me you can sing." I was so embarrassed that I started making excuses, trying to explain what I thought

Sonny meant by that. But Phillip said, "Oh, just get out there. All I need is noise."

NEDRA TALLEY-ROSS, The Ronettes: Phil started to say things like, "I need Ronnie to do this and this." No, you needed to spend the weekend with Ronnie at our expense. Phil was sort of quiet in his own way, he was just sneaky.

PART 3

Hitsville USA

1960–1963

CHAPTER 15

Motown's First Number One

The Marvelettes

KATHERINE ANDERSON, The Marvelettes: We lived in the projects then, and Georgeanna and Wyanetta lived on the street opposite mine. And so we would always sit up and play cards and music and stuff like that. I think Gladys's thing was, "What else do we have to do? So let's do this."

GLADYS HORTON, The Marvelettes: I already had in mind to ask Georgia Dobbins to be a part of my group. She was not only smart, but she was very kind. All the girls looked up to her, wanting to be just like her. I wanted her to be in the group, so I saved a spot for her.

GEORGIA DOBBINS, The Marvelettes: Gladys needed another girl. She just came over to the house and asked me to sing background with her.

GLADYS HORTON, The Marvelettes: I heard on the loudspeaker about the talent show.

KATHERINE ANDERSON, The Marvelettes: If we did win, we had a chance to go to Motown and do the song.

GLADYS HORTON, The Marvelettes: I said, "Well, I'm going to get some girls." I approached Georgeanna, and she brought Wyanetta and Katherine along.

KATHERINE ANDERSON, The Marvelettes: We came in fourth. Some of the teachers thought that we were exceptionally good and should have won and our teacher told us—Mrs. Shirley Sharpley—she told us that we were really good, and so she and several other teachers said that maybe we could go to Motown and sing.

SHIRLEY SHARPLEY, The Marvelettes' teacher: I thought they should have won. When I complimented them and told them that they should have won, they asked me if I would take them for the audition down at Motown. . . . The kids had the telephone number and I followed through. I just called. It was Gladys who gave me the number. I called and got an appointment.

KATHERINE ANDERSON, The Marvelettes: Oh, honey, oh, honey, please . . . yes, we were country girls—they didn't want us to do anything. They didn't want to be bothered with those country girls, because Inkster was a small community—Detroit is much larger.

GEORGIA DOBBINS, The Marvelettes: They looked at us like we were dumb. To them, we were little young, country, dumb-looking chicks. We were square, we weren't glamorous at all. We were country kids coming to the big city.

KATHERINE ANDERSON, The Marvelettes: Berry [Gordy] was the one who told us to come up with an original song. Berry said, "These girls are good, but do they have their original material? You can come back when you have your own original material." You always get that "but" in there.

GLADYS HORTON, The Marvelettes: I thought it would be a month or two before Georgia finished the song, but in just two or three days, she was at my front door singing it.

GEORGIA DOBBINS, The Marvelettes: I was standing by the window. I was waiting for the postman to bring me a letter from this guy who was in the Navy. That's how I came up with the lyrics. Then I made up the tune.

KATHERINE ANDERSON, The Marvelettes: That's the reason the song came out. You know when you're eighteen, nineteen years old—you have a problem. [*laughing*]

GEORGIA DOBBINS, The Marvelettes: I just hummed it over and over and changed it to the way it should be. I improvised.

KATHERINE ANDERSON, The Marvelettes: When we went to Motown with "Please Mr. Postman," they were excited because we had brought them original material. Here again, Motown was growing, it was building. So bringing in new material was like bringing in new blood. The few people there when we came, they were not necessarily of the magnitude you may expect them to be because you're a new company. You can't have everybody be perfect. You had a couple of writers, but you really didn't have a stable of writers. Therefore, it was vitally important to get original material. At that point Robert Bateman was there, Brian was there.

BRIAN HOLLAND, songwriter: She came to Motown, to Robert Bateman and I, with the idea of "Postman." We said, "Oh, that sounds great, that sounds great. Let us go and finish it—write this song."

MARC TAYLOR, music writer: Holland and Bateman made some adjustments to "Please Mr. Postman" in order to fit it to Gladys's voice and also arranged the background vocals; thus, they took part in the writing credits.

BRIAN HOLLAND, songwriter: It was really Robert Bateman and I and Georgia Dobbins that did the song. Then Freddie Gorman came in.

MICKEY STEVENSON, Motown A&R: And Freddie Gorman was a postman. You know, he was originally a postman.

MARC TAYLOR, music writer: Gorman, who was actually a mail carrier, also offered a few suggestions and became one of the five official writers of the song: William Garrett, an Inkster classmate who provided the title; Georgia Dobbins; Robert Bateman; Freddie Gorman; and Brian Holland.

KATHERINE ANDERSON, The Marvelettes: A lot of people are on that disc, but, see, if you can find one of the discs that came out earlier—you would only see the three names, which was Brianbert [Brian Holland and Robert Bateman's production team] and Georgia Dobbins.

BRIAN HOLLAND, songwriter: No, no, no . . . I don't really know that. . . . I can't answer that because I don't really recall that—I know she had a part of a song, but we had to finish a lot of that song—period. She didn't have a complete song—she had the idea of "Please Mr. Postman."

GEORGIA DOBBINS, The Marvelettes: We were going through rehearsals for about a week or so before they brought out the contracts. When it came time for the contract, I presented it to my dad and he hit the roof. He asked my mother, "How long has this girl been singing?" My dad did not know I could sing. My brothers and I were raised in the church and grew up a little strict. My mom would let me out. She knew I was having little rehearsals in the basement. I'm not knocking my parents, but they thought that when they signed the contract, that if we didn't make it, they'd have to pay that money back. That was their understanding. They didn't know anything but going to work and going to church on Sunday morning. And by them being Christian, entertainment and nightclub life was out of the question. That was unacceptable. Back then they'd call you "fast," "no good," "won't amount to anything."

My mother's illness was also the reason why they wouldn't sign for me. I'm the oldest child in the family with six brothers and my family depended on me totally. My mother was ill all of my life.

GLADYS HORTON, The Marvelettes: Georgia's mother was sick with a bad back, and Georgia made it clear that she was not going to leave her mother if we had to tour. Georgia wanted me to sing lead, so she taught me the song.

GEORGIA DOBBINS, The Marvelettes: When my dad wouldn't sign the contract, it was just like somebody had snatched the rug from up under me. It's like wanting something and somebody just takes it away from you. You want to go, you've got your outfit ready, but Daddy says no. That's the way it was for me. You've got your little dress and your shoes laid out, and you're ready to go to the party, but Daddy said, "No, you ain't going." I stayed in seclusion for about a year. I didn't even come outside. I was so hurt. I felt . . . robbed. I wouldn't listen to the radio or anything. It wasn't until 1978 before I sang again.

KATHERINE ANDERSON, The Marvelettes: Well, you know what? Yes—she was sad, but after you have plenty of time to think, after everything is all over, back in the day, we didn't think that much about it because we were busy performing. But then, after a while, you begin to think about it, and you say, "Georgia, who *wrote* 'Please Mr. Postman,' *that* was her claim to fame was 'Please Mr. Postman,' because none of us could write anything like that." But she didn't understand that for a while.

GEORGIA DOBBINS, The Marvelettes: Gladys had a lead voice and the rest of them didn't. When my dad refused to sign for me, I got Gladys and told her, "You've got to sing lead on this song."

KATHERINE ANDERSON, The Marvelettes: I do remember that the session was long and then, on top of that, Gladys had to sing the lead because Georgia wasn't any longer there. Then the background—Wyanetta, Georgeanna, and myself . . . we, and Wanda—because when Georgia left, Gladys took and recruited Wanda Young—so that means the four of us would be back there singing the background and Gladys would be singing the lead. Marvin Gaye played the drums. It was a *long*, long day.

MARTHA REEVES, The Vandellas: I think Gladys Horton gave her heart and soul, saying, "There must be some word today / from my boyfriend who's so far away / please, Mister Postman, look and see / if there's a letter in your bag for me."

KATHERINE ANDERSON, The Marvelettes: Then the rest of it *almost* was history.

BRIAN HOLLAND, songwriter: Let me tell you something—I was so elated when I first heard it on the radio. The Black station first started playing it. Then it became so popular, on CKLW—that was a big fifty-watt station at that time; it was the biggest station—they started playing it. That's when it erupted. It became huge. I mean, that was the most exciting time for me as a songwriter to hear that song on the radio. Can you imagine? I mean, Jesus, it was like a miracle. It was a miracle. I mean, for me, as a songwriter, to hear that?

KATHERINE ANDERSON, The Marvelettes: The next thing that we knew "Please Mr. Postman" was number one on the Billboard chart.

BILLY VERA, musician: Don't forget—the audience for rock and roll had now grown up to the point where they were out of high school. Even though there was no war on yet, a lot of boys went off to the draft. And so there were a lot of songs about soldiers—soldiers going away and the girl waiting at home for them.

BRIAN HOLLAND, songwriter: Motown's first big record was "Please Mr. Postman."

KATHERINE ANDERSON, The Marvelettes: Really to be truthful . . . when our record hit number one, they were not ready. They went and began to scurry around, trying to find people to do this and do that, and all of a sudden they made it seem like it was really, really big. But Motown was not as big as they wanted people to believe it was.

GLADYS HORTON, The Marvelettes: Everything happened so fast. It was like one-two-three-four. The talent show, the recording of the record, the release date of the song, the date it hit the number one spot on Billboard—all in the same year of 1961.

KATHERINE ANDERSON, The Marvelettes: But then they had five little Black girls from the suburbs of Detroit that took them there a little bit faster than they were ready for.

MARC TAYLOR, music writer: Motown needed to milk "Please Mr. Postman" as much as it could in order to generate some much-needed cash for the company.

KATHERINE ANDERSON, The Marvelettes: Motown had a tour that went out and Smokey Robinson and the Miracles were the headliners, and Mary Wells was on it. People began to start chanting—they wanted The Marvelettes. They caused so much noise, Berry called back and talked to Mrs. Edwards, which was his sister, to get us out there. Because if we didn't come out there, there would be five other girls that they would take and announce them as The Marvelettes. Mrs. Edwards told us that.

The album had a picture of a mailman, but our picture wasn't anywhere on it, because during that time, Black people weren't allowed to put their pictures on it, because the prejudices of some white people. We couldn't have our pictures on the front cover, I knew that.

GLADYS HORTON, The Marvelettes: Berry Gordy wanted The Marvelettes to quit school because we had a hot record out, people wanted to see us, and at the time, Motown was able to sell more records when people could see us.

KATHERINE ANDERSON, The Marvelettes: All of us began to start thinking that we need to get it together and go out there. Because if we didn't go out there to sing the song that *we* made, Berry would get somebody who would. We definitely didn't want anybody else going out there to be singing any song that we had made, so we all got together and began to pack our little rags and then we left. We went to Washington, DC; that's where our first major gig was.

DR. ROMEO PHILLIPS, The Marvelettes' principal: George Edwards, who was married to Berry Gordy's sister Esther, came to the school right after the girls, on their own, made "Please Mr. Postman," and he was encouraging them to drop out of school. In fact, I got on him because he did not stop by the office first. He just came into the building and walked straight back to the music room. He was talking to the girls, and they were expressing some ambivalence about dropping out of school. I think this was near the time they were about to graduate.

My experience in show business. . . . One hit does not a career make, and I was raising hell with Edwards. We belonged to the same fraternity. He was saying, "You have to strike while the iron's hot." And

I remember very vividly telling him, "You can strike while the iron's hot, but unless the iron's plugged in, it's going to get cool." I know they faced pressure from George Edwards and he went to the parents and the guardians of the girls and told them this is a chance of a lifetime, that they could always go back to school but they couldn't always have the chance. Once the record is out, they'll promote it . . . the usual things that a promoter says.

GLADYS HORTON, The Marvelettes: Mrs. Edwards and her husband became legal guardians of me. I was an orphan so early in my life, that it wasn't until I met her that I found out my real birth date, my middle name, my mother's and father's names, and place of birth. I had to send off for my birth certificate for the courts to acknowledge and sign the Edwards on as my legal guardians over my business and money affairs. That knowledge opened up a brand-new door for me. I discovered part of my roots and where I came from, the West Indies.

KATHERINE ANDERSON, The Marvelettes: Because Gladys was in foster care, and George Edwards was in the House, or something [Michigan state legislator]. They took Gladys and made her a ward of the court. That means that they would have to care for her and watch after her. But anyway, they made sure that the money and stuff was right, or whatever they did, and—because I was only sixteen years old then—all I can do is speculate.

DR. ROMEO PHILLIPS, The Marvelettes' principal: I tried to get the girls to stay in school. We did not want the girls to be caught out there with no marketable skill. But then George Edwards went by their homes and talked about striking while the iron's hot. I will never forgive him for that—he's dead now. I'm very disappointed in him and I'm sure that fate would have taken a different turn for those young ladies had they stayed in school and graduated. That would've served as a platform for them to move on to something else if show business didn't pan out.

KATHERINE ANDERSON, The Marvelettes: Unfortunately, that was the choice we had. We had a choice of staying in school or going out there and doing our record. So, why, if you were so family-oriented, would you think in terms of sending five other girls out there? Because the public doesn't know what The Marvelettes look like anyway.

At sixteen years old, how could I know? How could any of us? Georgeanna was sixteen, Wyanetta was sixteen. We had the choice of going out there or staying in school, and all of us ended up making the choice—we made the record, we made it popular, and we were going out there and representing ourselves.

CHAPTER 16

The Assembly Line

Making Girl Groups the Detroit Way

BRIAN HOLLAND, songwriter: I was with Motown before there was Motown.

JANIE BRADFORD, Motown executive: Berry Gordy, Smokey Robinson, Brian Holland, Robert Bateman, and myself were the first five. We would come together at his sister Loucye's house—Berry used to stay with her and we would go over there and write.

MARY WILSON, The Supremes: The family that ran the company—Mr. Berry Gordy's family—were all involved and they were all females, pretty much. They were responsible for always taking care of us, because of the girls there, because of the females—it was just a consideration that came down from . . . from various families, because the women were all very progressive women. They brought their ethics into it, which was cool because most of us had parents who had the same interests and values. That's the way it was in our neighborhood, in our Black community.

JANIE BRADFORD, Motown executive: Well, in the beginning, it was just a handful, really, in the office, so we had to do whatever had to be done. There was nobody—no money to pay a cleaning crew—so *we* cleaned the office. In fact, I remember several times we went out in the yard and pulled the weeds 'cause we didn't have a mower—couldn't pay nobody to cut the grass—but we didn't want our place to look the worst on the block, so we did whatever was required of us.

BRIAN HOLLAND, songwriter: I started working at Motown. You know what I was making? I was making twelve dollars a week. *Twelve dollars a week*. Eventually, I went to seventeen dollars a week, then when we started making money, I started making twenty-five dollars a week. I was so enthused by working hard because I wanted to make money—I wanted to buy me a car, take care of my family . . . matter of fact, I had a baby at that time.

JANIE BRADFORD, Motown executive: I remember once, Holland–Dozier–Holland, after the company had progressed and they'd had several hits . . . some girl that was studying music was there listening to whatever they were playing, and she said, "Oh no, you can't put those two notes together, that music don't go together," and they looked at her, they said, "How many hits have you had?"

BRIAN HOLLAND, songwriter: It was a place where you can go and achieve, you know what I mean?

MICKEY STEVENSON, Motown A&R: If you are a writer, we wouldn't take your song. In the Brill Building, you have to give up the writing, or part of it—this, that, and the other and all that mess—I thought that was a real rip-off for Black people and talented people, but they had no place else to go. So they had to go, and I understood that—other than the Brill Building, their talent will go nowhere—at least they get a shot. . . . So they had no choice. But we didn't play that game, and I made that *real* clear. That's why I hated that place.

JANIE BRADFORD, Motown executive: There were no restrictions on talent or who presented the talent, who came up with the ideas and had the opportunity to try them—we were free to do that.

MICKEY STEVENSON, Motown A&R: So it was like a gift for all of us, you follow me? And for Black artists it was a place to go and get into the industry. Other than that, you had to go out to either New York or Chicago, or something. But as we were growing, musicians came to Motown to be heard.

MARTHA REEVES, The Vandellas: Motown was the place everybody wanted to be.

CAL GILL, The Velvelettes: And thank God for the Motown music, because that music actually encouraged diversity. Because Berry Gordy wanted to appeal to a wide range of people. He didn't want Motown to be classified as "Black" music. He wanted to be classified as just "good" music that everybody who liked to hear music wanted to hear.

BERTHA BARBEE, The Velvelettes: The migration of African Americans—a lot of people migrated and they moved up to the North to get better jobs. Of course, Flint and Detroit had the factories—the Ford Company, Chevrolet and Buick and GM.

I love that whole history of Black music—where it came from—all of that mixed in together. I think that Detroit, Flint, Chicago, that music—yeah, it's there—but the influence came from down South.

So, you intertwined those and, Lord, I do know what I'm talking about with this piano thing, with the chords—you add a jazz seventh chord to this music, or it might have been a spiritual, you might make it a little faster—that's where gospel sort of came into play. And I think that's all part of Motown, you know what I mean? They mixed it all together—I call it sort of mixed in a pot, or something, and you stirred it all up together and it just came out with that beautiful . . . that sound that we hear.

MARTHA REEVES, The Vandellas: I'm from Eufaula, Alabama, and we grew up here in the city. We went south every summer when school was out while my dad worked in different places.

JANIE BRADFORD, Motown executive: Very few were born and raised in Detroit; they were born somewhere else—then raised in Detroit. So I think it was just a collection of people with various talents coming together and that was a release being able to let it out.

CAL GILL, The Velvelettes: My mother is from Mississippi. She didn't like the blues because she said the blues were depressing to her. She said . . . because she once told us, "I am the blues."

MARTHA REEVES, The Vandellas: Remember, we were collected too. Berry had producers and arrangers, headed by William Stevenson. They went from club to club, and house to house, and gathered those great musicians, and gathered the singers, and brought them to Hitsville USA.

BOBBY JAY, disc jockey: Berry decided to put together, you know, a permanent group of jazz musicians, the Funk Brothers, to play on all the records. It was more structured . . . it was more based on the assembly-line concept in Detroit. So it became, as Berry coined it, "the sound of young America."

BERTHA BARBEE, The Velvelettes: The Detroit sound . . . because Mickey Stevenson, who headed up their A&R at the time, where did they get the Funk Brothers? Got them from the clubs when Berry Gordy wanted musicians for his newly started recording studio. They got them from the clubs, you know what I mean?

JACKIE HICKS, The Andantes: You were there every day, it was like a little factory where you were just having fun, you enjoyed your job. You sat around, if there was nothing to do, as soon as you get up to leave, "Well, come on, we got this song here for such-and-such a group and we want to sing, you guys just sing on that." We practically lived up there.

LOUVAIN DEMPS, The Andantes: Stomping on boards and all kinds of stuff.

JACKIE HICKS, The Andantes: We had hand clappers and foot stompers . . . you couldn't flush the toilet because, in certain rooms, in certain times, it would come back on the tape—you would hear it.

CAL GILL, The Velvelettes: Berry Gordy was only in his thirties when he founded his Motown, or late twenties. So he was learning to . . . you know, he didn't have all the answers to everything.

BERTHA BARBEE, The Velvelettes: We signed in 1962. So we would see Pop Gordy, which was Berry Gordy's father. He was a carpenter and knew what he was doing. He was nailing . . . we'd see him some days nailing up mirrors in these little practice rooms—they'd call them practice rooms, where we could do our steps, and they'd have a piano in each of the rooms and then mirrors.

MARTHA REEVES, The Vandellas: It's a lot of people that were there working as a team. It sort of favored a factory kind of routine, like an assembly line—because the hits were coming so fast, and the artists were being so successful.

JACKIE HICKS, The Andantes: Every day, every week type thing—like when . . . when I say it was like a factory putting out cars—that's exactly what it was.

PETER BENJAMINSON, Florence Ballard's biographer: Berry worked in an assembly line, which is where he got the idea for how to produce records. Basically, the record moved from one department to another, right up the line.

BERTHA BARBEE, The Velvelettes: We would be the "car," so to speak, when we signed our contract.

MARTHA REEVES, The Vandellas: It was Berry Gordy's house. He invited his friends in.

CHAPTER 17

From Behind the Desk to Center Stage

The Vandellas

MARTHA REEVES, The Vandellas: And people say, "Well, who was first?" It was The Marvelettes—The Marvelettes were the first girl group at Hitsville USA. They were from Inkster, which is located a little ways out of Detroit, but they were Detroiters at heart. And then it was Martha and The Vandellas, then it was The Supremes. For history's sake, chronologically, that's how it happened. I did idolize The Marvelettes, and I was *thrilled* to meet Gladys Horton on my first day of working as A&R secretary, unofficially—I was asked to answer the phone. The next thing you know, I'm talking to the artists as well as the writers and musicians on the phone, people that I'd heard about and idolized.

MICKEY STEVENSON, Motown A&R: Martha was nonstop. She was determined to be in this business.

MARTHA REEVES, The Vandellas: I was discovered by Hitsville USA's A&R director, William Stevenson, singing as Martha LaVaille in a club that is now defunct but was one of the biggest in the city called the 20 Grand. I was asked to come to Hitsville USA with a business card, mind you.

MICKEY STEVENSON, Motown A&R: Okay, the A&R man is "artists and repertoire." So our job is to (a) find the artists, (b) put them together with the songwriters or producers, and make hit records. Now that's on the artist's side. . . . The A&R man's job was also to find writers and producers. In my case, I was given the authority to do anything I thought would make Motown great. So, I would find artists, writers, producers, *and* musicians. I was given the right to do whatever I thought would make the company grow. So it was a joy for me, because I interviewed a lot of people for a lot of reasons and was given the gift to pick the right ones for the best reasons. You with me?

MARTHA REEVES, The Vandellas: I went there the very next morning, Monday morning. And upon arrival, saw all of these people standing outside of Hitsville USA, waiting for an audition—maybe thirty people. It was a little cold, too, that January.

Anyway, I had a card so I could breeze by them and go to the front desk and ask to see William Stevenson. So when I got to the desk, Juana Royster, who was the beautiful receptionist, I'll *always* be indebted to her, she said, "May I help you?" And I said, "Yes, may I see Mr. Stevenson? I have a card." And she said, "You mean Mickey?" I said, "Okay, if that's what you call him." She buzzed the door—she didn't ask me my name or anything—I was just received. So, I just felt like it was an act of God. I was in the right place at the right time when I was buzzed through a door and on the other side of this little barrier—there was William Stevenson, the same man who gave me a card.

He was in the same clothing. He had taken off his jacket, he had loosened up his tie. He had been up all night after the 20 Grand closed at two o'clock, writing this song for a man named Marvin Gaye. I got in and I fit in real good because the minute he saw me, he asked me, "What are you doing here?" I said, "Well, don't you remember giving me this card last night and asking me to come?" And he said, "Yeah. But you're supposed to call for an audition. All those people outside had called for an audition. . . . Answer this phone, I'll be right back."

MICKEY STEVENSON, Motown A&R: I mean, she was taking messages like she was my assistant . . . and I really wanted to tell her a thing or two. And when I walked over to her and said, "Martha, what are you doing?" She said, "Just a minute," like *held me up*. [*laughing*] "Yes. Yes . . . well . . . okay. I'll give him the message." So I listen to her talk to whoever she was talking with, saying to myself, *That's pretty good*. So when she finished, before I could say anything, she handed me about five messages, "So-and-so called." And then I say, "Well, get this person on the phone right back."

MARTHA REEVES, The Vandellas: Anyway, he left me in that office and the four-line telephone was jumping off the hook, so I answered it, "A&R Department, may I help you?" To be asked, "Who are you, what are you doing here?" And I explained myself, "Mr. Stevenson said he'd be right back. May I take a message?" And I did that for about three hours. He was gone, but he was writing that song. That was the energy of the studio—people were always writing songs. There was seventeen guys working out of a small office referred to as the A&R Department. It was a little, tiny closet with some file cabinets, a telephone, a desk, and maybe a clock. Anyway, I got through that day and was asked to return.

MICKEY STEVENSON, Motown A&R: So when I finished my conversation, I said, "Martha, how would you like a job as a secretary?" [*laughing*] She said to me . . . this is amazing . . . she says, "First of all, I want to be an artist. But I won't be your secretary, I'll be your assistant." [*laughing*] And I said to myself, *Boy, she got a lot of heart*. So I was kind of sold on her there.

Because I wasn't interested in signing any more girls. We had *all* kinds of girl groups around. But she was so insistent on being with that company. And she had such an attitude about it and I took her on.

MARTHA REEVES, The Vandellas: That's right. I paid my dues on the inside and the outside—in the office and on my stage—I paid my dues.

MICKEY STEVENSON, Motown A&R: My deal with her was, "Okay, Martha, you know, see, I may be here all night and if you hang around I'm not paying overtime." She says, "I'm leaving when you leave." If I stayed there to eight, nine o'clock at night—because I go down and do some writing and producing—she'd be upstairs doing some other stuff. . . . She was amazing.

MARTHA REEVES, The Vandellas: And this went on for nine months of my coming to Hitsville USA, doing demos, taking notes, answering phones, making sessions, arranging for people to fill in the slots when it was session time. And he finally wrote that song for Marvin Gaye, a song called "Stubborn Kind of Fellow."

*

ANNETTE BEARD, The Vandellas: Well, Martha . . . I think she's always wanted to be a solo singer. It was never in my dream to become a singer, I wanted to be an RN—there was something about that white uniform and that white hat that I really liked.

ROSALIND ASHFORD, The Vandellas: I hadn't even had the slightest idea about being a singer. My intentions were when I got out of high school, I was going to try to become an airline stewardess. That's basically what I had focused on doing. But it turned out differently.

MARY WILSON, The Supremes: I don't think anyone had in their mind . . . I shouldn't say anyone—not us. We didn't have in our minds that we wanted to be singers. It wasn't something anyone was trying to do for a career back in those days. We were Black, obviously, and careers were not something that we thought about. Our parents and everything was just thinking about getting a job.

ROSALIND ASHFORD, The Vandellas: This guy, he was trying to start a girl group. So, I auditioned for him and I was one of the ones that was chosen to be in his girl group. He wanted, like, five girls and he had already had a lead singer.

ANNETTE BEARD, The Vandellas: I ended up at the same audition, but I ended up with a girlfriend of mine—she heard about the audition. When he pointed to me, he went, "You, come up here to the piano and give me an [*singing*] *ahhh*," and I'm looking around, like, "I didn't come to audition. I came with my girlfriend, right here. I don't know a thing." He said, "Oh, that's all right. Come on up here and give me [*singing*] *ahhh*."

After he got through auditioning all the young ladies that was running around YWCA, he finally said, "I have my group." He picked another young lady, he picked Rosalind, he picked the young lady that I went with, and then he picked me and said, "I have my group." And I immediately told him, "No, I can't sing in your group." I said, "My mother's going to kill me *and* you. I'm only fourteen years old." He said, "That's all right. I'll talk to your mom. Don't worry about it." And to this day, I still don't know what he said to my mother.

ROSALIND ASHFORD, The Vandellas: We practiced almost every day, at least three times out of the week.

ANNETTE BEARD, The Vandellas: We'd go to each other's house, move the coffee table out of the middle of the floor, and we'd practice and did some little steps.

ROSALIND ASHFORD, The Vandellas: We were doing the background behind Gloria, but we lost the two girls, so we needed to get another singer, and that's when Martha Reeves came in because Gloria knew Martha—she just went to her and asked her if she wanted to try out for the group. So, that's how we became four members.

MARTHA REEVES, The Vandellas: They were co-members and one of the members' family moved out of the city, making a need for a fourth singer to join them. And that I did, and we sang around locally. I'm referring to the group called The Del-Phis.

I didn't go to school with them. I had no idea of their personalities or their lifestyles. It turned out to be a real good combination and we sang so good together. We won amateur contests but dissolved when all of us reached an age, after high school, where we needed jobs, and to continue my singing, I sang as a soloist and was discovered.

ANNETTE BEARD, The Vandellas: We went to Motown to audition because Martha was there and she asked if she could bring her group down. Somebody had missed a session and they wanted to know if she could bring her group down to audition at Motown. So, that is literally how we got to Motown.

ROSALIND ASHFORD, The Vandellas: And it actually wasn't her group, it was just that she was a member of *our* group. She was the last member to come into the group.

MARTHA REEVES, The Vandellas: Annette was working for a soda fountain, Roslyn worked for the telephone company, and Gloria was working for the City of Detroit in the traffic department. And when I called them, they came to Hitsville USA to do a session behind this Marvin Gaye.

We looked at him and had beautiful harmony—we encouraged him to sing in a way that he had never sang before and it established his style. So, we were a group—a backup group. And one of our first gigs was Marvin Gaye. We were "Marvin and The Vandellas." But it was all about being at the right place at the right time.

Berry said, "Put on those girls that you brought and have them sing backup behind this demo." And that became my first record, a song called "I'll Have to Let Him Go."

ROSALIND ASHFORD, The Vandellas: We started doing some background work behind all the different artists.

MARTHA REEVES, The Vandellas: We're on about five of Marvin Gaye's first album cuts because we sounded so good and made him sing so soulful with us on one mic. We got to remember that—when we recorded with Marvin—it was only one mic for the vocals. We stood around him admiring him and just all up on him, just admiring Marvin Gaye. He was so handsome, and so sweet, and such a gentleman, and sang so good—so talented. And he could *move* you. I mean, here's a man who could sing "The Star-Spangled Banner" and make the girls go *woo*. Just because he was so handsome and so loving and had such a wonderful, gentle spirit.

BRIAN HOLLAND, songwriter: Yeah, I remember Martha. Are you *kidding*? She was a little skinny girl at the desk there. We thought about her and came up with a song for her—I knew she was singing at the time—but I didn't know how *well* she could sing. Anyway . . . we tried her out. She did well . . . she did well.

OTIS WILLIAMS, The Temptations: She was just doing her job there, answering phones and making appointments for Mickey, for sessions and songs. A song came up, and a producer couldn't get the singers they wanted to sing it, so Martha did it and that was the thrust of Martha and The Vandellas.

JANIE BRADFORD, Motown executive: They kept the song on Martha, and The Vandellas took off.

MARTHA REEVES, The Vandellas: Eddie Holland decided he didn't want to be a singer, he wanted to be a writer and a producer. He joined his brother, Brian, and Lamont Dozier. After a while, our record "Come and Get These Memories," written by Holland–Dozier–Holland, took off.

BRIAN HOLLAND, songwriter: Lamont and I did the producing—period. My brother came in just to do the songwriting. My brother came in, asked me, "Do you want me to write the lyrics with you and Lamont? Because y'all are great at coming up with these melodies—y'all come up with these melodies so fast that why don't you let me write the lyrics? We could do a whole lot of songs quick."

OTIS WILLIAMS, The Temptations: Next thing you know, Martha is no longer working as the secretary, she's working out on the road.

MICKEY STEVENSON, Motown A&R: Well, Martha was always around—but that's how we got "Dancing in the Street." We were finishing "Dancing in the Street," right? Producing it—Ivy Jo, myself, and Marvin Gaye.

MARTHA REEVES, The Vandellas: That was intended for Kim Weston. Her name comes up a lot. She wasn't in a group, but she was there and her husband was William Stevenson.

MICKEY STEVENSON, Motown A&R: So I said, "Okay, I got an idea—we'll have somebody dub it in like we want it. And then she'll listen to that and get the idea of how we want the song handled." Ivy Jo said, "Who are we gonna get to do it?" I said, "We'll get Martha." I said, "Then she won't keep bugging me about dubbing in on these records. And I'll have her do this, and I'll kill two birds with one stone." So I called Martha, she was upstairs. She came down, we told her how to dub in—we told her how we wanted her to sing. She did one halfway take working it out, and she said, "Okay, let's do it."

When she finished the song, Ivy Jo looked at me, Marvin Gaye looked at me, and said, "Do you hear what I hear?" And I said, "I sure did." I said, "That's a hit on Martha. This is what we're gonna do." . . . You know my word was whatever is the best—who's the best—that's who gets the song. So, now I got a problem [*laughing*] because Marvin Gaye said, "Okay, man, you know, you promised it to Kim Weston. What you gonna do?" I said, "Well, Martha's got the song. I got to figure out how to make that happen." And I did. Of course Kim didn't talk to me for about three or four weeks, but . . .

CHAPTER 18

The No-Hit Supremes

MARY WILSON, The Supremes: The first girl group that got the hit record was The Marvelettes—and that was no big deal for us. In fact, I remember Florence went into the studio and helped Gladys sing one of the lines in "Please Mr. Postman," because she was having a little difficulty with it. So what you hear about Motown in terms of being a family feeling, it was really right—we all loved each other and admired the talent that was coming in there.

GLADYS HORTON, The Marvelettes: Florence came in with Mary while we were recording. When we took a break, Florence asked the producer if she could have a couple of minutes coaching me, because of the ad libs she heard, she felt they would add to the song.

MARTHA REEVES, The Vandellas: My first encounter with The Supremes, I was in our department and they were sitting—basically, every day after school—in the lobby waiting to be discovered. Smokey Robinson introduced them to Berry Gordy, and after school, they would come in, they would sit in the lobby, hoping that Berry would see them. He said he didn't want to sign them to a contract or anything until they were at least twenty-one.

MARY WILSON, The Supremes: When rock and roll started, you had the doo-wop groups, but the girl groups were the ones that really interested me, because we were girls—so that was obviously . . . my ear was tuned in to them. The Chantels were one of the first female groups I listened to, with their song "Maybe." My favorite of everybody was The Shirelles.

Florence and I met at a talent show at our school. Florence sang "Ave Maria" a cappella. She and I just walked home together and we became friends right then.

A couple weeks later, she came up to me on the playground. Florence said her sister was dating a guy in a group called The Primes and they wanted to put a little girl group together, did her sister know anyone? She said, "My sister Florence can sing her butt off." So she asked Florence if she wanted to be in this group, and Florence said, "Yes, and my friend Mary." One of the boys was going to go across the street to ask this other girl Diane if she wanted to be in the group.

AUTHOR'S NOTE: Diana Ross was born Diane and later changed her name.

MARTHA REEVES, The Vandellas: There were all kinds of famous people at Northeastern High School who went on to big careers. I think I might've been one of the most celebrated. Mary Wilson went to Northeastern, so did Florence Ballard, and Sylvester Potts—those are people that we met again at Hitsville USA.

JANIE BRADFORD, Motown executive: I knew them as The Primettes before Motown. I knew The Primes and I had met them through The Primes before The Primes became The Temptations.

MARY WILSON, The Supremes: With The Primes and The Primettes, we were just some of the local groups who would just come up and sing to augment the recording artists. We did that for a couple of years before we actually started to go to Motown and audition.

We auditioned for Motown with the four of us, and Mr. Berry Gordy turned us down. He said for us to come back after we graduated from high school. Florence—when we walked out the door—Florence said, "He can't be that great if he doesn't know how good we are." To show you how good *we* thought we were.

People are not very aware of this—but there were four girls in The Supremes. Everyone always thinks we were three when we became The Supremes, but Barbara was still there. Our original groupmate Betty McGlown left, so we got another girl, Barbara Martin, who took Betty's place. She stayed with us until we actually signed with Motown. She signed with Motown. In fact, she recorded our first album with us, which was *Meet the Supremes*.

JACKIE HICKS, The Andantes: I remember their first audition because they weren't accepted because they were only sixteen. He couldn't have young girls . . . 'cause you know—unchaperoned and hanging around waiting to become artists, get a record or whatever . . . so he did insist that they went back to school and graduated. That's when they came back the second time, auditioned, and were accepted.

BRIAN HOLLAND, songwriter: Well, they were young girls that Berry Gordy told to go back home and finish school, then after they finish school to come back. You see, he can't really find them a recording contract at that time because they were really too young. . . . No . . . Berry, no . . . he didn't want that. He said he wanted them to be in school—graduate from school and come back. He was very big on young kids staying in school and trying to finish school—which was a good thing.

KATHERINE ANDERSON, The Marvelettes: What Motown said about school, "We want our people to graduate," this, that, and the other—that's crap. They didn't really give a damn if you graduated or not. When they were talking about how there were tutors and all like that, that is not true. Motown never told us to finish high school. So if they say, "We wanted them to finish high school," that's shit. It never crossed their minds about us finishing high school or anything else because we had a hit record and were out there on the road, so they really didn't give a damn.

If we had come out with another record before "Please Mr. Postman," then it would have allowed us time in order to finish school, but we didn't. . . . Unlike The Supremes, as soon as we came out of the box we had a million-selling record. Therefore, they didn't give a damn if we finished school or not.

MARTHA REEVES, The Vandellas: And so eventually The Supremes got in the offices, and eventually they got recorded.

MARY WILSON, The Supremes: Pretty soon, Barbara and her then-boyfriend, who she was just madly in love with, decided they wanted to get married and have children and this and that, so Barbara decided she was going to leave. At this point we just realized, *You know what? Everyone's getting married. No one wants us, so why don't we just stick with the three of us and just do that?* So that's what we did, we stuck with three.

ANNETTE BEARD, The Vandellas: When Rosalind and I first met Florence and The Supremes they were The Primettes. We met them before they became The Supremes, and before we became The Vandellas, we were Del-Phis. And to me, *she* had the better voice, *she* was the lead singer of the group. It later got to be Diana Ross, but it was Florence. Florence had that strong voice, Diana has that kind of sweet little voice, you know?

MARY WILSON, The Supremes: I was always in the middle of Diane and Flo. They were the strong ones and I was the one in the middle. I looked up to both of them.

BRIAN HOLLAND, songwriter: Smokey was the reason why The Supremes came to Motown. All I know is that when they got to Motown, they were in the studio and Berry called us down to listen to 'em. "So I've got these young girls . . ."

MARTHA REEVES, The Vandellas: Smokey did their first songs, "Let Me Go the Right Way, Mister" and "Buttered Popcorn." But evidently those songs were not hits and they were referring to them as "the No-Hit Supremes."

CHAPTER 19

Motown's Last Girl Group

The Velvelettes

BERTHA BARBEE, The Velvelettes: Well, I have to say that being brought up in Flint, we were called The Flintstones. We actually sung around Flint for a couple of years.

NORMA BARBEE, The Velvelettes: And we cut a couple of records—"Qué Pasa" and "The Wind." And my uncle wrote those two songs with Mickey Stevenson. And that's really who opened the door for us at Motown—Mickey Stevenson, who was working with Berry.

MILLIE GILL, The Velvelettes: After graduating from high school, I started Western Michigan University. That's when I met Bertha in the student center. I just heard somebody playing the piano and I just walked up the stairs. And lo and behold, I didn't know Bertha, but I met her that day.

BERTHA BARBEE, The Velvelettes: So, me and a bunch of the girls, one evening we went to the student center, we called it "boy looking," to find the cute boys. . . . [*laughing*]

So, we went to the student center to hang out, and there was a baby grand piano. And, of course, when I see a piano, I want to play it. I wasn't playing loud, but I played a little bit of classical stuff, and they were like, "Oh, Bird! Wow—yeah!"

MILLIE GILL, The Velvelettes: And after that, I said, "I have a sister that sings." And Cal was about fourteen at the time. Then she said, "Well, I have a cousin that can sing," and that was Norma.

NORMA BARBEE, The Velvelettes: Berry's nephew, Bob Bullock, he heard us singing and he said, "God, you guys are good. I want you to meet my uncle. I work with my uncle every summer when I'm not in college. And he's got these other girl groups and they don't nearly sound as good as you guys."

But we had to convince our parents. We would beg my dad because he was a hard worker. He had the two jobs—as a preacher and as a baker—he was tired, with seven children. I can remember him coming home, falling on the couch or going to the bedroom, and taking a nap, only to get up and go do his next job. So, it took some time but every day we would ask, "Daddy, please take us to Detroit. We want it, we want to audition for Motown Records," and by that time, the whole household knew what Motown was.

BERTHA BARBEE, The Velvelettes: So, finally, Cal's father said, "You know what? I'll take you girls down there." And we said, "Well, what do we got to lose? We'll try it." So, Norma, of course, met us down there.

CAL GILL, The Velvelettes: Betty Kelley spent the night here because she was my best friend. And so then Bertha, Mildred, and Betty got into the back of my dad's car, and it was starting to snow, but not too bad.

MILLIE GILL, The Velvelettes: My dad drove us down in the snow—it was horrible. We got down there, walked in the studio. . . . The lady says, "We don't do auditions on the weekend."

BERTHA BARBEE, The Velvelettes: She was very curt. And we said, "But we came in a snowstorm. It was just horrible. It took us four or five hours to get here." But she goes, "I'm sorry, but we just don't have auditions." I mean, she was just *really* rude. And finally, she said, "Well, where are you from?" And we said, "Kalamazoo." She goes, "Kalama-who?"

CAL GILL, The Velvelettes: I remember her saying, "Kalama-who?"

BERTHA BARBEE, The Velvelettes: We said, "You know, maybe it wasn't meant for us to do this." So, we sort of got tears in our eyes . . .

some of us were crying . . . we said, "Well, hey. We'll just turn around and go back."

MILLIE GILL, The Velvelettes: We were just crushed. But at that moment, this guy came walking through the studio and Bertha looks and she says, "Mickey?!" She recognized Mickey, Mickey recognized her.

CAL GILL, The Velvelettes: He recognizes Bertha and Norma because he used to record them with their uncle Simon in Flint, Michigan—with their group called The Barbees. And Mickey Stevenson, he was a little hustler young man, probably in his mid- to late twenties.

NORMA BARBEE, The Velvelettes: And he said, "Hey, what are you guys doing here? Come on in." So, that's how we got with Motown—from The Barbees, mm-hmm—from The Barbees. And he invited us in.

MICKEY STEVENSON, Motown A&R: And I didn't want to be bothered with them. And they—they were insisting. I mean, that was, they gave me a story about coming up with the car and all that kind of stuff. [*laughing*] . . . I think their father was a preacher or something like that.

So right there, I said, "Let me hear." I only did it because of all the trouble they had getting down there on a bad day, and I'm ready to leave the building. But I said, "Do it right now. Okay, let me see what you got."

NORMA BARBEE, The Velvelettes: And we played all of the songs that we had wrote. And because we went there, all of us could sight-read and we were all in college at the time—it was impressive, because the rest of the groups weren't in college—it was real impressive, I believe.

MICKEY STEVENSON, Motown A&R: And they blew me away. They blew me away. I told them right there. "You got it. Get back here." And I only had to see them one time because I say, "Wow, they got it." And they were so happy. And I was ready to get out of there. [*laughing*]

CHAPTER 20

Motown Makes a National Impact

MICKEY STEVENSON, Motown A&R: Motown was on that first—Motortown Revue. We took everybody, we took *everybody*—that's what was so wonderful about it. The biggest artists could do three songs, the other artists could do two songs—the ones we were grooming, you got me? On our Motown Revue everybody was on the show—Stevie Wonder's first time was out there—but I didn't have him any hits, but it didn't matter, we wanted them to see what we got.

MARTHA REEVES, The Vandellas: Our first Motortown Revue—which was three months of traveling, ninety-four one-nighters—everybody's records hit after we came back from that strenuous tour, on a broken-down Trailways bus that didn't have a toilet.

ANNETTE BEARD, The Vandellas: We actually toured the whole South and that was quite an eye-opener for us—being northerners and touring the South. There were things that we had seen on TV and heard about, but we got a chance to live it. It was a little scary . . . or quite a bit scary . . . because we were received well, but it was just the way in which we were received.

MICKEY STEVENSON, Motown A&R: And everything had to be absolutely on point with me, *everything*—no, nothing out of whack—everything has to be right on professional lines. And Berry insisted that I go. I said, "I'm in the studio, man, I ain't got time to go on no revue—going to the Apollo, running around theaters . . . stuff like that." He said, "Well, we'll sell more records when the people get to see what we got to offer." That's why he wanted me to go—because I'm gonna make it go right, period.

MARTHA REEVES, The Vandellas: Everybody doing two songs and the star doing maybe three or four or five. At that time being Smokey and the Miracles or Mary Wells, who had the, I guess, the biggest hits at the time and that's who was designated to be the stars of the show.

MICKEY STEVENSON, Motown A&R: I said, "Everybody that leaves the stage gets behind the curtain and sings the background to the artist that is on." And that's how we did it. We had the hottest revue in the country out there.

MARTHA REEVES, The Vandellas: We worked every night practically—maybe we'd have a night off if we had to drive a distance. And a one-nighter would be, get to the stadium—having rode the bus all night—not a hotel or anything. You'd get there, and you'd be assigned your dressing rooms. You'd try to wash your . . . excuse me . . . your *niceties* and hope they dried by the time the show started—get yourself together to go on your spot on the show and be prepared to do a finale.

And it was always fun to stand and watch each act do what they were doing—it was a joyous time. We managed somehow to get food in between those bus rides, and do our laundry and do our chores and meet that excitement on that stage when people gathered together and watched us perform.

MARY WILSON, The Supremes: We felt camaraderie. All the girls felt camaraderie together . . . unless you had an individual conflict of personality or something like that. In fact, on the Motown Revue tours, all the girls, we had to all be together. It's just like when you're teenagers and you go to a gymnasium party—the boys are on one side, the girls are on the other side.

ROSALIND ASHFORD, The Vandellas: Most of the time it was Annette and I, we roomed together. We had different . . . they kind of separated us. . . . We spent some time with all the girls, and sometimes you might have three or four girls in one room.

ANNETTE BEARD, The Vandellas: Berry put us in the rooms when we were on the Motown Revue. Florence used to share our room. I got some pictures in one of my photo albums with us in the room together—with our little cameras we used to take pictures of everything.

MARTHA REEVES, The Vandellas: So in order to regulate us, we only had one or two visits in hotels—most of the time we slept on that bus. But Mary Wilson was my roommate on two occasions. When they put us up, I think it was good . . . to just make sure that they could divide and conquer to control us and to keep us working—to keep us from rebelling as a group and changing things up or whatever, because we were under the guise of chaperones and tour managers.

ROSALIND ASHFORD, The Vandellas: Well, we had one chaperone. Her name was Miss Morrison.

ANNETTE BEARD, The Vandellas: Bernice Morrison—she was a sweetheart.

MARTHA REEVES, The Vandellas: But Bernie Morrison would sit and talk to us about morals—just standard ladyship—how women carry themselves and how to keep respect in our forefront. Make sure that the guys didn't disrespect us, or we didn't disrespect ourselves. I think it was very necessary to have a chaperone.

MARY WILSON, The Supremes: That's one thing I loved, we were always chaperoned. I'm sure that somewhere down the line they just said, "Make sure you take care of those girls," so that was something, we always had chaperones. In fact, we had chaperones until we were well into our twenties.

ANNETTE BEARD, The Vandellas: The guys weren't chaperoned. They was just chastised before we left Detroit, "Do not mess with them ladies."

ROSALIND ASHFORD, The Vandellas: They used to tell us, "Do not mess with The Contours!"

ANNETTE BEARD, The Vandellas: Stay away from those Contours.

ROSALIND ASHFORD, The Vandellas: After all that warning about stay away from The Contours, somebody always hooked up with one of the girls sooner or later . . . and ended up three or four girls married The Contours.

ANNETTE BEARD, The Vandellas: Two of The Marvelettes married The Contours, I think.

ROSALIND ASHFORD, The Vandellas: Gladys married Hubert. Georgeanna married Billy. And Wanda . . . Wanda was married to one of The Miracles.

ANNETTE BEARD, The Vandellas: Well, we were known by that time. The audience knew us, so they accepted "Heat Wave," and everybody would get up and dance.

I was glad that I had the experience of singing . . . all the traveling that we did. Because that is something that our parents would never have been able to do for us. So, we have had an experience of a lifetime.

MARY WILSON, The Supremes: First of all, it was very, *very* new to travel, and to travel with that amount of people *and* without your families. With the Motown Revue, this was the first time I had gone without my family, the chaperones were there, and it was very exciting . . . but probably the down part would be when we were faced with racial situations.

ANNETTE BEARD, The Vandellas: We'd be driving down the highway and we would actually . . . sometimes every now and then . . . see a rope hanging from a tree. That was a reality right there. That was enough to scare the heck out of you. Because you didn't know what had happened or if anything was getting ready to happen or what it was. Yes, that was very scary.

MARTHA REEVES, The Vandellas: We were mistaken for Freedom Riders on a lot of occasions. Like I said, we were in a Trailways bus—a broken-down bus that had no toilet. We had to stop some places. My first time ever being confronted with a shotgun was trying to exit a bus, thinking that we could use the facilities, and was told to get back on there. "*Get back on there*. And not another one of you niggers get off of that bus." But it was a misunderstanding, because they thought we came to freedom ride on him.

He told the sheriff when the sheriff showed up . . . he had called the sheriff on those phones where you turn the handle with the little hook on the hand—one of those antiquated phones on the side of the wall. And the sheriff shows up and they tell us to move on because we threatened him somehow with our showing up there like that. They were expecting some kind of protest or that was the attitude that they had.

We probably frightened him, that many Black people on the bus . . . because evidently we weren't seen much around there on buses. But I don't know, the newness of seeing that many people on a bus and being as happy as we were and going into his station saying, "Hey, man, where's the bathroom?" And not even speaking—that was a rule—that you wouldn't even speak in the South.

MARY WILSON, The Supremes: There were gunshots at the bus. I remember that being something really scary. We got on the bus and had to get out of town.

ANNETTE BEARD, The Vandellas: Yes, in Mississippi they shot at the bus. The bus driver said they missed our gas tank by an inch.

KATHERINE ANDERSON, The Marvelettes: And all of a sudden these shots were ringing out, and stuff, and we didn't know what to do. Then after that, the next day I said, "You know what? I want to go wherever there's somebody that sells guns," and that's when I bought my first gun. Because I'm saying, "Uh-uh." Yeah, see my life would be just as valuable as those guys' lives were. No, I didn't have to use it, but I was really afraid that I would . . . that I would have to use it, but I, you know, it just is what it is.

BETTY KELLEY, The Velvelettes, The Vandellas: I was born down South, so I wasn't surprised. I knew that this was the way it was. We moved to Michigan when I was in the third grade. There were things that happened. I used to go with my grandmother on the trucks to go pick cotton, so you would hear a lot of things. You're young, seven or eight, but you still realize this is what's happening.

MARY WILSON, The Supremes: But there were always policemen around to keep that in order, because we're talking at a time in the sixties when the segregation rules and laws were still being enforced. It was the law—let's put it that way. So a lot of times when we did those tours and we would go out there and we would be faced with this, many of us for the first time, it was what we had heard about, because our parents were all from the South, and they always told us how they used to pick cotton, and you couldn't do this, you couldn't do that, and if you're Black . . .

But in Detroit, even though we were segregated, it was still not really segregated the way it was in the South. When we saw this in the South, it was frightening, let's put it that way. Because you saw policemen telling people, "You can't go on this side, you've got to stay there."

We're face-to-face with something that maybe our parents had told us about and that we had not really experienced. In Detroit, you could go any place, but you *knew* your place. You didn't go where you weren't supposed to be.

MARTHA REEVES, The Vandellas: They were all segregated in the South. That was the rule. Some of the facilities had the Blacks in the balcony and the whites on the first level. This particular show there was a governor down in the South who would allow Blacks to be attacked with ax handles . . . these two guys had baseball bats with a handle sawed off and they were standing there.

ANNETTE BEARD, The Vandellas: You could tell that the younger people that attended the shows—they enjoyed the music—they just weren't able to come together. They actually had guards that was there to keep Blacks on one side, whites on the other side.

MARTHA REEVES, The Vandellas: And if anybody got up and moved or danced, they would attack them and beat them in their head and take them out of the auditorium. Smokey Robinson, who was the star of the show, when he got onstage, he said, "You two guys, we want you to leave because we've got people here that want to dance and enjoy the music and ain't nobody going to fight. Come on and let us dance and let us have a good time."

ANNETTE BEARD, The Vandellas: The guards were trying to break them up and Smokey Robinson said, "Leave them alone," and the guards backed off a little bit and they began to come together. They were dancing, they were just having a good time up on the floor.

ROSALIND ASHFORD, The Vandellas: Yeah, Smokey broke that line, broke that line.

MARTHA REEVES, The Vandellas: And we saw while singing "Mickey's Monkey," in our finale, in the last part of the show, everybody getting up . . . they pushed that barrier down and they danced and they were giving each other high-fives. They were mingling with people they wouldn't even *look* at in the beginning before the show started—when they were coming into the theater and being separated. We saw that remarkable change right before our very eyes.

ANNETTE BEARD, The Vandellas: I was very glad to leave from the South. I said once I left the South that I never wanted to go back that way again.

MARTHA REEVES, The Vandellas: They got us home safe. We all managed to come back and enjoy the fact that all of our records had charted. The whole point of doing that revue with them is to get all of our records on the charts. And it worked.

We toured the United States and when we arrived back to the city of Detroit—war-torn and had a few incidents—all of our records had charted. Very smart move . . . a team of people putting their efforts together to make us famous.

PART 4

Topping the Charts

1963–1964

CHAPTER 21

The Salute to Freedom, Birmingham, Alabama

The Shirelles Use Their Voices

RICHARD DUBIN, musician: AGVA, the American Guild of Variety Artists, were the principal organizers of this event, together with the NAACP. I'm a trumpet player. Whenever I was available, I would play the Apollo. So, it was through Local 802 that I initially got involved with the Apollo, and it was the Apollo orchestra or band, really—no strings, that was the band—the show band for that event. That's what I was doing there.

BEVERLY LEE, The Shirelles: I'll never in my life forget it. Joey Adams from AGVA, the union, contacted Scepter Records, and we were never told what this event was going to be like or what it was going to be for . . . who was going to be there.

JOHNNY MATHIS, singer: I was ready to do something because I'd taken a little heat. The people would say, "Why don't you help us out a little bit and do a little something for the Black community?" My mom and my dad were big fans of Reverend King and they said, "Oh, son, that'd be nice to show your appreciation of what he's done for our cause."

RICHARD DUBIN, musician: It was widely covered, that's why I'm surprised it didn't get more attention. The trip was loaded with significant people—Joe Louis, the boxer, was on it. Dick Gregory was on it, James Baldwin was there—then you know that Martin Luther

King was there for the whole thing—so it was a group of notables. I don't get why there isn't more writing about it, more of an understanding of how significant it was. Its purpose was to raise money for the March on Washington, which happened about three weeks later.

SHIRLEY ALSTON REEVES, The Shirelles: We did the first integrated show in Alabama. It was us, Johnny Mathis, Joey Bishop, and Nina Simone. We all flew down there in a private plane to do it. Everybody was quiet. It was kind of a solemn ride because we knew anything could go wrong.

RICHARD DUBIN, musician: I had a vague idea that it was a significant event, since we were traveling on private planes. We were guarded, the whole atmosphere was a little bit fraught.

SHIRLEY ALSTON REEVES, The Shirelles: I'd heard that they had some marches around the plane out there in the field. They had all kinds of stuff going on. This is what they were saying. We didn't know, because I didn't see it. There were different things they said were happening, things that would scare you.

RICHARD DUBIN, musician: We were all picked up at the airport by private people in their own cars, because there was no public transportation available to us. The authorities of Birmingham were doing everything they could to not make this happen, obviously. So we were shuttled off to [the A.G.] Gaston Motel, which was the Black motel in town. Gaston's was owned by the major Black entrepreneur. In those days in the South, the major Black entrepreneur in town would generally own a hotel and most significant funeral home, and so Gaston was that kind of guy.

BEVERLY LEE, The Shirelles: We found out later that the Klan had marched just before we got there. The National Guard had to guard the plane, they had to have their own security. They *had* their own security. We found out that Dr. King's car led the cavalcade from the airport to the hotel. When we got to the hotel, we couldn't leave out of the premises.

RICHARD DUBIN, musician: It was supposed to be at some civic center, and the permission to use the civic center was pulled at the very last moment. As a consequence, they needed to quickly build a stage out in a field, I guess it was a football field . . . I can't remember what it was, but in some large space at Miles College, which is a historically Black college just on the outskirts of Birmingham.

SHIRLEY ALSTON REEVES, The Shirelles: They set up a stage in the field out there and people had to bring their own chairs.

RICHARD DUBIN, musician: They built a stage in a hurry, because the permit was pulled for the civic center. This turns out to be significant because the show was a really, really big show—it was a big band, it was a lot of weight on this stage that was hastily built. And on the way to Miles College, we drove by thousands of people with candlelight and flashlights carrying chairs, because there was no preparation. All this happened at the last moment, and it was really profound to see thousands of people walking to this venue.

BEVERLY LEE, The Shirelles: I know that people . . . I was told that they walked miles and brought their own chairs.

CINDY ADAMS, writer: Those without chairs rented them on the grounds for twenty-five cents. Or brought pillows. Or squatted on the grass.

JOHNNY MATHIS, singer: I remember Nina Simone, she was a hoot. She was the most volatile one on the bus and everybody was telling us that there might be a disruption and what have you. And then Nina Simone was on the bus telling everybody in the most vulgar ways about what she would do, "These sons of . . . if they do anything to me, I'll kill them."

CINDY ADAMS, writer: An additional forty-five-minute delay was caused by the late arrival of Ray Charles. His bus couldn't proceed to the stage because opening the gate would have meant thousands could pour in helter-skelter. Near mayhem was averted by the Reverend Dr. Martin Luther King who quickly stepped forward toward the helmeted policemen on duty, he formed a human chain to stem the onrush. It wasn't needed. His presence was enough.

RICHARD DUBIN, musician: The crowd was big, enthusiastic, boisterous—couldn't believe that this thing was going on, that this was actually happening. The show was slightly integrated. There was a smattering of white people on the stage and in the audience, but just a smattering. It was overwhelmingly Black.

CINDY ADAMS, writer: The "stage" was an elevated slab of plywood put together with spit.

BEVERLY LEE, The Shirelles: It was heavily guarded. When we were doing the show, we finished our songs. I'll never forget, I was watching Johnny Mathis—all of a sudden, there was a lot of popping. I've heard and read about a lot of different versions of this story, but I was standing right there.

CINDY ADAMS, writer: Near the three-quarters mark, when Johnny Mathis was eight bars into his opening song, the entire bandstand collapsed. With it went some invited guests. I was one of them, so was Leo Shull, Johnny Mathis, William B. Williams, James Baldwin. It was like an earthquake. Two sections of the stage suddenly split.

SHIRLEY ALSTON REEVES, The Shirelles: I remember Johnny Mathis was on and the stage went down—it collapsed.

RICHARD DUBIN, musician: He was singing "I've Got a Lot of Livin' to Do." The first thing I noticed was him diving off the front of the stage as it collapsed. So he dove off the stage and I fell backwards off the stage.

CINDY ADAMS, writer: Simultaneously, all electrical equipment went dead. Some of us were slightly injured. Several had broken limbs, one had both legs broken. All of us were badly shaken. We'd been repeatedly warned of possible violence. In the ensuing darkness and chaos, we wondered if it was to hit now.

BEVERLY LEE, The Shirelles: I knew what was happening. The light bulbs had overheated, and some of the gel or something got on there and they exploded. Some people may have thought it was gunshots, and I was told that people started panicking, running. I didn't see one person get up and run.

SHIRLEY ALSTON REEVES, The Shirelles: The people started running. We were running and didn't know which way to go. We didn't know if anything was going to happen. It was a scary thing, it was so scary. I was trying to get up under the car. It was a scary moment, but not because someone did anything. It was one of those freak accidents. We never heard anything about it, as far as there being any kind of sabotage.

JOHNNY MATHIS, singer: The problem was that everybody thought it was sabotage from some people who were in the audience to disrupt the performance. But I just thought it was . . . going onstage as I have all my life, things like that happened.

RICHARD DUBIN, musician: When the stage collapsed, these thousands of people began to sing "We Shall Overcome." So there was this moment of chaos, followed by silence for a second, and then the voices of thousands of people singing "We Shall Overcome."

CINDY ADAMS, writer: In true show-must-go-on tradition, [the] Alabama Christian [Movement for Human Rights] Choir struck up a gospel. The remaining performers did their turns sans lights, mics, and music since many instruments had been broken.

RICHARD DUBIN, musician: That moment when everybody started to sing, I was being picked up by two very large men, very large Black men, one of whom was named Thad Jones. Thad Jones is a *major, major, major* figure, and he was in the trumpet section together with me. So he and Joe Louis the boxer were over me to see if I was okay and ultimately lifted me off the ground. These are two giant, big, strong, scrappy Black men and there's this chorus of thousands of people—I think there were about fifteen or sixteen thousand people there. So all those voices . . . I thought I was in some kind of heaven for a moment. I was in an altered state, but not panicked. Then I got back to business and went back to playing.

JOHNNY MATHIS, singer: The minute the stage collapsed, all the pandemonium started, and they hustled me out of there and took me back to the hotel. Those things—when they hire someone like myself—they hide me away and then they rush me on the stage and do what I do and then they hide me away and take me home.

RICHARD DUBIN, musician: They got the power back pretty quickly, but it was cut down and clearly there wasn't a whole band playing arrangements, it wasn't the show as planned, but my horn was fine, thank God. Amazingly, very few people were injured, and the ones that were, were only slightly injured. I was not at all injured, so I continued to play. There was a rhythm section that played, so the drums survived—they were played by a very notable drummer called Panama Francis. Billy Taylor, he was a piano player, he was still there. I can't remember who the bass player was. So I played, the trio played, and I'm sure a saxophone player or two . . . we cobbled together music in a catch-as-catch-can way.

BEVERLY LEE, The Shirelles: We were a part of the civil rights movement and didn't know it with a lot of these shows we were doing. But when I saw the picture with Dr. King to my side, my heart just went out of my body. Tears just came down. It was one of the proudest moments of my life.

RICHARD DUBIN, musician: After the show . . . a kind of relief that this whole thing is over, none of us are dead, and we'll go back to the hotel. Honestly, my feeling was . . . I met a woman, and so my feeling was, *Let's get back to that hotel.* Then we got rushed out in the middle of the night because there was a bomb threat at Gaston's. So the FBI was there and they rushed us out and we left by plane in the middle of the night.

SHIRLEY ALSTON REEVES, The Shirelles: On the way home, everybody was quiet. No one was saying anything on the plane.

CINDY ADAMS, writer: At 9:00 a.m., twenty-one hours after this weary band of minstrels took off, they returned.

CHAPTER 22

Summer of '63

The Angels

RONNIE SPECTOR, The Ronettes: "Be My Baby" hit the charts in the last week of August 1963.

JOEY DEE, Joey Dee and the Starliters: We were commuting from Jersey, and they, from New York. We drove down together to Wildwood. We had six weekends—it was summertime, so the Jersey Shore is a hot place for entertainment during the summertime. Touring with them was fun and they always kind of stole the show because they looked so pretty and they sang so greatly, danced well. But you know, I had the hit record, so I'm the one who got us in the door. But we did some dates and Wildwood, New Jersey, was our first engagement.

NEDRA TALLEY-ROSS, The Ronettes: Wildwood, New Jersey. We ran into the Mafia there. The Mafia in Wildwood, New Jersey, going, "You're going to do another week." And I had an aunt—Aunt GoodGood—that's about five-foot-two, redhead, freckles, and she said, "No, we're leaving." And they were like, "No, you're staying. And we're going to pay you the same amount of money." They were really being hostile, so my Aunt GoodGood—you got to see her—she's five-foot-two, red hair, buxom, very pretty. So she just turned around, she said—back to the room, "Call the uncles."

We had seven blood uncles and then we had all the women whose *husbands* were uncles, so we had about fourteen uncles in Manhattan. They were characters because, you got to realize, in New York City, my uncles walked down the street—they had the fancy canes, cowboy hats, suits on, boots—those were *the uncles*. And they were very good-looking men, their presence was something else. They just went, "Who are the uncles?" They know the Mafia, but who are the uncles? It was so funny. [*laughing*] And she was so small, but she was so strong. She backed them down—he goes, "Well, we don't want a problem."

RONNIE SPECTOR, The Ronettes: The first time I heard it, The Ronettes were on tour. We were lying in bed watching Dick Clark's *American Bandstand* when he said, "This is going to be the record of the century." And it was us!

NEDRA TALLEY-ROSS, The Ronettes: Once we got "Be My Baby," we were an overnight sensation. My father said, "If they have a hit, I'll eat my hat." We were standing near the window, I wanted to snatch his hat and not throw it out the window but stuff it down his throat.

JOEY DEE, Joey Dee and the Starliters: One day I turned the radio on and I hear "Be My Baby." I'm saying, *What the heck is going on here?* The Ronettes—I was very happy for that. I'm always pleased when some of the people from my group become successful, because that's the idea. We had some wonderful engagements together, albeit short-lived because their success happened immediately thereafter.

PAUL SHAFFER, musician: When I heard "Be My Baby," it was like a voice reaching up to me in the hinterlands and saying, "Paul, come down to New York, you know, participate in this music with us. Maybe there's a girl like me for you down here. I may not be of your faith, but, you know . . . we could work something out."

RONNIE SPECTOR, The Ronettes: When we showed up at the Brooklyn Fox for our first show after "Be My Baby," we took one look at the marquee and had to pinch ourselves.

NEDRA TALLEY-ROSS, The Ronettes: And I remember walking out on the stage at the Fox that Labor Day, because we were really loved, because we were hometown girls. So that was a difference—this wasn't somebody coming in—we were *from* here—New York, *New Yorkers*. And we do love our own. We had to come a long way to get that hit.

RONNIE SPECTOR, The Ronettes: We knew we were big-time, because Murray the K didn't just put anybody's name up in lights.

NEDRA TALLEY-ROSS, The Ronettes: So you became, for the neighborhood, the people that made it. And so you have to treat that with a lot of respect, because people have dreams in this city and they don't make it. But if you're a part of their neighborhood and you make it, *they made it*.

JIGGS ALLBUT, The Angels: We played the Brooklyn Fox Labor Day show 1963, when our record was number one. That was Murray the K's show. When Murray had booked us for the show, he heard the guys play the record before it was even a hit. He booked us for that show—at a low, low, low, low price. I went to the stage manager and was saying to him, "You know, our record is number one, could we get a little bit better introduction? Could you say, you know, that 'it's the number one record in the country' today when you introduce us?" Finally, they did, but we had to ask them to do that.

RON DANTE, musician: Summer nights were not the same without girl groups.

RENEE PAPPAS, music executive and ex-wife of Jerry Wexler: They were always pretty cute girls. But there was not . . . I don't think you ever thought of them as being sultry. I don't think they were ever sold as sexy, per se.

BILLY JOEL, musician: Girl groups had a lot of hit records back in those days. I remember in the early sixties, when I was an adolescent and everybody had a transistor radio. We used to take them to the beach and you had your little leatherette case, and everybody would play their radios.

BIBS ALLBUT, The Angels: We were in demand.

PEGGY SANTIGLIA, The Angels: I was at the beach, the Jersey Shore, with my family, and Bibs and Jiggs called up. They said, "Peggy, you have to come home! This is flying up the charts—it's going to be a big hit!"

BIBS ALLBUT, The Angels: "Come home, Peggy, we have a hit record!" The record was so in demand that they couldn't press it fast enough. They were up all night and all weekend.

JIGGS ALLBUT, The Angels: One time I was riding in the car and going from station to station—from WINS to ABC, CBS. I remember going from one station to the next—all three big stations—and it was playing the same time on all of them. That was really stupid, but that was *thrilling* to me.

BIBS ALLBUT, The Angels: We met Peggy when she was in another group called The Delicates, and we performed with them in a concert. And when we needed a new lead singer, we thought of her.

PEGGY SANTIGLIA, The Angels: The funny thing is, we were kids then. With my group The Delicates, people thought, "Oh, they think they're delicate. Isn't that sweet?" It was really after Denise's family because they ran a delicatessen. Her uncle or father, he said, "You're always here eating and practicing in front of the mirror"—shortened *delicatessen*.

JIGGS ALLBUT, The Angels: We called Peggy and asked if she wanted to come sing with us, and she did.

PEGGY SANTIGLIA, The Angels: Years before, we had been on a show called *[The] Joe Franklin [Show]*, which was an old-timer New York show. At that time they were The Starlets, and I was with The Delicates. They had us stand on boxes and lip-sync to our songs. At the time, we said, "We have to sing out loud." I mean, it was just . . . we felt too phony just moving our mouths—although that's what they wanted us to do. But because we sang out loud—they had to pay us. And I remember Jiggs calling . . . the phone rang, "Oh, hi. This is Jiggs from The Starlets. We just want to know, are you keeping the check that *The Joe Franklin Show* sent?" I said, "Yeah." It's the first TV show that we got paid—evidently, the producers called all of us and asked us to return the check, because they said it wasn't right—they told us not to sing out loud. But we didn't, we didn't return the checks.

JIGGS ALLBUT, The Angels: We said, "What are you going to do?" And so we all decided we were going to keep our checks. So we did, and that was the first thing that we did together—defy Joe Franklin and keep our money.

PEGGY SANTIGLIA, The Angels: Bibs was more serious and determined. She would be the mother hen, sort of. "We have to rehearse. You have to be here at one o'clock." And we were lucky that she was that way, because I certainly wasn't that single-minded and neither was Jiggs, so that was a big help. And I just don't really think The Angels would have come to be if it wasn't for Bibs.

BIBS ALLBUT, The Angels: I started piano lessons at age five and I started writing little songs with Jiggs. We used to sing duets. My sister's great—she's . . . she's just a great person.

JIGGS ALLBUT, The Angels: Our birthdays are on the same day, two years apart. Bibs taught me how to sing harmony.

BROOKS ARTHUR, sound engineer: Bibs and Jiggs were fun ones, they kept you on your toes.

BOB FELDMAN, songwriter: One of my ex-partners, Jerry Goldstein, was going out with Jiggs.

RICHARD GOTTEHRER, songwriter: Jiggs was one of the girls in The Angels. And we all became friends and we wrote this song specifically for them.

JIGGS ALLBUT, The Angels: Jerry Goldstein told us about this hit that would be perfect for Peggy's voice. So I was the first one to hear it, he played it on the piano, and I loved it. I loved, loved, *loved* it.

BIBS ALLBUT, The Angels: We did background . . . started doing some background for FGG [the songwriters Bob Feldman, Richard

Gottehrer, and Jerry Goldstein]. So they wrote the song "My Boyfriend's Back" for us, and we decided to record it with them.

BOB FELDMAN, songwriter: There was a sweet shop across the street from Lincoln High School. Trump [Sr.] was building a huge apartment complex and they were closing the sweet shop. It was a Friday . . . because I came in not only to say goodbye to them, but because I would come into Brooklyn to have dinner with my parents on Friday evenings.

In the back of this sweet shop is where we used to hang out. As I'm sitting there having my last egg cream, there's a girl, young lady . . . but thank God the statute of limitation is over because *she* wrote the song. She's screaming at a guy dressed like the Fonz—leather jacket, the DA [duck's ass] haircut—she's yelling at him, "My boyfriend's back! You're going to be in trouble! You've been saying things about me that aren't true—when he gets a hold of you, he's going to kick the crap out of you!" I grabbed a napkin—and I always carried a pen or a pencil—and I wrote that. I called my partners and I said, "Do not leave the office! I'll have a quick dinner, then I'm coming into the city. I heard a number one song today." I had a quick dinner, hopped on the train, went into the city, and we wrote "My Boyfriend's Back" that night—except for one line. Every hit song really has a signature line. It took us ten days, I think, then Richard came up with the "If I were you, I'd take a permanent vacation" line.

JIGGS ALLBUT, The Angels: At every session we did, after that we would say, "We aren't gonna do that much more background work, because we are gonna have a hit record."

RICHARD GOTTEHRER, songwriter: But the publisher we were with at that time, April Blackwood, thought it was so great, and that it was a perfect song for The Shirelles. They didn't want us to do it with The Angels. Because we were sort of amateur producers at that time, no one knew we were that good, and they tried to push us toward The Shirelles. And it broke up our relationship with the publishing company—we got kicked out of there.

BOB FELDMAN, songwriter: They wanted to give it to The Shirelles, who were, really, the top girls at the time. We said no. They just changed the lock on our office and fired us, basically.

RICHARD GOTTEHRER, songwriter: And we went and produced the song ourselves—our own money—with The Angels.

JIGGS ALLBUT, The Angels: In order to get that, in order to be able to sign with FGG, Bibs and I had to get out of our old contract with a man named Gerry Granahan.

BOB FELDMAN, songwriter: Well, oh boy . . . they were signed to Gerry Granahan, he had promised to release them, and he didn't. Richard Gottehrer and I were in a bar around the corner from 1650 Broadway waiting for our cars, and we were talking about . . . just spouting off what we'd like to do to this guy—*he promised this, he promised that*. Anyway, somebody tapped us on the shoulder, he was wearing a sharkskin suit, he was a slender man of color with a broken nose, and he said, "Who do you want eliminated?"

Excuse me? We're talking about nice Jewish boys here, who went to Yeshiva. He opens up his jacket, and he was like Pancho Villa—he had two shoulder holsters.

At any rate, there was a meeting set up. We were able to work out a deal to get The Angels so that we could sign and produce them, and the fee for that was Sonny Franzese and Nate McCalla became their management. Why not? Tit for tat, you know?

AUTHORS' NOTE: Sonny Franzese was an underboss of the Colombo crime family. Nate McCalla was a well-known associate.

JIGGS ALLBUT, The Angels: In order to get out of our contract, Jerry Goldstein made us sign a management contract with him, Nate, and Sonny—they needed to get something, so he made the deal with the Mob, and they became our managers. And I'm sure Jerry was getting a cut out of everything they gave us.

BIBS ALLBUT, The Angels: Well, it was very behind-the-scenes.

RICHARD GOTTEHRER, songwriter: Well, that's a complicated story. But Sonny and Nate were helpful in establishing a relationship.

JIGGS ALLBUT, The Angels: Nate was great. He was fun. He was a really nice guy.

BIBS ALLBUT, The Angels: I liked him a lot.

RICHARD GOTTEHRER, songwriter: Because it was a lucrative business, there were a lot of elements of the business that were outside of the "traditional" business, but were still used as influencers.

BIBS ALLBUT, The Angels: Nate became our manager. Sonny was just involved from the outside. Big Moishe was our road manager—I can't remember his real name, but we called him Moishe.

JIGGS ALLBUT, The Angels: It kind of made me laugh. *Oh, I'm managed by the Mob.* I was like, *Okay, what's next?*

PEGGY SANTIGLIA, The Angels: I didn't really know how much FGG might've been into . . . beholden to them . . . I don't know how else to put it . . . but I certainly never imagined that they were *our managers.*

JIGGS ALLBUT, The Angels: Sonny, he was kinda this frumpy old Italian guy. He once asked Bibs to go out with him, and she was like . . . she was . . . how do I explain how she was . . . she was like . . . she turned him down.

PEGGY SANTIGLIA, The Angels: Now, I want to tell you something, I never heard that they were our managers. I never knew that. I only knew Nate at the time, and he wasn't in the picture a lot, but I thought of him as a bodyguard. And Sonny Franzese . . . I did know after meeting him that he was a gangster.

I only remember once, in some restaurant FGG and we were all together and when we got up to leave, he patted me on my butt and said, "Do you want to be in the movies?"

BIBS ALLBUT, The Angels: They were very good to us. Yes, they were very good to us. Sonny wanted to take me to Chicago with him. They treated . . . they treated us well. And I just felt like nobody was gonna, you know, bother us. When Moishe was around on the road with us, and Big Nate was in his office at home, they were taking care of us.

RICHARD GOTTEHRER, songwriter: We were never part of that world. So, as long as you're not *part* of it, you're not deeply engaged in it. And you're not held responsible for anything that goes on, and you're not even threatened. In fact, in a minor sense, you're almost protected.

BOB FELDMAN, songwriter: Murray the K, remember him? Murray the K could pick a hit. He was wonderful. I don't know how many contests we won with records we would send him. At any rate, The Angels, we brought them to him before the record actually hit the charts. But he bought them for the show early, okay? He treated them really poorly, *harshly*. So the manager went and had a talk with Murray. They got their second song back, and they were treated with great reverence. . . . "Why didn't you tell me who managed them?!" "Listen, we didn't think you'd be outrageously rotten to them."

BROOKS ARTHUR, sound engineer: They were hysterical. And then you had the three guys, Feldman, Goldstein, and Gottehrer, who were jokesters also, but they meant serious business in terms of getting down what they wanted to get down. No mistake about it. They were hitmakers, they went on to prove it.

JIGGS ALLBUT, The Angels: They were like schleppy guys from Brooklyn just trying to make it. We had a lot of fun, and they wrote great stuff, and we had a hit record with them. It was later on, when you have this huge hit record, and you haven't made any money, then you're not so happy about the people who made so much money.

BOB FELDMAN, songwriter: They made some good money working a lot of gigs because of that one record. We got lazy . . . as writers, we got lazy. We started using other people's songs for follow-ups. We forgot what got us there, which was our songwriting.

PEGGY SANTIGLIA, The Angels: There was a promotion man, I won't say his name, and he was a young guy at the time, similar age, in his twenties, and I was nineteen. And the promotion man and a really famous baseball player at the time asked Jiggs and myself to go out to dinner. And we were all staying at the same hotel, but we didn't want them to come to our room, maybe because it was a mess or something when we were getting ready. So, we said, "Okay, we'll stop by your room, then we'll go to the restaurant together." The promotion guy was the one that would drive you around to the different shows and stuff. So, we dress up and we go down, and knock on the door. . . . They open the door and they're both stark naked—as if that would really lure us. We were much more interested in what we were going to have for dinner, and it wasn't going to be them.

JIGGS ALLBUT, The Angels: We were all a little too innocent, too uninformed, to make any business decisions, to be good at business, and to realize it *is* a business. We weren't concerned about the future, as long as we could make money to live, to have fun, to sing.

PEGGY SANTIGLIA, The Angels: We were all innocent at the time. I did get myself in some situations that weren't good. The Angels were performing at a big outdoor show, and there were lots of motorcycle people there—bikers. And they didn't have security around.

So, as we're leaving the stage, we had to go back through this semi-tunnel kind of thing . . . and as we came offstage, we were really thirsty—I guess somebody handed us a bottle of water—and the next thing I knew, Bibs clubbed one of them over the head. Well, evidently he grabbed her crotch. And he just looked around and he said, "Oh, I love her." He was so flattered that she beaned him on his head.

CHAPTER 23

All Over the Radio

The Chiffons

MELANIE MINTZ, writer: Girl groups took over. They were all singing about young love. Boy meets girl, boy gets girl, boy loses girl.

BROOKS ARTHUR, sound engineer: Each girl group had their own style and their own attitude. Because each group had their own personality and that personality wound up in the grooves of the recording, you know? That's hard to do. Some records are just boring—not our groups'.

JUDY CRAIG, The Chiffons: To tell you the truth, I think we were the first pop artists. Because, when I think back on the artists that came out before us, they were basically rhythm and blues—R & B. And we came along, our stuff was pop, I really believe it.

BILLY JOEL, musician: I think they were pioneers in the recording industry.

DARLENE LOVE, The Blossoms: And it took a few years for all that to start melting, to start becoming a trend. And that started happening in the sixties when the girl groups were really big and popular. Of course when the sixties hit, my goodness, girl groups exploded, right? I mean, there must have been a hundred of them on the radio at one point; at least it felt like that.

LA LA BROOKS, The Crystals: They were starting groups every month in our neighborhoods.

MELANIE MINTZ, writer: Girl groups were the hottest thing.

ELLIE GREENWICH, songwriter: Girl groups were making hits. Everybody became a girl group. Every writer wanted to write for the girl groups and producers wanted to produce girl groups. And they were available. But one or two girl groups make it and everybody jumps on the bandwagon and then there were twenty-four thousand girl groups and a sound is created. The girl groups are in.

BEVERLY LEE, The Shirelles: Well, each girl group had their own sound which was wonderful and unique. You knew who The Shirelles were, you knew who The Supremes were, The Crystals, The Chantels, The Marvelettes.

BROOKS ARTHUR, sound engineer: Even though it was all from the same period, they have to have a similar sound because it was an attitude about that period of time. But through it all, they all had developed—or even walked in with—their own individual sound. I had done some magic with microphones and out-of-phase things, but all of that just gelled with the girls' sound. Put it all together and it spelled magic. How bad could I feel? That was my day-to-day work, you know? How bad could it be going from The Chiffons to The Shirelles to The Cookies in one day?

*

JAY SIEGEL, The Tokens: We started our own record company.

JUDY CRAIG, The Chiffons: The Tokens is the group that had a song called "The Lion Sleeps Tonight."

PHIL MARGO, The Tokens: It became a monster. By Christmas, it was number one. This was in 1961.

JAY SIEGEL, The Tokens: Neil Sedaka knew someone who brought us to a record label, and that person there, he came up with the name

The Tokens. But we didn't want to be known as a subway token or a bus token. Why would we want to be named after a subway token? We wanted to be known . . . tokens of affections or tokens of love. But everybody used to kid around with, "Oh yeah, with you and ten cents, I can get on the subway."

We heard this term *one-hit wonders*. What happens if we never have a hit record again, you know? We could be a one-hit wonder and nobody ever hears of us. But we were all very involved and wanted to remain in the music business, so we really studied and learned about the publishing end of it, starting a record company and becoming record producers.

PHIL MARGO, The Tokens: Okay, we get to a point where we have made some of the worst shit ever in recorded history—I mean—it was *awful*. The songs were *awful*. We had no taste whatsoever, but we were learning. It was like kindergarten, right? First grade.

JAY SIEGEL, The Tokens: Bright Tunes was formed because we lived in Brighton Beach. Get it? So, Brighton, that's how we got that name, Bright Tunes Productions.

PHIL MARGO, The Tokens: Now we have no money left in our recording budget. We do have some money left in our demo budget for the publishing company. And a buzzer rings, and it's Millie the receptionist. She said, "There's a group out here that would like to audition." And we could say, "Come back next week or set up an appointment for that," but we saw them. In comes Ronnie Mack and Patricia Bennett and Sylvia Peterson and Judy Craig and Barbara Lee. And they sing these songs, amongst which was "He's So Fine."

JUDY CRAIG, The Chiffons: Ronnie wrote that song because I had a crush on one of his friends and he said, "No, it's not going to work. He's too old for you." So he wrote "He's So Fine." And I'll never forget that friend's name, his name was Andrew. Mm-hmm, yep.

JAY SIEGEL, The Tokens: Ronnie Mack, a young guy, a very nice guy, he brought up these four girls to the office and they worked for the New York Telephone Company, and they came up on their lunch hour.

JUDY CRAIG, The Chiffons: Ronnie Mack happened to be my best girlfriend's brother. We all came up in the same neighborhood. Ronnie did the legwork and The Tokens asked him to bring us in. When he came to us that day and said, "Listen, I got some people that want to hear you guys." I said, "Really?" Of course, we were all very scared. We were shaking like, *Oh wow, we have to sing?*

BILLY VERA, musician: There was the four of them—Sylvia lived in Harlem, but the other three lived in the Bronx.

JUDY CRAIG, The Chiffons: Bronxdale Houses, Soundview Houses, Castle Hill—basically in walking distance of each other. It was a long walk, but that's what we did back then. Nobody had bus fare and cars, or anything.

I know some people think of the projects as, *Oh my goodness, all the crime*. It wasn't like that when I came up. We just didn't go through all of that; we just had a *ball* in here. We would have real bands when we had our little block parties, we had real musicians.

And it just seemed like for us it happened overnight. I know for Ronnie it didn't because he had been working on it so long . . . because he wanted, you know, to really be a recognized songwriter. I know he put a lot of work into it, but it just happened for us because of him, you know?

JAY SIEGEL, The Tokens: When we presented it to Capitol Records, the president wrote us a letter that they're going to turn down "He's So Fine," because, in his exact words, they thought that the record was "too trite."

JUDY CRAIG, The Chiffons: Yeah, that's another thing, too, The Tokens even played on "He's So Fine." They played the instruments and we recorded it.

PHIL MARGO, The Tokens: We went to eleven other record companies, and they all passed. They weren't interested.

BOB FELDMAN, songwriter: They were turned down by every record company, and I brought Hank [Medress of the Tokens] and the master up to Laurie and helped sell the master to Laurie Records.

ERNIE MARTINELLI, manager, The Chiffons: As far as I was concerned, The Tokens were a plus *and* a minus. Because they were also eighteen, nineteen, twenty years old—and they thought they were geniuses. They thought they knew everything about *everything*. And they could have destroyed the girls' careers.

JAY SIEGEL, The Tokens: The promotion man at Laurie Records, his name was Doug Morris. He was very young at that point as well. He said, "No, that's a hit record—we want this record. We think that's a hit record." So, Laurie Records put out "He's So Fine." Doug Morris then became in his career the chairman of Universal Music—he became very successful in the music business. Also, he was one of the cowriters of "Sweet Talkin' Guy," another hit record we had with The Chiffons.

JUDY CRAIG, The Chiffons: "He's So Fine" came out in '63, I was eighteen. And it went to number one and it stayed number one for seven weeks.

PHIL MARGO, The Tokens: And after "He's So Fine," I got a call from Carole King. She says, "We just wrote a song that I think will be perfect for The Chiffons, we did a demo with Little Eva and invite you to take a listen to it." Wouldn't say no to Carole King.

BARBARA ENGLISH, The Clickettes: The Cookies were the hot group for background in New York.

RON DANTE, musician: They had their own hits. I mean, "Chains" was a great hit. "Don't Say Nothin' Bad (About My Baby)," those were *great*.

MARGARET ROSS, The Cookies: We was like a family—especially with Carole and Gerry and [Carole's daughter] Little Louise. We used to go to Carole's house all the time. We did have a lot of fun with them. They didn't live too far from where we lived—I live out in Coney Island.

Once Gerry came to pick us up, and the police stopped him because he thought we were prostitutes. Gerry says, "No, I'm a songwriter, and I'm taking them to my house, and my wife and my kids are there. We're going to rehearse." They thought he'd picked us up because he saw the three of us in the back of a car, and by us being Black, and he's white, and he was driving. . . . We all laughed about it later, but it wasn't funny at the time—we thought that was terrible. That wasn't the first time that happened to us. If we were in the car with two different colors, they would stop and ask, "What's this about?"

BROOKS ARTHUR, sound engineer: A woman in Philadelphia called Dee Dee Sharp did this song called "Mashed Potato Time," and Donnie Kirshner wanted Carole and Gerry to write a follow-up for her, and they wrote a song called "The Loco-motion."

CAROLE KING, songwriter: Eva invented the dance. . . . Gerry wrote a lyric based on words having to do with *train*.

ARTIE KAPLAN, session musician: Donnie Kirshner, the day after the session, he immediately called Cameo-Parkway Records—he called Bernie Lowe; Bernie owned the company. Donnie sent me up there, and I took a bus to Philly that afternoon, sat in Bernie's office—I wanted to meet the man because I had great respect for him, but he wouldn't allow me to sit at his desk while he listened. So I waited in the waiting room, and I heard him play the record. Then he lifted the needle off the record, gave it back to the girl, and said, "No, thank you." I came back to New York City on the next bus and gave the news to Don Kirshner.

BROOKS ARTHUR, sound engineer: Eva came in and knocked out a vocal and they sent the record to Philadelphia, to Bernie Lowe, the producer—he and Dee Dee Sharp turned the record down and Donnie Kirshner got so pissed, *so* irate—and Al Nevins was *so* angry—that they started their own little record company called Dimension Records.

ARTIE KAPLAN, session musician: That was the first record on Dimension Records.

MARGARET ROSS, The Cookies: The Cookies is the one that brought Little Eva to them, because she lived down here in Coney Island also. We found out that Eva could sing, it was like, *Oh my goodness, we* *didn't know Eva could sing like that.* Earl-Jean took her to meet them because they needed a babysitter. I don't know whether you would realize it, but if you listen to "Chains," you can hear Eva very clearly, because she has that Southern drawl.

RON DANTE, musician: The first day I walked in, of course, I picked up a *Cashbox* magazine in the lobby and there was a picture of Don Kirshner and Goffin and King and Little Eva—right on the cover standing on a locomotive.

JAY SIEGEL, The Tokens: Everybody was trying to get the next hit record. If somebody had a hit record, like, we had "He's So Fine," everybody wanted to get the follow-up. And we got the follow-up record, which was written by Carole King and Gerry Goffin, and that was "One Fine Day," which was another smash hit record, you know.

PHIL MARGO, The Tokens: She sends over the demo and I listened to it and I say, "Okay, Carole, we're going to do it. The only thing is I want the demo. I want to use your track." Because that's her playing the piano and I couldn't make a better track—all we did was add a saxophone, solo, and the background "*Shoobie doobie doobie doobie doo wop wop.*" There was no background on it at the time. A few other little odds and ends and it was "One Fine Day."

JUDY CRAIG, The Chiffons: "One Fine Day," Little Eva did the demo, but the music was already laid out 'cause Carole played the piano, everything. The track was already there. It was originally done in Eva's key, so we didn't have to really do anything but sing.

MARGARET ROSS, The Cookies: I don't know whether you were aware of it, but we did "*Shoobie doobie doobie doobie doo wop wop.*" That's The Cookies in the background, you know? They never took the background out—they left it in there. I didn't even realize it. When I would listen to the radio when it was playing, I always used to say, "I know that's me," because I'm on top, I'm a soprano. I kept hearing, and I'm saying to myself, *That has to be me. They didn't take the background out.*

ARTIE KAPLAN, session musician: The Cookies appeared on every session that she came, that Carole did.

MARGARET ROSS, The Cookies: Jay said to me, "Margaret, you don't remember? We didn't take you girls out. That's you girls still." I said, "What? All this time, and all these years that I had heard myself?" He said, "Yeah, you girls, they didn't take your voices off." He said, "You can't say this, but I mean, don't tell nobody too much, but you all sounded better. I mean, your background was much better." They left our background, she just put her lead voice in.

BROOKS ARTHUR, sound engineer: It could be The Cookies with Dorothy, with Earl-Jean and Margaret. Or it could have been the three of them plus Carole.

TONI WINE, session singer: Well, I gotta think about that . . . the demo was Carole. Could be Carole and The Cookies, because Carole and The Cookies did *tons* of sessions together. But if they kept the background singers, you can't prove it. In listening to the record—and I've heard it from many, many people—and listening to it myself, I know The Cookies' voices—and it sure sounds like The Cookies to me. But the truth is, if you don't have contracts, you don't have shit—that's just the bottom line.

I can tell you that if Margaret tells you that she sang on a record, you can bet your ass she sang on that record. She is just as true as the day is long. And her voice and The Cookies' voices are so identifiable that I would take it as gospel.

JUDY CRAIG, The Chiffons: "One Fine Day," I think, went to number five. But "He's So Fine" went to number one.

PHIL MARGO, The Tokens: We went and brought him the gold record—to Ronnie Mack in the hospital room. He did see that, but because of his death, the world didn't get to hear, see what he could do. It was sad and he was a terrific gentleman too.

JUDY CRAIG, The Chiffons: Ronnie unfortunately died early. When he died, he was twenty-three and he had Hodgkin's disease. "He's So

Fine," yeah, he was alive for that. But after that, he started getting sick. But he went to a few of our performances.

PHIL MARGO, The Tokens: He had a way with lyrics and they were authentic, you know what I mean? It was the authentic stuff from his gut. That was the saddest thing—that he was young and not having known what he would have written.

JAY SIEGEL, The Tokens: When we went to the BMI awards dinner for "He's So Fine," his mom sat at our table. His mom was there accepting the award for him.

JUDY CRAIG, The Chiffons: If he had lived, I think he would have been on top with a lot of the good ones.

JAY SIEGEL, The Tokens: Sylvia, she had a great voice and was very beautiful. She was a stunning, stunning, *stunning* girl . . . beautiful dimples, a beautiful smile. And we made a record called "My Block." We put it out as the Four Pennies, and Sylvia sang the lead on that. It was a pretty good record, but it never got to be that successful. They didn't seem to have any, you know, kind of competition between them as far as who's singing, who's doing what.

JUDY CRAIG, The Chiffons: We met different people, we went different places, other countries, so it was good, it was good. A lot of people are all like, "You got robbed. You didn't make any money." I say, "Yeah, but hey, what are you going to do?" It wasn't like we were held hostage, we just didn't make a lot of money, but we had a good time.

*

TONI WINE, session singer: We as the family of Aldon . . . we knew talks were being talked, so we were not surprised. We were just wondering, *What is it gonna mean?* We knew things would change.

ARTIE KAPLAN, session musician: Aldon sold to Screen Gems because they made Donnie the president of the music division. They also paid Donnie a serious amount of money for that move, so they did well in getting him there. He certainly had a wonderful suite of offices. We continued to have all the same writers . . . but it was just different.

RON DANTE, musician: We were all, like, blindsided. Nobody had heard he was negotiating with Columbia. We had no idea . . . yeah, it surprised everybody—even the top teams—Goffin and King, Mann and Weil, and Greenfield and Sedaka—they were kind of like, "Oh, we're going to be sold off to another company." I think it was for $3.5 million—something like that. It would be three hundred million today, you know, like Motown's catalog.

MARGARET ROSS, The Cookies: We weren't even told anything until it was sold. And we no longer were a part of . . . we thought we were. It looked like they just threw everybody away.

TONI WINE, session singer: When we moved out of Aldon, we were in 1650 Broadway—it consisted of maybe four or five offices in one open, you know, one door—601. When it was sold to Screen Gems/Columbia Music, which was Colgems, they took the whole seventh floor of 711 Fifth Avenue.

RON DANTE, musician: We had to leave that office—that magic office—and go to this very sterile environment over on Fifth Avenue, right near the Trump Tower now. The Screen Gems/Columbia building was at 56th and Fifth, so all of a sudden we're Fifth Avenue people. We're all West Side people . . . it was a whole different, a different thing—there were no subways near that place.

GERRY GOFFIN, songwriter: I knew it was the beginning of the end.

TONI WINE, session singer: Of course when you are in an office of thirty, then all of a sudden you are in an office of hundreds or thousands, it's a different situation, but exciting nonetheless.

RON DANTE, musician: It became, like, antiseptic.

TONI WINE, session singer: It became corporate. Like all wonderful things that start out small and mom-and-pop and easygoing . . . when it became corporate, it was a whole 'nother ball game. But also it opens up all kinds of doors for so many of us. You can't say it was not a good thing, nor can you say it *was* a good thing.

GERRY GOFFIN, songwriter: He screwed us both. All of us. We were stuck writing for Screen Gems. They gave us assignments. We couldn't write what we wanted.

CHAPTER 24

The British Invasion

RONNIE SPECTOR, The Ronettes: Our first big trip was to the UK, where we met The Beatles before they even came to the States and the Rolling Stones were our opening act.

NEDRA TALLEY-ROSS, The Ronettes: We went over there in '64; I turned eighteen over there. I called my mom and said, "I'm eighteen, Mom. I think I'll have a drink." Not that I hadn't drank before that—I just didn't tell her that. [*laughing*] So she was so happy—*Oh, my darling daughter called and said she'd like a drink for her eighteenth birthday*. But anyway, so yeah, we partied over there *hard*.

RONNIE SPECTOR, The Ronettes: But when we got to the UK, we felt like real stars for the first time. [*laughing*]

NEDRA TALLEY-ROSS, The Ronettes: The Stones came into our room, you know . . . just talking and dressing in regular clothes. And we're going, "Well, we got to get dressed." And we were dressed to the T—all of that. So we were like, "Guys, the show's going to be starting." And they said, "Yeah, we're going to go on." But they didn't change—they were sitting there in regular street clothes—and we're going, "We came from New York where The Temptations and Smokey and the Miracles and stuff were doing shows and they were so dressed." I mean, they were, like, *perfect*—cuff links, here we go, shiny suits. And they had on just street clothes. We're going, "What's wrong with these people over here?"

LA LA BROOKS, The Crystals: The Crystals met The Rolling Stones in a restaurant, but they were so obnoxious—jumping on tables. We were like, "We don't want to be near them," because they were wild, you know? We were more conservative, like quiet.

VICKI WICKHAM, manager, Labelle: In England, we didn't have any . . . okay . . . artists didn't *perform*. They sang. But that was kind of it until the Stones or The Who or any of those acts came along. To watch someone like The Shirelles perform was just amazing, and yes, the clothes to me were *just*!

ERNIE MARTINELLI, manager, The Chiffons: That's what put The Beatles in the business. Without The Shirelles and without The Chiffons, The Beatles wouldn't have come into the business. England had *no* music.

ANDREW LOOG OLDHAM, manager, the Rolling Stones: They were so white and naff, all these English groups. Either they were schoolgirls or they were people who had just come out of the nightclub period. But then the great thing about these American acts that came in was they were *sexy*. Yeah, I mean, The Ronettes, you know, they were American and—calling it on face value—they were American and they were Black. And then you suddenly had this very pop structured stuff, but you know, England wasn't that interested, really, in Leiber and Stoller, Big Mama Thornton.

LA LA BROOKS, The Crystals: I know we played one job—I was petrified. . . . It's because there were so many fans. When they get to the car and they rush and the car is shaking, and you think they're going to turn it over. But they were very receptive—I think they were more receptive than America. They still are.

NEDRA TALLEY-ROSS, The Ronettes: You didn't do that in America. You sat in your seat, you enjoyed, you stood up, you clapped. But they were just going, "All of them, we're going to touch them." And the guards, were going, "No, you're not." [*laughing*] And then they pitched them out.

RONNIE SPECTOR, The Ronettes: They were a bunch of scraggly-looking guys. But I loved them and I especially loved Keith, because I love that rugged look he had. Mick was, like, a pretty boy, maybe. Keith used to say, "Oh, we would have great babies because you have that black, thick hair and I have black, thick hair."

NEDRA TALLEY-ROSS, The Ronettes: We came out and we closed the show. The Stones were, "We love you guys . . . you sound good," and we were going, "You guys were good. . . ." We said nothing about the clothes. [*laughing*]

Then we got, "Oh, there's this group, The Beatles, they want to"—they weren't on that show—"they want to give you a party," so we said, "Okay, let The Beatles." *What a stupid name*, we were thinking. *Who would name themselves The Beatles?*

RONNIE SPECTOR, The Ronettes: They knew us, but we didn't know them.

BEVERLY LEE, The Shirelles: We were on the tour in England and some of the musicians would always ask, "Do you like The Beatles?" I said, "Who are The Beatles?" When they came over, that's when we heard that they liked our music. John Lennon said that we were his favorite group.

NEDRA TALLEY-ROSS, The Ronettes: They gave us this party—it was part of the production group over there. So we were listening to all these new accents, we played games—literally, games, and then running around—I think it was just pent-up energy that we ran around this living room.

I was going up the stairs. I felt something *tap tap tap* on my butt . . . and you would have thought that I got the movie star role of the year. I turned around. I slapped him so hard. *How dare you touch my butt?* It was the drummer for The Kinks. I'm sure he was so shocked, but I'm like, *How dare you tap with your drumstick on my butt?* It was just from my gut—reflex. *How dare you? I don't even know who you are. Guess what? You're nothing to me and you're not even cute. I can't even dream about you.*

RONNIE SPECTOR, The Ronettes: "You've got the greatest voice," George told me. "We loved it the first time we heard you." The guys had just seen us on an English TV show called *Sunday Night at the* [*London*] *Palladium*, and they couldn't stop raving about it. "You were so great," John Lennon told me. "Just fucking great."

NEDRA TALLEY-ROSS, The Ronettes: George Harrison and Estelle had a little thing going on. I won't say *affair* because I don't know what affair would . . .

RONNIE SPECTOR, The Ronettes: Estelle and I went out on double dates with John and George a couple more times before we left London. They'd take us to these romantic white-tablecloth restaurants, but once we got there, all they'd want to talk about was American rock and roll . . . so we'd just go down the list, telling them stories about all the acts we worked with at the Brooklyn Fox. And as we'd talk, John and George would sit there like they were hypnotized.

BRIAN HOLLAND, songwriter: They studied the producers and the writers, not the singers. They wanted to know about the people behind the scenes, who wrote the song and produced the song. That's what they wanted to know. Man, I tell you, they were very, very thoughtful about that stuff—period.

RONNIE SPECTOR, The Ronettes: It was very scary, because I really liked John Lennon and I was saying, "Oh my God, I've got to think about Phil." John really had a big crush on me. I'll never forget sitting on the windowsill, looking out on the lights, and I said, "London is so beautiful." And he said, "You sure are," because he was looking at me. It made me want to cry, because I really felt like such a star then. That moment, I knew I'd made it.

CHER, singer: I still remember her dragging me into the ladies' room at Gold Star to tell me how The Beatles thought she was cute, and how John Lennon had a big crush on her. "And, Cher," she told me, "you wouldn't believe how much the kids over there loved our music!"

NEDRA TALLEY-ROSS, The Ronettes: Paul of The Beatles said they felt like they were impersonating—they couldn't dance and do those things. Like the American groups could do . . . *smooth*. American groups were just *smooth*.

RONNIE SPECTOR, The Ronettes: We went out one last time, but my mom came along that night and it was a disaster. What happened was John and George were making conversation with my mom before we left the hotel. Then, out of politeness, John invited her to come along, never dreaming she would take him up on it. Estelle and I walked into the room just in time to hear Mom give her answer. "Dinner? Oh, that sounds like fun. Let me get my purse."

NEDRA TALLEY-ROSS, The Ronettes: Sounds like Aunt BeBe—she liked her pocketbook. She really did.

RONNIE SPECTOR, The Ronettes: There we were at this fancy candlelit restaurant in London with John Lennon, George Harrison, and my mother.

NEDRA TALLEY-ROSS, The Ronettes: People tried to put me with Ringo—there was nothing there. He was just a friend. Nothing more, nothing, nothing, nothing.

KEITH RICHARDS, musician: We toured with The Ronettes on our second UK tour and I fell in love with Ronnie Bennett. . . . She was twenty years old and she was extraordinary, to hear, to look at, to be with.

RONNIE SPECTOR, The Ronettes: We were on the bus and they never spoke to us. I said, *What's going on? Why weren't these guys speaking to us?* So I went over to Andrew Oldham, which was their manager at the time, I says, "Hey, how come you guys are so cold? This is supposed to be England." He said, "No, honey, Phil Spector sent us a telegram saying don't talk to you guys." I said, "You gotta be kidding me, he's crazy!" And then we made friends.

ANDREW LOOG OLDHAM, manager, the Rolling Stones: Yes, we did date them. Yes, there may have been a telegram from Phil Spector going, "Stay away from my girls."

NEDRA TALLEY-ROSS, The Ronettes: Ronnie liked the Rolling Stones and Keith liked Ronnie, that's why Phil said that. Phil had a chokehold on Ronnie . . . just not letting her be around them. If he could keep her away from being around them, then he didn't have to worry, you know?

KEITH RICHARDS, musician: It all had to be kept very quiet. . . . She had to be in her room all the time in case Phil called. And I think he quickly got a whiff that Ronnie and I were getting on, and he would call people and tell them to stop Ronnie seeing anybody else after the show. Mick had cottoned to her sister Estelle, who was not so tightly chaperoned.

RONNIE SPECTOR, The Ronettes: Well, we were on the front pages of every paper over there, until my ex-husband came over and he got me out of there.

DARLENE LOVE, The Blossoms: He wouldn't let Ronnie . . . Ronnie was a huge success in Europe with The Ronettes. And he got so upset because they were hanging out with The Beatles and the Rolling Stones.

RONNIE SPECTOR, The Ronettes: The Beatles were leaving to start their first US tour in a few days when John asked me if I wanted to fly back with them on their chartered jet.

NEDRA TALLEY-ROSS, The Ronettes: With Phil, he was separating Ronnie for his personal benefit. He was saying all the things. You know he was paying out of our money, the record money—it wasn't like he was fronting us anymore. We were fronting ourselves, because it was the money that was coming from "Be My Baby" and other things. So when he was with Ronnie, he was getting the privilege of having her with him, now as a girlfriend, *and* deducting things under The Ronettes.

RONNIE SPECTOR, The Ronettes: They wanted us to come over, be on the plane with them, so they wouldn't be so nervous to come to America.

DARLENE LOVE, The Blossoms: He made them come back home. But it was *them* that were famous, you know, at this time, along with The Beatles and the Stones, and he wasn't having it.

RONNIE SPECTOR, The Ronettes: We couldn't fly back with The Beatles, but there he was, standing in front of all the cameras after The Beatles got off their plane.

NEDRA TALLEY-ROSS, The Ronettes: But we were so received over there, it was like they went crazy. Later, the craziness was brought over here.

CHER, singer: I think that was the first time any of us realized that people all over the world were actually listening to these little records we were making at Gold Star, and that just blew our minds.

RONNIE SPECTOR, The Ronettes: I was at the peak of my career when I was with The Kinks, The Beatles, and the Rolling Stones, and we were all so happy together. And then all of a sudden, I was taken away from it.

*

NEDRA TALLEY-ROSS, The Ronettes: The Beatles hit America like nobody had ever hit America. I think they saw what happened over in England and then they said, "Oh, this is what we're supposed to do—we're supposed to act stupid and faint and go crazy."

RICHARD GOTTEHRER, songwriter: By '64, that change was happening because of the British Invasion—The Beatles, Stones, Kinks. At first, they were using Brill Building songs but then started writing songs themselves—because they'd use these blues and use these Brill Building–style songs as frames of reference.

JUDY CRAIG, The Chiffons: The Beatles were so huge then. That was their first time coming here. The crowd just wanted to see them, so when we were on the stage singing, they were throwing jellybeans, or something, at us. They wanted us to get off. We didn't even get a chance to meet them because that's how wild it was—we got off the stage and we just left.

ERNIE MARTINELLI, manager, The Chiffons: They didn't come to see The Chiffons. They came to see The Beatles. The people that bought a ticket didn't come to see The Chiffons or anybody else who was on the show. We were just there to be there. They were there for The Beatles.

NEDRA TALLEY-ROSS, The Ronettes: Beatlemania did catch me offguard because I thought, *They're good*. I think they're good, but that side of just people going crazy, I wasn't used to it, not in America. I didn't think it was going to come off in America like that.

BRIAN HOLLAND, songwriter: The Beatles sang "Mr. Postman." When they sung it . . . I made more money when The Beatles sung it than when we did.

MARGARET ROSS, The Cookies: The Beatles took "Chains" and sang it and put it on a record and made big-time money on it, singing it. We were furious when we found out that The Beatles had our song, redid our song. Oh, we was *mad*. I mean, they came over here and they just took over and pushed us out. And that's when everything slowed down. They just knocked all of us out.

RONNIE SPECTOR, The Ronettes: The Ronettes were lucky—1964 was actually our biggest year ever.

NEDRA TALLEY-ROSS, The Ronettes: George Harrison would come over to see us, so he did like Estelle, you know. When you're young, you're not thinking of anything except, *Oh, I think he's cute* or *I think she's cute*—that kind of thing. And that he had a girlfriend

The Chantels: (*left to right*) Sonia Goring Wilson, Jackie Landry, Arlene Smith, Lois Powell (*at piano*), Renée Minus White.
(Photo by Michael Ochs Archives/Getty Images)

The Bobbettes: (*left to right, back*) unknown, Jerry Wexler; (*front*) Jannie Pought, Reather Dixon, Laura Webb, Helen Gathers, Emma Pought.
(Photo by Michael Ochs Archives/Getty Images)

The Clickettes at the Apollo in 1959: (*left to right*) Barbara English, Jean Bouldin, Sylvia Hammond, Barbara Saunders. *(Photo courtesy of Barbara English)*

The Shirelles: (*left to right*) Shirley Alston Reeves, Beverly Lee, Addie "Micki" Harris, and Doris Coley are presented a record to commemorate sales for "Will You Love Me Tomorrow" from Florence Greenberg (*center*). *(Photo by Michael Ochs Archives/Getty Images)*

The Chordettes: (*top*) Margie Latzko with (*left to right, bottom*) Lynn Evans, Carol Buschmann, Janet Ertel. *(Photo by Michael Ochs Archives/Getty Images)*

The Cookies: (*left to right*) Dorothy Jones, Earl-Jean McCrae, Margaret Ross. *(Photo by Michael Ochs Archives/Getty Images)*

An early version of The Blossoms: (*left to right, top*) Fanita James, Gloria Jones; (*bottom*) twins Nanette and Annette Williams.

(Photo by Pictorial Press Ltd./Alamy Stock Photo)

The scene outside the Peppermint Lounge in 1961.

(Photo by Pictorial Press Ltd./Alamy Stock Photo)

The Ronettes backstage: (*left to right*) Estelle Bennett, Nedra Talley-Ross, Ronnie Spector. *(Photo courtesy of Nedra Talley- Ross)*

The Exciters: (*left to right*) Herb Rooney, Lillian Walker, Brenda Reid, Carolyn Johnson. *(Photo by Gilles Petard/Redferns)*

Phil Spector, Darlene Love, and Cher at Gold Star Studios.
(Photo by Ray Avery/Redferns)

The Marvelettes: (*left to right*) Gladys Horton, Georgeanna Tillman, Wanda Young, Katherine Anderson.
(Photo by James Kriegsmann/Michael Ochs Archives/Getty Images)

The Vandellas: (*left to right*) Martha Reeves, Annette Helton, Rosalind Ashford. *(Photo by James Kriegsmann/Michael Ochs Archives/Getty Images)*

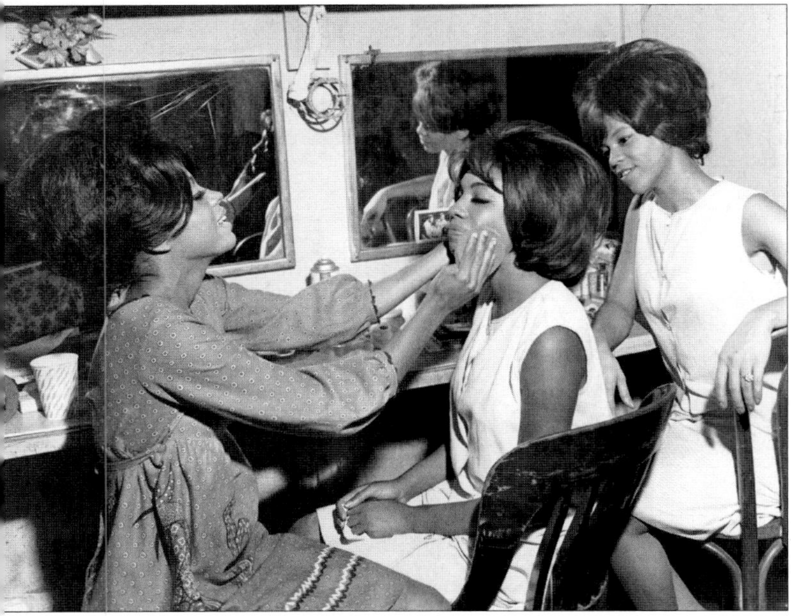

The Supremes: (*left to right*) Diana Ross, Mary Wilson, Florence Ballard. *(Photo by Michael Ochs Archives/Getty Images)*

The Velvelettes:
(*left to right, back*)
Mildred Gill,
Bertha Barbee,
Carolyn "Cal" Gill;
(*left to right, front*)
Betty Kelley,
Norma Barbee.
(Photo by Pictorial Press Ltd./Alamy Stock Photo)

The Shirelles perform for Martin Luther King Jr. (*seated, at right*) at the Salute to Freedom benefit concert on August 5, 1963.
(Photo by Grey Villet/The LIFE Picture Collection/Shutterstock)

The Angels: (*left to right*) Barbara "Bibs" Allbut, Phyllis "Jiggs" Allbut, Peggy Santiglia. *(Photo by Don Paulsen/Michael Ochs Archives/Getty Images)*

The Chiffons: (*left to right*) Sylvia Peterson, Judy Craig, Barbara Lee, and Pat Bennett in the studio with Brooks Arthur.
(Photo by Michael Ochs Archives/Getty Images)

"Loco-Motion" promotion shot with (*left to right*) Al Nevins, Carole King, Little Eva, Gerry Goffin, and Don Kirshner.
(Photo by PoPsie Randolph/ Michael Ochs Archives/ Getty Images)

Murray the K's Big Holiday Show at the Brooklyn Fox Theatre, September 1964, featuring The Vandellas, The Ronettes, Marvin Gaye, The Temptations (*in back*), Murray the K (*middle*), and The Supremes, among others.
(Photo by Michael Ochs Archives/Getty Images)

The Crystals in London, 1964: (*left to right*) Barbara Alston, Dee Dee Kenniebrew, Fran Collins, La La Brooks. *(Photo by Keystone/Getty Images)*

The Ronettes in 1965: (*left to right*) Nedra Talley-Ross, Estelle Bennett, Ronnie Spector. *(Photo by Michael Ochs Archives/Getty Images)*

Left to right: Ellie Greenwich, Jeff Barry, George "Shadow" Morton.
(Photo by Michael Ochs Archives/Getty Images)

The Dixie Cups: (*left to right*) Rosa Lee Hawkins,
Joan Marie Johnson, Barbara Ann Hawkins at the Apollo Theater, circa 1965.
(Photo by Don Paulsen/Michael Ochs Archives/Getty Images)

The Shangri-Las: (*left to right*) Mary Ann Ganser, Mary Weiss, Marge Ganser.
(Photo by Michael Ochs Archives/Getty Images)

Diana Ross and The Supremes: (*left to right*) Cindy Birdsong, Diana Ross, Mary Wilson.
(Photo by James Kriegsmann/Michael Ochs Archives/Getty Images)

The Vandellas on the Ford Motors assembly line for Murray the K's special: (*left to right*) Rosalind Ashford, Martha Reeves, Betty Kelley.
(Photo by Michael Ochs Archives/Getty Images)

Labelle: (*left to right*) Sarah Dash, Patti LaBelle, Nona Hendryx wearing Larry LeGaspi designs.
(Photo by Gijsbert Hanekroot/Redferns)

The Andantes:
(*left to right*)
Jackie Hicks,
Marlene Barrow,
Louvain Demps.
(Photo by Donaldson Collection/Michael Ochs Archives/Getty Images)

The Blossoms with Elvis Presley on the '68 *Comeback Special*: (*left to right*) Jean King, Elvis Presley, Fanita James, Darlene Love.
(Photo by Michael Ochs Archives/Getty Images)

or whatever . . . guys weren't telling you if they had a girlfriend when they're trying to take you on a date.

When George started coming over, it was just . . . they understood, just like we understood. When you're a performer like that, your world becomes very limited. Your world is big, but where you can go and who you can go with becomes small. So with other performers, they know that you're not needing them to pat you on your back and tell you how good you are, you just don't need to do that with them.

I was just young, Ronnie was just hot stuff but without the substance, and Estelle just evoked . . . *boy*. And I mean even *gay guys* fell in love with Estelle. I was like, *What the heck is she got that . . .* you know—George Harrison, George Hamilton, Sal Mineo, Johnny Mathis came to pick her up to take her out on a date.

RONNIE SPECTOR, The Ronettes: I remember them coming to New York the first time, and John Lennon called me, saying, "Ronnie, we don't know what to do. We're prisoners here." They were in either the Warwick or the Plaza Hotel. "You gotta come up and get us out of here." They didn't know anybody in America. So me, Estelle, and Nedra—the three Ronettes—would go up there. He said, "Please bring the forty-five records." So we'd sit there on the floor and listen to records. We had the best time.

NEDRA TALLEY-ROSS, The Ronettes: People were fighting to get into the hotel.

RONNIE SPECTOR, The Ronettes: The Beatles picked us up in a limousine for a feast of ribs and chicken at Sherman's Barbecue on 151st and Amsterdam in Harlem. . . . The Beatles were no big deal up in Harlem. The people at Sherman's weren't exactly Murray the K's crowd.

NEDRA TALLEY-ROSS, The Ronettes: Did we dance? Yes. Did we sing together? Yes. Did we travel together? All of those things. So when it came time for them to come here, there was a competition between the Stones and The Beatles.

RONNIE SPECTOR, The Ronettes: That was in June 1964 during the Stones' first trip to America.

NEDRA TALLEY-ROSS, The Ronettes: I did date Brian of the Stones later on when he came to America and dressed up and put some clothes on. Ronnie was dating Keith and Estelle dated Mick Jagger.

KEITH RICHARDS, musician: We were twenty years old and we just fell in love. What do you do when you hear a record like "Be My Baby" and suddenly you are? But same old story, can't let anybody else know. So it was a terrible thing in a away. But, basically, it was hormones. And sympathy.

RONNIE SPECTOR, The Ronettes: Phil always liked them, so he let them sleep in the offices of Philles Records on York Avenue.

NEDRA TALLEY-ROSS, The Ronettes: No. The Rolling Stones stayed with my husband, who was my boyfriend at the time, Scott Ross. But the Stones came to Riverside Drive, to my house at 157 Riverside Drive. The building—it's a sixteen-story building and people yelling across the court, "The Rolling Stones are in the building!"

RONNIE SPECTOR, The Ronettes: These guys were so poor—let me tell you—they had nothing, they were so *skinny*. So they came to America. They didn't have "Satisfaction" or any of those hit records yet, so they came to America. Where do you think they came? To my house. They slept on the floor, not in my bed. They slept on the floor. My mom and dad were still there. And so my mother would . . . every morning, "You guys want some bacon and eggs?" and they were so polite.

NEDRA TALLEY-ROSS, The Ronettes: Estelle can't drive. She really can't. She had a Jaguar, she had a beautiful Jaguar. She couldn't . . . they shouldn't have sold it to her—dark brown, beautiful.

So we're in the car, the Stones are in the back and Estelle is driving. And you know how lights will have one change green, and then two seconds later the next light turns green, and if you catch it, you can get all the way down? That's the whole thing to New York City driving—catching the lights. So it would change to red and Estelle would keep driving.

I said, "Estelle, you need to stop the car! It's a red light, *red light*!" Estelle said, "Well, it changed too fast." They lit up pot. Mick and Keith going, *I may get arrested, but I gotta get high, because she is killing me.* Keith was on the ground in the back, going, "I can't look at it! No more!"

Then she lost the Jaguar in New York City. Parked it someplace and couldn't remember where she parked it. [*laughing*]

CHAPTER 25

Crossing the Mason-Dixon Line

The Dixie Cups

BROOKS ARTHUR, sound engineer: We were all touched by this magical sort of invisible breaststroke—heaven above you, you know. We had the Dimension girls, often referred to as the "Dimension Dolls," and then we had the Red Bird girls.

RON DANTE, musician: One side was Don Kirshner and his Aldon crew, and the other side was George Goldner and Red Bird Records—Jeff and Ellie, Leiber and Stoller. So, that was a whole different crew.

ELLIE GREENWICH, songwriter: Before Red Bird really got going and Jeff and I were still cutting demos and trying to sell the songs, we would always be in competition with someone at Aldon. If they got the record, I'd envy them, but it wasn't a kind of negative, resentful reaction. I wish I could've gotten it, but I was happy for them and really wished them the best. Sometimes we'd be waiting outside a demo studio for our time and Gerry and Carole would be in there cutting something, and we'd turn to each other and say, "Gee, that really sounds good." But that only made us try harder—the competition was fierce.

BROOKS ARTHUR, sound engineer: Red Bird had the most astounding run. It was . . . it rivaled the Aldon Music publishing run. Except this run was helmed by Jerry Leiber and Mike Stoller and their general manager named George Goldner.

MELANIE MINTZ, writer: [*singing*] "*Going to the chapel and I . . .*" I mean, *everybody* thought that you got married and your life was going to be great for the rest . . . would you think that if you were thirty? No. Would you think that if you were even married a year? No. But you'd think it if you were sixteen or seventeen and you just met a boy and you're hanging out in school or something.

JEFF BARRY, songwriter: Very few songs are about anything other than love. I've always said if anybody figures out the love thing, songwriters are out of business.

VICKI WICKHAM, manager, Labelle: Ellie and Jeff, of course, were really writing their story. I mean—going to the chapel—those type of things were what they did together.

JEFF BARRY, songwriter: I'm just not a metaphor kind of guy. I say it very directly. Growing up with a blind father and a disabled sister, communicating with two-thirds of my family had to be simple for my sister, and succinct and visual for my father. And I was always aware that I was trying to entertain kids, not adults.

ELLIE GREENWICH, songwriter: That song had originally been cut by The Ronettes. Phil Spector had cut it with The Ronettes, but never put it out. Why? Do not ask me. And we always believed in that song. . . . Jeff and I said, "We *have* to do something with it." And just at that time, a gentleman named Joe Jones came up from New Orleans with a whole slew of people. Amongst them was three girls, which we eventually named The Dixie Cups.

MIKE STOLLER, song writer: It all came in through Joe Jones. Joe brought in a number of different performers and there was the girls that I renamed The Dixie Cups, he had called them The Meltones. The Meltones were two sisters, Barbara Ann and Rosa Lee Hawkins, and their cousin, Joan Marie Johnson.

BILLY VERA, musician: They actually had a guitar player with them, a guy named Alvin Robinson, Alvin "Shine" Robinson, and he played a little thirty-five-buck Sears and Roebuck Silvertone guitar.

MIKE STOLLER, songwriter: We released him on Blue Cat—which was the sister label to Red Bird.

JEFF BARRY, songwriter: Joe Jones was their manager, I suppose was the word. I sensed that he was very much . . . in control of them. He was involved, as opposed to bringing them up to New York and handing them over. He was very, *very* . . . it was *his* group, people-wise.

BARBARA ANN HAWKINS, The Dixie Cups: This talent scout had gotten in touch with my friend and asked her to come and see him. Well, she didn't want to go by herself, so she asked me to go with her.

So, we went to meet him at the labor union hall, but he wasn't there, but he left a note to go to his house. So, we went to his house, and when he opened the door for us, he kept looking at me all the time he was talking to my friend . . . he kept looking at me and I'm getting uneasy. *Why is this man looking at me like this?* So then he says, "You were on the talent show, too, weren't you? You were the girls that wore the green dresses. . . . I've been trying to get in touch with you." He said, "You all were magnificent." And then Joe, that's his name, Joe Jones, he brought us to New York.

ROSA LEE HAWKINS, The Dixie Cups: I'm sitting here in this car smashed in between however many people, snow on the ground—I'd never actually been in snow before. And Joe got some apartment for us to live in, and I'm walking around and I see this ugly gray color on every room in the house. I'm saying, *Is this the New York I've been waiting to see?*

BARBARA ANN HAWKINS, The Dixie Cups: This was in 1963 that he brought us to New York. It was us—The Meltones, the Five DJs, there was a single artist—Moody Scott, a young lady—Vivian Bates, and his whole band. So we caravanned, it was two or maybe three cars of us, we caravanned to New York, and he put us all in this hotel, it looked like seventy-two people to a room. Then he started . . . they call it "pounding the pavement."

ROSA LEE HAWKINS, The Dixie Cups: And it was so cold. My mother knew that I was very cold-natured and I still am. I called her up crying one day. She said, "You have a coat with you, don't you? And you have sweaters." I say, "Yeah, but we have to walk everywhere, every place you go, and these people up here, they are so ungrateful—they'll knock you down and keep going." She said, "Well, sweetheart, welcome to New York. That's the way the New Yorkers are. Yes, they will bump into you and turn around and look at you or they may not turn around and look at you." I said, "Oh man." So it was a shock to me, but then I . . . soon, I kind of got over it because then we did move up to Manhattan around the corner from the Brill Building.

BARBARA ANN HAWKINS, The Dixie Cups: Well, my first impression when we got to this hotel . . . it was so many people in there. What he did is, he went to the front desk and registered, I don't know how many people for how many rooms. And then, of course, you couldn't go through the lobby—going up there with your suitcase. So, he has whoever registered—he had them bring the suitcases up—we had to go in the back door and go upstairs to the room. Now, anytime we left, we could leave through the lobby because we could have been visiting somebody—but when it was time to actually go in for the evening—we had to go up the back way.

We got dressed and he took us to the different record companies. Well, every record company, every record company we went to wanted to record us. But Joe kept saying no until he got the deal that *he* wants. We thought it was what was best for us, but it was what was best for him. So we landed up at Leiber and Stoller, and they put us with Ellie Greenwich and Jeff Barry.

JEFF BARRY, songwriter: They hit the harmonies and could sing—I guess that's why Joe Jones brought them up to New York, because he saw that they had something.

MIKE STOLLER, songwriter: They were already working with Jeff and Ellie. Ellie was very good at picking out parts for vocal groups. The song "Chapel of Love," which I . . . it was, how can I put it? It was so simple and, in a way, silly, but it was so right. I really liked them. . . . Jerry did not, particularly.

BARBARA ANN HAWKINS, The Dixie Cups: Even though Jerry and Mike liked one of the songs we did, they obviously wanted one of *their* songs to be the A-side. So they put us with Jeff and Ellie and they went over some songs with us. When they first played "Chapel," we kind of looked at each other and said, "Do you want us to sing it like *that*?" Because the way they played it, it kind of had a country flavor. And, coming from New Orleans, the land of jazz and blues, it didn't sound like something we wanted to do. And when we asked, "Do we have to do it that way?" Ellie said, "Well, how would you do it?" So we say, "Give us a minute." And we went in the corner and we came up with the way we recorded it.

ROSA LEE HAWKINS, The Dixie Cups: And when we sang "Chapel of Love," Ellie said, "Wait a minute." She just played the first notes and, well, Barbara said, "Okay, that's all we need." And we sang the whole song a cappella, and they couldn't believe it—they were blown away. That's the one thing that we had different from a lot of the girl groups in the sixties. They were lead and background, so they had one lead and however many other people were their background.

BARBARA ANN HAWKINS, The Dixie Cups: We had three-part harmony on everything.

ROSA LEE HAWKINS, The Dixie Cups: When we finally finished with the song, when we gave it back to Ellie and Jeff, they said, "Oh, that is so beautiful. We never heard it that way."

BARBARA ANN HAWKINS, The Dixie Cups: We didn't know at that time that we were actually doing arranging on "Chapel of Love," but we did.

ROSA LEE HAWKINS, The Dixie Cups: Wardell Quezergue *actually* did the arrangement. He was the one that sat there and put the horns and said, "The guitar does this," and so forth and so on. Mike and Jerry, they didn't have nothing to do with it, either—Wardell did it, but Joe Jones got credit for it.

BROOKS ARTHUR, sound engineer: And before that, I was in the studio with Mike Stoller, and it was just me and him getting ready for a session and then, [*singing*] "*Spring is here, bdam, bdam, bdam,*" and he was not happy with what was on tape. So he . . . well, there was a little toy cello sitting in the studio, keyboard cello, like somewhere between a toy piano and a cello, and Mike went out there and he pulled in Ellie Greenwich and in one take he went, [*singing*] "*Spring is here, bling, bling, bling, bling, da, da, da, da, bling, bling, bling, bling,*" and in one take he nailed it. I was so amazed at how quickly he did it, how proficient it was, and what a great choice to use that piano. It was useful, it had *pride*.

MIKE STOLLER, songwriter: When I hear "Chapel of Love," it makes me feel good, it makes me feel happy. I feel a relationship to it because I'm playing on it and I was involved in it. My good friend of many, many years, Artie Butler, came into the studio, and as it happened there was a set of orchestra bells there, and I said, "Artie, play these bells at a certain point when I point at you."

ARTIE BUTLER, musician: I said, "Mike, I came by to say hello, see if you want to have lunch afterwards." He said, "Nice to see you, Artie, you have to play the chimes."

MIKE STOLLER, songwriter: And he went, [*singing*] "*ding, ding, ding, ding, ding . . . going to the chapel,*" and then the bass player always came in, *bom bom*.

BROOKS ARTHUR, sound engineer: And Ellie was quite the singer herself and could *lay it down*. She went out there by herself, "Roll the tape." I hit the red light for *record*. Next thing I know, she goes, [*singing*] "*Yeah . . . yeah, yeah, yeah.*" And that's Ellie, that's Ellie at the end of that record to this very minute.

*

MIKE STOLLER, songwriter: United Artists didn't want to pay us for "Chapel of Love," so we had this record sitting around, and Jerry encountered George Goldner one evening at Al & Dick's restaurant, which is where people in the music business hung out. He wanted to know how we were doing, and Jerry said, "Well, we're starting a record company." We had a start-up label. It wasn't called Red Bird yet. He came to the office and listened to all of the stuff and he picked that one out.

JERRY LEIBER, songwriter: When I walked in, Goldner was talking to Mike. George immediately turned to me and said, "This is it." And with that, he handed me an acetate without a label. "Which song is it?" I asked. "Put it on and play it," Goldner replied. I did. *Oh God*, I thought, *it's that piece of shit*. "'Chapel of Love,'" George declared. "I'll bet my life on it." I wanted to say, "You don't value your life very much," but didn't. Guys like Goldner possessed special genius for divining hits.

MIKE STOLLER, songwriter: He said, "That is a smash!" Jerry said, "Oh my God, I hate that record."

JEFF BARRY, songwriter: He really got excited about the music. He would come to the studio and listen to a new record and get really excited and throw chairs around and yell, "Smash! That's a smash! That's a hit!"

MIKE STOLLER, songwriter: He said, "All right. If we're going to be in business together, who's going to run the business? Who's going to make the . . ." And Jerry said, "Okay. You're the guy." That was our first release on Red Bird Records.

JERRY LEIBER, songwriter: I hated the record. I thought "Chapel of Love" was insipid, a trifling based on nothing but clichés. I wasn't even in the studio when Mike produced it. I couldn't stand listening to it. On the other hand, I was the guy who recruited the great George Goldner to go through our inventory and see if he smelled any hits.

GEORGE "SHADOW" MORTON, producer: Goldner got his hands on "Chapel of Love." He had a theory. He said anything that has to do with a name, a number, or going someplace to be in love is a hit. Going to the *chapel* . . .

JERRY LEIBER, songwriter: How come Donnie Kirshner and George Goldner were the best pickers in the business? I finally figured it out. They both had the soul, temperament, and minds of twelve-year-old girls. And those are the people that buy pop records.

JEFF BARRY, songwriter: I remember the ad that they took out, the first ad for the first record for Red Bird. There was a picture of the record in the center of the page, and above it, it said, "This is a hit." That was the ad they took in *Billboard*, *Cashbox*, and *Record World*. . . . But is "Chapel of Love" fabulous? I don't know. "We'll never be lonely anymore"? That's a lie.

ELLIE GREENWICH, songwriter: I knew it would be a hit because of the way they said "maaaaried."

JEFF BARRY, songwriter: Sure enough, it knocked The Beatles out of number one.

MIKE STOLLER, songwriter: All the other British groups were at number one, one after the other after the other. And we were the first American artist record to break through.

ROSA LEE HAWKINS, The Dixie Cups: The Beatles came over here in '64. They had, I don't know, how many records in the Top 100. In the Top 10, I believe they had two. One of their records was number one and had been there for many weeks.

JEFF BARRY, songwriter: I think it was good programming, too, because it came out in the spring, so what they call a good "summer record."

BARBARA ANN HAWKINS, The Dixie Cups: We had heard, after "Chapel" was recorded, that there was somebody bootlegging copies, they were making copies and selling them. And for some reason, their whole place burned down.

ROSA LEE HAWKINS, The Dixie Cups: Everybody thought we made money off of "Chapel of Love," which actually, in reality, they handed each one of us an envelope, and we getting all happy and said, "Oh, well, we'll go shopping and buy us some new things for stage," and yada, yada, yada. And when we pulled the papers out and it had the sheet that said what the money had went for and it showed where X amount of dollars went for recording. You paid for the rental of the studio, the tapes that they used, the people to run the tapes. If there was lunch served, you paid for that. You paid for everything.

In the big printout "advance," "advance," "advance," and each entry had a date and amount. So we went to the bookkeeper, whose name was Florence, to complain because we had never come up to her office to ask for money—ever. Our mother had a good job in New Orleans and didn't need our help. Florence said to us, "Your manager was always coming up here saying you needed money to send to your parents for rent or this or that." When she saw the tears streaming down my cheeks, Florence said, "I'm really sorry."

BARBARA ANN HAWKINS, The Dixie Cups: It was four-hundred-something each person got—each one of us. So that was like $1,200 for a number one record.

Joe looked out for Joe. He called it "front money." So they might say, "All right, but what is the front money for?" And he would come up with, "Oh, I have to send money home," or blah, blah, blah, blah.

ROSA LEE HAWKINS, The Dixie Cups: Your chance at making a number one record is 150 million to one. We—three young ladies from New Orleans—went to New York, recorded "Chapel of Love," it was released and shot its way up. It dethroned The Beatles—not just dethroned them for a day or a week. "Chapel" was number one for three weeks before anybody else could get in there.

*

BROOKS ARTHUR, sound engineer: We were editing and mixing "Chapel of Love." We told them, "We'll be with you in a few minutes." And then we closed the door—it was halfway open so we could hear what was going on.

ROSA LEE HAWKINS, The Dixie Cups: And it was just the three of us in the studio. So we started playing around with something that we had done before and talked about and everything, and we sang "Iko."

ELLIE GREENWICH, songwriter: One girl starts singing "*My grandma and your grandma . . .*" and I said, "What's that?" And they said, "Oh, it's just some old New Orleans traditional song called 'Iko Iko.'" And I said, "I like that—keep singing it."

JEFF BARRY, songwriter: I think that's the basis of . . . it is an old New Orleans funeral song. They would march along and sing those songs.

ELLIE GREENWICH, songwriter: And Jeff starts hitting the wall, and I'm banging on the console, and I told our engineer Brooks Arthur, "Hold it, Brooks, we're not done for the night yet." So we went out into the studio and we all grabbed something—a Coke bottle, whatever. I said, "Girls, let's go."

BROOKS ARTHUR, sound engineer: I press the red light on the recording machine and . . .

ROSA LEE HAWKINS, The Dixie Cups: Since there were no musicians, we had to make our own music. So somebody had a drumstick on a Coke bottle, a drumstick on a chair.

BARBARA ANN HAWKINS, The Dixie Cups: Aluminum chair and aluminum ashtray.

JEFF BARRY, songwriter: I'm playing a screwdriver on a plastic ashtray for the main rhythm on that.

BROOKS ARTHUR, sound engineer: Jeff Barry grabbed an ashtray. Mike Stoller grabbed a shaker . . . then it became like a little jam in a circle around the microphone that we recorded. [*singing*] *"I-ko, I-ko, un-day."*

ELLIE GREENWICH, songwriter: We had this Jamaican box in the corner—Jeff and I had gotten it down there on our honeymoon—and that's the only real "instrument" you hear on the tape.

MIKE STOLLER, songwriter: The engineer, Brooks Arthur, had been in Jamaica and brought back an instrument, I think they called it a kalimba. And you could tune it and make the notes adjust by pulling them further in or out, changing their lengths. It had a bass sound, so I played that.

BROOKS ARTHUR, sound engineer: That became the bass, [*singing*] *"du du, du, du, du, du and I-ko, I-ko, un-day, Hey, now."*

JEFF BARRY, songwriter: As I recall, Ellie and I brought that from our honeymoon in Jamaica.

BROOKS ARTHUR, sound engineer: It was an instrument that I had brought back from Jamaica, and I kept it in the studio just for grins. Just, maybe, someday we'll use it or maybe we won't . . . but it also reminded me that maybe we should apply it somewhere and make the sound live forever, and it did. The sound that certainly grooves me, I don't know if it grooves you.

ROSA LEE HAWKINS, The Dixie Cups: And after we sang it down one time, Jerry or Mike, whichever one, said, "Hey, can you do that again?" So we did. So, that was two takes on "Iko."

ELLIE GREENWICH, songwriter: The original tape went on forever. So we picked out the best section, went back and spiced it up a little, added the background vocals and some little things here and there, and that was it. We listened to it and said, "I don't believe it—that should be the next single."

ROSA LEE HAWKINS, The Dixie Cups: So then they ask us, "Who wrote it?" And we told them we did. They immediately brought out the writer's sheets. We filled them out and they sent them to Washington. Well, when Joe came in and found out we had recorded it, he blew up because he said it was something that *he* wanted to introduce to them later on. Well, it was already done. So they put it back—they called it, putting it in a can. But they did send it to a DJ in Europe. And what happened? He played it. And when he played it in Europe, it was hot. And it was so hot in Europe that Leiber and Stoller *had* to release it here in America. But it was a hit over there before it became a hit here. And that's how "Iko Iko" was born.

CHAPTER 26

The Not-So-Bad Girls

The Shangri-Las

ELLIE GREENWICH, songwriter: I knew George from Long Island. He came by, and after he and Jeff played some verbal games, he said he'd come back in a week with a hit record.

GEORGE "SHADOW" MORTON, producer: He turned to me and said, "Well, just what is it you do for a living?" So I said, "Well, actually, some people would call it being a bum, but I'm a songwriter, just like you." So he said, "What kind of songs do you write?" And I said, "Hit songs."

BROOKS ARTHUR, sound engineer: "All right, if you're a songwriter," Jeff said to Shadow, "if you're that much of a writer and you want to work with us, go home or go to a studio. Show me the group, show me the song, and then we'll talk about it."

LAURA WEINER, Ellie Greenwich's sister: I just thought he was like a—I don't mean it in a negative way—a bad boy. He was different, he had his long coat on. . . . I thought he was very good-looking. And remember, I'm younger than my sister, so to have this hot-looking guy coming in with the long raincoat or whatever, he was just like, *ahh.* Almost like a tease, *Should I or shouldn't I?*

GEORGE "SHADOW" MORTON, producer: I had never really written songs—it was a complete lie. I was just on the spot and pissed at Jeff's attitude. Left there, went back to Long Island, and called a friend,

Joe Monaco, who had a studio in his basement. I said, "I've got a record company that's interested in hearing some of my material." He said, "You don't have any material." I said, "Don't worry about that." He gave me the studio. Then I called up George Stermer and said, "Listen, I need a band." He said, "What for?" I said, "I've got this record company, I've got a studio," so he got me a band. I called up another friend of mine and said, "I need a group." He said, "How come?" I said, "I got this band, I got a record company, I got a studio." He told me about some girls who were singing in Cambria Heights, Queens. So I saw them and gave them the same routine. "I got a band, I got a studio, I got a record company. . . . " It was all bullshit, it was all a lie.

BROOKS ARTHUR, sound engineer: Shadow came in with The Shangri-Las. That was his creation.

MIKE STOLLER, songwriter: The group consisted of four girls—twins Mary Ann and Marge Ganser and two sisters who looked like twins, Mary and Betty Weiss. The Weiss girls were blondes, the Gansers brunettes. They dressed in leather boots, overtight jeans. The Shangri-Las were the perfect white "bad girls" of the day.

ELLIE GREENWICH, songwriter: They would come in and they were like kind of a little tough and they would come in chewing gum and they would have stockings with runs in them.

GREG SHAW, rock critic: They were like the tough sluts, the kind of girls who would go out with leader-of-the-pack kind of guys. That would carry stilettos in their hairdos and yet they had soft hearts inside. It was just such a fake image, but yet I think it appealed to a teenage kind of fake emotional view of life.

MARY WEISS, The Shangri-Las: I've heard we were tough, and I just find that so hilarious. If you really look at the old tapes, I don't think that word would even come up. I saw a clip recently. . . . How do you get "tough" out of that? It makes me laugh. People liked to put people in boxes back then, especially the girls. Maybe it was the boots.

ARTIE BUTLER, musician: The Shangri-Las . . . well . . . they were young. Mary was drop-dead gorgeous. Oh my God, she was a shiksa goddess—even at that age.

ARTIE RIPP, music executive: Listen to Mary sing "Remember (Walkin' in the Sand)," and that is probably the most . . . Mary's performance is, I think, the most powerful out of all the records that Shadow made with her.

GEORGE "SHADOW" MORTON, producer: For a long time people said "'Remember (Walkin' in the Sand),' wow! That's so weird. How did you come up with that?" I don't know, South Oyster Bay Road and a Buick?

ELLIE GREENWICH, songwriter: Well, he came back and played us this weird little record. It was like seven minutes long with this long narration by George in the beginning. I knew there was no way we could put out anything like that, but I thought, "Gee, that girl's voice is so strange, and the song is so interesting." We played it for Leiber and Stoller and they said, "Go cut it."

MARY WEISS, The Shangri-Las: I had enough pain in me at the time to pull off anything and get into it and sound believable. . . . I think you can hear it in the performances. It was very easy for me. The recording stuff was the place you could really release your feelings without everybody looking at you.

GEORGE "SHADOW" MORTON, producer: I brought it to Jeff Barry, who was sitting there ready to tear my heart out, and he heard it and said, "Do you mind if I play this for someone else?" Then I was frightened; up until now it was a joke. So he took it and came back thirty minutes later with a guy [Jerry Leiber] who had one brown eye and one blue eye who said, "What would you like to do?" I said, "What do you want me to do?" He said, "I'd like you to write songs." I said, "Okay." He said, "I'll give you a hundred a week, off the books." I said, "Do I have to come here to write?" He said, "You can write anyplace you want to." I said, "I'll take the job." He said, "Incidentally, that record you made is coming out in two weeks."

JERRY LEIBER, songwriter: We thought it was, you know, very corny but very sweet and finally, somewhere, touching. It wasn't synthetic. It was for real, like he was.

MIKE STOLLER, songwriter: It wasn't my cup of tea, but I appreciated what he was doing and I really liked him.

ELLIE GREENWICH, songwriter: Shadow was about as interesting a character, in a different way, as was Phil Spector. He was very eccentric and he wanted total control. He created what I call these little soap operas on vinyl, and he got ultra-involved with them, and things had to be his way. He was kind of hard to deal with at times, and the only people he would listen to would be Jeff and myself—there was a mutual respect among the three of us. Sometimes he would drink a little too much when he was getting involved in what he was doing, and we'd have to revive him before he went on with the session—sometimes eventually we just said, "Let him sleep," and I think he was involved with some of the most interesting records that ever came out.

BROOKS ARTHUR, sound engineer: Jerry Leiber named him Shadow because he would be standing next to you one minute and then disappear the next.

JEFF BARRY, songwriter: I grew up with *The Shadow* as a radio show. "Who knows what evil lurks in the hearts of men? The Shadow."

JERRY LEIBER, songwriter: I called him Shadow, and just like that, he became Shadow Morton, a guy who appeared in the room without your realizing that he ever walked in. And he was never there when you looked for him. Shadow was elusive.

JEFF BARRY, songwriter: You could be talking to him and you'd turn away and go to the bathroom and come back, he's gone for days.

BROOKS ARTHUR, sound engineer: Billy Joel played on one of those demos too. He might've played on the master.

BILLY JOEL, musician: I didn't realize at the time. I thought I was playing on what they call "a demo," which is just a sample of what the recording was going to be. But I believe my piano part ended up on the actual master recording by The Shangri-Las, and that was my first recording experience.

ARTIE RIPP, music executive: Billy was a Long Island kid and Shadow somehow wound up using him as the pianist for the demo, but a demo that was, like, *brilliantly* done.

BILLY JOEL, musician: I knew the guitar player on the session. It was a guy named Sal DiTroia. And he was from Long Island and he invited me to do this recording, which again, I thought was just a demo. The girls were not there. They laid down the instrumental part first, and that was the basic track. And then The Shangri-Las came in and did their vocal parts at another time. I didn't even know what the song was.

I was so overwhelmed with the whole experience. It was a blast. I really had fun doing it. I wasn't even in the union, so I didn't get paid. I mean, I was only sixteen years old. I didn't realize the ramifications of what I was doing—it was just fun. The lesson I took away was, you better join the union if you want to get any more work.

ELLIE GREENWICH, songwriter: We started getting together with the girls working on arrangements and vocals, and just when we were getting ready to go into the studio, all of a sudden everything came to a halt, because in walked Artie Ripp and the Kama Sutra Records people, they had contracts with the girls and there was nothing we could do about it. . . . So all of a sudden, George and I are off the label as producers and Jeff and Artie Ripp share production credits. And you know, Artie Ripp *wasn't even there.*

ARTIE RIPP, music executive: No, that didn't happen that way. A finished record arrived on George Goldner's desk, and then Jeff Berry put his imprint on it.

I had met Phil Steinberg, who had a company called Kama Sutra Productions; he was partnered with Hy Mizrahi. And so as Phil and I came to know one another, he said, "You know something? We don't know anybody in the record business. I burned down a store, got $60,000 in insurance money." Or . . . um . . . he hadn't burned down the store . . . the store burned down. And he got sixty grand in insurance money—Italian lightning. And so he and I become pals. And he says, "Well, why don't you become a partner at Kama Sutra?" I said, "Well, what have you got?" "Well, you could come and see our offices."

And the first thing I did was go through their filing cabinet. I listened to every single song that there was, and there was a demo of this group, The Shangri-Las, who were starting, at that time, at Mercury Records and put out a record called "Simon Says" that didn't go anyplace. And the demo I picked out was, like, seven- or eight-minute-long opera, and it was called "Remember (Walkin' in the Sand)." And it was The Shangri-Las, and it was Shadow Morton, George "Shadow" Morton, his song, and I said, "Ah, this is the goods."

And I went into the studio and produced a shorter version, in my opinion, of "Remember (Walkin' in the Sand)," and I took that to George Goldner, who was now in partnership with Leiber and Stoller at Red Bird Records. Artie and George are back in business with one another! And I have the blessing to get a relationship with Jerry Leiber and Mike Stoller.

BILLY JOEL, musician: When I heard it on the radio, I was at Jones Beach listening to my transistor radio. And I heard this and I went, "Wait a minute, that's me!" Oh, I knew it as soon as I heard the recording on the radio, I knew that was this thing I had played on.

BROOKS ARTHUR, sound engineer: I finished a recording session at Mirasound in Manhattan, and I was driving to my apartment in Queens. We were stopped at the red light there at Queens Boulevard and a guy rolls up with a girl. He's got his arm around the girl and he's listening to "Remember (Walkin' in the Sand)" and singing along with it. And I looked over, and I rolled down my window, and I said, "Hey, buddy," you know—and he's really hugging and kissing his girl—and I said, "Hey, buddy, I just want you to know that I engineered that record just the other day and now it's on the radio!" And he looked at me like I was nuts and he pulled away into the night, *zoom*, never to be heard from or seen again.

DAVID JOHANSEN, the New York Dolls: I think the beauty of those songs is that they're so kind of vulnerable in a way that guys aren't in that stage of their careers. So it gives you a lot of insight into that. But as far as, like, serious or not is concerned, if things are serious, I'm not really on board with them so much. I think rock and roll should be interesting, but most—it should be fun, and the people who stretch the boundaries of what's fun are talking to me, you know?

ELLIE GREENWICH, songwriter: They were as they looked—they were tough yet very vulnerable—I think that was part of the appeal. At the beginning we did not get along—they were kind of crude, and having to deal with them on a daily basis used to get me very uptight—with their gestures and language and chewing the gum and the stockings ripped up their leg. We would say, "Not nice, you must be ladies," and they would say, "We don't want to be ladies."

MARY WEISS, The Shangri-Las: I think the clothing . . . and I think when you perform music, people are always looking for a box to put you in. It's not necessarily true. It never was true.

JAY SIEGEL, The Tokens: The motorcycle—the bad girls of rock and roll—they were good girls to us. No, they weren't like that at all. It was just their image, you know, especially "Leader of the Pack."

DAVID JOHANSEN, the New York Dolls: You get your taste set at a certain age and it kind of sticks for a long time. So they were just made for me, and people like me—you know, they were, like, *mine*. Whereas older people, I mean, older, you know, two years older or whatever, would kind of, like, tut-tut them.

GEORGE "SHADOW" MORTON, producer: Leiber and Stoller wanted me to collaborate with people in the business because I was an "outsider," I didn't have any track record or background. They were right. They were worried. All of a sudden, they had a hit with a new artist and things were taking off with Red Bird Records. I didn't want to do that, so when the record hit number one, they walked into the office and said "Hey, what do you want to do for the second record?" I said, "I got an idea for a song. It's called 'Leader of the Pack.'"

JEFF BARRY, songwriter: My first really big hit was "Tell Laura I Love Her," which is about a kid getting killed in an auto racing stock car race. That's why he wanted to get to us, and me in particular, to hear his ideas about this group, and this kid getting killed on a motorcycle—which did obviously strike a chord.

Mary was sixteen when she sang "Leader of the Pack." And you know the part where the kid gets killed on the motorcycle and she screams, "Look out, look out, look out!" And you hear the sound effects and the cry . . . she wasn't giving me that drama that was necessary.

She's at the mic doing the vocals, and anybody I've ever produced knows when I come up to talk to them that the mic is shut off and nobody in the control room can hear it, what we say. And I went out there and I said, "Mary, you know . . . think about it. You're on this rainy night and you went and told your boyfriend that you couldn't see him anymore because your folks wouldn't let you. And he's on his motorcycle and he's like, 'Well, to hell with it,' and cranks it and he spins around on a rainy night, he doesn't see the car and he gets killed right in front of you. You know—you gotta feel it—you got to get your head into that." And I stayed out there with her sitting across the mic from her and when you hear that record, she was crying, practically. When she was screaming, "Look out, look out, look out!" she really meant it.

MARY WEISS, The Shangri-Las: They don't realize how young I was back then.

GEORGE "SHADOW" MORTON, producer: I mean, I made demands of Mary Weiss that were extraordinary. When you listen to her records today and imagine that it's coming from a fifteen-, sixteen-year-old girl. I was asking her to be an actress, not just a singer.

JERRY LEIBER, songwriter: As a producer, Shadow threw in everything but the kitchen sink.

DAVID JOHANSEN, the New York Dolls: The Shirelles could really sing. The Shangri-Las just had to throw everything in there to come across, I think, but I just thought they were great.

ELLIE GREENWICH, songwriter: After the session, I knew it was a number one record. "Chapel of Love" and "Leader of the Pack" were the only two I was dead sure about.

BROOKS ARTHUR, sound engineer: My assistant engineer, he had his Harley-Davidson parked in front of the studio every night. We had to go . . . we had that *vroom, vroom*, we needed that, and we took—this was before wireless microphones—so we took a long microphone cable through the whole building and out onto the street and it was plugged directly into the tape recorder in the control room. And we made a series of starts and stops. It's *vroom, vroom*, loud, soft, brakes screeching.

JEFF BARRY, songwriter: But George, actually after the success of The Shangri-Las, or during that success, he bought me my first motorcycle.

JERRY LEIBER, songwriter: "Leader of the Pack" reached number one for The Shangri-Las.

GREIL MARCUS, music writer: The songs most often celebrated a shadowy male of wondrous attractiveness, and on a superficial level, such figures surely represented the producer's or the lyricist's fantasy of himself.

JEFF BARRY, songwriter: When Ellie passed, there was an obituary. It was in the *New York Times*, somebody said how Ellie had the ability to get, feel, and represent the feelings of teenage girls at the time, but *I* wrote the lyrics.

MELANIE MINTZ, writer: They started writing about teen angst.

JEFF BARRY, songwriter: And it was kind of fun doing Jeff Barry at that time, walking around in my cowboy outfits.

JERRY LEIBER, songwriter: It was teen melodrama and the teens went nuts for it.

DAVID JOHANSEN, the New York Dolls: Listen to the records. The Shangri-Las' "Remember," that's, like, such a masterpiece of recording and singing. And "The Leader of the Pack," "Out in the Streets." They're, like, masterpieces.

BROOKS ARTHUR, sound engineer: "Walkin' in the Sand," . . . "Give Him a Great Big Kiss," "Leader of the Pack," all those are little mini-movies.

DAVID JOHANSEN, the New York Dolls: They were "teen dramas."

JERRY LEIBER, songwriter: He wrote another sappy mini-saga for The Shangri-Las, "I Can Never Go Home Any More." I was sure this one was just too cornball to hit. I was wrong. It soared to number six in 1965.

PART 5

Motown Becomes the Sound of Young America

1964–1966

CHAPTER 27

Motown University

MARTHA REEVES, The Vandellas: We are a selected group. They went and collected everybody and made a school—made a Motown University. I'm glad to have studied those four years there.

MARY WILSON, The Supremes: You're speaking of artist development. Again, I want to go back to Mr. Gordy's family, who were . . . all the women were . . . a couple of the women had gone to one of the schools, the House of Beauty, and the person who had her own modeling studio there was Ms. Maxine Powell.

CAL GILL, The Velvelettes: She had a modeling school, Immaculate House Finishing School, and Berry Gordy's sisters attended it. They told him about her and what an asset she would be to the company and see what you think about hiring her and to train the people—not just the women—correct body posture, body carriage, how to present yourself in a professional way, the right way to talk, and manners. She taught us etiquette that we may not have had in that detail had she not been chosen by Mr. Gordy and his sisters to do so.

MARTHA REEVES, The Vandellas: If we weren't on the road singing somewhere, we would be there for lessons.

CAL GILL, The Velvelettes: Everybody went to Maxine's house, you know, within Motown—we all had to attend.

MAXINE POWELL, Motown etiquette instructor: Mr. Gordy and I both said, "You don't have to do any of the things that I suggest to you, none of them. You do have a choice. It's just that you can't stay here. We like you just the same, but you can't stay here." So, they knew from the beginning that if they wanted to grow and develop and be top stars, they had to participate.

MICKEY STEVENSON, Motown A&R: And, yes, it's going to take up some of your time. Yes, when you leave the studio with the singing—you can't go home right now—you got an hour and a half, you got to stay across the street, get the routine down on the song that you're going to deal with, we got choreographers over there. And if you didn't—mainly, the girls—if you didn't go over there, I wouldn't record you. You know, if you've found reasons not to go to the second level, you can't come into the studio.

MAXINE POWELL, Motown etiquette instructor: At the time, some of them thought it was a waste of time; youngsters, you know how they are. Some were from the projects, but they were not rowdy or disrespectful, but neither did they have class or were they gracious or did they know anything about being a great, great performer. That's why the finishing school was opened, so they could learn to be beautiful, unique human beings onstage and offstage. First, you have to learn to be who you are and to be great within yourself so that when you go onstage all you're doing is being natural.

MARTHA REEVES, The Vandellas: They showed us how to perform, how to give us music theory. They gave us the social graces, they gave us choreography from vaudeville through Cholly Atkins, our choreographer. We had the best teachers—the most learned, experienced professors of music and theater. Berry trained us all. We were all trained and programmed to be what the Motown sound afforded us.

MICKEY STEVENSON, Motown A&R: Because of the natural format of things, girls and women—especially Black—were not looked at in the right light—period. We couldn't just be—especially for girls—you couldn't just be an artist. You have to be as polished as you can be, because everybody's watching.

MARTHA REEVES, The Vandellas: We paid for the instructors. It was part of our royalty returns to pay for the people that were professional and taught us. That's an investment that Berry Gordy decided to take, but it helped everybody. I mean, they didn't do all of that training for free and Berry made it possible for our royalties to include instructions and costume designers and music directors.

MARY WILSON, The Supremes: Maurice King was the person who did a lot of the music and the harmonies with our group. Prior to that, he had been a big band leader, worked with all the greats—the Lena Hornes and Nat King Coles and everyone.

Then you had, of course, Harvey Fuqua, who was one of The Moonglows, he was brought in as well. Of course, then someone brought in Mr. Cholly Atkins. All these older professional people who had been in show business themselves became members of this artist development. Their jobs were to pass on all their professional skills and train all of us younger rock and rollers, because these people had worked in vaudeville and we used to call them the chitlin' circuit, so they were well-polished, professional entertainers, all of them, in their own field.

MICKEY STEVENSON, Motown A&R: The record is one thing . . . but if they see *you*, enjoy *you* as artists, the record gets bigger, and they love you as a person, and they take from you and learn from you and it turns into a whole 'nother world. So that's what it was really all about for us.

DEE DEE KENNIEBREW, The Crystals: That's one thing I can say for Motown, whether they paid them or not, whether they dissed them or not behind the scenes, they always promoted their acts.

BERTHA BARBEE, The Velvelettes: Lady with a capital *L*. She was always a lady. That was one thing she taught us; "When you girls are out in the public and representing Motown," she'd tell us, "you act like ladies, you sit like ladies, you talk like ladies."

MAXINE POWELL, Motown etiquette instructor: I always had high standards. They went to school for two hours every day; not one day, but every day. I had them sit in a circle. I don't believe in anybody sitting behind anyone because everybody is somebody. I wanted them up front. I didn't want them to be shy, or whatever their problem was, they were still coming up front. I told them that I was going to open up a department that had nothing to do with singing. I can't even hold a note. I said, "You're going to be trained to appear in the number one places around the country, and even before kings and queens or at the White House." Those youngsters looked at me and laughed and said, "That woman's crazy. All we want is a hit record." This is 1964. They didn't have the vision at the time. I began to work with each one of them as to what they needed. I started with, "Who are you and what makes you tick?" and I helped them find out what a unique, beautiful flower they were. I gave them stage technique and stage etiquette. This is what I worked with—no bending over, no making faces when you sing, no holding the mic so close to your mouth so it looked like you were going to swallow it. They were taught how to do that and sing pleasantly. They were lifted from being a singer to being a performer.

ROSALIND ASHFORD, The Vandellas: She taught us how we should get into a car and how we should get out of a car, she taught us how to sit.

BERTHA BARBEE, The Velvelettes: How to get on a stool—because sometimes we would have a stool onstage. So, you have to know how to put your leg and your knees . . . so a lot of times when you see people perform, a lot of times you don't know all the rigmarole that they've gone to, to look like that or to act like that.

ROSALIND ASHFORD, The Vandellas: She used to have us walking up and down the stairs. Posture, trying to get us to have proper posture.

BERTHA BARBEE, The Velvelettes: The stool deal was you put your fanny on . . . you have to go up to the stool sideways, and you put your fanny on first, then make sure that your skirt is a certain way, and put one leg on, and then have the other leg next to it. I'm telling you, it was a step-by-step-by-step. And we had to go through those singularly.

MICKEY STEVENSON, Motown A&R: Right down to the wardrobe, everything was laid out.

CAL GILL, The Velvelettes: Mrs. Powell used to tell us it's one-third glamor and the rest is hard work. And you must remember that it's good to look good, but your bodies are gonna take a beating at times, you know.

MARTHA REEVES, The Vandellas: We were made into a good product and the proof is in the pudding. So one hand helped the other, one hand washed the other. It was a plan that worked and it's still working, thank God.

MARY WILSON, The Supremes: Maxine Powell was one who was more of our mentor. She was giving us inspiration in terms of how to become proper ladies. Everyone contributed to the grooming, let's say, of the act.

*

KATHERINE ANDERSON, The Marvelettes: For us, it was just the excitement of we're going to do a record. My mother did have a copy of the contract and she had gotten together with a couple of the other parents and did try to find an attorney that could help them in regards to the contract, but no one in the Inkster area was of entertainment and entertainment law. In Michigan, with the entertainment industry being so new to the area, there was no such thing as an entertainment lawyer. So, therefore, many of the attorneys, though good, were ignorant to the point of entertainment law. The only thing they could basically tell us was that we were contracted to them for X amount of time and X amount of this, that, and the other, and that technically, the contract didn't necessarily benefit us as the artists, but it benefited the record company. There was nothing in the contract to protect us.

Through the years when you're working, you don't necessarily pay attention to what is going on and what is transpiring in your business. You're called in to sign your contract; there may be an increase in it, there may not be an increase in it. As you get older, you realize what a major conflict it was having Motown serve as your record label and also as your manager, but it was point in fact that there was no other record company in the area.

MARC TAYLOR, music writer: The eight-page document each Marvelette received was Motown's standard boilerplate agreement. There were numerous stipulations that any experienced entertainment attorney would have questioned.

Motown would choose all of the songs the group would record, and the group would record each song until "the satisfaction." However, Motown "shall not be obligated to release any recordings," meaning that just because a song was recorded it would not necessarily be issued to the public.

The Marvelettes received a 2 percent royalty rate of 90 percent of the suggested retail price for each record sold in the United States, less all taxes and packaging costs. They received half of that amount for overseas sales. This was a group figure that had to be split five ways.

Per the terms of the contract, Motown was obligated to pay the costs of the arrangements, copying, accompaniment, and all other costs to each recording session, whether the song was released or not. However, these expenses and others were to be recouped by Motown from the royalties generated by sales of the records that were released. This was a particularly troublesome practice for The Marvelettes, as well as other artists at Motown who would record numerous songs that would not be issued.

If any of the girls were to leave the group, she would have no further right to use the group's name for any purpose. And Motown could replace any member of the group with any person the company chose, or could require the group to record and perform live without a new member.

MARTHA REEVES, The Vandellas: I knew nothing about contracts—and had I had that experience as a lawyer, I probably would have found a better deal for myself. Gloria decided right away that she did not want to sign a contract, she wanted to keep her job with the city—which was a hard job to get—and she wanted to stay at home with her children.

ROSALIND ASHFORD, The Vandellas: That's how Martha became the lead singer, because Gloria had to step out. We had talked to her much, much, *much* later—years, years, years later—and she did say she was upset that she had to do that, but the way it was, she had to do what she had to do.

MARY WILSON, The Supremes: When Mr. Gordy wanted to finally sign us to a contract, which we had been there a couple months or whatever, he said that he wanted to change the name to another name. When we got there the day that we were signing the contract, no one really had a name picked out. We certainly didn't get together and say, "Maybe we should be called this and be called that."

JANIE BRADFORD, Motown executive: Mr. Gordy said The Primettes name needed to be changed, so I put three names in a hat, in a bag, that Florence Ballard pulled from those three names the name "The Supremes."

MARY WILSON, The Supremes: We had no idea about contracts. All we knew was that to be signed with Motown meant that they were going to be sponsoring us and this and that, so that's pretty much all we thought a contract was. We didn't know it was going to have all these legal things in it.

We did not get a lawyer or anything because, first of all, we were too poor for that. My mother couldn't even read and write. Getting the contract was, for us, a surprise, but we didn't really mind signing because as I said we would've done anything to be at Motown, to be anywhere if someone wanted us to sing. We were just happy, and when Mr. Gordy said, "Don't worry about getting a lawyer, we'll take care of anything," okay, cool. We've got it made. They're going to take care of everything. What we have to do is just sing. They were—in those days—they were our managers. They were managers, they booked us, they did everything. So we were thrilled because we didn't have to do anything outside. Everything was in-house and everything was taken care of there.

Of course, later on, it did become a conflict and they had to change.

CHAPTER 28

Standing Out from the Crowd

BOBBY JAY, disc jockey: The Supremes were lucky they weren't dropped. We called them "The No-Hit Supremes." They went through almost six, seven, ten records with no hits.

MARTHA REEVES, The Vandellas: I think what really helped The Supremes' career and their music was when they started touring with Dick Clark.

MARY WILSON, The Supremes: The funny thing about that, however, was that we didn't get on "Dick Clark's Caravan [of Stars]" because we were good or because we had hit records. In fact, we got on the show because Motown had coerced Dick Clark and everyone to have us on the show. Because the show, really, their show was all about people who had hit records. Gene Pitney was on that show, The Shirelles, The Dixie Cups—all kinds of people.

DEE DEE KENNIEBREW, The Crystals: I remember what they wore the first day. It was a green . . . a lime-green, three-tiered, almost like an empire waist, but it was a three-tiered dress with spaghetti straps, and they were rehearsing. We were all in the same room.

CAL GILL, The Velvelettes: When we went out on that Dick Clark tour in '64, "Needle in a Haystack" was a greater hit than "Where Did Our Love Go."

MARY WILSON, The Supremes: So the record was released just prior to us going on the show, but it hadn't really been played a lot on the radio. Once we were on the tour, the radio started playing it and it became a hit.

BEVERLY LEE, The Shirelles: I'll never forget a Supreme asking me what it was like for this, that, or the other. I said, "Don't worry, girls, you're going to get your turn." A few days later, we were in a hotel, we checked in and we heard all this screaming out in the hall, we looked out our doors, and they were out in the hallways jumping up and down. Their song "Where Did Our Love Go" had went to number one, and they took off like a rocket.

MARY WILSON, The Supremes: Then once the record started being played everywhere on the radio . . . it was *then* the applause and the recognition and the screaming would be the same for us as it was for Gene Pitney and the other acts.

ROSA LEE HAWKINS, The Dixie Cups: By July 13, when the Caravan rolled into Pittsburgh to play the Syria Mosque, a popular venue, The Supremes pushed past The Shirelles as the headliners.

BARBARA ANN HAWKINS, The Dixie Cups: Once their record hit, Berry took them off the tour.

*

JANIE BRADFORD, Motown executive: Everyone knows that The Supremes did not want to do "Where Did Our Love Go." They did not like it, and at the time, they did not know that it had been a Marvelettes reject. 'Cause Holland–Dozier–Holland had tried to get The Marvelettes to cut it—then The Marvelettes *wished* they had taken it.

BRIAN HOLLAND, songwriter: Listen, we wrote it for The Supremes. I know contrary to what I'm saying Lamont Dozier said he did it for The Marvelettes. But anyway, we did it for The Supremes. Maybe he got bored saying the same thing over and over in interviews, so he made up some new stuff. [*laughing*] Yeah . . . he does that often . . . he did that often.

MARTHA REEVES, The Vandellas: Holland–Dozier–Holland, the most prolific writers, went on to be so successful for The Supremes after our records, "Heat Wave," "Quicksand," "Jimmy Mack," and "Come and Get These Memories." But they had been successful with Martha and The Vandellas prior to The Supremes.

BRIAN HOLLAND, songwriter: How I got involved with The Supremes is that Berry just came to us and said, "I need a song for these girls." He was working with them. He wrote a song called "Buttered Popcorn," and I said, "I don't particularly like that song." He put it out—it didn't do nothing much.

KATHERINE ANDERSON, The Marvelettes: And then when Berry Gordy stepped into the picture, everybody was out. I don't really know when it happened, but I know that everything we did on the buses—she [Diana Ross] always used to say she's going to call Berry. And so then I just said, "Well, go on and call Berry. It makes no difference to me." But then again, whoever she called, it made a difference because, you know, it is what it is.

MARTHA REEVES, The Vandellas: Their success was mainly because they were concentrated on. The company concentrated on them. Everybody had a turn. There was a time when they were concentrating on Stevie Wonder, then it moved from there to another artist. He was good at making an artist and moving on to the next one. And the machinery changed and got better.

MARY WILSON, The Supremes: I told Eddie Holland, "If we don't get a hit record, our parents are going to make us go to college." I became the spokesperson at that time, I don't know how *I* got to be the spokesperson.

MARTHA REEVES, The Vandellas: There are reasons why they became more successful and it wasn't all of a sudden. They worked real hard to get hits with Holland–Dozier–Holland. Smokey Robinson was the first writer for The Supremes when Holland–Dozier–Holland found success with Martha and The Vandellas.

ANNETTE BEARD, The Vandellas: It was that Diana went to Berry.

ROSALIND ASHFORD, The Vandellas: Mary used to always say she wants a hit like The Vandellas, because they never could get a good hit. It took them quite a while to come up with something. That's how we lost our writers, because they had to focus on working for The Supremes.

ANNETTE BEARD, The Vandellas: Florence, to me, she had the better voice. She was the lead singer of the group—I don't know if a lot of people know that, but she was the lead singer of the group.

BRIAN HOLLAND, songwriter: Eddie told me Mary could sing it, but actually Lamont and I—we always thought Diana Ross would be the one to sing it. So we argued back and forth, it was the, "Oh, let Mary Wilson sing it 'cause she got a softer sung voice." And I said, "No, Diana Ross is a much better singer." So, we argued over an hour, then he said, "Lower the key and let Diana Ross sing it." So we lowered the key and she sung it.

DEE DEE KENNIEBREW, The Crystals: Sometimes the strongest singer is not the one who makes the hits, you know. That's just not the voice that they want to hear. There are a lot of people out there that have hit records that don't have strong voices, but if you're rehearsing with a group and you've always been the lead when you rehearse, and this record company comes along and says, "No, I want this other girl," well, that's going to cause resentment.

BERRY GORDY, music executive: While The Supremes sparkled through their own cycle, they stayed great friends for a long time before trouble started.

BRIAN HOLLAND, songwriter: The guy who was in charge of promotions, he told Berry, "Look, this record is so big that we've got to stick with this group, because something is magic about this group and this song. We've got to keep pushing *this* group because it will open up doors to cross over to white folks, you know what I mean?"

KATHERINE ANDERSON, The Marvelettes: Let's see . . . it makes a difference as to who's zooming who. So then it was what it was.

BERRY GORDY, music executive: Though we were discreet, it was common knowledge that we were together.

DIANA ROSS, The Supremes: The girls had treated me very badly. They had gone against me with a vengeance. They had blamed me, acted as if everything was my fault, that the press had not written about them, that Berry had chosen the songs that he wanted me to record. They were so blinded by jealousy that they never stopped to think that maybe, just maybe, my voice was better suited for the songs that Brian, Lamont, and Eddie wrote. That our records were selling because of my sound.

BRIAN HOLLAND, songwriter: Well, listen, I will tell you this much—I truly was in love with her. And matter of fact, Berry understood it and he wanted Diana and I to get married. But I couldn't do that, because I was already married. I had a child, and I couldn't do it. I just couldn't pull away, you know? But even so, I was truly in love, I wanted to marry her and all . . . I mean, I thought she was a very special and compassionate person, you know. But maybe she kind of changed. I think making money and all that took her whole emotional thing away, I mean she just kind of changed.

DIANA ROSS, The Supremes: I didn't know much about HDH as people, what they might have been experiencing in their personal lives and where they eventually ended up. Beyond the brilliant music they created, I have to admit I didn't pay much attention them.

JANIE BRADFORD, Motown executive: The focus was on them because it was hit after hit nonstop—which we had never experienced before. I think they had six number ones before they stopped—and they didn't stop. After "Where Did Our Love Go," it just kept going, so *definitely* the focus was on The Supremes.

MARTHA REEVES, The Vandellas: Just like any other business, if you have a product, when you put it out and it is a hit, as it grows, you add to—you modify. You have a better engine to promote your music, to get people to listen to it, and to put the best foot forward.

BRIAN HOLLAND, songwriter: We cut three songs in one session, and all three of them went to number one. It was "You Keep Me Hangin' On," "You Can't Hurry Love" . . . I can't think of the other one.

MICKEY STEVENSON, Motown A&R: They were twenty-four-hour writers. They didn't just write a song—I'd have to put them out of the studio, you know they were *nonstop*. They just . . . forget it . . . they had no lives.

*

DEE DEE KENNIEBREW, The Crystals: So, that happens a lot, they pit—they even do that with the guys at Motown—they would pit one guy against another, one group against another. "Okay, so you want your money? You don't think we gave you enough royalties? Guess what? We're not going to record you for a year. We're going to let you sit, because, see, we got the Four Tops over here, and we'll just give them all the songs. Or we've got so-and-so over here." So, that's enough to drive you crazy right there. And that's what they would do—things like that to control the acts, which I feel was horrible.

CAL GILL, The Velvelettes: He always wanted to bring the competition.

LOUVAIN DEMPS, The Andantes: I think that Berry liked to have a competition, and it's good that it did not get out of hand because it could have, you know, like, pushing people, like, "Oh, they got this and you got to do this" . . . and it could create some hard feelings with the women mostly. *Hellooooo.*

JACKIE HICKS, The Andantes: "And don't think that you the only apple in the barrel. So, you're talented, but we got some people that's as talented as you and some of them are even more talented." You have to recognize that in this business, and it's just what it is.

MICKEY STEVENSON, Motown A&R: It happens in any company with any artist. When one starts taking off in another format than the other, then they form a jealousy—envy comes into the picture. It's normal. It should be inspiring the other artists to do better and be greater, but some of them take it as a threat—and it should go the other way. I kept trying to tell artists, "You can do that and more—why don't you take some classes in acting? Why don't you get some dance classes? You want to go further? You got to pay for it." It's hard to convince people of that. Some people would rather get mad, you know, say, "You're choosing that person over me."

MARTHA REEVES, The Vandellas: They had been put on a pedestal and put in a different area. None of us could relate to The Supremes. They were just *that*. They were put in a category where they were untouchable—unreachable—and set aside as being the superior act in Berry Gordy's eyes.

DEE DEE KENNIEBREW, The Crystals: I know that Florence resented the fact that they changed Diana to the lead singer. And she felt it was because of Diana's relationship with Berry, how she got to be the lead, because she was actually the stronger singer.

MICKEY STEVENSON, Motown A&R: I cannot say enough about the difference between Diana Ross and the other ones. Mary was next—she had that desire. My thing—which I learned earlier—is that eight hours you work, eight hours you sleep. Now what are you doing with the *other* eight? You can make use of that time you lose.

SMOKEY ROBINSON, entertainer: Books have been written about Diana Ross and Berry Gordy, their love affair, his favoritism, her bitchiness, his unfair treatment of the other Motown women. Berry managed Diana because Diana was a tremendous talent. Diana followed Berry because Berry was a tremendous businessman. These were two powerful but practical people. Interested, more than anything else, in success.

BERRY GORDY, music executive: Diana meant more to me than she could ever imagine. It is absolutely true that at one time I was obsessed with her. In the heyday of The Supremes, I saw the butterfly emerge from the cocoon and I was dazzled. She was magic and she was mine. Diana was willing to let me make her a star and I knew that she had the talent, drive, and stamina to go the distance.

BRIAN HOLLAND, songwriter: Oh, she *wanted* to work. Never had a problem like that. She was very enthused about working, doing something, you know.

MICKEY STEVENSON, Motown A&R: Diana Ross would go to rehearsal time and it's supposed to be two hours—hour and a half whatever—she would say, "Well, where is so-and-so? They coming in—the ones behind me? Can I stay here 'til they get in?" One of those kinds of people—if that person didn't show up, she takes *their* time.

DEE DEE KENNIEBREW, The Crystals: Diana knew what she was about. She stuck with it. She might have done things that someone else might not have done, or that somebody else might have said, "Well, that was wrong." But she knew what she wanted, she did what she had to do, *and* she was able to deliver once she got there.

*

BERRY GORDY, music executive: Traveling together, there were many times of fun and closeness before the cycle tightened its noose and a major cold war developed among the girls.

BEVERLY LEE, The Shirelles: A lot of time the writers would write about friction between girl groups, but we got along with them all, we never had any problem. As a matter of fact, we were on a Dick Clark tour with The Supremes and The Crystals and The Dixie Cups, and we all shared dressing rooms.

ROSA LEE HAWKINS, The Dixie Cups: Whenever we had a day off . . . you never really had a heck of a long time to be off. When we arrived in a town, all the girls would get together. When I say "all the girls," that would be The Supremes, The Shirelles, The Dixie Cups, and The Crystals—*everybody*. The bus driver would drop us in the middle of town after we had unpacked our suitcases and what have you. And he brought us to where downtown was or the shopping area was.

Unfortunately, Diana walked by herself. She didn't want to walk with anybody. Eventually, the rest of us—we were all together, and we shopped until we were ready to drop, and we get back to the hotel and everybody's showing what they bought—the shoes or the dress or lipstick, whatever. Diane didn't want to show anything to anybody. And then she said, "Oh, well, this is the lipstick that I bought." And Mary said, "Oh, I have the same lipstick." And somebody else in some group had it—we all ended up with the same lipstick. And you know what Diana Ross did with hers, unfortunately? Threw hers in the garbage can. And we kind of looked at each other and said, "This girl really has a problem."

BARBARA ALSTON, The Crystals: It was quite obvious to everyone on the bus that Diana thought she was the Queen Bee.

CAL GILL, The Velvelettes: When we roomed together on "Dick Clark's Caravan of Stars" tour, Diane said, "You know, I'm gonna be a star one day all by myself."

ROSA LEE HAWKINS, The Dixie Cups: She didn't get along with Florence in her group and she didn't get along with La La.

DEE DEE KENNIEBREW, The Crystals: There was a guy on the tour named Bobby Freeman and he had out a song called "Do You Want to Dance." And he was a really cute guy. I think he was flirting with La La and Diana. So, that kind of set up a little rivalry.

LA LA BROOKS, The Crystals: Diana Ross was always showing off, she's always there someplace in the wind. You know how somebody . . . you always see a showoff when they always have on a dress and they swing it around like Baby Jane, like *Whatever Happened to Baby Jane?*—that was Diana Ross. [*laughing*] So she came down in our dressing room and our shoes was lined up . . . and they dressed very nice, too—their clothes for the show—she was just being cocky and she said, "Oh, so those are the shoes you guys are wearing?" They were in sacks of . . . like a potato . . . you know how you have your shoes in a sack that has a string?

DEE DEE KENNIEBREW, The Crystals: It was something about La La's shoes . . .

LA LA BROOKS, The Crystals: And I said, "I'll beat her, I'll kick her butt." She was scared, because I'm a bigger person than her, and she must've told Florence and her mother.

So next thing I know, I'm between the two buses—me, Florence, and Diana's mother. And she says, "La La, I just want you guys to get along." I said, "But you know, Ms. Ross." I said, "Diana gets on people's nerves." And her mother was like, "I know she does. That's Diana." And I said, "But I'm not the one, you know? Because I'll beat her butt." And then Florence comes in and says, "*Oh, no you won't!*"

Because Florence was bigger than me and Florence is older, and Florence was like a little bit more *Detroit-Detroit*.

ROSA LEE HAWKINS, The Dixie Cups: And her mother was so opposite of her. It was unbelievable, her mother was very sweet—a nice, soft voice, and she would tell Diane, "Why don't you go with the girls? Why don't you eat with the girls? You know, the girls are going down to the swimming pool." And she always had a reason why she didn't want to mingle.

LA LA BROOKS, The Crystals: Dick Clark separated us.

BARBARA ALSTON, The Crystals: When Dee Dee told us what had happened, I laughed so hard my side started hurting. I knew what Diana had said was probably true, because La La was *hard* on some shoes.

DEE DEE KENNIEBREW, The Crystals: This was 1964. We had been out since '61, and there were five of us. We did not have any money, so to speak, to keep up everything.

BARBARA ALSTON, The Crystals: But The Supremes had been sent on tour with brand-new outfits because their record had just been released.

DEE DEE KENNIEBREW, The Crystals: That was only the sideline of it. The real thing was, I believe, that Bobby was flirting with both of them. But it really was about the rivalry between the two girls—because La La always thought she could out-sing Diana, and, which *she could*. But the bottom line is, *who's getting all the hits?* Diana. So, it doesn't matter if your voice is stronger.

CHAPTER 29

Putting a Face to a Name

The Girl Groups Hit Prime Time

PAUL SHAFFER, musician: The Murray the K *It's What's Happening, Baby* special—it was a two-hour rock-and-roll music special that Murray the K had talked to the US government—in particular, the Job Corps at a youth job program that Sargent Shriver organized—Murray the K sold them on a two-hour special which would not only show all the hottest acts of the day, but he would do live commercials for the Job Corps. But his commercials were so hip, you know, he talked jive and that—the government didn't understand. The commercial said, "Baby, your government is a groove." You know, and that's all he would say, and they felt cheated, I think. Nonetheless, up in Canada, I saw this as the most magical thing I ever saw.

And he had videos too. The Ronettes were on Mott Street singing "Be My Baby" on the street . . . and then they had some live stuff at the Brooklyn Fox, from one of the shows there, including Dionne Warwick singing "Walk On By."

And we saw that footage of The Vandellas going through the assembly line in Detroit, singing "Nowhere to Run." And this was, you know, way, *so long* before MTV, but that was like, that was *a video*.

MARTHA REEVES, The Vandellas: Berry was very clever. He talked Ford Motor Company into doing something no one else has ever been able to do—go in the actual factory and see the men working and putting a car together.

ROSALIND ASHFORD, The Vandellas: They just had us taping it, going through the plant. And, it was actually . . . everything was moving. Everything was for real. They did not stop the assembly line—the assembly line was moving while we were running through there and dodging the hoods of the cars and all that stuff—it was all real.

MARTHA REEVES, The Vandellas: All that was done in such a short amount of time, but it was six o'clock in the morning when we showed up at the factory and we was told and sort of cursed at by some of the workers, saying, "Hey, get the women out of here! We're trying to do a job."

BETTY KELLEY, The Velvelettes, The Vandellas: It wasn't a thing where they were going to stop the assembly line because we were in there filming.

ROSALIND ASHFORD, The Vandellas: They were playing "Nowhere to Run" while we were running through the plant.

MARTHA REEVES, The Vandellas: They would start the tape and stop the tape. And get off of one car—get off the car, let them put a fender on—and get back on and ride down.

ROSALIND ASHFORD, The Vandellas: It was scary. Especially when the hood of the car was sliding down the assembly line, because they did not stop that, either. We had to dodge it and run in between it. It was fun, but it was scary. It was definitely scary. All they did was tell us, "Just be careful." That's all they had to say. They told us, "Be careful because you're on your own."

MARTHA REEVES, The Vandellas: I think we did a good job of making the first music video ever. That car—Murray the K got the keys and drove off at the end of the video. I never heard a thing about that car.

ANNETTE BEARD, The Vandellas: No, that was not me on the video. I did not record "Nowhere to Run." It came out, I think, two or three weeks after I left the group. I was a little hurt by that, because I felt like Berry could have came and got me and put my voice on there.

MARTHA REEVES, The Vandellas: She left to marry her childhood sweetheart, Morris. I remember her saying, "See ya."

ANNETTE BEARD, The Vandellas: By that time, I had stepped out of the group because I had gotten married and I had gotten pregnant with my first child. I was the first one to step out because I was in love with my high school sweetheart and he went to the military. He came back and proposed marriage, and we got married.

ROSALIND ASHFORD, The Vandellas: It was really depressing because I had been so used to singing with her. And we had been together for so long that it kind of upset me when she said that she wasn't going out with us anymore.

ANNETTE BEARD, The Vandellas: I was showing. I was pregnant by that time, and I just made up my mind that I cannot get onstage with a big stomach. Like *no*, that's not going to work. And they were telling me, "Well, we'll have some uniforms made and we'll have them made kind of big," but I didn't want to get up there with a big stomach—that's why I stepped down.

MARTHA REEVES, The Vandellas: Berry was very clever. He knew exactly what to do when situations came up, like one of the group members dropped when you have a hit record like "(Love Is Like a) Heat Wave" ready to go international.

BETTY KELLEY, The Velvelettes, The Vandellas: When the secretary calls and says that Mr. Gordy wants to see you, you're thinking, *Oh, what did I do? What is he going to do? Is he going to take me out of the group?* These things were going through my head. When I actually got there, I saw Rosalind and Martha sitting outside his office. When I went in to talk to him and it finally hit me that he was going to pull me out of The Velvelettes and put me in The Vandellas for a trial, it was kind of scary. They were already out there and had some hit records.

It was different. The Velvelettes hadn't really traveled and been on the entertainment circuit.

BERTHA BARBEE, The Velvelettes: So Berry Gordy was like, "Ooh, wow, we got to get somebody," and they looked at The Velvelettes and they saw that we had so many . . . with five, we really wouldn't miss Betty.

So Cal said, "Hey, girl, go for it. We got four left in the group, we're fine." So we gave her our okay kind of thing. We did our thing because we had four and she went on, bless her soul, to be on "Dancing in the Street." *Hello*—"Nowhere to Run." *Hello!* These are *hit-hits*.

BETTY KELLEY, The Velvelettes, The Vandellas: The initial decision was hard. I called Carolyn [Cal] and said, "I really don't know what to do. They need me to fill in because Annette is leaving. It's an opportunity." We talked it over and she said, "Go for it." I had to make a decision . . .

Well, the decision was already made for me because it was supposed to be a trial. I had to learn their songs and their steps. Rosalind was so great at accepting me, taking me under her wing, showing me the steps, and rehearsing with me. She and her mom were just wonderful. They really made me feel welcomed. Rosalind and I clicked right away.

MARTHA REEVES, The Vandellas: Betty Kelley was a plant. I had recorded and I came out and saw this girl who looked a whole lot like Annette. She approached me and she says, "Hi, how are you? Are you Martha?" And I go, "Mm-hmm," and she said, "I understand you need a girl in your group." I looked at her and she looked like Annette to me a little bit, and so I said, "Okay." We got to talking and the next thing you know I moved her into my house from Kalamazoo, Michigan. She was on her way to . . . I don't know where she was going.

*

MARY WILSON, The Supremes: Our record had become number one, and then we had five consecutive number ones. When that happened around the world, I would say that we started realizing that our dreams were coming true.

The artists we mentioned earlier—The Chantels, The Shirelles, and a lot of the shoulders that we stood on, the Sammy Davises, the Lena Hornes—they didn't have the TV thing back then. So, therefore, even though they were very famous and popular, they still didn't really hit the market worldwide.

WHOOPI GOLDBERG, entertainer: You didn't have the same exposure for somebody like The Shirelles. You saw The Lennon Sisters, you saw a lot of other groups, but you didn't see a whole bunch of Black women.

MARY WILSON, The Supremes: In fact, I think The Shirelles probably were bigger than us in terms of the amount of records they had, but the record business was not as prominent as it became in the sixties, so it was a different thing.

SHIRLEY ALSTON REEVES, The Shirelles: Florence tried to get us on *The Ed Sullivan Show*, and he turned us down. We had a number one record, but he said no because he was afraid for his ratings. She said, "What do you mean?" He said, "If they were Sammy Davis Jr. or Lena Horne, I would take them, but a Colored rock-and-roll group, I don't think so." Then, the next thing I know, The Supremes came. That was afterwards. Things evolved in the business. I guess their people were more insistent. The first time they were on, he had to apologize to them because he cut them off. He put them on near the end and cut their time. He gave them a return engagement and issued an apology.

WHOOPI GOLDBERG, entertainer: No one looked like them. You didn't see women dressed like that who were Black and singing. You saw all kinds of folks on Andy Williams, but you didn't see *these* girls. To be on the same stage as Ed Sullivan—it was a *huge* deal. It was a huge deal. And they *were* supreme. They looked amazing, they sounded great, you know we all knew the words to the songs, and there they were. It was really quite good.

MARC TAYLOR, music writer: The Supremes, they didn't really fall into that quintessential teenage girl group era. By the time The

Supremes had a hit, they were just beyond teenagers—in their early twenties—so they didn't have to grow with their audience because they were already grown when they started having hit records.

MARY WILSON, The Supremes: In the very beginning, we were just awfully thrilled to be wearing all these gorgeous gowns. And from doing the television show here in America, we ran into great designers because in those days the designers used to work on television shows.

WHOOPI GOLDBERG, entertainer: And so the first time they were on, I think they really stunned people because you saw pictures of them in places, but you never really got to see them in performance mode. And it was kind of wonderful to watch and say, "Oh yeah, there's some Black girls. There's some Black girls," and, "I'm not going to look like any of them, but if they can get on Ed Sullivan, anything is possible. I could do it." So it wasn't a building block, but it was part of the mortar.

MARY WILSON, The Supremes: Ed Sullivan was one of those shows that . . . I did *Dancing with the Stars* last year . . . and it was the same kind of show in the sixties that the entire family watched. It wasn't where rock and roll was listened to by the young people; the TV show was watched by the entire family.

If you had a hit record out and you were on *The Ed Sullivan Show*, obviously that record would go to the top of the charts, and that's what happened to The Supremes. We were on sixteen times, probably more than most other people except that little puppet [Topo Gigio].

WHOOPI GOLDBERG, entertainer: For me, I knew, because my mother said, "There is nothing that is not within your reach, but it might be a little harder than it is for other people. So you have to really decide whether this is what you want." And when you looked at *those* girls, I knew that that was the kind of commitment that *they* made. This is what they really wanted and they were willing to go for it.

MARY WILSON, The Supremes: Because with the three of us—we're three totally different individual girls or females—but we still blended so well. We *really* did blend well, and we were friends.

And we, as I said many times before, we dared to dream at a time when, for Black people, it wasn't really a possible dream to come true.

WHOOPI GOLDBERG, entertainer: Their ability to do what they were doing just fueled the fact that change was happening. I was glad to be born in a time when it was happening because I couldn't imagine what it must've been like for my mom and her mom—they weren't singers. They weren't these, *these* girls, but they were really glad to see them.

PART 6

The End of an Era

1965–1970

CHAPTER 30

A Girl Group Grows Up

The Shirelles

BILLY VERA, musician: The Shirelles, they had more hits than anybody.

STEVE TYRELL, producer: They became the first super girl group, and then finally The Supremes took over for them.

BEVERLY LEE, The Shirelles: We were always in the studio, that was constantly. Whenever we came off the road from a show, they had songs all prepared for us.

SHIRLEY ALSTON REEVES, The Shirelles: We went about our daily lives like nothing happened. We went to the same shoe stores to get the $19.99 shoes. . . . We'd take the bus from Passaic, New Jersey, and walk up Broadway. The people would come outside and say, "Oh boy. You Shirelles got another chart record."

BEVERLY LEE, The Shirelles: They were proud of us in our hometown. Quite naturally, some people would say things that weren't true, like we were out one night and we came through dragging our minks—which we didn't do, we never did that. We were always . . . when we were back home . . . we did the things we always did. We didn't change—the people changed their concept of us.

STEVE TYRELL, producer: I thought Shirley had the best voice and the sexiest voice of anybody I'd ever heard. You think about it, she had something in her voice that made her different from everybody else, you know? It was kind of a sexy thing, right? Shirley had this kind of cry in her voice that was just so *sexy* and she knew how to use it too, *boy*. She'd go out there and knock everybody out.

I had a crush on Shirley, I'm telling you. . . . And I just would look at her and she would just *knock me out*. I was happy to watch her sing. I liked the other girls, but Shirley used to take her shoes off, sing in her stockinged feet. I'd go mad. . . . I remember her dresses. I just remember that she didn't have shoes on and she was singing her ass off and I thought, *That is so sexy*.

BEVERLY LEE, The Shirelles: I didn't know what was going on with Luther Dixon. Now I know it's hearing different melodies or an instrument playing this or that or the other. He was composing in his head. When we did "Soldier Boy," he and Florence disappeared. We had finished up a session, we had a little bit of time left over, and they disappeared and they came back.

We did it in three takes. "Soldier Boy" sold well over fifteen million copies thanks to God and so many people.

STANLEY GREENBERG, producer: Florence, she and Luther wrote "Soldier Boy," in a hotel room.

STEVE GUARNORI, author of *Scepter Wand Forever!*: He certainly played around. Let's not mince our words about this. If you look in *Jet* or *Ebony* magazine, he was hanging around with socialites and things like that when he was seeing Florence. So she had her hands full keeping him under control, in that regard. She was desperate to keep him, and it probably showed through—she was very worried about losing him as a partner. Which, again, goes into this kind of socialite type, you know? He's in a nightclub mixing with all these beauties and all this sort of stuff, who wouldn't be worried? But I got the impression that he could play around a bit, but she was very much keen to keep the relationship going for as long as possible.

ARTIE RIPP, music executive: Well, I think that one of the things was Luther . . . what happened between her and Luther. Luther decided that this should be Luther's world and how she wanted to, again, control everything.

STANLEY GREENBERG, producer: "Mama Said" was a Luther Dixon record, "Baby It's You" was a Luther Dixon record. That was in his heyday at Scepter—everything he touched was successful. Then "Soldier Boy" was the biggest one, then after "Soldier Boy," he was leaving and going to Capitol Records.

MARVIN SCHLACHTER, music executive: He started to write songs for other artists and other labels. So we then decided that he couldn't do that, and we bought him out.

STANLEY GREENBERG, producer: The Shirelles had one big hit after "Soldier Boy," and you would think, with "Soldier Boy" being as big of a hit as it was, it would generate hits after it, but it didn't.

SHIRLEY ALSTON REEVES, The Shirelles: The sad part to that was the day he called us into the office. We had been working together for years and couldn't think of working without him. He called us all into the office. We were wondering what we were going to do. Maybe he had a project for us. He said to us, "I have nothing else to give you. I've given you everything that I have." We were so sad and were crying. Tears were falling out of my eyes. I felt like somebody had died. It was awful. It was like an end of an era. . . . That was the end of that. He went his way and we went our way.

BEVERLY LEE, The Shirelles: The other producers didn't know how to produce us the right way. Like I said, Luther was a genius, and it was a big void after that.

STANLEY GREENBERG, producer: The company has a personality, especially with music people—creative people—and when you change one of them you change the personality.

STEVE TYRELL, producer: I took Luther Dixon's place. Can you imagine? I was eighteen years old. . . . I moved into his office, but Florence wouldn't let me take anything out of his desk for, like, six months. I'm thinking, *Is this guy going to come back and I'm going to be over with?*

Well, "Foolish Little Girl" was their last hit. That was when I got there, I was at the end of The Shirelles, at the end of their hitmaking.

MELANIE MINTZ, writer: Even look at the end of some of their careers, like the last few songs The Shirelles recorded, some of those songs are great. "Foolish Little Girl" is one of their last hits—*fabulous*. I loved that, right? But the time had kind of passed a little bit. It wasn't anymore that we were thinking like foolish little girls. You *didn't* love him.

SHIRLEY ALSTON REEVES, The Shirelles: With that song, I said, "First of all, I'm getting a little old for lollipop stuff." That was sort of like a little lollipop song. She wanted me to do it, and I did. That's Beverly singing the little three-part [*singing*] "*But I love him.*" She has a cute, little voice. I think we were all very unique. We all had our own little thing. Doris had the R & B. They had me geared for the pop market. Micki was sort of our little clown in the group. She'd come out there and dance up a storm. She was light on her feet. We used to have so much fun. I do miss them.

BEVERLY LEE, The Shirelles: We were told that there was a trust fund for us. We were always told, "Girls, you're going to be rich." We heard it so many times, "Girls, you're going to be rich." We turned twenty-one and there was a pause, and we asked about the money.

MARC TAYLOR, music writer: The Shirelles, once they started asking them about, "Hey, you know, where's our money?" I mean, that's always kind of a no-no.

STEVE GUARNORI, author of *Scepter Wand Forever!*: They expected to get paid for some of their past royalties, bearing in mind that Beverly had also written some of the songs.

MARVIN SCHLACHTER, music executive: I don't know anything about that aspect of Florence's involvement with the girls and a trust. That's something I was not aware of.

BEVERLY LEE, The Shirelles: We were crushed, we thought we were going to get a large sum of money like we were told, and we didn't.

STEVE GUARNORI, author of *Scepter Wand Forever!*: They got an allowance. But they didn't get royalties on any of their songs.

SHIRLEY ALSTON REEVES, The Shirelles: We were told—when we were young and first started—that she was making a trust fund. When we got to be twenty-one, they bought a couple of buildings where they moved their offices to. We didn't get anything. We were always in the red on the books at Scepter. I never could get it; I never could figure it out.

BEVERLY LEE, The Shirelles: There was a lot of "somebody" did this or that or the other. "Somebody" stole the money. There were different stories we heard. But we didn't get no money at twenty-one.

MARC TAYLOR, music writer: You know, you have to mature with your audience. And most of these groups, you had a few members who wrote their songs, like the Beverly Lees, you know, but they were pretty much at the mercy of whoever was available to write or produce for you, they were definitely not letting you do it yourself—even if you get a small percent of the songwriting credit for your work—more times than not you get cheated out of it. And if they're not writing and producing at the rate that your audience is growing and becoming adults . . .

ARTIE RIPP, music executive: I think the minute Florence got involved with Dionne Warwick, okay, that was the end of The Shirelles. Now she only has to deal with one woman—Dionne. It was a good business relationship that she had with Dionne Warwick. Getting involved with her destroyed, I believe, the relationship between her and Shirley, in particular. Shirley had to feel like you're the only thing, and all of a sudden the new baby comes along in the house, and mama doesn't even remember who you are, you know?

DIONNE WARWICK, singer: I had the extreme pleasure of being a Shirelle for all of three and a half weeks. It was during the period of time Shirley was about ready to give birth to her daughter . . . so they asked me to come and rehearse with them and I did and I had a zillion songs to learn and then they wanted me to do routines.

BEVERLY LEE, The Shirelles: Dionne filled in for Shirley, so Dionne was a Shirelle for a while.

DIONNE WARWICK, singer: Well, after about two and a half hours of me trying to figure out left from right, Micki finally said to me, "Tell you what, you should stand there and sing, we'll do the routine." And I was so happy to hear her say that. I am so indebted to these ladies because they taught me how to walk onto a stage. Doris, who was the tallest, told me always, "Shoulders back, head up, and smile." Beverly, the prissy one, I called her, said, "You don't walk onto the stage, you *prance* onto a stage." And the bad girl Micki, Micki said, "Well, while you're prancing, *switch*."

STANLEY GREENBERG, producer: The centerpiece of Scepter became Dionne Warwick.

ARTIE RIPP, music executive: But anyway, Florence's life went past The Shirelles. She had enough talent, taste, tenacity to go beyond The Shirelles.

STEVE GUARNORI, author of *Scepter Wand Forever!*: Dionne was very talented, clearly very intelligent, and clearly a hitmaker. . . . For Florence, it was another money spinner, and a bigger money spinner than The Shirelles.

SHIRLEY ALSTON REEVES, The Shirelles: She told me that she never took any money from us personally, that she used our money to build the company and to help the other artists like Dionne, Chuck Jackson. This is what she told me. Nobody can tell me anything else. I know what she said to me.

ARTIE RIPP, music executive: You're yesterday, but that's the way it is. The music business, entertainment business, is a cruel business. It isn't that we're here to make you happy; we are here to take everything you give us, and once we've had enough of it, you are cast aside. You're now a memory.

STEVE GUARNORI, author of *Scepter Wand Forever!*: I think that's why they were aggrieved—because Florence was leading a pretty high life. I don't doubt that Florence kept some of it back—no, no question. I'm not going to try and pretend the books balanced . . . because clearly they didn't.

STEVE TYRELL, producer: I got along terrific with all of them. Florence would send me on the road when they started having troubles between Florence and The Shirelles. She sent me to Atlanta when they were doing a gig. I would be like an ambassador for the company, "Okay, now, what's wrong with you girls? What can we do to fix this?"

STANLEY GREENBERG, producer: The chemistry changes—that's not a criticism. It's not something to be ashamed of or upset about. When you are dealing with music and people's feelings, it's very difficult to hold that together.

BEVERLY LEE, The Shirelles: Deals were always made with record companies and whoever had written a song, or who was producing, we had no knowledge of. We found out people owed other people favors, and some instances the group paid off that favor.

SHIRLEY ALSTON REEVES, The Shirelles: I wouldn't have had any career without her, so I can't be bitter. I used to be bitter. All of us were. We really looked up to her. We used to call her the mother hen. She always acted like she was protecting us. We just felt like, *What happened?* It was like there was nothing for us—nothing. We had to just keep fending for ourselves like we're doing now.

BEVERLY LEE, The Shirelles: The love of money is the root of all evil.

STEVE GUARNORI, author of *Scepter Wand Forever!*: One of them didn't want to go on strike. In the end, they all did. I mean, if you're a recording star, and you're popular, and you're having hit records, to turn around and say, "We're not going to make any more records" is a pretty drastic move. It's not one you would do lightly. I think they must have had some prior negotiations and attempts to get money from Florence that failed. It's very much a last resort, when you're in a contract, to say, "Well, we're not going to go in a recording studio anymore."

BEVERLY LEE, The Shirelles: There were lawsuits, but I really wouldn't like to get into it. We did finally wise up and start suing to get our royalties back.

STEVE GUARNORI, author of *Scepter Wand Forever!*: What Scepter did was put out a load of old B-sides, and you know, records that hadn't been good enough for release. . . . And the public kind of could see through it. They put out a couple of budget records when The Shirelles were on strike. But having their recording strike, they were on the Pricewise record label—which is Scepter's budget label—that, and the emergence of the Motown sound really did it for The Shirelles.

STANLEY GREENBERG, producer: When you get to the point where you are working together, making records together, singing together, and traveling together on tour—you have a relationship which transcends friendship. And, yes, they *were* friends . . . and then they *weren't* friends.

ERNIE MARTINELLI, manager, The Chiffons: Things have changed. None of my business, but there was some very hard feelings amongst The Shirelles and Beverly Lee, and so forth. I don't know if there was any kind of love. So, I don't know if you're getting all the truth.

BEVERLY LEE, The Shirelles: We left Scepter because we knew that time was winding down. We weren't being produced correctly—we were growing up, we had more knowledge of the business.

STANLEY GREENBERG, producer: People go through phases in their lives, sometimes it has to do with how old they are, sometimes it has to do with how they are getting along with one another. The

Shirelles grew up together—they were kids together, their relationship was different from what it was at the very beginning. The chemistry all changed, and that's the way it is with groups. It's not just that way with singing groups, but all kinds of people do all kinds of things, and it changes, you can't always create the same thing every time and come out with the same results.

CHAPTER 31

Things Fall Apart

The Crystals

DEE DEE KENNIEBREW, The Crystals: Barbara said Pat was going flat a lot and Barbara was very meticulous about the harmony.

BARBARA ALSTON, The Crystals: We had been talking about the harmony problems with Patsy for quite some time. We all agreed it was something that needed to be dealt with, but nobody wanted to do it.

LA LA BROOKS, The Crystals: Patsy was, like, very sensitive, basically. Sometimes her feelings used to get hurt because she was always on the wrong note to them. I didn't know any notes because I was the lead singer. But Dee Dee and them used to fuss, and when they'd come up onstage, sometimes she'd cry, and I could hear Barbara and them say, "But you was on my note." And they'd rehearse with her again backstage, so when she goes on again, she won't do it. But she'd do it again.

DEE DEE KENNIEBREW, The Crystals: Barbara and Patsy were the best of friends.

BARBARA ALSTON, The Crystals: So I assumed the responsibility of breaking the news to Patsy because I didn't want it done where it would hurt her too badly.

DEE DEE KENNIEBREW, The Crystals: Patsy just left in tears and took the bus back home and she was out. So that only left three. Just me, Barbara, and La La. So we got this girl, she was a dancer, but she could sing, and *very* pretty girl—her name was Fran Collins. And that was the four of us. And we were just on the road traveling and doing shows, getting our salary. We didn't know you have to have money in a kitty to pay your driver, keep the car up, keep your clothes in the cleaners. We just thought if we made a certain amount of money, we should have divided it up between us, not knowing that you have to have these things. We were not sat down and told how these monies would be worked out, just told, "This is what you're going to make." So we were doing a lot of shows and doing Dick Clark, and we were doing the tours and all of that, but we really were still on a salary.

LA LA BROOKS, The Crystals: When Phil [Spector] went to California, he forgot about us. He moved the company to LA, and that's when he stopped recording us. And that's where the problem came. He left, and we needed to work.

DEE DEE KENNIEBREW, The Crystals: When we first met Phil, we had gone by his house one time and he was living in a one-room little dark studio apartment, I believe it was on Eighth Avenue and 58th, somewhere like that. It was a little dinky dark studio apartment, but by the time "Uptown" came out, he was living over near Sutton Place, it was on, like, 61st Street and York Avenue. Had an office on the first floor of this high-rise and then a penthouse apartment and we still haven't gotten any royalties.

BARBARA ALSTON, The Crystals: We worked constantly, traveled regularly, did numerous shows, and never received the money we made ourselves. It always went to somebody who said they were taking care of all our expenses and whatever else they could find to spend our money on. We were always manipulated and lied to by someone. Like my grandmother always said, "Too many hands in the pot spoils the soup." Our soup had gotten real spoiled because we had more hands than we had soup.

LA LA BROOKS, The Crystals: We had a contract with him, and he wasn't obeying the contract; that's when Joe Scandore was interacting with him, trying to get him to record us, and he was just in his own little producing selfish world.

DEE DEE KENNIEBREW, The Crystals: The only way we really even got out of the contract with Phil is because Joe said, "Come on. Give the girls a little bit of money and let them out of this contract. You're not recording them anymore."

LA LA BROOKS, The Crystals: Joe Scandore was affiliated with the Mafia. He kept calling Phil, saying, "Listen, Phil, The Crystals started you, you started The Crystals. They need a record out." And so, one day I go up to Joe Scandore's office and he's sitting at the table, and this big guy is standing there named Jim, and he says to me, "Jim, tell La La what you just did when you went to California with Phil."

I'm standing there looking at Joe Scandore, like, *What did Jim do?* Jim says, "Yeah, La La," he was very Italian, he said, "Yeah, I just flew back from California," he said. "I ran Phil around the fucking table." *Excuse me?* I'm a child, standing up getting ready to cry because . . . *why did you do that to Phil? Why you going to hurt him?* I adored Phil, because I know no better. This is in my head, and Joe Scandore and Jim is talking, and Jim is a big mafioso, big Italian guy, and he said, "Yeah, La La, I ran Phil around the fucking table, and I told Phil if you don't put a record out on The Crystals, I'll break his legs, and I'll kill his fucking mother."

So I'm like, *Oh my God. Why are you going to do that to Phil?* Then Jim says, "Yeah, Joe, and you should have saw him with his short ass running around the table, trying to get away from me."

DEE DEE KENNIEBREW, The Crystals: William Morris became our booking agents and it was a guy named Wally Amos, the one who made the Famous Amos cookies. He was one of our agents from William Morris—so we were booking with a big agency.

We had a guy who put Sam Cooke's act together, who we had toured with for many months—we had his guys put together a completely polished nightclub act for us.

LA LA BROOKS, The Crystals: And he put us in this club with the gowns and all—$5,000 act. You had to do, [*singing*] *"I can only give you love that lasts forever."*

DEE DEE KENNIEBREW, The Crystals: And $5,000 from us was a lot of money at that time. But we paid it because we thought it would pay off in the long run. We were looking to go into the better clubs and we never did get there. He didn't put us there. I don't know why, but he didn't. He put us in his club.

LA LA BROOKS, The Crystals: He owned the Elegante on Ocean Parkway in Brooklyn. We'd have to sing songs like, [*singing*] "*Kansas City, here I come.*" I hated them songs. But anyway, he had the audience for that, right? Like the Copacabana. When I used to come offstage, there used to be rich men in the audience—producers—and they'd grab me as a kid and they'd hand me their card and they'd say, "Here, take this card. You don't need them." 'Cause my voice was big and I was strong. "I'll make you the biggest star. Your voice is *too unique, too different* to stay with them. I'll make you a singer." And I'd say, "No, I can't leave them."

DEE DEE KENNIEBREW, The Crystals: Joe really didn't put us in better places. We had the costumes, we had the act down, we had the vocals . . . but they just didn't put us where we felt we needed, you know, we wanted to go. So of course this again caused dissension.

LA LA BROOKS, The Crystals: They used to tell me to leave them and I always was saying, "I could never leave them." But I guess he was grooming me, because I could sing so well, and I was a pretty little girl. So he said, "I'm going to make her a star, and just get rid of The Crystals." Because that's how *they think*, try to make you big.

DEE DEE KENNIEBREW, The Crystals: One of The Playboys on one of the Dick Clark tours, oh, he was funny and everybody liked him—really handsome kid. And I think he started liking me and I think she got jealous of that . . . because then she began to be kind of mean to me. And I didn't know why because we were . . . you know . . . she was my closest friend and ally in the group.

LA LA BROOKS, The Crystals: Dee Dee would check on everything and Joe didn't like that. And when I used to go up to his office, he said, "I want her out," and I was close to Dee Dee and then we sort of . . . kind of fell apart.

I think I went through missing my sister at home and Dee Dee became my sister. And then when she started dating, it was like I lost my sister on the road and I got mad at Dee Dee. We used to always have the room together . . . and it was like I was being . . . she just was my sister.

BARBARA ALSTON, The Crystals: Dee Dee and La La would gang up on the rest of us on varying occasions. I remember walking out of arguments with the two of them on several occasions and just throwing up my hands and giving up. I should have known that anybody with half a brain knew not to argue with Dee Dee. La La would always laugh at me and Dee Dee would always nag at me. Mary and I used to call her "the nag." After a round with her, I always felt like I needed a joint.

DEE DEE KENNIEBREW, The Crystals: "A woman can't do this" and "a woman can't do that"—and a lot of times the girls didn't really want to hear it. Because, *remember,* I'm one of the youngest. Who am I to lay down the law? And I'm trying to be like my mom was to me. "Don't do that because guys are going to talk about you, don't do this because of so-and-so. We don't want to wear those clothes." Unless you really were focused on what you wanted to do in your life, or you had a manager or somebody who really was, you know, in your corner, which we never had, you just really weren't going to make it.

LA LA BROOKS, The Crystals: I loved her, Dee Dee was my sister. And then when she was wanting to date, I didn't want her to date 'cause she's my sister. So I think that was the problem.

DEE DEE KENNIEBREW, The Crystals: But she started getting mean to me, she started to tell lies on me, and I just was like, *Okay, I'll just stay away from her because I don't know why she's doing that.* I didn't do anything to her, but it was her own insecurity.

La La had a very envious nature, and I don't know why—I didn't think I was that pretty, but she began to then, you know, say things about me behind my back and just childish, stupid stuff. I guess had we had stronger management and been more mature it wouldn't have happened . . . you know, but it did.

LA LA BROOKS, The Crystals: Joe used to tell me, "You are the group. You have the voice. I can make you the star. You can get anybody to background sing."

DEE DEE KENNIEBREW, The Crystals: So eventually the group broke up and La La put me out. She put me out. She told Joe Scandore, "I just can't work with her anymore."

LA LA BROOKS, The Crystals: How the *hell* is a seventeen-year-old going to put a girl out of the group? I may have been pissed with her and said, "I don't care if she leaves," but she held that against me. "La La put me out of the group." I didn't even have that weight. Joe wanted her out and he was the Mafia and he definitely wanted her out because she . . . Dee Dee was smart, and she would look at everything, you know.

DEE DEE KENNIEBREW, The Crystals: She got Joe to put me out. She told him, "I can't work with her anymore," and she brought in her niece.

LA LA BROOKS, The Crystals: Today Dee Dee thinks I put her out of the group and Joe Scandore gave everything to me and I started a group without her.

DEE DEE KENNIEBREW, The Crystals: I was just, like, in total shock.

LA LA BROOKS, The Crystals: Joe took me underneath his wing, like a daughter. He told my mother, brought my mother in the office, and said, "I'll make her the biggest star." But then I got afraid of him when he did something with Dee Dee's husband—put a gun to his head in the street and told them not to work as The Crystals. There was only gonna be one Crystals—that was me.

And then what happened was when I started seeing my husband, I was seventeen . . . which I shouldn't have been seeing him . . . but anyway, Joe Scandore ended up taking everything from me. Because there's one thing the Mafia don't want you to do, they don't want you to fall in love, because he can't control you then.

He took me to the side and he said to me, "Do you have a boyfriend?" I say, "No . . . sort of." He says, "That's not what you want. You don't have a boyfriend." Joe says to me, "La La," with that Italian accent, "you like any boys? You think about dating?" And I'd say, "No." And he'd say to me, "Okay." He says, "If you're thinking about dating, you have feelings for guys or whatever like that," this is what he told me, I've never forgotten, he said, "and they want to do something, have sex with you," he says, "don't ever have sex." He said, "Just let them feel on you."

DEE DEE KENNIEBREW, The Crystals: It's very hard for a woman. You get caught up in so many things, especially young girls, you know. You have to do the right thing, you have to make the right choices, and you can't do *this*, you can't do *that*, or people will call you names.

LA LA BROOKS, The Crystals: So I'm sitting here feeling so uncomfortable, because my dad didn't talk like this. So he said, "You hear me?" I said, "Yeah, Joe." He said, "Because all girls get pregnant and I don't want you to get pregnant. So don't let him go inside, just let him feel on you." I said, "Okay."

But then he found out that I did have a boyfriend. He took the car.

BARBARA ALSTON, The Crystals: They quit a few months later. La La became pregnant and decided to get married.

LA LA BROOKS, The Crystals: He found out that I was dating, and I had the car, and my husband—he was my boyfriend at the time—he used to drive it. And one time I told my husband to take it to his house, because I couldn't keep it on my mother's street, and I went there and it was gone. So he made sure he took everything back and I never investigated it 'cause I knew it was serious, like he must have got Mafia people to take it right from the street. I never called him. I never asked him, I never said anything. I let them have it because he was angry because he was wanting to make me a big star. I was at seventeen when he took the car. And then I married at nineteen.

CHAPTER 32

A Family Divided

The Ronettes

SCOTT ROSS, Nedra Ross's husband: I had left WINS and gone to a station in Long Island, and I was a disc jockey. I was really quite successful, actually, in New York, Connecticut, etc. And then The Beatles came in. I saw Nedra with the girls, and we went up to see them. So through that, we started talking more.

Nedra was always something. . . . I don't know how to explain it really. . . . She was very non-showbiz. I remember going to a party at the Dakota and Nedra was supposed to come, but she went home. It was a very *big deal*, 'cause it was a party for the Stones. And I saw so many people using each other and lying and wheeling and dealing. Nedra was not like that.

The Ronettes were doing a show in Long Island and I went to the show, and then after the show, because I had a car, I said to Nedra, "Are you going back to the city?" She says, "Yeah, I'm going to a family party."

NEDRA TALLEY-ROSS, The Ronettes: I asked the girls if I could ride back to the city with him, because we didn't separate. And I started introducing the family to him. I had known him for probably five years, so I wasn't concerned about my safety with him.

So the next day—it was December, we were putting together Christmas toys for my little cousin. It was a nice little apartment on Riverside Drive. And I'm thinking, *I've been liking him since I was sixteen years old*. Finally, I'm in this galley kitchen with him . . . so he came towards me and he kissed me . . . and it was like the song "Then He Kissed Me," and I swear—I hadn't been dating anybody for about eight, nine months—and I saw stars and steam came out my ears, the top of my head got hot . . . like, the blood pressure—I had a high blood pressure attack at nineteen years old. [*laughing*]

SCOTT ROSS, Nedra Ross's husband: There were obviously many members of the family comparing me with Phil Spector and how important and successful Spector was. I was on trial in many ways, but I never for a moment compared myself to Spector, nor did I envy him at *all*.

✻

RONNIE SPECTOR, The Ronettes: I didn't even go on The Beatles' tour.

SCOTT ROSS, Nedra Ross's husband: The Ronettes were on—they came on right before The Beatles. The Beatles wanted them *and* the Stones wanted to tour with them. I got close to Brian Epstein, The Beatles' manager, and he was asking me what I thought about The Ronettes, and I, *of course*, espoused them and spoke highly of them. [*laughing*]

NEDRA TALLEY-ROSS, The Ronettes: I did the lead and Ronnie was in the midst of . . . our producer sort of going, "Well, I need you to do this." He was just jealous.

MELANIE MINTZ, writer: It was one of these things, which is very common, by the way, he didn't want her to perform. Why? Because if she went on the road with The Beatles, you think people weren't trying to get in her pants *every day*?

NEDRA TALLEY-ROSS, The Ronettes: He didn't want her near The Beatles because of insecurity for himself. It was probably valid. I'm not saying anything more than that . . . it was probably valid. [*laughing*] And she listened to him and didn't do it. So she didn't do what she should have done. But *we* had a great tour. . . . Jimi Hendrix was our guitarist. He traveled with us on the road.

RONNIE SPECTOR, The Ronettes: And The Ronettes did go on tour. But I didn't. It was an ultimatum. My ex-husband said "me or The Beatles." He said, "I'm gonna make your hit record bigger than 'I Want to Hold Your Hand.'" I said, *Is he crazy? Or am I delusional or is he delusional for thinking he can do this or pull it off?*

NEDRA TALLEY-ROSS, The Ronettes: He promised that he would make her a star, but only if you don't do the show with The Beatles, and she went for it. That's when she began to think, "Well, I could do this on my own and he loves me and he wants me." And I'm going, "He's playing you. He's not stable." That's not love—possessing somebody—you're squeezing them to death—but it's slowly squeezing, and you don't know that you're being choked to death.

SCOTT ROSS, Nedra Ross's husband: Their other cousin Elaine looks a lot like the girls.

NEDRA TALLEY-ROSS, The Ronettes: She was a singer herself and she was very pretty. She was our cousin, so she could fit into the clothes. But I did the lead for all of those times and it was fun.

SCOTT ROSS, Nedra Ross's husband: My radio show, it got so popular that Sid Bernstein, who brought The Beatles into Shea Stadium, said he was being inundated by phone calls of people that wanted me to be one of the emcees.

After that Shea Stadium event, we were in the car and trying to drive out. Now, it's a Bentley, it's a British car—and then people see Estelle, they see me—I had long hair then. They jumped the car and were going *nuts* because they thought it was a Beatle, and there was one of The Ronettes. They were rocking the car, beating on it, everything else. And the police on horseback came and rescued us from that event. They got us out of there. It was scary, *really*. Estelle was yelling, "We're going to die, we're going to die!"

NEDRA TALLEY-ROSS, The Ronettes: I didn't go with them when they left Shea Stadium that night because my mother called and said, "I need to talk to you, I really need to talk to you, Nedra." I got in my car and I left at the end of the show and I went to my mom to talk to her and she asked me not to marry—to call off my plans to get married. I didn't have the date set, but we were going to get married that year, and she said, "Just give me a year to see if I feel this is right." And I respected what she wanted, and I called it off.

SCOTT ROSS, Nedra Ross's husband: I had a good relationship with almost every member of Nedra's family *except* Nedra's mother. Nedra had never had a New York City boyfriend. I kept arm's length from her and she always also tried to influence the rest of the family against me. That was *quite* a clan, but they were a great family. I would go to their events and go to their houses and their apartments and eat there and everything else—but they didn't let Sue know that. They had to keep it under cover. I did it on the sly.

NEDRA TALLEY-ROSS, The Ronettes: So the night of the big Shea Stadium Beatles—you know, fifty-five thousand people—I was at the house, calling off my engagement, breaking my heart. *But* I did it. My mother was not pro me marrying my husband. She had groomed me for more than what she felt I could have had with Scott.

SCOTT ROSS, Nedra Ross's husband: Her mother lived on the bottom floor downstairs and her other cousins lived on an upper floor. I would go into the elevator to go to the upper-floor apartment and bypass Sue and Nedra. Nedra would come there and meet me—it was a clandestine kind of relationship.

NEDRA TALLEY-ROSS, The Ronettes: She was a strong woman and she was a force to reckon with, and I had never busted my mother on *anything*. My mother was so upset, *so upset*. She was like, "Nedra, give me a year to adjust to this." I was twenty years old, and she's asking me to give her a year . . . to not be with him, and if she was okay then, she'd give her approval.

*

NEDRA TALLEY-ROSS, The Ronettes: I felt that Phil was controlling Ronnie, but sometimes people can make you think that they love you *so* much, that they're only asking things of you because they love you. And so many women want to believe, *It's only because he loves me that he's doing these things.*

RONNIE SPECTOR, The Ronettes: Phil said, "I don't want anybody to see you but me," so I wasn't allowed to go with Cher anymore, or Darlene, I wasn't allowed to see the other girls. I was sort of just left with him all the time.

NEDRA TALLEY-ROSS, The Ronettes: We would be on tour and we would always sleep together. So we'd be in the room trying to go to sleep, he would call and say, "Don't hang up the phone." We didn't have cell phones back then . . . he wanted her to not hang up the phone so at any point he could say, "Ronnie," and she'd say, "Yeah." So he knew where she was at.

RONNIE SPECTOR, The Ronettes: I'd just leave my phone off the hook all night.

NEDRA TALLEY-ROSS, The Ronettes: And I'm sure for her, she was thinking, "Well, he's Phil Spector, he's a producer, he'll be producing me."

RONNIE SPECTOR, The Ronettes: In the morning I'd pick it up and there would be Phil, yawning and saying, "Good morning, baby. Did you sleep well?"

NEDRA TALLEY-ROSS, The Ronettes: I was saying, "He's controlling you, Ronnie, and he's a married man, so this is not doing good at all. This is not the way you go."

RONNIE SPECTOR, The Ronettes: So I never got a chance to be in the studio having fun. They would turn off the microphones and I could see their faces and see them having fun, but I didn't know what, 'cause I was always sat in the control booth with Phil. And from that day on it got worse and worse. I just got more secluded from everything.

NEDRA TALLEY-ROSS, The Ronettes: He did have little man syndrome—there is such a thing as little man syndrome—and *he had it*. I knew Phil was not her type of guy. Because when you grow up together, you know what look is there. Phil had none of those things. All he had to offer was his gift as a producer. . . . And he was a *great* producer.

*

SCOTT ROSS, Nedra Ross's husband: I went to Maryland because my draft board wanted me to get drafted and go to Vietnam. My mother was a praying mother, always praying for her son. We sat there and a preacher preached some sermon, the pastor preached—he did what was called "an appeal" for anybody there who wanted to make a commitment to God and to Christ to come forward. Nedra grabs my hand and says, "This is for us," and I said, "This is for *you*." She said, "No, I'm going up to the front of the church."

NEDRA TALLEY-ROSS, The Ronettes: The word was, from the preacher, "There are two that are here today." I knew it was us.

SCOTT ROSS, Nedra Ross's husband: She grabbed my hand. Anyway, I went up with her and knelt down and then so much of my teaching that I've been taught from my childhood and younger years started washing over me. . . . It was a revisitation. . . . I remember slamming my head into the wall, my fist, and saying, "God, I want you! I don't want church!" I made a tentative commitment, but I knew *something* had happened. We went back to New York, but things had changed. I knew they had changed.

NEDRA TALLEY-ROSS, The Ronettes: The family thought, "You've got to be crazy. You need to get a psychiatrist for her." That's how serious it was, the change—it was like, "What are you talking about? You belong to Convent Avenue Baptist Church since you were nine years old," but it was a whole 'nother thing. When we went to New York, the sky was different, the air was different. It takes *a lot* for New York to be different.

RONNIE SPECTOR, The Ronettes: We never made a big plan to split up.

NEDRA TALLEY-ROSS, The Ronettes: We were a trio. We always shared the money three ways, thirty-three and one-third for each girl. And so then Ronnie said, "Well, I sweat more than you when we dance, so I work harder than you." So I was going, "No, your glands are more active than mine." [*laughing*] I thought that was a very good answer. *No, you don't work harder than me, you're out front.* But we had a great sound, it was working, so why would we not keep it going?

RONNIE SPECTOR, The Ronettes: It just seemed like the natural thing to do.

NEDRA TALLEY-ROSS, The Ronettes: We had hints of that when Ronnie was dropping little things, and my whole thing was we were a trio from childhood. You're not going to change midstream and not be a trio. I used to only think in thirds.

Estelle was softer. Estelle would go, "Well, if Ronnie wants it, just let her have it." And I was like, "No, I can't." I just *couldn't*, because it was the principle of the thing, we were a *trio*.

It was Ronnie saying, "I want to be a single star." You see that in a lot of groups. But for us it was always a trio. So for me, I said, "The day we're not a trio, I'm out. The day we don't split five dollars, a hundred dollars, or a thousand dollars three ways—I'm out."

It was the end of '66 and I said, "You know what? I'm okay." She was like, "Oh, well, Phil's marrying me." I said, "Well, good, let him marry you. I'm going to marry Scott Ross. That's what I'm doing. I'm going to have a family. That's what I've always wanted." I lived out my contract that I had. I did the shows. I went to Germany for two weeks.

RONNIE SPECTOR, The Ronettes: Germany turned out to be The Ronettes' last tour.

NEDRA TALLEY-ROSS, The Ronettes: I guess I was so family-oriented, it did not bring me my satisfaction. My satisfaction was my family. I enjoyed the applause, all those things I worked towards . . . but there were other things. I said, "You know what? You can have it. I just don't care."

I had sort of come into my own . . . my own strength. Now, this is a year after I called off the wedding, and so I felt that my mom had to accept that, you know, this is what I wanted to do.

SCOTT ROSS, Nedra Ross's husband: It was a very, *very* bold thing for Nedra to do—for her to choose me over her mother. It really was quite humbling. But it was the God factor, because we really do believe that the Lord brought us together. When we came to that juncture in our lives, we were putting the Lord first and prayed about things and believed that we shared that—that the Lord expressed his will for us.

NEDRA TALLEY-ROSS, The Ronettes: I knew that I was in love with Scott. I knew we had a chance, which was really God, because I didn't marry the year before with him being in the state that he was—the showbiz and all of that. At that time, he was smoking pot and all those things. The marriage would not have made it. Mommy was right.

SCOTT ROSS, Nedra Ross's husband: Prior to that, as Nedra mentioned, I was smoking dope, I was dropping acid, I was running around partying. We would have never made it, not as a marriage. We never would have.

NEDRA TALLEY-ROSS, The Ronettes: We got married on Lexington Avenue, 62nd Street, at the Rock Church in March of '67. Ronnie married Phil April of '68. Phil Spector took us where we went with his sound . . . but it split us.

BILLY VERA, musician: He moved her out to Los Angeles and then we didn't see them again. They sorta went off the radar.

NEDRA TALLEY-ROSS, The Ronettes: But once we married, when I said, "Mom, we got married last night," she said, "What God put together, let no man put asunder," and she gave us a big reception. A catered reception at our home. She accepted it totally.

SCOTT ROSS, Nedra Ross's husband: Fifty-six years later, it proved to be right.

CHAPTER 33

Lost in the Shuffle

Red Bird Closes Its Doors

BARBARA ANN HAWKINS, The Dixie Cups: We went back home. And it was the record company that called us and told us that we had a number one record on our hands and we had to move to New York. We said, "Move to New York?" So they made arrangements, or somebody did, for us to stay at the Bryant Hotel. It had a really rickety, rickety elevator. Every time you got on the elevator, you didn't know if you were going to make it up to where you were going or not.

ROSA LEE HAWKINS, The Dixie Cups: When we moved to New York, we learned that New York was overrun with girl groups, between New York and New Jersey.

BARBARA ANN HAWKINS, The Dixie Cups: And then there was this new apartment building, 300 West 55th Street.

TONI WINE, session singer: I moved to 300 West 55th Street, which was called the Westerly, and the building had a yellow awning, and the entrance was on Eighth Avenue between 54th and 55th. Diagonally across the street was 888 Eighth Avenue. Brooks Arthur was at 888. Those were the two buildings that most music people would be living in. Especially singer girls, because no woman would want their daughter on any of the side streets there, it was really not a safe area. But 888 and my building were doormanned apartment buildings and were both within walking distance of 1650 Broadway, the Brill Building, and every studio.

BARBARA ANN HAWKINS, The Dixie Cups: So we got an apartment there on the fourth floor with a doorman and everything. A lot of the people that lived in the Westerly were in the entertainment field. There was a guy who did a commercial—the Man from Glad, he lived there.

TONI WINE, session singer: The whole entire music industry was between 46th Street and 58th Street. You could walk to any appointment and just be as safe as possible in such a wonderfully seedy area. Howard Johnson's was three blocks away, and I would get my lemon ice cream. Farrah Fawcett was on my floor.

ROSA LEE HAWKINS, The Dixie Cups: The manager of the apartment building liked us, realized we were in a situation not of our own making, but having observed Joe Jones as a tenant, he warned us, "I keep an eye on you ladies, and you really need to get away from that man. He is not doing you all any good." The Dixie Cups didn't take the warning seriously. . . .

At some point, Joe had shelves put into our dining room and made it his office, telling us when we were on the road that he was going to use our place. So he changed the locks, keeping a key for himself. That meant he could get in and out of the apartment anytime he wanted. He wouldn't even ring the bell, just walk in. . . . We had only one bedroom—Barbara and Joan slept in the double bed in the bedroom, and I had the pull-out bed to myself in the living room. . . .

He knew I slept in the living room, and one night after our European trip, he came into the apartment. Everyone was asleep, but I woke up. When he came to the pull-out bed, he whispered, "I know you're not sleeping." And proceeded to take off his clothes. I tried to keep pretending I was asleep, but before I knew it, he was on top of me. . . .

I was just out of high school when we came north to New York. I really never even had a boyfriend. I had a date to prom, but it wasn't as if we were really tight. Not only was I a virgin, I never even watched these kinds of sexual situations at the movies or on television. I was so naive, I didn't even realize what was happening to me was rape. . . . This went from one night to two nights to three nights to whenever we were home and he felt like doing it. If I complained or fought back, he would say to me, "I'm going to send you back to New Orleans on a

Greyhound bus." He said he would then call my mother and tell her that I had been with the men in the band and they all said they had had me. He would tell my mother that after the tour, all the guys bragged I had been with all of them. I was a teenager, but emotionally and experientially I had not yet grown up. He had guardianship over me . . . he knew he could do whatever he wanted to me.

*

JERRY LEIBER, songwriter: I was walking down Broadway, not far from our offices in the Brill Building. I had just bought two pairs of red suspenders from a street vendor for my little boys when an enormous Black hand draped itself over my right shoulder. "Sal wants to see you."

BILLY VERA, musician: Goldner was a degenerate gambler. And so he was always getting into trouble with these Mob guys. And so, one day they show up, and really the gangsters own their company.

MIKE STOLLER, songwriter: George was a bad gambler, loved the horses—always bet on the horses—always lost. He'd lost a few labels that he'd started that were successful. He'd lost them at the track, so he was always borrowing money. Some of the people that he borrowed from were starting to hang around our office and we decided that we didn't want to hang out with them.

ARTIE RIPP, music executive: He was disappointed in himself. He was embarrassed that Morris Levy got him three times. He put himself in the hands of the devil. And the devil was nearby to suck his blood, take his talent, and benefit from it—and that was sad. Because George was an artist. Morris wasn't an artist. Morris was a tough guy. He was like a commander. George was wonderful.

MIKE STOLLER, songwriter: It was a Monday in March of 1966. Monday seemed like the best day to do it. Jerry and I had talked about it all weekend and we didn't see any other way out. . . .

"George," I said, "how in the world could you do this to us? Put us in jeopardy by bringing in the wiseguys?" "It's only temporary," George said. "Once I pay them off, they'll be out of here. It's nothing to worry about." Jerry and I, two nice Jewish boys, were somehow in the business with the wiseguys.

JERRY LEIBER, songwriter: He was always into some *very heavy* shylocks, and they'd come up, and they were always polite and always well dressed. But you could look in their eyes, and you could tell that you could disappear in thirty seconds.

BOB FELDMAN, songwriter: They just closed down Red Bird. That's it—partnership was over—they didn't want what's hanging over George to touch them.

BROOKS ARTHUR, sound engineer: Rumor has it . . . I think that they sold it to George Goldner for a dollar.

BILLY VERA, musician: "Here's a dollar. Go away."

JEFF BARRY, songwriter: It just all went away. Just all went away.

BOB FELDMAN, songwriter: What happened with it? Closed shop. And they ended their partnership with George. I mean, he was gambling and owed a shylock some money and all that. I tell you, Jerry and Mike, they were upstanding. You never heard a bad word about either one of them, correct?

MIKE STOLLER, songwriter: We started our string of little labels at the end of 1962. By spring of 1966, we were out. It had been a helluva run. We were amazed at the number one hits. The last one to chart, ironically enough, was called "Past, Present, and Future," sung by The Shangri-Las. History would establish Red Bird as one of the most successful independent labels of the era.

Our material rivaled the best of Motown. But the great bulk of our material was generated by others—primarily Ellie, Jeff, and Shadow. True, our supervision was critical. We helped sculpt the songs and oversaw many productions. But the girl group aesthetic was not our aesthetic. We appreciated it, we encouraged it, we profited from it, but we did not love it the way we loved the blues we had written for Big Mama Thornton or the rollicking R & B we had written and produced for The Coasters.

JEFF BARRY, songwriter: I think it was twenty releases and seventeen hits, or something like that. So it was great, it was fun and great.

And, did anybody ever get paid everything they should've during that whole time? Probably not, probably not.

*

LAURA WEINER, Ellie Greenwich's sister: One of the things my sister always used to say, she was so fortunate that she met the guy that she could really harmonize with. They were able to just share this wonderful talent that they both had. It was wonderful that they were able to, but then again, it was not a good thing, at some point.

ELLIE GREENWICH, songwriter: I grew up in Levittown, Long Island, on the corner of Starlight and Springtime Lane. . . . I really believed in that little house with a white picket fence and together forevermore, and absolutely, I was really a dreamer. I think that still could happen—unfortunately, it didn't happen for us. I think that was partly the business split, but, yes, I was very much a hopeful romantic.

JEFF BARRY, songwriter: Our time together . . . it was more about creating and writing than it was as a romantic couple—as a male–female relationship, honestly. That's the way I emotionally recall it.

BROOKS ARTHUR, sound engineer: I couldn't help but notice. They were family—brother and sister to me. They were my kids' godparents. They were facing some trying times. And we still had to power through it to get our work done . . . and there were difficulties at times doing that. You couldn't—for lack of a better term, and in pure honesty—sometimes you couldn't get it up, you know, because you felt so down.

LAURA WEINER, Ellie Greenwich's sister: It was very hard for her. Definitely. Because I think that she was hoping that maybe they could maybe fix what was wrong. But at that time, I guess it wasn't meant to be.

JEFF BARRY, songwriter: Yes, it of course was uncomfortable. Not so much working with, but, you know, I went on and had another relationship. So yeah, it was uncomfortable. How could it not be?

LAURA WEINER, Ellie Greenwich's sister: That was the thought process then when you got married. You work it out. You got to work everything out, and they couldn't work that part of their relationship out. I think the music was in the way a little bit. Not that that's what broke them, but I don't think it helped the relationship.

ELLIE GREENWICH, songwriter: We tried to write together right after the split-up, but it was awful. We couldn't sit and write "Baby, I Love You" with divorce papers sitting right next to us.

SUSAN COLLINS, singer and best friend of Ellie Greenwich: When Jeff and Ellie split up, Ellie became a recluse. When they split up, she was still under contract with Leiber and Stoller. And they were pretending they were together, but they were not. And it was very difficult for Ellie because she still had to work with Jeff. After that ended, she became a recluse . . . a real recluse.

LAURA WEINER, Ellie Greenwich's sister: But, yeah, my sister was unhappy at that time. Very, very unhappy. And it was not as accepted then either, in that time. You were almost like wearing the letter *A*—you would read the letter *D* for Divorced.

ELLIE GREENWICH, songwriter: It was a very devastating time for me with the British Invasion coming in, Jeff's and my divorce. I had a hard time for many years trying to adapt to all this stuff . . . because I had only known one thing, and it was so wonderful. Then all of a sudden to have all these misses happen. . . . I was never quite able to put it in proper perspective.

SUSAN COLLINS, singer: Ellie couldn't handle anything to do with Jeff, just nothing.

ELLIE GREENWICH, songwriter: One of the things that did happen, fortunately for both Jeff and I, I discovered a guy named Neil Diamond. And at that time, we opened up a company called Tallyrand Music. And Neil actually wrote for the company, and Jeff and I coproduced all his early records.

NEIL DIAMOND, singer, songwriter: If I hadn't met Ellie Greenwich, I wouldn't have had a career. I met her at a demo session. I had enough in my budget to hire a few background singers, and even though Ellie was one of the hottest writers in the country, she still did background dates just because she liked to hang out with her girlfriends. She liked my voice or she liked the song or something, and she took me back to meet her husband, Jeff Barry, and they got me signed to Leiber and Stoller, and that lasted a year.

I got canned from that job, but Jeff and Ellie said, "Hey, how 'bout we produce you?" We got a record deal with Bang Records and the rest is history. Ellie was the best background singer ever. She did all the background parts on my early Bang Records, "Cherry, Cherry"—"she got the way to move me"—"Kentucky Woman"—all of those records were Jeff and Ellie. They just had this great knack of singing all kinds of background parts and they were great at it. She invented the background parts to "Cherry, Cherry." The background parts of "she got the way to move me" were not part of the song.

SUSAN COLLINS, singer: She made up the backgrounds on every single session she did. And back in the day, singers, we're not getting credit as arrangers. You know, now it's a whole different ballgame.

ELLIE GREENWICH, songwriter: So we sort of, we were now not writing for people but we were producing and had a little company and we had our own self-contained person. And Neil, that's when his career started, it was, like, in the mid-sixties, '66–'67, in there.

JEFF BARRY, songwriter: I packed up and moved out of New York in 1970 and moved to LA. Just took all my artists and moved everybody out here.

ELLIE GREENWICH, songwriter: And I got involved in doing jingles, commercials, radio spots, the singing on them, and that wasn't what . . . you know, I didn't feel totally alive, like writing songs and doing what I did made me feel. But it did eke out a living and it did allow me to still do my music. The seventies, for me, was not my best time . . . and I didn't go to drugs and I didn't go to alcohol, but I did fall apart.

MELANIE MINTZ, writer: Ellie was only wife number two, and it only lasted for a few years, which was what their career lasted. She wasn't writing hits anymore and it was different. . . . It didn't evolve, but that was because of Ellie's choice. She stayed; they all went to LA, every single one of them because that's where the music business moved. And they were working with those people.

STEVE TYRELL, producer: Pretty much the whole Brill Building. Everybody ended up going on to LA.

BROOKS ARTHUR, sound engineer: Everybody started going west.

ALLAN PEPPER, nightclub owner: Jeff was the cowriter of *The Jeffersons* theme.

MELANIE MINTZ, writer: Jeff, he went on, but Ellie could never go on. She never recuperated from that whole thing. You can never say Ellie was exploited. She had every opportunity in the world. It didn't work for her.

ARTIE BUTLER, musician: I moved to Los Angeles in '67, and out of sight, out of mind. I only spoke to her when I went to New York. I'd have dinner with her, a lunch or breakfast, or even a cup of coffee. I talked to her once in a while and I tried to get her to move out here. I said, "Ellie, my son doesn't live here anymore, he's out on his own, come and stay here as long as you want and stay in his room." But she wouldn't make the move or even come out and visit. I don't know. All I can tell you is that I love her dearly and I send her a kiss right now.

✳

ROSA LEE HAWKINS, The Dixie Cups: Joe Jones, he broke the contract. He asked for money for something and they refused him. So he said, "I'm going to show them." So he went over to ABC-Paramount and they were interested in us because of our harmonies. They said they would make us the next McGuire Sisters. So we did an album for them and it was being played—they released one of the songs and the song was going up the charts. But then we were the ones that got shafted because Red Bird wanted to sue ABC-Paramount, so they were fighting. So there we are, caught in the middle. Now we don't have a song on the charts because they pulled it.

GEORGE "SHADOW" MORTON, producer: The girls of The Shangri-Las became "The Shadowettes." I mean, they disappeared. They vacated and a lot of the other groups who were with Red Bird, it just seemed . . . like dust. It just disappeared, as if it never was. Except we can still hear the music.

MARY WEISS, The Shangri-Las: My mother kind of signed my life away when I was fourteen. . . . I'm laughing. Thirty years of litigation. There's a storeroom of litigation up to the ceiling. That's one of the reasons I walked away. The litigation was much thicker than the music. I couldn't go near another record label for ten years. Everybody around us was suing each other. Basically, to me, the litigation just got so insane and it wasn't about music anymore.

ROSA LEE HAWKINS, The Dixie Cups: Barbara and I decided to continue our career without Joe. Other agents were not going to touch us as long as there existed an association with Joe Jones.

MARY WEISS, The Shangri-Las: I moved out on my eighteenth birthday. I moved into a hotel in Manhattan . . . and then I moved to San Francisco for a while. It was hard to get into the music business and it was even harder to get out. I couldn't go near another record company for ten years.

ROSA LEE HAWKINS, The Dixie Cups: Joe was going to the different companies and asking them for money if they wanted to book us, and what have you. So some of the agents would stop booking us. And we had one guy at a very famous company and he said, "Listen, I love you ladies. You're one of the best female groups I've seen in a long time. You work hard." He said, "But as long as you're with Joe, I can't book ya." And of course we were hurt and we even had some tears there and they said, "I just don't want to get into that," because he had talked to his lawyers and his lawyer said it's "not worth it," "yes, they are great, but maybe one day they'll get away from him." . . . As far as the music industry was concerned, The Dixie Cups had fallen through the cracks.

MARY WEISS, The Shangri-Las: I lost my way. It was real rough.

ROSA LEE HAWKINS, The Dixie Cups: Joe would say if they booked The Dixie Cups, he was going to throw an injunction at them.

MARY WEISS, The Shangri-Las: I could have pursued it further, but how much deeper do you want to get into legal nonsense? At some point you just have to cut it off. I always thought that someday I'd go back to music, I just didn't know when.

ROSA LEE HAWKINS, The Dixie Cups: That's when Barbara and I opted to find jobs outside the music industry, thinking if we could just hold on long enough, Joe would be out of the picture. . . . Joe figured out we were working and came to our apartment asking for money. . . . We sold all our furniture to a girlfriend who was moving to the big city. By the winter of 1969, The Dixie Cups had returned to New Orleans.

CHAPTER 34

A New Music Business for the Next Generation

TONI WINE, session singer: When Aldon became Screen Gems, you had the door open to anything Columbia Pictures was a part of—and that would have been songs for movies, songs for television, songs for series. It just became a very big, big, *big* business. It also wasn't as personal . . . but sometimes there are good things that come from not being that personal. All of a sudden, we could go to LA for a couple of months and stay at the corporate apartment and write for some situation that may be happening out there. Just a lot of different doors were open.

RON DANTE, musician: After the Screen Gems thing, people kind of left when their contracts were up, although Kirshner got them tons of money. I mean, he did great things for them. . . . But people kind of floated apart and did their own thing.

CAROLE KING, songwriter: *Wait a minute, what's happening? Things are changing. How do we write this stuff? What do we write?* Innocence started to go away then.

GERRY GOFFIN, songwriter: I wish we had tried more to write songs that really meant something. We wrote about eight throwaways for The Monkees.

CAROLE KING, songwriter: I knew that he had a gift. But I didn't realize how great the gift was until much later, but he had a gift for taking the most simple words and expressing profound concepts. I mean if you look at . . . taking all those words, there's no fancy words. There's no fancy rhymes.

And he was a very, very sensitive person. I mean, this is before the mental illness came upon him and everything. He was deeply sensitive. He was driven, in part, driven by money, as I mentioned, because he was the provider of our family and it was really important to him to succeed at that. But he was also driven by these concepts of justice and what was right and what was fair and, you know . . . but the way he did it, he was in his head all the time.

MELANIE MINTZ, writer: Gerry was trying to go off in one way . . . then Carole was going . . . they had kids and they would try to live a normal life, which Gerry wasn't interested in.

CAROLE KING, songwriter: When Gerry told me he was going to move to California without me, I didn't break down until he walked out the door. I didn't know I had that many tears. I had dreamed of that mythical man with whom I would have four beautiful, healthy children, live in a big, cheery house, and spend the rest of our lives as a happily-ever-after family.

GERRY GOFFIN, songwriter: That was the whole thing that led to Carole's and my breakup. I wanted to be a hippie—grew my hair long—and Carole did it modestly. You know, we smoked some grass together once in a while. . . . She never wanted to go overboard. And then I started taking LSD and mescaline. And Carole and I began to grow apart because she felt that she had to say things herself; she had to be her own lyricist.

CAROLE KING, songwriter: When we wrote a song, Gerry often guided me towards the realization of a concept I didn't fully understand until later. Though we worked as a team in the studio, he was credited as the sole producer and paid accordingly. At the time, this seemed logical. Production credit was customarily given to the person in control of the booth, and Gerry's contribution was essential. But I arranged and conducted, sometimes I was a band member. Sometimes I sang background, and I often directed other singers with hand and body movements from a position close by in the studio. We both did what we did because we loved the work, but because I believe credit was so important to my husband, it never even occurred to me to ask for coproducer credit on any of the Dimension recordings. Clearly, I could have benefited from the women's liberation movement, but women's lib didn't fully come into its own until later in the sixties. I had no trouble valuing Gerry, but I didn't know how to value myself.

JEFF BARRY, songwriter: He certainly changed after . . . I was never really clear on the incident, whatever. Well, I heard he accidentally ingested something that altered his thinking. But in the later years, it was more difficult . . . just very difficult to communicate with him.

CAROLE KING, songwriter: I don't believe Gerry knew he was dropping acid the first time he ingested it. I believe someone who thought he was doing him a favor slipped it into his coffee. It wasn't a favor. After that, Gerry took LSD many more times on his own. He lost touch with reality at first for days, then for weeks at a time for many years afterwards, with intermittent periods of lucidity, creativity, and wisdom.

MELANIE MINTZ, writer: So there were other issues going on.

CAROLE KING, songwriter: At first a doctor had diagnosed Gerry as schizophrenic. Then they decided he was manic and treated him with massive doses of Thorazine to bring him down. Not unpredictably, he went into a deep depression. Though his doctors adjusted his medication this way and that and brought him in for psychiatric sessions, Gerry remained in a severely depressed state. The next treatment the doctors recommended was electric shock therapy. Because their patient was incapable of rational thought—hence the need for such a drastic remedy—the decision to give consent was legally in the hands of his young wife. To say that this is one of the most agonizing decisions I've ever had to make is to grossly understate the difficulty. I was twenty-three, Gerry was twenty-six, and our daughters were five and three. I didn't see how I could possibly decide something of this magnitude on behalf of someone else, especially when every muscle in my heart, throat, lips, and tongue wanted to shout "NOOOOOOO!" But the doctors assured me that all the less obtrusive options have been exhausted and a shock treatment would restore my husband to his normal state.

STEVE TYRELL, producer: I loved Gerry and they had some issues. . . . Gerry messed around a little bit and he shouldn't have . . . but he was a sweetheart, and he was a genius too, man.

MARGARET ROSS, The Cookies: Earl-Jean and Gerry had something going on. She says it doesn't bother her anymore . . . and if you saw the daughter, she is the spitting image of Gerry. *Very* beautiful girl, *beautiful* girl. . . . She looks just like Gerry. That was a mess, but not getting into that.

RON DANTE, musician: It was pretty common knowledge, at least, in the office, and it would get Carole really upset. It was, you know, not a great time for their marriage, but, boy, their songwriting was great.

And he took care of it, I heard. I heard he supplied money for the child. He didn't run away from it.

DAWN REAVIS SMITH, Gerry Goffin and Earl-Jean McCrae's daughter: I always knew Gerry was my father, and from the time I was five, he always told me I was "planned." He said, "You were wanted, from the beginning." Later, when I was going off to college, I talked to my mom about it. She said they did plan to have me.

BARBARA BEHLING GOFFIN, Gerry Goffin's ex-wife: They had a lot of money and the Reavises were poor, it was a simple decision for them. . . . Carole's attitude was, Gerry was responsible for the baby, so they would do this.

MARGARET ROSS, The Cookies: I don't . . . because I never did . . . I didn't want to see it. Because I love Jeannie—Earl-Jean—but I just didn't . . . I didn't like that. But it was nothing I could do about it. I mean, I didn't have anything to do with it. And I got married and had my two children and moved back to Coney Island. And I've been here ever since.

BROOKS ARTHUR, sound engineer: A couple of years go by . . . the end of all the music . . . and the birth of *Tapestry*.

CAROLE KING, songwriter: It might have been the pull of all the music and media celebrating California. It might have been because

I didn't want to be left behind. But one thing above all compelled me to turn west. With Gerry moving to Los Angeles, there was no way I would deny my daughters proximity to their father. In March 1968, [daughters] Sherry, Louise, Lika [the family dog], Telemachus [the cat, who appears on the cover of *Tapestry*], and I moved to California.

✳

ALLAN PEPPER, nightclub owner: In its own way, FM radio contributed to the demise of girl groups and doo-wop.

What was happening in the country was more young people writing the music. The FM radio game went to—not the professional songwriters, the Ellie and Jeffs, the Carole Kings, you know—those were the professionals who worked in the Brill Building. They gave way to younger people who were writing about stuff that was directly affecting *them*. Because Ed Sullivan exposed a lot of rock groups—more young guys wanted to be in bands and play guitars.

DARLENE LOVE, The Blossoms: We woke up one morning and it was British music, and it was no more American music—they just came in and took over completely.

RONNIE SPECTOR, The Ronettes: The British Invasion took the girl groups away, it took the guy groups away, it took your Black artists away. There was just no room.

NEDRA TALLEY-ROSS, The Ronettes: As an American artist, I can't say I was always so happy, because what about our American artists? It was like all of a sudden the British Invasion was *it*, you know. Thank God for the Beach Boys and Frankie Valli and them, they kept the boy music going in America because people went stupid crazy.

ELLIE GREENWICH, songwriter: In came this infiltration of British artists that were a self-contained group, writing their own stuff, and we're now going, "How are we gonna place our songs?"

ALLAN PEPPER, nightclub owner: So, whereas before this, you had songs being passed on to artists who were relying on writers from the Brill Building, *now* you had young people writing *their* own songs, and the music reflecting the social ills of the country as it directly affected *these* young people.

SCOTT ROSS, Nedra Ross's husband: You listened to AM if you're more into hits, the latest hits or whatever, but FM gave us an expression outside that format. Almost kind of like independent radio or like an independent film.

JERRY LEIBER, songwriter: Records were being made differently and certain efforts by publishers were no longer required. They became anachronistic, they didn't need them anymore.

RONNIE SPECTOR, The Ronettes: All these writers just stopped. I mean, you couldn't go on because you weren't selling.

ALLAN PEPPER, nightclub owner: And on top of that, you had the Vietnam War. And you had the pushback from a lot of young people—mostly males—who didn't feel it was a just war, and they had a draft and once they had the draft, anybody was now open to going into the military. And you had all these songs that were being written having to do with criticizing society by all these young people who this war greatly affected.

MARC TAYLOR, music writer: A lot of times your appeal to the mass audience is dependent upon what's going on in the world. President Kennedy was killed, Bobby Kennedy was killed, Dr. King was killed, I mean the riots—you know—it wasn't okay. It's the Vietnam era and the Black Power movement and everything, all of a sudden. It wasn't a fun time anymore. It's just too many things happening that are really kind of sobering this country up a little bit. As the sixties came to a close, it just got more serious and the fun of those songs kind of went out of it. That's no longer fitting in 1967, 1968. And then you have the glossy, upscale soul music of Motown and the more Southern get-down soul of James Brown, Stax, Chicago soul—they dominated on the R & B charts, but none of these got to number one on pop.

But was the girl group era R & B? The major ones that we talk about, you know, like The Shirelles, it's hard to say. Who really supported the records? I mean, take The Shirelles. I don't think people really consider them Black records even though they were an African

American group—and their main writer, Luther Dixon, was African American. I think in retrospect, their music was more pop oriented—and you had people of both races enjoying the songs. Whereas, like, once the British Invasion hit, The Beatles—none of their songs chart on the R & B charts.

ARTIE BUTLER, musician: That's the thing about the records that we made in that period of time—it'll never happen again. Every generation has their statement, but this generation that I'm talking about that I came up with, it was about the *emotion*. It was about making sense of a lyric and getting the lyric across with an honest melody, with an honest deliverance from an artist. It was all about honesty and a simple emotion. You can't get any simpler than a song lyric and a great vocal performance.

ALLAN PEPPER, nightclub owner: Like, The Beatles swept some of *these* artists off charts, FM radio came in and it just changed the nature of pop music. AM was fashioned for those two-minute little short stories, "Leader of the Pack," you know, stuff like that.

So record companies were now signing more individualized artists and bands who wrote their own material, as opposed to performers who relied on the repertory created by a certain group of people. And all that came together and led to an explosion of this new generation.

SCOTT ROSS, Nedra Ross's husband: FM radio gave me the opportunity to play music that no one was hearing anywhere, except the people who bought albums.

ALLAN PEPPER, nightclub owner: The promoters of Woodstock advertised, basically, on all these hip FM radio stations. They didn't advertise on AM radio; they advertised on FM. They got a quarter of a million people—*holy shit!* And the record companies realize *there's a whole audience out here that we are not reaching and this represents a lot of money.*

Ten years later, you're not at the Fox, you're at the Fillmore East. You have young people who are now playing guitar, playing drums . . . young people see that and want to be like them—they want to play instruments, they want to write songs. It's a *whole* shift. Everything shifts and it's just as ritualistic.

PART 7

Motown Outgrows Detroit

1967–Present

CHAPTER 35

Detroit, 1967

MARTHA REEVES, The Vandellas: We were getting ready to sing "Jimmy Mack." It was going to be our next release, and I was excited about it, actually. After being held for years in the archives, Holland–Dozier–Holland was able to release "Jimmy."

ROSALIND ASHFORD, The Vandellas: When the Detroit Riots happened, we were on at the Fox Theatre.

MARTHA REEVES, The Vandellas: Robin Seymour [a Detroit DJ] called me to the edge of the stage, just as I was getting ready to introduce it and sing it, and said, "There's a riot starting in the city—if you listen, you'll hear the sirens—there are tanks in the city and we have a curfew. You must go back to the mic and announce that everybody should leave in an orderly manner, so as not to get hurt, or stampede out of the theater, but to leave, in a quiet manner. *They've got to go home.* There's a curfew."

ROSALIND ASHFORD, The Vandellas: Martha told them that they was going to stop the show—they were wanting everybody to be careful and everybody had to leave and go home.

MARTHA REEVES, The Vandellas: I was able to do that, spontaneously. Then I ad-libbed *beautifully*, being frightened myself.

ROSALIND ASHFORD, The Vandellas: Because they hadn't actually got where the Fox Theatre was—they hadn't actually got that far down in the neighborhood yet.

MARTHA REEVES, The Vandellas: It took five minutes to empty the theater out. I went back up to my dressing room. I had three or four children in there whose parents had left them with us—we'd do four shows, and sometimes the parents would bring their kids and leave them—we were actually babysitting some of the kids . . . but to get them into my personal car, and to drive them to their homes, and try to make it to our homes, because we had to leave town the next morning, as Detroit burned.

ROSALIND ASHFORD, The Vandellas: They had somebody there that was driving for us, and they picked us up and they took us straight home and had us pack. That was scary, too, because all the way home we could see people walking across the street and taking everything—anything they could find or anything they can carry, people were carrying.

MARTHA REEVES, The Vandellas: I don't know how it started, but there are rumors that there were different events in the city that caused them. The one called to my attention, by one of the people involved, was where the policemen had raided . . . they raided an after-hour joint, which used to be popular—they called them speakeasies in the forties, but in the sixties, they were after-hour joints—where people gathered and went on until the morning, with drinking and gambling or whatever activities. Not that there was any violence in the after-hour joints, they just were *caught* actually having entertainment and selling alcohol after two o'clock, whatever the law was. They raided one, and they had the men and the women lined up on the sidewalk. They were going to put some of them in jail, but they actually assaulted a lady of the night—we would call her a prostitute, I guess—she was caught in the after-hours joint on that morning. So, they took their foot, and they kicked this woman—the only woman in the crowd. That incited a riot. Those twenty or so men that were standing about wouldn't stand that. They couldn't take that brutality against a woman, no matter what her walk of life was.

That was the beginning of the riot in that particular area, on the west side. Men rebelled and actually attacked the four policemen. They called for help and backup, and that started the violence all over the city. It escalated. It was almost like this explosion of fireworks. All over the city, there was violence, and fighting, and not necessarily shooting, but rioting.

ROSALIND ASHFORD, The Vandellas: We left that night and went to the airport in order to be able to catch a flight out of Detroit.

MARTHA REEVES, The Vandellas: We had a series of one-nighters and headed for Myrtle Beach, South Carolina. We left there the next day, to Elizabeth, New Jersey, where the riots began. It ignited all over the United States. We were held up in a hotel for a day or two.

It was escalating all over the world. We left Elizabeth, New Jersey, and we flew to Harlem. From Harlem to Watts—to Los Angeles, where the riots were starting. It was like a series of explosive, eluding, fighting, shooting, and actually a rebellion of Black people.

ROSALIND ASHFORD, The Vandellas: It was a while when we came back, but everything had kind of calmed down.

MARTHA REEVES, The Vandellas: In about a week, it was calmed down. We were all relieved, the fact that the rioting had stopped and that the incidents stopped. We all tried to pick ourselves up and get back to our normal.

CHAPTER 36

Diana Ross and The Supremes

BRIAN HOLLAND, songwriter: Well, you know what? What happened was Berry said Diana Ross was gonna be "Diana Ross and The Supremes." And they—you know, Mary and Florence—they didn't particularly like that . . . 'cause Diana Ross became such a popular figure, you know what I mean?

ROSALIND ASHFORD, The Vandellas: It was '67. And that's when they started with the "Diana Ross and The Supremes."

MARY WILSON, The Supremes: The thing about it is . . . when the name, when it was said they were going to change it, it wasn't, no one said, "Great, let's do it." It was something that was very *not* what we wanted. We liked ourselves as a group.

However, if that was going to keep us at Motown, and Motown was still pushing us—whatever . . . whatever's good for the group is what we want . . . that's where it was. Obviously, I'm not talking for Diane, because I'm sure it affected her totally differently. She was *thrilled* about it. I would've been thrilled too. Florence would've been thrilled too.

MARTHA REEVES, The Vandellas: We had nothing to do with the turmoil between The Supremes. We weren't around them and didn't know what was going on with them. They were singled out. They were specialties of Berry Gordy's.

MARY WILSON, The Supremes: It wasn't something that we were happy about, but Florence and I never sat down and talked about it.

It was no longer three, it was now one and two. That was where Florence's head was, and all of her previous problems started getting bigger because they were never taken care of.

DIANA ROSS, The Supremes: Florence was not easy. She had a strong personality, just like her voice. Everything about her was big. When she was happy, it was contagious. Everybody was happy. When she was unhappy, everybody around her felt miserable. She was terribly moody, constantly up and down. And she was hard to figure out; we could never really understand what drove her moods. We never knew if we had done something to offend her and she wouldn't tell us. She'd be in some dark mood and then, miraculously and suddenly, it was over.

MAXINE BALLARD, Florence Ballard's sister: Flo told me that it was getting to the point where they couldn't be in the same room together without an argument or fight.

ROSA LEE HAWKINS, The Dixie Cups: So I'm kind of standing there, you know, 'cause everybody kind of stood off the stage to watch your act . . . and whoever it was, was announcing The Supremes when Diane said something nasty to Florence. And all of a sudden I saw somebody's fist come out somewhere—and I had to duck—and Diane and Florence was—I mean, *they were going at it*. And Mary's going, "Oh God, girls, we got to go onstage! Please stop!" They call some of the guys that was on the show and, you know, they're the ones that really just pulled them apart and said, "No, y'all can't do this. They calling you onstage."

MARY WILSON, The Supremes: There was turmoil within the group, there was turmoil with Motown. By this time, Diana was emerging as the star of The Supremes.

DIANA ROSS, The Supremes: Mary, Florence, and I were not true sisters. Other groups like The Ronettes and the Jackson Five were actually blood relatives and had been brought up in the same house. The girls and I started out as three strangers who were randomly placed together. Mary and Florence had already been friends for a short while when I was brought in, so I was the new girl who was introduced into this already existing unit. I think we did very well together considering the fact that we had just met. When difficulties arose, we did not have the kind of bond that automatically exists between family members. We didn't have the kind of commitment or understanding that, no matter what happened, we were together forever.

MELANIE MINTZ, writer: The truth is, as I said, with the exception of some of these girl groups that had these voices connected to them . . . like, there's no voice like Arlene Smith, and I feel Shirley Alston had a different kind of voice, and Diana Ross, clearly. That's why they all started to say, "What do we need them for?" Because the truth was, any other girls could do backup singing for their stuff. But other than that, The Cookies or The Chiffons and all, who was the lead singer? Who knows? And who cares? Even though they had huge hits, you just didn't know who the singer was. Diana Ross had whatever you needed to have.

MARY WILSON, The Supremes: I never really resented my role. I didn't think of it as being backup. The roots of R & B music, soul music comes from Africa, and the way . . . there's always the callers and the chanters and it's all equal. And I always felt my role in The Supremes, I was a star at what *I* was doing.

BRIAN HOLLAND, songwriter: It was great early . . . then there became a problem because Florence, she liked to drink, you know what I mean? And so that became a problem, you know. I don't want to say anything negative about Florence. I mean, I really liked Florence. But her drinking . . . you know drinking . . . that drinking will cause a whole lot of problems for a lot of people, you know what I mean?

DIANA ROSS, The Supremes: With Florence, there always seemed to be a problem. Nothing was ever right no matter how hard we tried to please her. It was difficult. Mary and I both cared for her, and we wanted her to be happy. I wanted everyone to be happy.

BERRY GORDY, music executive: There was another problem—Flo's drinking. She was showing up late for shows and interviews, skipping rehearsals, putting on too much weight.

DIANA ROSS, The Supremes: I can't remember when she started drinking, but it was sometime during the period of constant touring. At first, it was beer, but after a while, that wasn't enough to drown out her pain, she went on to hard liquor. Often, when we went onstage, she would be completely out of it and seemed as if she just didn't care. I'll never forget a show we did at the Flamingo Hotel in Las Vegas. Mary and I were thrilled to be there, it was one of the places that we never imagined at the beginning of our careers we'd get a chance to play. But here we were, as excited as we could be, and then Florence showed up, late and drunk. Our costumes were tuxedos. Florence had gained so much weight, her stomach was bulging out of her costume. We were embarrassed to go onstage with her.

PETER BENJAMINSON, Florence Ballard's biographer: Mary Wilson pointed out that Flo may have been allergic to alcohol. She'd have one drink in, like, clubs in Puerto Rico after they were offstage. You know, Diane and Mary would have one glass—they all have one glass of champagne—and Flo would start to go woozy immediately. She was alcohol affective. That's why the confusion. . . . I think she didn't drink that much. But every swallow of alcohol went right through her system.

DIANA ROSS, The Supremes: By the mid-sixties, life was becoming very difficult. We were basically living out of suitcases, touring endlessly, doing one-nighters all across the country, and recording albums, laced with touring through Europe. It was very tough to maintain stamina to keep going. You had to love singing so much, you had to want it so bad, in order to work at it that hard. Florence loved to sing, but she just didn't seem to be able to keep up with the lifestyle. She was always tired and angry, and eventually, the pressure became too much for her.

PETER BENJAMINSON, Florence Ballard's biographer: The first big blow was that Flo wasn't allowed to sing her leads anymore. She became a background person woven with Mary. Then, she noticed that

Cindy Birdsong was showing up and riding in the limousine, either the same limousine or another limousine. If I were Flo, I would have said, "Who is she? What are you doing here?" But she didn't. She was beaten down, metaphorically, by that.

FLORENCE BALLARD, The Supremes: We got to the Copacabana, and Cindy Birdsong was there. They had been grooming her with tapes for a whole year, and I didn't even have any knowledge of it. They had a whole tape of the show we were doing—the nightclub act, so she was learning the tunes and everything with the tape. Having Cindy at the Copa caused me to feel more pressure because it was as if they were saying, *We're getting ready to put you out now.*

AUTHORS' NOTE: All Florence Ballard quotes are from a series of interviews done in 1975.

PETER BENJAMINSON, Florence Ballard's biographer: So, eventually, one night when she got to the concert, they said, "I'm sorry, you're not singing—Cindy is, in your place." But that's it. That was it. She should have tried to stand up for her rights initially. You know, "I've got a contract. You're paying me. Who is she? I want to be lead." But she had been beaten down.

MAXINE BALLARD, Florence Ballard's sister: One day, Flo called to me downstairs during one of my rehearsals and said, "Mac, guess what? They think they can replace me with Cindy Birdsong. They have lost their mind." By that time, Flo had already tried to sue Motown. I can't say if she ever received any money from Motown, but I know she lost the right to identify herself with The Supremes or to collect royalties.

FLORENCE BALLARD, The Supremes: To be depressed and drink with depression can cause a whole bunch of turmoil, especially when you are actually angered, as I was toward Berry, and I just began to lose all respect for him.

BERRY GORDY, music executive: Finally, in July of 1967, we all knew she had to be replaced. At the time, we decided not to publicly disclose the reasons for Flo's dismissal. In the sixties, alcoholism was not dealt with the way it was today. It was something to be kept a secret.

FLORENCE BALLARD, The Supremes: At the particular incident at The Flamingo in Las Vegas, I had me a few drinks . . . and they kept calling me fat so much until I went onstage and I poked my stomach out as far as I could. Gordy called me up the next morning and said, "You're fired." They had Cindy already there. I don't know how long she had been there, but they had her there, and I flew back to Detroit.

CINDY BIRDSONG, The Bluebelles, The Supremes: I had twenty-four hours to get fitted with the gown. Florence wore the same dress and shoe size. She was just one inch taller than me. They didn't have time to really hem it. When I went onstage, no one even knew that it wasn't her. It happened so quickly. It was a hard thing because I loved my group, The Bluebelles. I'd been with them seven years then. Mr. Gordy had spotted me somewhere and, looking back now, they wanted to get rid of Florence because of problems. Smokey Robinson called my house in New Jersey. . . . They found the Birdsong name in the phone book. It's an unusual name.

DIANA ROSS, The Supremes: Cindy Birdsong had been singing with Patti LaBelle and The Bluebelles and we approached her. She was the same physical size as Florence, all the costumes fit her, she sang in the same key, and they had similar personas. She ended up staying on until I left three years later.

CHAPTER 37

A Girl Group Evolves

Labelle

SARAH DASH, The Bluebelles, Labelle: I have to be careful in the wording of this story. I orchestrated Cindy's leaving, but not knowing it, okay? There was a man by the name of Larry Maxwell. We were playing the Uptown Theatre and Larry was always sauntering around Cindy, or I would catch him lurking. . . .

After the show one night, I went back to [fiancé] Sam's apartment with him and the phone rang. Sam says, "Larry Maxwell is on the phone. He wants Cindy's number." And Both Sam and I thought, *Oh, wow, that's so beautiful. He wants to date her. We're in love, so we want everyone to be in love.* So, I gave Larry Maxwell Cindy's phone number. I did not know he was pursuing her to take Florence's place in The Supremes.

NONA HENDRYX, The Bluebelles, Labelle: A manager in Philadelphia, he put us together with Cindy Birdsong and a young lady called Patricia Holt, as we know as Patti LaBelle. . . . And we recorded a song. Well, Sarah and I were in a group called The Del Capris. Patti was in a group called The Ordettes with Cindy Birdsong. The two of each came together and made The Bluebelles song called "I Sold My Heart to the Junkman" that became a hit record. And next thing, I went from being going to school in Trenton High in Trenton, New Jersey, to being on *Bandstand* in Philadelphia.

PATTI LABELLE, The Bluebelles, Labelle: We were inseparable back then. Whenever you saw one, you saw four.

BILLY VERA, musician: Patti LaBelle and The Bluebelles. They were one of those acts that nobody wanted to follow 'cause, when Patti started hitting those high notes, you know, it was over. You could not follow them.

PATTI LABELLE, The Bluebelles, Labelle: I knew something wasn't right the minute [the group's manager] Mr. Montague got the call from Cindy. We had a club date in New York in a few hours and she said she wasn't going to make it. She wouldn't say why. All she would say is that she wasn't sick and we shouldn't worry about her. But worry was all I could do. . . . The only time Cindy had ever missed a show was the year her father died and she went home to handle his arrangements and grieve for him. But then everything had been worked out in advance. This was strange. Something was definitely wrong.

SARAH DASH, The Bluebelles, Labelle: Okay, so we're supposed to go to North Carolina three days later, Patti and The Bluebelles, and we're waiting for Cindy to arrive. . . . So she never showed up and we never—we didn't get a call. When we tried calling her home, no one. . . . Her mother said, "No, she's not available," and we were like, *This is really weird.* So, finally, I called her and I said, "What's going on?" I said, "I gave Larry your number, are you okay? Because we're in North Carolina and the club owner is docking us because he hired four girls and now we have only three." And she was like, "Well, I'm leaving the group because I'm going to join The Supremes," and I was like, "You're going to do what?!" "Yes, I mean, I'm going to join The Supremes. You know, Larry Maxwell called me. . . ."

And so there we are walking around in a circle and you can imagine Patti LaBelle versus Diana Ross, you know, that fever pitch. "You're coming to come and take one of my girls?" They have since made up, of course.

CINDY BIRDSONG, The Bluebelles, The Supremes: A lot of people were very, very angry with me because I left The Bluebelles and they wound up being a trio. I think it was the best thing that happened to them.

VICKI WICKHAM, manager, Labelle: Although they were really good about it, I think it really hurt, the fact that you could be that close to people . . . and she never told them. There was no conversation. It was just she didn't show up. I think that's really tough. I always thought that was really unfair.

PATTI LABELLE, The Bluebelles, Labelle: In my whole life, I had never felt so close to anyone. For a while, Sarah, Nona, and Cindy became my sisters. There was a time when people would show me early photos of The Bluebelles and I'd get this sick, hollow feeling in the pit of my stomach.

CINDY BIRDSONG, The Bluebelles, The Supremes: I didn't see them for a whole year. I just disappeared. I really felt bad about that.

PATTI LABELLE, The Bluebelles, Labelle: Sarah, Nona, and I were the last to get the word. It felt like someone had put a knife in my heart. No, it was more like a knife in my back. It was bad enough that Cindy had abandoned us. What made it worse, what turned the knife over and over was that she never even told us . . . she didn't even say goodbye. After six years of sharing everything—our dreams, our secrets, our sardines, our makeshift beds—she just got up and walked away. At first I was hurt. Then I got pissed. In interviews whenever people would ask me about her, [Patti's alter ego] "Priscilla" answered, "Cindy who?" and said a lot of mean and ugly things. Things I regret, but I just wanted to forget her. Remembering was too painful. Cindy's defection had another effect on me. It made me feel even closer to Sarah and Nona. We were all we had left, and we circled the wagons. Cindy appeared onstage as a Supreme for the first time in July of 1967. And from that day forward, The Bluebelles were a trio. As the saying goes, the show must go on.

SARAH DASH, The Bluebelles, Labelle: The next time we saw Cindy she was on the stage with The Supremes, and there she was. She wasn't apologetic. She didn't say, "I'm sorry," but moving forward, Cindy did an interview with a newspaper and they asked her about Patti LaBelle and The Bluebelles—she had since, at that point, become a minister. And she said, "If I had to do that over again, I wouldn't do it that way, not the way that I did it." To this day, Cindy has health challenges and the three of us are involved in her welfare, so we still love her.

VICKI WICKHAM, manager, Labelle: Of course, she did make the right move because after that . . . after all, Patti LaBelle and The Bluebelles were really floundering and having a hard time, it wasn't specifically because she'd left. It's just that times were changing. They were continuing as they'd always been, with clothes, with presentation, with the songs. People weren't interested anymore. Everybody else had moved on.

NONA HENDRYX, The Bluebelles, Labelle: Things had changed. We'd gone to the moon. We had the British Invasion. We had the West Coast, Haight-Ashbury, sex, drugs, and rock and roll, Flower Power, and taking all kinds of stuff to do inner exploration. All of that stuff had happened, or was happening, so all of that was a part of my life and thinking.

PATTI LABELLE, The Bluebelles, Labelle: Well, by the end of 1969, we were so far down we had to look up to see the bottom. As the sixties ended, it seemed like everything was also coming to an end for us. Our record contract with Atlantic, our management contract with Mr. Montague, even our popularity with the public had begun to slide. We were only in our twenties and were already being booked as an oldie-but-goodie act at the time. At a time when we should have been soaring, we were sinking.

NONA HENDRYX, The Bluebelles, Labelle: We had met Vicki Wickham in England when we first went over in '62, '63, somewhere in there, I think.

SARAH DASH, The Bluebelles, Labelle: I was writing back and forth to her and I told her we were tired, we needed a change, and I don't know whether we were going to stay together because it was tiring us out. We had a couple of managers in between and they weren't working out. So Vicki called me from London at my parents' home.

NONA HENDRYX, The Bluebelles, Labelle: Patti stayed in touch with her, when she was a part of a record company called Track Records that signed Jimi Hendrix, and The Who was the big act they had. They were coming over, and she said, "Well, you have to see this group called Patti LaBelle and The Bluebelles." We were The Bluebelles. They came up to see us at the Apollo Theater. They came up to Harlem. Loved us. Said, "We want to sign them." Signed us, took us to London. And we were there for probably about eight months, going through a metamorphosis or a transformation into Labelle.

VICKI WICKHAM, manager, Labelle: We went through The Bluebelles, Patti LaBelle and The Bluebelles, to Labelle, with Pat fighting all the way because she did not like change at all—being told by me, "You're never going to sing 'Over the Rainbow' onstage again."

PATTI LABELLE, The Bluebelles, Labelle: The fight started early on from day one; they were intense. Even before Vicki started managing us formally. She began telling us her ideas about the direction she saw the group taking. Vicki is a visionary and her view was radical. She saw us doing things I had never even imagined.

Our future, as Vicki saw it, was rock and roll, but rock and roll with an edge, a message. Our music could be political, progressive, passionate. Vicki saw us as Labelle, three Black women singing about racism, sexism, and eroticism. Nona shared Vicki's vision. From the beginning, they saw eye-to-eye. That left Sarah in the middle. She became the buffer, the shock absorber, and the peacemaker. I didn't want to give an inch and Vicki, Nona, and I were miles apart. When I tried out Vicki's concept on other people, I knew their reaction was the same as mine. "You can't be serious."

But Vicki didn't want to hear any of it. She said the sixties were over and a new decade was dawning. For Vicki, it wasn't about keeping up with The Supremes. She wanted us to be pacesetters, pioneers. She wanted Sarah, Nona, and me to change the face and future of women in rock music.

SARAH DASH, The Bluebelles, Labelle: One night we were down in Cherry Hill [New Jersey] playing in a club there and I had come in from Atlantic City and I saw another group's act and I said, "You know what we have to do? We have to get three mic stands just like we are three people and we are going to *sing*. And we are going to blend like we never blended before." I said, "We have to get over this."

When we changed from Patti LaBelle and The Bluebelles, we were going to sing all of our parts, if they were backgrounds or leads, sing them like lead singers. And that's where we got that force from. And that's how we developed that sound.

VICKI WICKHAM, manager, Labelle: When we first started Labelle, they would wear jeans and a T-shirt. It was anything to get away from those frocks and gloves and pumps that they knew that they wore as Patti LaBelle and The Bluebelles. It was just to dress them down. All three of them loved dressing up, so when we got them into all the silver and feathers and [fashion designer] Larry LeGaspi came onboard for Pat, the audience obviously reacted. The audiences were brilliant. They sometimes looked as good as the girls, and we had a lot of fun with it.

PATTI LABELLE, The Bluebelles, Labelle: In 1972, we were playing this club circuit in New York's Greenwich Village. I remember drawing a large following of gay men. When we did a show at the Village Gate, we met an innovative designer, Larry LeGaspi, who had followed our career since we were The Bluebelles. Larry was a true fan and a true original. He told Vicki our sound was cutting edge, but our look was yesterday's news. He convinced Vicki to let him design some clothes for us, and people have been talking about his creations ever since. It was Larry who conceived the whole Labelle look, designing and sewing that unforgettable drag that writer Jamaica Kincaid once described as a "Puerto Rican's idea of Negroes from Mars," the silver, the cabling, the breastplates, feathers, the platforms, the spacesuits, the helmets—they were all LeGaspi originals, Camp Vamp.

VICKI WICKHAM, manager, Labelle: Thank God Larry LeGaspi came to the Village Gate and said to me, "I really could dress the girls. I have really good ideas." I said, "Larry, we've got no money. How am I going to pay you?" "Don't worry, let me just do it, and we'll go from there." He came up with the whole silver, which is beautiful-made jewelry, beautiful jewelry that went with the clothes. That's where the look came from, literally Larry LeGaspi was solely responsible for the look. The more we got into it, the more people reacted. People loved the fact that they didn't look like anyone else.

PATTI LABELLE, The Bluebelles, Labelle: To everybody's surprise, no one had to talk me into this change. I melted right into that drag. I am the original drag queen. Whenever Larry brought his sketches by, I thought, *This is me, baby*. Once Larry told me the concept behind the outfits, I loved them even more. He said his spacesuits did not mean we were from outer space or spaced out but that Labelle was futuristic, miles ahead of all other girl groups. Thanks to Vicki's vision, we were about innerspace, a head trip to everybody, everybody's surprise. It may have taken me a while to see eye-to-eye with Vicki and even longer to get with the program. But, eventually, I did think she was right. Not only did people accept us as Labelle, they begin to hear the message in our music. Larry's clothes got their attention.

VICKI WICKHAM, manager, Labelle: I never want to see a feather or silver in life again. [*laughing*] Nona would come out with handcuffs around her waist and a whip. I mean, outrageous. Sarah would have these wonderful—and it's ludicrous, but they really were made of silver—bra. The most beautiful bra in the world; it cost a fortune. I don't know who paid for it. Pat at first didn't like the clothes at all, but as we got more into it, and Larry began to realize what she did and didn't like, of course they all move a lot, but Pat *really* moves. She got hot, we had to work out things that were comfortable for her. Yeah, Larry LeGaspi was just a genius.

Had we *not* at that stage changed to Labelle, the look, the music, and the approach . . . they played a lot of white clubs, things like the Bottom Line. Anyway, it was a new day and, of course, then it became a new audience. The audience was very mixed. Yes, there were a lot of gay audience, but it wasn't just gay. It was . . . you'd get women in hats who were from the church, a real mixed Black and white audience.

NONA HENDRYX, The Bluebelles, Labelle: I think it allowed me to bring into *that* time things that had been a part of my consciousness from when I was four years old. It was always kind of being woven through my life, being interested in science and technology or electronics. I think it allowed me to bring those interests into a musical expression, in that Labelle was not yet *another* girl group, that we thought beyond "My man has left me. My man is coming back. I love you. I hate you. I'm going to break up with you." It was to get beyond that.

VICKI WICKHAM, manager, Labelle: Nona was the one who suddenly started saying, "I write poems." Okay, you write poems, what does that mean? Does that mean you write lyrics? Yes? Okay. What about melodies? Oh, yes? Suddenly, she turned into the writer for the group. She wrote for Pat's voice, which is why some of the early songs are so amazing. "Going Down Makes Me Shiver," just beautiful, beautiful songs that nobody else but Pat could have sung. Equally so, the three of them became, if you think of things like "The Revolution Will Not Be Televised," where they all take individual solo verses, whatever, you can hear all three voices separately. Sarah was the one that kept the group together. When Nona and I would argue or Pat and I would argue, it was Sarah that would come in and go, "Okay, this is what we should . . . this is fine." She was great. She just was the leveler, the one who stopped it getting out of hand. I guess it was really helpful with Pat, who was uncontrollable, but I see now that's what makes Pat, Pat.

PATTI LABELLE, The Bluebelles, Labelle: With Vicki's advice and guidance, we had our own production company, our own management company, and our own publishing company. Before Vicki, we had allowed men to control everything. They told us what to do and how to do it. We didn't do any thinking for ourselves. Now we were doing it all—thinking, planning, and speaking up for ourselves. And for others. It was clear people were getting the message. After one performance, a woman told me how she much appreciated our having the courage to say things that we were saying and our music. She said we were singing for anybody whom society discriminated against because of who they were. Blacks, women, gays. She paid us one of the biggest compliments anyone ever could. It was so touching and real. I just started crying.

CINDY BIRDSONG, The Bluebelles, The Supremes: It was the best thing for them. Several years later, they had "Lady Marmalade."

VICKI WICKHAM, manager, Labelle: Of course, we had success with "Lady Marmalade." Pat said to me, "*Voulez-vouz coucher avec moi, ce soir*? What does it mean?" I told her, and she said, "No, we can't do that." I said, "Yes, you can."

CINDY BIRDSONG, The Bluebelles, The Supremes: If I had been with the group, my mom wouldn't have let me sing on something like that. My mom was a church mama. It worked out well that they became hottest as Labelle with hit songs that were not the kind of songs we did when I was with them. We did little classical clean songs. My mom wouldn't have let me do that.

VICKI WICKHAM, manager, Labelle: *Voulez-vous coucher,* yeah, right. She hadn't got a clue what it was. I said to her, "Okay, think about this. You're going to teach people French that don't know what it is." Okay, and of course, they did it and it was the biggest hit they ever had.

CHAPTER 38

Behind Motown's Curtain

The Andantes

MARLENE BARROW, The Andantes: I stood in during the time that Florence formally left the group. I think that they had Cindy in mind from the start, but they had to straighten out everything with the contracts. I knew the songs, so they didn't have to teach me the songs. I also fit her gowns.

JACKIE HICKS, The Andantes: I think they were considering Marlene, but if Marlene was to join The Supremes, she'd have to leave The Andantes and tour, which is something she didn't want to do.

MARY WILSON, The Supremes: The Andantes were three girls, and they backed up everyone at Motown. So they became the backing vocalist choir, or ensemble, I guess you could call them, and did all the background vocals for every act there. They were like the choral group who sang extra parts.

BRIAN HOLLAND, songwriter: Yeah, listen—we used The Andantes on all the songs—all of the songs in some kind of way because The Andantes had such a big sound, you know what I mean? A big, round sound. The voices was immaculate. Them girls got great-sounding voices. We used them 90 percent of the time—period.

JANIE BRADFORD, Motown executive: I would be afraid to even quote a number—to stab at a number. It's easier to say how many songs they *did not* record on.

JACKIE HICKS, The Andantes: There's not a day go by that I don't hear my voice on the radio.

LOUVAIN DEMPS, The Andantes: I think the first biggest thing, I think, was "My Guy."

JACKIE HICKS, The Andantes: That was the first one-million seller that we were on.

JANIE BRADFORD, Motown executive: Oh yes, they definitely were on most of the girl groups tracks.

JACKIE HICKS, The Andantes: We're on The Supremes things, The Vandellas, you name it.

LOUVAIN DEMPS, The Andantes: The Marvelettes . . . just, you know, everybody's voices.

JANIE BRADFORD, Motown executive: It was not like a competition.

JACKIE HICKS, The Andantes: You get a little dissension with girl singers, but not the musicians. What they wanted was our voice and that is what they got.

LOUVAIN DEMPS, The Andantes: Right. Even if they turned somebody else's voices down and turned us up.

MICKEY STEVENSON, Motown A&R: When I felt something was better for someone that could make it happen, I would do that no matter what it is—in my head and in my heart, it's gotta go that way. And some people didn't like me for that. And some love me for that. I would take it from you and give it to them—even in the group.

JACKIE HICKS, The Andantes: There was jealousy . . . but there was . . . some of the things there was nothing they could do about. And it wasn't something that they show, "Now we mad at you," and we fought; no, it wasn't like that. But, heck, if I'm the lead singer, or whatever, and somebody kind of slips in—or I got to share the song with them, or whatever, you're going to be a little jealous, but you don't be crazy because a hit is a hit. This person might've helped you, but you're the one that's going to get the money—so, what's the problem?

LOUVAIN DEMPS, The Andantes: When it came up or somebody came up against me, it was just . . . I said, *Well, you know what? Okay, so you're angry, but you got the royalties. So don't be angry. Just take the money.* Because when the hits started coming and the road's looking good, and they were on it and going places . . . you know they had *that* kind of fun, but we had ours.

JANIE BRADFORD, Motown executive: Louvain was there very early doing backgrounds. She came over when they would be cutting some of the early sessions and needed various backgrounds before they got all the different groups. So Louvain formed The Andantes herself later on.

LOUVAIN DEMPS, The Andantes: I had a girlfriend that wrote some poetry, and she wanted me to go over to the people that were putting this stuff together. It was Berry's wife, Raynoma Liles Gordy, and Berry Gordy. Raynoma asked me to join their group and it was called the Rayber Voices—it's a combination of Raynoma and Berry. And so I became their soprano.

JACKIE HICKS, The Andantes: I met Marlene, I might've been six and she might've been four, but we met in church because we were all churchgoers in our entire neighborhood and her mother happened to be minister of music at our church. We went to school with Popcorn Wylie of [Motown house band] the Funk Brothers, and so he knew that we sang in church and he wanted to audition for Motown and he needed background voices. He wanted the full package. We were just going to sing with Popcorn, but it ended up that Motown was just getting off the ground . . . and so they needed singers to background some of the artists that would be coming in and some that were already there.

And so they kept calling. Finally, with the pushing of my mom, we responded. But when we got back there, we told them that we wouldn't really be able to sing because we did not have a soprano. And they told us that there was a young lady already there that could sing and perhaps they could bring her in with us and see how it goes. And that was the start and the beginning.

LOUVAIN DEMPS, The Andantes: One day these two ladies came in, and they were kind of cute and they didn't have a soprano voice, so they put me with them. And I was so *excited*. I was . . . oh man . . . I could . . . oh, I just was *so excited* to be able to sing and sing with people that *really* could sing.

JACKIE HICKS, The Andantes: We were always there so long and, you know, basically, every day. You know, we'd be walking out the door sometime after the session and they would say, "Well, come back. We just got one more song."

LOUVAIN DEMPS, The Andantes: They would call us any time of day and night, and I was *always* ready to go. And it got so that, after a while, we were doing so much they gave us an office upstairs.

JACKIE HICKS, The Andantes: We went from Mondays to Sundays, so I can't remember a week, really, that we were not at the studio. We practically lived up there. "Just come on downstairs and start singing."

JANIE BRADFORD, Motown executive: They were basically all the time at the studio.

JACKIE HICKS, The Andantes: One thing about traveling, it was impossible for us to travel the way we sang every day.

LOUVAIN DEMPS, The Andantes: I never could dance, but I wanted to be with and learn in Ms. Powell's class, you know?

JACKIE HICKS, The Andantes: If we would have been out of town, that would have shut Motown down for background, putting the voices on songs.

LOUVAIN DEMPS, The Andantes: We sang onstage. Remember the Motown Revue? And they finally let us come from behind the curtain.

JACKIE HICKS, The Andantes: We didn't have uniforms and all of that. We just had to put on a black dress or something ugly—to put it mildly—some ugly black dresses. Now that I think about it, I wouldn't be caught dead in none of that stuff—bury me in pink, you know?

LOUVAIN DEMPS, The Andantes: We were on a few of those shows, but other than that our job was mainly in the studio.

JACKIE HICKS, The Andantes: It was *amazing*, the audience's response to those shows. It was just amazing. This is something that they went through all the time on the road. So they were accustomed to it, but that little bit was enough to me.

LOUVAIN DEMPS, The Andantes: For me, I think it hit me later on down the line. I was so happy with being on a record . . . I didn't think about that they didn't put our names on. I didn't think about that till later.

JACKIE HICKS, The Andantes: Well, I've always felt like that would've been nice recognition. And that's something that I would have appreciated, and I did think about that back at that time, but it wasn't anything that I was going to push or harp on or get bent out of shape about or anything. But, yes, I think that should have happened. 'Cause it would be an amazing amount of records to look at and actually see your name on it . . . you know you're singing on it . . . but it would have been really nice to get that, and that was just something that we didn't get.

LOUVAIN DEMPS, The Andantes: And then, too, when you hear something on the radio and you get excited and you say, "Hey, that's us!" *Oh, who is us?* You know, people don't believe you.

JANIE BRADFORD, Motown executive: After Motown became so popular and so famous all over the world, then the fans—everybody knew even who the lady in the kitchen that cooked us chili—they knew *everybody*. They knew the band members, they knew The Andantes. So it was then like, *Well, why didn't Motown give them credit?* No other record company has ever given band leaders or musicians or people like that credit; it just happened to be that Motown became a phenomenon. And I'm glad that they *did* finally get recognized because right now each one of them—the Funk Brothers and The Andantes—they're legends.

JACKIE HICKS, The Andantes: We were content with being in the background. Some people . . . *well, look, I made everybody else famous, how come* . . . Uh-uh—we were background singers. And, hey, I did what I did, and I did an excellent job. I didn't do a good job, I did an *excellent* job.

LOUVAIN DEMPS, The Andantes: Oh! It's just wonderful. Sometimes, like when I look at the things where The Supremes and The Temps or Tops are together on TV, I said, "Boy, they look good, but we *sound* better."

CHAPTER 39

Martha and The Vandellas

ROSALIND ASHFORD, The Vandellas: Diana was the first one it happened to. That's when they changed the name. I don't know who in Motown did it, but they just come to you . . . "Okay, we changing the name to 'Martha Reeves and The Vandellas,'" and that's the end of it. Nothing you can do about it.

MARTHA REEVES, The Vandellas: Berry realized that it should be "Martha Reeves," since I was doing all the work. I brought them to the company. I did all the singing. I did all of the appointment makings. I did all of the schedules. I was making costumes or buying costumes with my portion of my income and had basically the responsibility to keep going, to continue.

ROSALIND ASHFORD, The Vandellas: Once Martha did not want to sing with Betty, it was already set up that she was going to put her sister in the group. And then they explained things to me, "Well, you're not a lead singer. We can't take you out and just let you be out there by yourself. But, with Martha . . . if you're gone, all we got to do is just take two more people and put them behind her and call them whoever." So, that's the story.

MARTHA REEVES, The Vandellas: My sister traveled with me for a year and observed my show. She was just my companion. Mom taught us all to sing, and she could very well have been a part of the group before Betty Kelley. When Betty left, she had a hearing problem that wasn't announced. That was one of the reasons why she left.

BETTY KELLEY, The Velvelettes, The Vandellas: I look at the stuff on the internet on Wikipedia that says, "She was fired because she missed some gigs." I never missed a gig. This is crazy. People get what they think are facts, but they're not facts. I tell people that when I left, the feeling was mutual, but, yes, there was a problem with Martha. It was a problem on her side, not my side.

ROSALIND ASHFORD, The Vandellas: When they put Lois in the group, they kind of explained to me . . . you never know who actually did it, but the words just come down . . . "Well, we know that Martha, we feel she can get along better with her sisters. So, that's just the way it's going to be. We putting her in the group." And I had no say-so. . . . I didn't even have a choice as far as choosing who got in the group, because that was already set up.

MARTHA REEVES, The Vandellas: My sister had been observing us perform from backstage and realized that she could very well do the show. It was a rough exchange, because shows were continuous, and there was no break, and no time to stop, and let one go, and train another. It's just a coincidence that Betty's leaving the group was of her own design. She wasn't told, "Betty, you're fired." She wasn't told that. It was that she was let go because of the ability of her not being able to sing and hear.

BETTY KELLEY, The Velvelettes, The Vandellas: I'm not saying that it was easy and that everything fell into place overnight, because it didn't. At one point, you were doing this constantly, and here, now, you have to make a decision as to what's going to happen in your life and get attorneys to try to straighten this out and that out. Your royalties are messed up and there were all kinds of things.

ROSALIND ASHFORD, The Vandellas: But, I mean, it was a big, big disappointment. But my thing was I just had to go along with it if I wanted to keep my job—that was it—I had no choice.

BETTY KELLEY, The Velvelettes, The Vandellas: You adapt to it and go on to the next phase of your life. That's what life is. I wasn't going to lie down and die. You have to focus on your health, decide what you want to do in your life, and that's that.

MARTHA REEVES, The Vandellas: There had to be a change made. Sensitivity of it was overshadowed by the fact that we could continue, and I could have my sister put in her clothes and her shoes, and go on and make an appearance . . . with Betty sitting in the audience, objecting and shouting out insults to my sister and causing her to be a little uncomfortable. But my sister was only doing what the time called for—she was being trained by Cholly Atkins. Because one of her next engagements after the Fox Theatre was the Copacabana in New York.

CHAPTER 40

Lost on the Road They Paved

The Marvelettes

KATHERINE ANDERSON, The Marvelettes: After a period of time, it makes a big difference if the people that you were singing with . . . if they're the same people that you started out with. Then it came to the point that we no longer had the same people we started with and stopped. Georgeanna had sickle cell. And then on top of that, some way or another, she developed lupus. It was the point in fact that Georgeanna, that she was leaving. Gladys left not too long after Georgeanna left. . . . It really hurt my heart because then two of my friends were leaving or had left.

GLADYS HORTON, The Marvelettes: Like a fool, I left because I was having a baby. I needed someone on my side to say, "Gladys, don't leave this. It's not that easy outside." Maybe things would've been different for me. I got married and stayed married for maybe a year. I don't even know if I actually got married. The guy who married us wasn't even an ordained preacher. My first child was born with cerebral palsy.

KATHERINE ANDERSON, The Marvelettes: I asked her if she was going to be coming back after she had the baby. She would have to hire someone to take care of her son. She said no, that she would not be coming back. I was really hurt because it seemed like the group was falling apart. When Gladys was there, there was balance. When she wasn't there, there wasn't one, because of the fact that it was me against Wanda.

MARTHA REEVES, The Vandellas: Sadly, Georgeanna passed away before Motown moved.

KATHERINE ANDERSON, The Marvelettes: We weren't getting that much attention. You know, they say that we're this, that, and the other. But you know what? They are lying. By then, Martha had come along, and then The Supremes had come along. So why would they?

MARTHA REEVES, The Vandellas: The Marvelettes paved the way for Motown's girls, The Supremes, everybody. If they hadn't worked, we wouldn't have worked.

KATHERINE ANDERSON, The Marvelettes: Everything had changed. Everything had changed. Georgeanna wasn't any longer there. Then after a while, Gladys wasn't any longer there. There was only Wanda and myself. Wanda had gone off the rocker—basically, there was no . . . nobody in that I could talk to. . . . To have Wanda to deal with is more than a notion.

BRIAN HOLLAND, songwriter: Wanda married Bobby Rogers, of The Miracles—Wanda was a pretty girl, strange-sounding voice, nice-looking girl. Smokey started writing songs for them. "Don't Mess with Bill," that was one of them. I loved that song too. [*singing*] "*Don't mess with Bill, leave my Billy alone.*" That was a pretty good, popular song. It was not a big record, but it was a little light hit.

KATHERINE ANDERSON, The Marvelettes: "Don't Mess with Bill" was a shot in the arm.

MARTHA REEVES, The Vandellas: Wanda was under a lot of stress and was hospitalized. . . . It's just personal things that happened to The Marvelettes and they didn't continue.

BOBBY ROGERS, The Miracles: I think [Wanda's sister] LaMona's death had an effect on Wanda, but I think something else happened to her. Something when she was in Europe, something happened to her. When she came back, she was different. A couple of things happened, and it was like she had changed. Her friends had become her enemies and her enemies became her friends. She took on a totally different thing.

KATHERINE ANDERSON, The Marvelettes: I wrote a note more or less asking for help. Basically, I wanted to get it to Berry, and I don't know if it ever did reach him. When there was no help to be gotten, I just figured our time had come. I would have liked for Motown to take an interest in what was going on, and if they had, I would think that maybe they would have tried to get Wanda some help. . . . I would've liked for them to try to get Wanda some help in the early stages instead of letting it go on.

BOBBY ROGERS, The Miracles: She was really nice. She just got sick along the way . . . mentally. When somebody does something to you and you don't know it, you think it's you. Usually at a bar when somebody puts something in your drink, you don't know it. That's why, unless you leave your drink with someone who you know and trust, when you come back to it, you just don't drink it.

KATHERINE ANDERSON, The Marvelettes: If she could've gotten help at the time, then perhaps she would've been able to have been drawn back into reality from what was going on, but she didn't get help at that time and later in years they tried to get help for her, but then it was too late.

BEBE YOUNG, Wanda Young's sister: Her problems started when The Marvelettes came back from overseas. . . . When they came back, that's when she started being hospitalized. Then with her drinking and experimenting, that just made it worse. I think she started having difficulty in her marriage, then my sister [LaMona] got killed, then with the drinking and experimenting, everything just exploded. That's when her drinking really took off.

KATHERINE ANDERSON, The Marvelettes: Smokey was a person that usually took the lead singer and then the rest of them . . . he'd just say, "Go ahead and do it." She basically sang with The Andantes.

We were almost through. And then they called and asked me if I would do the photo for the album. And I told him, I said, "There's no way in hell I'll be doing this album because you used somebody else and didn't use me. So then whatever." So it ends up being like that.

CHAPTER 41

Left Behind

Motown Leaves Detroit

JANIE BRADFORD, Motown executive: Well, it became historic. It became an identity for Detroit. At first it was the cars . . . and still you kind of relate it to cars—but before you mention cars, you think of Motown. And a lot of people don't even say Detroit. They call Detroit "Motown."

JACKIE HICKS, The Andantes: They actually left the state of Michigan and went to California, and then it just all changed. It was just all gone.

LOUVAIN DEMPS, The Andantes: The musicians found out because there was a note for them. It was . . . it was cold. It was . . . all the way around, it was just cold, you know?

JACKIE HICKS, The Andantes: They were not going out there to sing, they were going out there to do the movie business. And if they felt like they could elevate themselves, you know, well, I guess that's what you work toward, is gaining the most that you can gain.

KATHERINE ANDERSON, The Marvelettes: I looked around and there was nobody there that I really particularly cared for. Then under that situation, it was all good. I didn't leave The Marvelettes, I just stopped singing. I married somebody outside of Motown, but then again *with* Motown—in other words, he was a road manager and a lighting person.

MARTHA REEVES, The Vandellas: When we were first on the label, we were managed. We were told where to live, we were given opportunities to live in houses that we didn't own. . . . We were guided, and trained, and nurtured, and chaperoned, and cared for—as managers are expected to do. But when the management company dissolved, they decided they weren't managing us anymore. . . . They left us on our own to do our own thing. Some of us were strong enough to continue, and some of us were completely deserted and abandoned and orphaned, so to speak.

NORMA BARBEE, The Velvelettes: They was leasing the cars—there's certain things, I guess, he would do to make it look like these people were making a lot of money. I think the writers weren't making tons of money, like Holland–Dozier–Holland.

BRIAN HOLLAND, songwriter: I really would not bore you to death. . . . You want all the information you can get, but listen, I'll tell you this much—we wasn't getting along with Berry at the time, that's all I can tell ya, you know?

NORMA BARBEE, The Velvelettes: They later went back to court to get money from him. And the bottom line, the point that I'm making, I don't think anybody was getting money, a lot of money.

ROSALIND ASHFORD, The Vandellas: A lot of the groups were broken up.

MARTHA REEVES, The Vandellas: Rosalind left to get married or have a baby, or whatever, I don't know. Girls do that. Girls will decide, "I want to be with a man. I don't necessarily want to be in the business," or "I don't like what's going on, so I'm going to go and do this." Well, you can sign a contract to sing, but you can't sign a contract to make someone oblige to the rules, and when their lifestyle is involved, they make a choice for their own personal happiness.

ROSALIND ASHFORD, The Vandellas: In '69, somebody from Motown called me down to the studio and to the office, and they said, "Martha doesn't want to sing with you anymore." Period. And, like I was saying, they told me, "Well, we can take her tomorrow and we can put her out there, and she can do a show. Because all we have to do is get two more girls to put behind her and she can go do a show. But *you* can't just do that. You can't just up and go out and do a show," so you have to take it or leave it . . . not take it—you're gone . . . so, that was it. I was gone.

JACKIE HICKS, The Andantes: They came to, they called us in the office, said, "You're fired," more or less. [*laughing*]

MARTHA REEVES, The Vandellas: I had no idea that Motown was moving to Los Angeles. I had no idea that my contract was expiring that year. I just had my son, I was recuperating—my mom was the kind of mother that would make you wait a month before you get active and do something after having a baby. I had my baby out of wedlock. So, when I recuperated enough to call the studio, to ask for my next assignment—which was the routine—I was told, "Girl, don't you know that Motown is moving to California?" To my dismay, I went, "Oh my God. What am I going to do?"

JACKIE HICKS, The Andantes: It was a shock. It was a shock to *everybody*. But it was one . . . hey . . . when I was told, I was like, *Well, let me put in and get me a job with a pension and a retirement plan. Because I'm not going to California.*

LOUVAIN DEMPS, The Andantes: It just really devastated me. . . . I mean, I just got, I just kind of felt like there was nothing there for me anymore. Some things bothered people differently, and I guess I just took it to heart . . . and it was just too much for me.

JACKIE HICKS, The Andantes: A lot of those talented people actually ended up doing nothing—just all that talent went to waste. . . . Because there was nowhere to express and direct all of that energy.

LOUVAIN DEMPS, The Andantes: Well, you know what? As time went by, I'm glad that it didn't happen, because I'd probably be one of the ones going on the street saying, "You want me to wash your car windows?"

ROSALIND ASHFORD, The Vandellas: Martha moved to California for a while, and then she moved back to Detroit. . . . She just continued to sing herself.

LOUVAIN DEMPS, The Andantes: When they moved to LA, from the musician's standpoint, at first they thought that they were going to be used, and instead a lot of them came back home. They lost a lot of stuff by going out there, and it didn't work. So a lot of them were bitter.

JACKIE HICKS, The Andantes: And this is why some people are still angry today—because they were not considered and taken there or asked to come or compensated for being there. . . . And there's just a lot of people that were bitter about it. And rightfully so, rightfully so.

MARTHA REEVES, The Vandellas: I felt abandoned and I felt like I had been betrayed, because Motown was my all-in-all. Being an adult and realizing that my contract was up—they had no obligation to me to even tell me they were leaving.

LOUVAIN DEMPS, The Andantes: They were really sorry that some of them went out there because, no matter what they did, it never was the same for them.

MARTHA REEVES, The Vandellas: I moved out to California too. Got my son and I thought I was marrying somebody that loved me, a husband . . . took my car and drove to California and recorded with Universal. Fought my way through the fact that I'm . . . from apartment to apartment, not really having a secured residence, but taking a chance on the business, and Mom and Dad helping me with my child, and I continued my life, continued my career.

NORMA BARBEE, The Velvelettes: Martha had a lawsuit against Berry Gordy, some of the writers too. Well, when you sue somebody, as you probably know, or maybe you don't know, you sign an agreement that you can't discuss it. . . . Yeah, these people sign agreements that they cannot discuss certain things about the lawsuit or retrieving royalties, past royalties. You can't talk about it. That's in the agreement.

BRIAN HOLLAND, songwriter: He paid every one of his writers money what they earned. He was not . . . if I said that in my book, then I misspoke. I was not right because Berry Gordy was a great man. He really was.

MARTHA REEVES, The Vandellas: Motown leaving Detroit was something that Berry had planned to do. Rightfully so, because he made new. . . . Everybody was happy. Everybody found a way and I continued recording for the three major labels. I faced it and took the challenge and succeeded in continuing. That was the point—to continue. Some of us fared well, and some of us were just lost by the wayside.

CHAPTER 42

Flo's Story

PETER BENJAMINSON, Florence Ballard's biographer: For several years, I covered City Hall for the *Detroit Free Press*. In 1975, a friend of mine came over and said that he just got a tip that Flo Ballard was on welfare, and asked, did I want to check it out? And I immediately got enthusiastic about it—*a Supreme on welfare?! This is a great story!* His source, who was a woman, a female friend of Flo's, had called up and said, "You got to do something about it. How could this happen?" You know, "Send someone over there" so the story would help her out.

BERRY GORDY, founder, Motown: A lot has been written and said about the tragedy that surrounded Flo's life after she left Motown—the stint at ABC, the legal action she brought against a lawyer she accused of misappropriating her funds.

FLORENCE BALLARD, The Supremes: Things looked good when I first started out as a single. I had signed with a new company and was pleased with the initial releases, and even had a few engagements lined up. Then all of a sudden it seemed as if I was blackballed. My records weren't being played and there were no bookings.

PETER BENJAMINSON, Florence Ballard's biographer: She thought she could parlay her stature as a Supreme into another recording career. But she was very bad with all the legal paperwork she'd get—people would present stuff to her and she'd go, "All right . . ."—not even read—and she'd sign. And one of the things she signed banned her from publicizing that she was a former Supreme—and that would have made her career.

FLORENCE BALLARD, The Supremes: You're not supposed to ever say you were a Supreme or had anything to do with The Supremes whatsoever. You can never call yourself an ex-Supreme. But I chose the name "Supremes" and Berry Gordy took it away from me.

PETER BENJAMINSON, Florence Ballard's biographer: I mean, if she could have been billed as "Former Supreme Florence Ballard in Concert Tonight," that would have attracted a lot of people. But she wasn't allowed to say that . . . and, you know, not everyone even knew her name. Sure, the real aggressive fans who really bore in knew that Florence Ballard is one of The Supremes—but she couldn't even mention that she was a Supreme. So that eliminated 75 percent of the possible audience, and *Why should we pay forty dollars to see her?* That was a big deal. But she just signed that. She tried to get it back, but there was all this legal paperwork that she'd signed being used against her by these high-price lawyers and everyone else higher. And then her lawyer was a cheater—he was disbarred, finally, for cheating her and other people.

FLORENCE BALLARD, The Supremes: I respected the guy for what he was. He would tell me, "Your money is being invested in stock, whatever; your money is in an account," with his signature on it and mine, he couldn't draw without my signature; I couldn't draw without his signature. Where that account went, I don't know. Where the stock went, I don't know.

PETER BENJAMINSON, Florence Ballard's biographer: The lawyer that negotiated her settlement with Motown just took all the money that Motown gave her, which *was* several hundreds of thousands. But he just took it, basically, and then was disbarred. Every lawyer that dealt with her—apparently, they saw that she didn't pay any attention to any of this stuff—so they just took as much as they possibly could.

MAXINE BALLARD, Florence Ballard's sister: I always believed that if she did get anything from Motown, then Tommy Chapman, Flo's husband, probably had gotten hold of the money and it was never seen again.

PETER BENJAMINSON, Florence Ballard's biographer: He was really Berry's chauffeur, you know. When he left Motown, he got a job at a supermarket stocking the shelves; I mean, he wasn't a businessman. He was just a laborer, basically a chauffeur, which is fine, but then he tried to manage Flo's post-Motown career. That was a disaster—he had no idea what he was doing—I wouldn't either. I mean, she should have hired someone—a business manager for a percentage—who then would have been motivated to get her into big clubs, and try to avoid the prohibition against saying that she was a "Supreme." I mean, there was nothing that prevented entertainment writers or people on the radio or TV from saying "Former Supreme Flo Ballard is going to perform tonight." Motown's prohibition didn't apply to them. If the manager could have told these people, "Look, just say 'former Supreme,'" as long as *she* didn't say she was a former Supreme . . .

Tommy Chapman's idea of publicizing your new record was to carry them around himself to various record stores in, like, cardboard cartons. Try to sell them . . . you know, thirty copies or something. That's not what a manager does. You should be getting your gigs, big clubs, you know—"former Supreme"!

FLORENCE BALLARD, The Supremes: I began to go into a complete depression, where I would just withdraw from people completely, just stay locked inside, wouldn't come out. I didn't want to be seen or anything. . . . I guess I was drinking because I wanted to feel happy. But that only made it worse.

PETER BENJAMINSON, Florence Ballard's biographer: I mean, not only did she go way up and then way down, but then it started getting worse—she lost her house . . . her kids had to go somewhere else. She lost her husband. She ran out of money. She lost the car. She then . . . she drank and staggered on the street, she was robbed at least twice. She had gone from the very top . . . to really . . . to close to the very bottom in, like, a couple of years. It must have taken a tremendous toll.

FLORENCE BALLARD, The Supremes: Sometimes I have regrets and wish I was back in the group, but a lot of times I say to myself, "Would it be worth it to go back into it and have the same thing happen again?" Because, basically, Mary Wilson, the only original Supreme now—she's still singing, but she didn't get what she deserved, either.

PETER BENJAMINSON, Florence Ballard's biographer: She gave away all the records—people would ask to see if they could get an album from her, and ask her to sign it—she was either generous or depressed, or both. She'd just give them to them, so she had no albums left. . . . Nothing to remind her of The Supremes—anything. She turned off the radio.

But eventually, she started to reconcile with things. Because Mary Wilson invited her to a concert that she was giving—she invited Flo to sing one song. Flo did sing it successfully and the audience, *did they love it!* The audience was yelling for an encore.

MARY WILSON, The Supremes: When she died, I just wanted people to realize that she had been dealt a really hard hand to handle. . . . I wanted to make sure that people understood that.

I would do the same for Diane because we all loved each other equally. That was one thing that we had, that people just don't know, we really did. And so just . . . Florence, she's not here to speak. Diane can—has—but Florence is not here. So it's not that I love her *more* than anyone else, it's just that, I'm just . . . keeping her voice there as well.

Because we were three wonderful friends who dared to dream . . . and we made our dreams come true. It should be all of us. . . . I'm here to speak for myself, Diane's here to speak for herself, and Florence is not.

PETER BENJAMINSON, Florence Ballard's biographer: I think she was very wounded, psychologically. She became an international star two years after she got out of the house—she didn't even graduate from high school. Then she was thrown out back down below, where she'd been before. It was . . . I don't know what to call it medically . . . it hurt. I think that's what killed her. I mean, she had a coronary artery thrombosis. But what causes that? I'm sure there was some psychological stress.

MARY WILSON, The Supremes: She told it to you like it was. If she wasn't happy about it, she would tell you. That's what was going on and why there became a time when, for her, it was just too much. People knew The Supremes from our television appearances and what we did on the outside. But they didn't know what motivated us and who we were as individuals.

People did not know Florence's story—how she had been brutally raped when she was fourteen years old. When we were singing, we had these great hopes and dreams, and then this really destroyed her . . . that really destroyed her self-confidence—we were all virgins, so she was never the same. You can't be the same . . . that haunts you all your life. She just had her grief at that time, and after that . . .

I think Diana and I just felt that when we went back to Motown, and we started recording, our life as a group was going on, and Florence would get over it—because now we're famous, you know what I mean?

MAXINE BALLARD, Florence Ballard's sister: I tried my best to help Flo take her mind off her horrible experience. Flo didn't want to tell anyone what had happened, because the boy was well known.

PETER BENJAMINSON, Florence Ballard's biographer: It was Reggie Harding, the basketball star. He was a big guy, I mean, he was a big star . . . but he never got far because he got . . . criminally, he was arrested for stealing a car—some stupid shit. He could have been, probably, a wealthy basketball star because he was very good. He didn't make it through his twenties, either; he was shot in the street and died.

MAXINE BALLARD, Florence Ballard's sister: She felt like no one would believe her. In those days, most people didn't talk about such things, but you knew they happened all the time. Young Black girls were raped daily, suffering at the hands of men sometimes in their own families. Because of her attacker's popularity, Flo almost became just another silent victim—afraid to tell who he was and bearing the brunt of the pain she felt and the blame she internalized.

PETER BENJAMINSON, Florence Ballard's biographer: She never told me about that. She was much too ashamed or embarrassed or something. She never mentioned it. I had no idea that she had been sexually assaulted. She said, "Oh, I cried a lot. I sat on the steps to cry," she never told me why. That was obviously why.

MARY WILSON, The Supremes: Those type of things . . . they find their way up. So, eventually, it was Florence's own problems that were magnifying the things that were happening in the group. Because obviously I felt the same way she did about the name change—I didn't want it to change—I didn't want to become two backup singers . . . we weren't backup singers in our mind.

We didn't have a "Me Too" movement then. Her parents didn't try to get her help. They were trying to care for her and prevent her being exposed to certain things. Therefore, what should've been done for her was to get help and to talk about these kinds of things, like what's happening now. She was suffering because of not knowing what to do. Things were not going right, nothing was going right for her.

I don't think people knew it until I told them, until I put the word out. Because Florence was too embarrassed to talk about it . . . she never talked about it. She wasn't the kind of person to complain or *me, me, me*—that just wasn't who she was.

So, no—people didn't even know. So, all they could go by would be how she acted. They saw her drinking, *Oh, she's an alcoholic,* and that hurt my heart because I knew that wasn't what was going on.

DIANA ROSS, The Supremes: On the day of her funeral, I had no idea the extent of the angers and resentments I was facing. It was like a lion's den.

MARY WILSON, The Supremes: Being at the funeral, just Florence . . . knowing she was no longer with us . . . sitting there, I just wished no one was in that church but me and Flo. *What is all this about? I want to say goodbye to my friend.* And there was just so much going on.

PETER BENJAMINSON, Florence Ballard's biographer: The real big thing was Diana Ross hadn't been invited—for some obvious reasons . . . obvious reasons that were later exposed—she hadn't been invited because she basically forced Flo out of the group. Flo's family said later, "Of course, Diana knew that she would be welcomed there." I'm not so sure that's true. I guess that's what they said later, and no one stopped her, and she arrived uninvited.

DIANA ROSS, The Supremes: I showed up because I wanted to show my love and friendship and concern for her three children. I wanted to be supportive and helpful. It was like walking straight into the fire. The funeral was a mess—utter chaos.

PETER BENJAMINSON, Florence Ballard's biographer: As soon as Diana Ross got out of the car, people—they were hissing, booing, and stuff—they were very upset.

DIANA ROSS, The Supremes: I went straight for the kids. My greatest concern was trying to protect the children, but I was pushed around on every side by disrespectful, intrusive people.

PETER BENJAMINSON, Florence Ballard's biographer: Diana marched down the aisle of the church and joined Mary Wilson up there. She picked up Flo's daughter and put her on her lap and the daughter was sucking her thumb. Diana was looking very motherly . . . one of my colleagues at the *Free Press* took the picture . . . that was the world-famous picture.

MAXINE BALLARD, Florence Ballard's sister: I think that picture that was taken of Diane was almost as famous as the picture of the King children at Dr. King's funeral. I was upset that even in death Flo was pushed to the background.

PETER BENJAMINSON, Florence Ballard's biographer: I mean, it was a great picture, but also was nicely symbolic. . . . She always knew what she was doing, she's very smart—she outsmarted everyone. But it's little stuff—she took all the publicity from the funeral, moved the light, spotlight from Flo onto herself, which is what she did in life too. So, she was totally consistent.

DIANA ROSS, The Supremes: I got a lot of bad press for it later, but I only did it because I wanted to make things right for Florence.

PETER BENJAMINSON, Florence Ballard's biographer: Then people were trying to crowd in. They were crowding to such an extent they prevented the hearse company vehicles from taking Flo's body to the cemetery. To distract them without using clubs, the various funeral workers threw all the wreaths and flowers into the crowd. The crowd ripped up the flowers, because they wanted them.

DIANA ROSS, The Supremes: I finally gave up. I didn't go to the cemetery. I got into my car feeling terrible and went home to grieve alone.

MARY WILSON, The Supremes: I just wanted to be there with her myself. You know, at the end, the Four Tops were there and the parents, and everyone left me, and I was just there with Flo at the last minute. . . . And I said, "Flo, don't worry, we are the greatest."

CHAPTER 43

The Legacy of Motown

BRIAN HOLLAND, songwriter: The Vandellas stayed longer because Martha Reeves, she kept going on and on.

ROSALIND ASHFORD, The Vandellas: Around '89, Martha had asked me back in the group. I called Annette, and I talked to her, and I talked her into coming back to do that show. So, we were supposed to just do that one New Year's Eve show.

ANNETTE BEARD, The Vandellas: We were surprised that after the amount of time we had been separated from each other, that when we started singing the background to the songs, that we could still harmonize the same as we did on the records. And everybody loved it.

MARTHA REEVES, The Vandellas: I really like being grouped in the specification of girl groups, but I'm a single performer. I'm a solo artist. I *chose* to sing in groups because I like harmony. But my career was a single effort.

ROSALIND ASHFORD, The Vandellas: Everybody was excited. Everybody seemed to have enjoyed it. And then there was a comment that said, "Well, Martha really needed you girls." So, she made a comment to whoever said that, "No, they needed *me*."

ANNETTE BEARD, The Vandellas: Me and Rosalind looked at each other, like, *We didn't ask to go back to the group. You asked us back.*

ROSALIND ASHFORD, The Vandellas: We would sing with her on weekends or whatever. And she had even came to us and said, "Well, you guys can quit your jobs." But that was not going to happen. We had put in too much to give away our time. That's when we said, "Well, we'll travel with you, but on weekends—that's the only way we'll do this."

MARTHA REEVES, The Vandellas: They didn't write anything. They didn't invest in anything. They didn't have any loyalty to me whatsoever or give me any credit for working as hard as I did to get us in Motown. So, it was a different thing. They were strangers and it didn't last very long.

ANNETTE BEARD, The Vandellas: We went back with her for close to ten years. We traveled extensively with Martha. But we had seniority in our jobs, so we were going to continue to work our jobs, which we did. We both retired off of our jobs.

ROSALIND ASHFORD, The Vandellas: I did my thirty years, believe it or not, and I retired from Meritech.

ANNETTE BEARD, The Vandellas: I ended up getting a job at, long time ago it was Detroit Memorial Hospital, working in a laboratory. I was a phlebotomist; I drew blood. There at Detroit Memorial, I learned quite a few things about the lab, because I'd been sending over some of the techs asking questions and they'd be like, "You want to know how to do this?" And they would teach me how to do all of those different things. I didn't have no degree, no nothing, but they taught me everything that I knew. Everything that I learned, I learned hands-on.

And I started that job at $1.66 an hour. That's how I raised my children. I tried to get help from the state—they said I made too much money.

MARTHA REEVES, The Vandellas: I was miserable! We didn't grow up together and I didn't go to school with them. I didn't know them. We just sang good together. When we got back together, they didn't remember that most of the planning and most of the singing and all of the arranging, and the bookings and the interviews and everything I had done.

ANNETTE BEARD, The Vandellas: When we got back to the dressing room, Martha confronted us and said, "What gave you guys the right to continue to sit there and sign autographs after I had left the table?" And I looked at her, I was like, "What?" She said, "What gave you the right to sit there?" She asked me, she said, "Who pays your salary?" I said, "Saint John Hospital." She looked at me like—if looks could kill, I would be dead right now.

What I made with her was what me and Rosalind would carry in our pocket as chump change. I mean, it's not like we were making an overabundance of money or anything like that. We were doing it because we felt like we should. She looked at me like, *How dare you?* I was like, well, I told the truth, "I depend on Saint John Hospital to give me a check every two weeks. No, not you."

MARTHA REEVES, The Vandellas: I think Annette was away from the business twenty years. When she came back, she was not the same person. They were different, real different, personality-wise. They hadn't experienced anything other than what we had done in the past. It was hard to go forward with them. They were even at the point of secretly going in my briefcase, trying to find out what contracts looked like, and what their cut of it was, and all that. Which was . . . I thought it was very disloyal and inappropriate.

ROSALIND ASHFORD, The Vandellas: Then next thing you know, we were gone again.

ANNETTE BEARD, The Vandellas: She never said, "I don't want to sing with you guys anymore, I'm using my sisters." Never said anything like that.

She has really, really changed, and people talk about her all the time. We go to different places and we work with different groups—and they're like, "Ooh, we worked with your girl last weekend," and we're like, "You didn't work with our girl." And they was like, "She was her same old self, bitchy as hell." I was like, "Well, y'all know her."

MARTHA REEVES, The Vandellas: By some of the reports from Rosalind and Annette, I'd be offended by some of the things they'll report, if you have plans to interview them.

ANNETTE BEARD, The Vandellas: But our peers, some of the band members, and the people we knew from Motown were like, "You guys are the original Vandellas. Why don't you get you a lead singer and get back out there and start singing?" It was something that Ros and I never even really thought about. I mean we felt like, *Well, that part is over.*

MARTHA REEVES, The Vandellas: But they're still going around saying that they're "The Original Vandellas." They've got some girl singing my songs, doing a terrible job of it. It's like I'm dead—and I'm not. It offends me.

ANNETTE BEARD, The Vandellas: We got back and when we started doing shows again, when she found that out, she was really pissed at us. She really stopped talking to us. We've been to functions at Motown and she has walked in the room and spoke to everybody *but* me and Ros. She'll just pretend like we don't even exist. And I think it's for that reason—the fact that we got a lead singer. She'll say she doesn't want nobody singing her songs because she's still alive and she can sing them herself.

MARTHA REEVES, The Vandellas: I've had over fifty backup singers and that's why I said you can't really categorize me as a group, because I sang the lead on all of the songs. *I'm* the voice that sold the records. *I'm* the one who showed up to Hitsville USA and did the role for nine months as a secretary to be there—to get records and to stay involved in music and in my dream. I didn't know them. I didn't know their life. I didn't know what they would do or were subject to do. I had a dedication and it's been to show business, and to sing, and to do what I'm told to do with the talent that I prayed to God for.

ANNETTE BEARD, The Vandellas: She thinks because she's Martha Reeves that she's supposed to get the bigger of it. But I have to remind people that I talk to—the first time we did a big show, which probably was the Apollo—we stepped out as three young ladies on the stage. She did not walk out on that stage by herself—she had me and Ros with her, and that's what the people saw. *That's* what the people heard.

MARTHA REEVES, The Vandellas: We don't have the same frame of mind. We're not on one accord, never have been and never will be. I sang with people who sang backup for *me* and I'm continuing with members of my family—who I help to nurture and teach to sing—who join me now, in my career, in my effort to be a performer.

*

MARY WILSON, The Supremes: Well, Motown folks, we are a family. Not by blood, but we are because we all came together when we were all very young. And so there is this family reunion situation that, whenever we're together, that's what it is. For your own family, there you've got drunk Uncle Louis, you got Aunt Lucy, you got all these different people, but you all love each other. So it's the same thing with the Motown family—we maybe have different personalities, different this, different that, but we all love each other still.

JACKIE HICKS, The Andantes: Hey, I'm proud of myself. I'm proud of Motown . . . and I seriously have no regrets looking back now, wishing so-and-so could have gone this way instead of that way. It went the way that it was. I do see everyone now on a regular basis. We're friends and, you know, we celebrate each other.

MARTHA REEVES, The Vandellas: That love was put in the grooves on those records.

LOUVAIN DEMPS, The Andantes: Anything now that I hear, I always say, "Boy, didn't we sound good?"

BRIAN HOLLAND, songwriter: I tried to get in touch with Diana Ross. I even talked to Berry Gordy. I said, "Berry, give me Diana Ross's phone number." I wanted to talk to her about something, but anyway, he said, "Man, well, I got the number around here somewhere. . . ." I know he's lying, [*laughing*] but anyway, I just took it for what it was. . . . Hey, listen, you don't have to tell me about Diana. She is different. Like I said, she's a mystery wrapped up in an enigma.

MARY WILSON, The Supremes: If I were to say what The Supremes' legacy is, it's that hopefully we have inspired many people—not just women, not just Black women, but many people in terms of who they were and who they could become in life. What I would say is that four little Black girls from the Brewster projects in the 1950s and 1960s dared to dream—and we made our dreams come true. I think that's what we ended up doing without even realizing that's what we were doing—is helping other people to dare to dream and to make their dreams come true.

KATHERINE ANDERSON, The Marvelettes: You know, we performed many, many times, many, many times. After we did the performances, everybody would say, "You all were really good," but then again—the thing in the back of my mind was to graduate from high school. That really, *really* bothered me—that we couldn't graduate from high school during the time that we should have.

So, then I went back after I had my first stroke, and I studied—which it really was rather hard to do because I had a stroke. I got it together, I went on and studied and got my high school diploma. Yes, I did get it. I got it with honors, and I was *quite* thrilled about that.

WHOOPI GOLDBERG, entertainer: As I said it, it wasn't the building block, but it was the mortar that runs through everything that says, "You know, go for it. See what happens. Don't be afraid to go for it." I think that particular time with The Supremes, The Marvelettes, and Martha Reeves and The Vandellas, that was a really moving and shifting time in the country as well as in neighborhoods and realizing that there was no door that could keep you out if you were willing to knock the door open.

Just that if these girl groups sounded as great and did all of the stuff that they were able to do, it meant that there was no barrier. If you had talent, you know, something great could happen. There was never a question in my mind about talent and that was *real* talent. You had to be able to sing. You had to be able to do what all of these girl groups were doing. It was the mortar that runs through everything that says, "You know, go for it. See what happens. Don't be afraid to go for it."

MARTHA REEVES, The Vandellas: We did try, and we endured, and yes, we are queens. Yes, we are.

PART 8

Coming Back Together and Saying Goodbye

1970–Present

CHAPTER 44

The Chantels, The Bobbettes, The Clickettes, The Super Girls

LOIS POWELL, The Chantels: It's interesting because I had met Darlene Love at some point. She came to the Apollo Theater to see our show, and so we formed a relationship and became pen pals. She would write to me from California. I still have her letters. She sent me her graduation pictures, and when she got married—her first marriage—she sent me pictures of her husband, and after she had her child . . . whenever she's in a space where we are, it's like old home week with her.

BOBBY JAY, disc jockey: I still host a lot of shows, and I notice the audience coming in with their defibrillators and their oxygen tanks, they're coming in their wheelchairs. The audience is old, but the music is still the same.

LOIS POWELL, The Chantels: I try to build relationships because we didn't have that opportunity. They all came after us.

EMMA POUGHT, The Bobbettes: We've all sat backstage and talked. Basically, we were all going through the same thing. . . . When you do a girl group show, that's a lot of fun, that's a lot of fun with all the different groups—The Marvelettes, The Clickettes, The Chantels, The Shirelles—all women.

DARLENE LOVE, The Blossoms: Let's face it, you know, as James Brown said, this a man's world. It takes us all helping one another. We all have to be on the same page, you have to help one another. And fortunately, I did have help from other women. Nobody gets there by themselves—somebody helped you.

JUDY CRAIG, The Chiffons: It feels good to see that everybody is still doing well, and they're able to still do it like me. It feels good, it really does. Like when I first ran into La La, I said, "Oh wow, La La, I didn't know you were still out here." She said, "Yeah, girl. We're still doing it. We're just going to make this money tonight and go home." I said, "You're right."

EMMA POUGHT, The Bobbettes: You run into people on that "circuit," as they call it. A lot of them had just stopped singing.

BRENDA REID, The Exciters: As we got to know one another back in our era, the next time we saw each other, it was like a reunion. And everybody would get together and have a good time from one dressing room to the other—laugh and talk between shows, you know. And if we had to stay there for a week, everybody was getting a hookup with somebody bringing us a cake they baked, cookies, or something like that.

SYLVIA HAMMOND, The Clickettes: I got a call in 1999 about a doo-wop thing up here on Strivers' Row, and Barbara called me and said, "Would you like to come back? We can be a group again." I said, "I don't know if I can do it again." I didn't know how my voice was, because I hadn't really sang with anybody since 1950-something—during that particular time, those years, we were getting married, working, and whatever. So it was kind of hard.

BARBARA ENGLISH, The Clickettes: It was a doo-wop day in Harlem. Only Trudy and I were there—we ran into some people who were very much in love with The Clickettes, and they convinced us to reunite.

SYLVIA HAMMOND, The Clickettes: We've been staying in touch, and we still stay in touch. I spoke to Barbara, of course, Trudy—we all stay in touch.

BARBARA ENGLISH, The Clickettes: All the time. They're like family. They're my sisters. . . . Yeah, those that are here. You know, Barbara Saunders passed. Charlotte passed—she was original. Barbara was the alternate, she's gone. But Jean and I talk at least once a week. Yesterday Trudy just called me; she's with me two times a month—stays at my house. Sylvia, I speak to all the time, so we're still close.

TRUDY McCARTNEY, The Clickettes: I talked to Barbara today. She said, "What time is your interview?" I said, "You're so nosy." [*laughing*]

SYLVIA HAMMOND, The Clickettes: Barbara is good with putting words together. . . . She's a good writer—she's phenomenal in her own way.

BARBARA ENGLISH, The Clickettes: "Because of My Best Friend" and "To Be a Part of You," "Lover's Prayer," which did not do big-time, but it's considered . . . I mean it is a classic among record collectors.

MARC TAYLOR, music writer: There are so many other girl groups out there who had a hit record that was just local, regional, or sometimes only R & B but didn't really chart nationally on the pop charts, so they're not necessarily coming up in conversations.

JEAN BOULDIN, The Clickettes: When we left Zell, we could not use the name The Clickettes, so we became The Fashions, but everybody just sort of . . . I started going to dance school more and I wouldn't show up because I was taking my dance classes, and so everything just, you know, just fizzled out.

BARBARA ENGLISH, The Clickettes: I started working as a receptionist at a music publisher at 25 West 52nd Street, but also as a demo recording artist. It was frustrating, disappointing, and painful. So I stopped singing completely for about seven years. . . . I wouldn't even sing in the shower. It was just awful for me until 1971.

JEAN BOULDIN, The Clickettes: I got a job as a secretary, but I was still going to dance school, and I went to a lot of Broadway auditions to try to work Broadway as a dancer. Finally, I ended up with a group that was going to Europe for six months, went with them as a dancer, and ended up staying in Europe for about fifteen years.

BARBARA ENGLISH, The Clickettes: Well, Lord, in the seventies I was recording for Alithia Records [as Barbara Jean English]. I made a lot of records, more than I can ever imagine. They were not super successes, but I became a working cabaret singer—you know, I worked on stages now rather than the recordings. I made my living for twenty, thirty years working in various venues—Atlantic City, cruise ships, opening for major comics—got my start at Rodney Dangerfield's, worked there for, like, four or five years. Got my legs at the Catskills, the Poconos, Europe, India, Ghana . . .

SYLVIA HAMMOND, The Clickettes: I said to Barbara, "I always wanted to come back." During the years that I was married, all those years, I said, "Boy, it would've been nice if I could go back. . . ." Well what do we have to do? Because I got to get my voice together because I haven't sang with the group. So we had to go through and just rehearse all over again—getting ready to get back up there. I'm nervous as what—I don't know if everybody else was, I'm quite sure, but Barbara had the expertise, and she had the connections because she had been out there.

And going back up and getting back up there was frightening. And people were saying, "The Clickettes . . . sing this song, sing that song! Oh wow." So it's like, *Oh boy.* And we had practiced all of that, so I felt good, thinking, *Wow, they remember back—all the way back, people still remember all of this?* This is what I'm thinking to myself, *They remember all of this?*

TRUDY McCARTNEY, The Clickettes: My prayer, you know, is when people hear the music they'll say how beautiful it is. But, yet, and still, it didn't get anywhere. That's The Chantels. . . . That wasn't us—that was them. They got the recognition, we didn't.

BARBARA ENGLISH, The Clickettes: I did not know that we had impacted so many people, you know, because we were not The Chantels, we were not The Shirelles. We were The Clickettes and were small.

But there's a group of people who say, "I don't know whether you were big or not, you were bad."

TRUDY McCARTNEY, The Clickettes: We weren't that . . . that . . . big. But you know, it was big to me . . . that first time, oh my heart. . . . You know, it was just like heaven, *That's me on the radio?*

BARBARA ENGLISH, The Clickettes: I can't describe the feeling, the feeling when I heard our song on the radio. I ran up and down 10th Street. "Everybody listen!" By the time I got back to the house, it was over, you know what I'm saying? [*laughing*] I ran up and down to tell everybody, "Put on the radio, put on the radio!"

✳

LOIS POWELL, The Chantels: I didn't care if I ever sang "Maybe" ever again. I hated it, and I didn't start to like it until maybe 1998 when we did a show and a guy came up to me and said, "The only reason I'm alive is because when I was in Vietnam I played 'Maybe' every night in my foxhole, and I knew if I could play that song and hear it, I would come home." At that point the hair on the back of my neck stood up. I couldn't breathe. I was taken so aback, and I said, *If this man could appreciate this song, then I'm missing something*. And that's when I . . . and even now, when we sing it, well, not only because we lost Jackie [Landry]—we get very emotional.

TRUDY McCARTNEY, The Clickettes: Jackie lived in my block and then I met the rest of The Chantels through Jackie. We became friends and all sang together. We were close friends growing up. . . . Her brother was my first boyfriend. So you know, we were little, but that was my first boyfriend. [*laughing*]

RENÉE MINUS WHITE, The Chantels: Regrouping after Jackie's passing was difficult. I had to learn all of her notes to fill the gap in our harmony. There were times when we would simply stop singing a song while onstage and just start crying.

LOIS POWELL, The Chantels: But she comes with us wherever we are. We never forget her. Before we go out and sing, we say, "Jackie, we know your spirit is with us. Just hang out with us onstage." Sometimes we can do it without crying, and other times we can't.

EMMA POUGHT, The Bobbettes: I remember when Jackie died. . . . She was a nice person. We was at the Apollo together. It really was fun because we were nothing but children.

LOIS POWELL, The Chantels: I really was out of the loop until the late nineties, when a friend of mine called and told me that The Chantels were getting inducted into this United Group Harmony Association Hall of Fame. Arlene Smith was there, and the agreement was we were going to sing "Look in My Eyes," and Arlene was going to do "Maybe."

And so, while Arlene was singing "Maybe," Jackie decided that why don't we just all go out and sing with her? The other girls were hemming and hawing, and I said, "No, she's not expecting it. How would you feel if somebody walked out?" But nobody could hear me, and then Jackie just started walking out. So, then we walked out, and then we started to sing with Arlene, and people were on their feet. It was like, "Oh my God, a reunion!" Which was not the case, but that's how they saw it.

We both received our awards separately. She got her plaque, and then we got our plaques. It was cordial, and it was fine. We didn't have any beef with Arlene, but we hadn't sung with her since 1959. This is 1995. We won't talk about each other to anybody. We don't talk about Arlene to anybody. And we *certainly* will not listen to anything if anybody says something negative about Arlene. We don't want to hear it. But that's who we are.

EMMA POUGHT, The Bobbettes: The Chantels is good because they got most of them still alive. We started getting people for substitutes and I had to go through this long training period, how we moved onstage, how we interacted with each other. And that's very difficult for somebody that's been working together for forty years, forty-five years, for you to come in from nowhere.

LOIS POWELL, The Chantels: Jackie and I were the closest of the group. We were the same height. We pretty much weighed about the same and we would dress alike and tell people we were twins. So we did everything together. She was at my house. I was at her house. She spent the night at my house. I spent the night at her house. And so we were like two peas in a pod. So I was closest to her in terms of friendship. We had made a promise that if either of us got sick, we would not let the other die alone. She died in my arms. So that's what I can say about Jackie. I kept my promise.

I stayed with her, and I slept there, and then I went home again for another change of clothes, came back, and then I knew that was going to be the day. And so that's . . . the nurse came and told me she was taking her off the life support, and I said, "Okay." And then we went in and we got her prepped, because I was a nurse. And so we did that and then she stopped breathing and her son had gone out across the street to get some coffee, and I said, "Jackie, not now." Because I wanted Chris to get back there. And she knew better and then she started breathing again and then she stopped breathing and I said, "Jackie," and she didn't move. I knew she was gone. So she didn't want her son there, that was obvious.

EMMA POUGHT, The Bobbettes: We were a group for years and years and years, I would say from children, we grew into everything together from childhood into adulthood, marriages, debt, you name it, divorces. We've been through it all right together. And we were like sisters more than like a group—you would call it like that because you live and eat and sleep and everything together. And that's what we did.

Reather died from a heart attack. She was the last one that died about six years ago. Laura died from colon cancer. Helen died from a heart attack too. It was all sickness except my sister. They had it out that somebody stabbed her, which was not true. She was killed in an accident in 1980. What happened was she carried a screwdriver—she always kept a weapon on her because where she lived was a bad, bad area. So she had a screwdriver that she laid crossways of her bra; you can put it down in your bra, a woman can do that.

Well, anyway, what happened was two of her friends got into a fight, and she tried breaking them up. The man pushed my sister, but when he pushed her, he pushed her in the chest—like, "Get off of me"—and the screwdriver bent inwards. It stuck into her lungs, and nobody realized that she had been stabbed. All of a sudden, she collapsed against a car—she leaned back and she took a deep breath, and when she did, my younger sister who was there—I wasn't there—she said, "I saw blood trickling down the front of her blouse." That's what happened to her.

This is the most I've talked about this business in a long time, because I'll tell you, I don't do interviews, I just don't. And I try to keep my mind away from it, because I think about the girls so much at times. I really miss them. I really miss them.

✳

MARGARET ROSS, The Cookies: The Super Girls got together because we didn't have our girls. Somebody said, "You are a leader from The Cookies, you're a leader from The Hearts and The Jaynetts—that's Louise Murray. Then you have Lillian Walker-Moss, who is from The Exciters, and then you have Nanette Licari from Reparata and The Delrons, and Beverly Warren, who used to sing with The Raindrops. Why don't you girls get together and be The Super Girls?"

LILLIAN WALKER-MOSS, The Exciters: I had left The Exciters in 1972; it was a lot of things going on. You know, I used to suffer from some clinical depression. Music has always been my passion. I never wanted to do anything *but* appear on the stage. But I started becoming robotic. . . . I felt like one of those little windup dolls—you know, dress me up pretty, sit me out onstage, turn the key in the back, you know, and I'll perform—instead of really being into it, you know, getting into it, and really enjoying myself. I knew something was wrong when that happened to me, because I feel music *very deeply* since I was a little girl. And I stopped feeling, I stopped feeling the music. . . . I wouldn't want to be bothered with singing and everything. And all my personal issues started rising. I guess it was part of my depressive symptoms . . . but I started getting, I started feeling like I wasn't a person, I was just an object.

BRENDA REID, The Exciters: I'm just beginning to really accept who I am. Because I tell you why . . . things happened so fast with my career and with all the things that happened in between after having children.

LILLIAN WALKER-MOSS, The Exciters: I went to college and I did my undergrad in social work, I did guidance and counseling at Hunter College, and I got my master's, then I got my postgraduate certificate in expressive arts therapy. I learned so much about myself, and how I felt concerned when I was young, how I felt when I was a teenager, why I quit my group and about my own clinical depression, which I'm proud of that—I beat clinical depression.

BRENDA REID, The Exciters: The women in the business encountered so much, they have so much to tell, I know they have all got stories to tell. I was afraid to tell my real story because I have cried, and I didn't want my fans—which are the best fans in the whole world—I didn't want anybody to see any blemish on me at all in any kind of way.

LILLIAN WALKER-MOSS, The Exciters: In 1992, United Artists had this thing called The Legends of Rock and Roll, and they were rereleasing a lot of their acts who were on their label in the sixties. I went to the party and after the party I kept getting this *gnawing* feeling in my guts. And I'm like, *What is it? What is bugging me?* I *never* sang . . . you know, it was crazy . . . with clinical depression, I *never, ever, ever* sang—never—not even in the shower. Not even if I'm playing a record, you know how you sing along to a record? I never sang one note. After the party, this gnawing feeling one day reached my throat and, all of a sudden, I'm in my house, and I started *singing* at the top of my lungs. And then I said, *Oh, I must want to sing again.*

MARGARET ROSS, The Cookies: I love to sing. I do. I do. I'll be in the house cleaning up and I'll be singing to my neighbor upstairs. [*laughing*]

LOUISE MURRAY, The Hearts, The Jaynetts: It would always seem like we'd be in the same place when things were going on, singing.

LILLIAN WALKER-MOSS, The Exciters: I knew Margaret and Louise, but we hadn't seen each other in years. . . .

BEVERLY WARREN, The Raindrops: I reunited with Margaret. After all those years, we talked about the time we were onstage together.

And somehow, you know, like the continents moving closer and closer together, we all came into contact. And it's pretty amazing—these were my favorite artists growing up, and my idols, and now I'm appearing with them and I'm singing with them, which is like, *Is this real or am I dreaming?*

NANETTE LICARI, Reparata and The Delrons: Every one of my musical dreams have come true. I did backup for The Hearts and so many people. . . . I backed up Little Eva. Oh my goodness, I just love harmony.

BEVERLY WARREN, The Raindrops: You have all these legendary ladies from the sixties. Again, I don't know how legendary *I* was, but certainly I was *with* a bunch of legendary ladies.

NANETTE LICARI, Reparata and The Delrons: Total honor. And when you hear the sound of all of us together, it's a beautiful thing—and so we're still singing, enjoying it.

BEVERLY WARREN, The Raindrops: They sing their hits and all back each other up.

MARGARET ROSS, The Cookies: And as long as God gives me the strength, I'm going to still try to get out there and do a show every now and then. I like to make people smile.

CHAPTER 45

The Shirelles

BILLY VERA, musician: The Shirelles were a different story. They had never stopped working because they had so many hits.

BEVERLY LEE, The Shirelles: We left Scepter because we knew that time was winding down. We weren't being produced correctly. We were growing up, we had more knowledge of the business.

STEVE GUARNORI, author of *Scepter Wand Forever!*: They had a fairly good run after they left Scepter, and they might not have been successful, but three of them at least were singing together for several years afterwards.

BILLY VERA, musician: I was doing my little club dates with my band, and when The Shirelles worked, I went out with them.

BEVERLY LEE, The Shirelles: A lot of people didn't work beyond that, but we were prepared because we had different material. We had different formats of our show, which I still do today. We didn't just do the oldie shows; we had supper clubs we could perform at.

BILLY VERA, musician: At the time I joined The Shirelles, they were trying to update their act and they were doing current songs in addition to . . . they'd do, like, "Will You Love Me Tomorrow" and "Soldier Boy" and a couple of the big hits, but they'd bring in Carole King songs from *Tapestry*. And you know, I said, "Listen, people don't really care about you singing all these new songs. They want to hear your hits, the songs that they love you for." So, I got them to do what were their old hits. And, of course, the audience response got better.

BEVERLY LEE, The Shirelles: Yeah, Billy he's a sweetheart. . . . We did colleges, we worked a lot of colleges. We were able to work. There were always three out of the four original members, unless somebody was sick.

BILLY VERA, musician: Shirley, Micki, and Beverly. Doris had left the group to raise a family. She came back many years later. And I even got them to do "Met Him on a Sunday." [*laughing*] They said, "Oh man . . . that's a very primitive song." I said, "That's what they like about it. Do it, do it." And they did, and it went over great, of course.

SHIRLEY ALSTON REEVES, The Shirelles: I had my baby in 1976. . . . I called Doris and asked her if she would take my place. Doris had left years prior. She had twins and she had left. I asked her if she would take my place while I was pregnant. First she said no, but then she said, "Okay, but only until you get well enough to come back." When the baby got to be a few months old, I decided to go back with them.

BILLY VERA, musician: They were a few years older than me, and I was the only male that traveled with them other than this old guy, this forty-five-year-old gay guy who was sort of their bodyguard and their emcee—he was kind of part of the act. He had worked with Pearl Bailey before them, and he had been with The Shirelles for about thirteen years by that point.

SHIRLEY ALSTON REEVES, The Shirelles: I came back out and I felt like a complete stranger. I felt like I just met them. They would be talking and I felt left out. . . . They actually came to my house and told me that they decided they were going to keep Doris as lead. I said, "Fine." I looked at Doris because she had told me she didn't want to stay and was only going to stay for a little while. Things happen. I guess you get back out there and it's fun to you again. I said, "Well, if that's the way you want it . . ." That was it.

BEVERLY LEE, The Shirelles: It was me, Micki, and Doris touring most of the time.

SHIRLEY ALSTON REEVES, The Shirelles: Beverly still works as "The Shirelles." I can't, because she owns the name. She and Doris owned the name. They both went to court. I could've owned the name, too, but I chose not to go to court. We were friends for all of those years, and I wasn't about to go in there and fight about a name. No, thank you. I just do what I have to do.

BEVERLY LEE, The Shirelles: I legally . . . I got the name because I was the only Shirelle who never quit the group. I kept the group intact.

SHIRLEY ALSTON REEVES, The Shirelles: I didn't say, "Well, I quit. I'm going out on my own. I want to be Diana Ross." I didn't—I did not do that. It was never "Shirley Alston and The Shirelles"; it was always just "The Shirelles." They built Diana into that. You have to work to do what she did. It would be more difficult for me to just get out there and do what I did. I had to struggle to really get out there because I was only allowed for a while to use "Shirley Alston." Beverly took me to court so I couldn't use "The Shirelles." She had them put down that "The Shirelles" had to be 25 percent smaller than my name.

BEVERLY LEE, The Shirelles: My attorney told me that I had the right to the name. Oh gosh, in '82, somewhere around there, '82, '83, I believe, don't hold me to it.

SHIRLEY ALSTON REEVES, The Shirelles: What was happening was that they were trying to stop me from using it at all, but it's a statement of fact. You can't say that I wasn't the original lead singer of The Shirelles. Even now, when they're doing a show, what do they do? They play all of the songs I'm singing on. I was hurt and was crying. I couldn't talk about it. It was like something had a grip of my whole heart, but I'm over it. It's still a little sensitive area, but I'm happy within myself. I'm not doing anything spectacular, but neither is anyone else. We're just traveling along, riding into the sunset.

AUTHORS' NOTE: Addie "Micki" Harris McFadden died from a massive heart attack on June 10, 1982, at the age of forty-two, following a performance in Atlanta, Georgia. Four years later, in 1986, Beverly and Doris split the rights to The Shirelles' name. Each formed their own act. Doris would stay primarily on the West Coast, and Beverly primarily toured the East.

FANITA JAMES, The Blossoms: Beverly had a group, and Shirley had a group, and Doris had a group.

GLORIA JONES, The Blossoms: They told Shirley that she couldn't use the name "Shirelles." It could only be so high. They had to say "Shirley Alston, formerly of The Shirelles," and that would be down at the bottom. Then Doris and Beverly had to share the name.

FANITA JAMES, The Blossoms: It was in '92.

GLORIA JONES, The Blossoms: And that time, Doris moved out here to Sacramento. So we were on the same coast. She asked me to come and sing, and I said, "Okay. I'm not doing anything." I always had a job where, if I wanted to take off to go do something, they were so impressed that I was singing with The Shirelles, they didn't care.

FANITA JAMES, The Blossoms: Oh, we toured everywhere. We went all up and down to places I had never been in California.

GLORIA JONES, The Blossoms: We did a show in Caesars Palace, in Atlantic City. It was a New Year's Eve party. It was on TV. . . . We did it before—we filmed it. So a man came out and he said, "I'm going to tell you girls, they just finished this floor and it's slippery as hell. So be careful." The announcer was announcing, and from backstage Doris sings, "This is dedicated . . ." and fell and hit the floor. But she never, ever stopped singing.

FANITA JAMES, The Blossoms: "This is dedicated . . ." And that's all she had to sing . . . first notes out, the audience would go crazy. "To the one I love." Oh my goodness.

GLORIA JONES, The Blossoms: We were trying to pick her up off the floor . . . because you couldn't see us backstage. And then we walked out. We all walked out, and thank God, I was praying the whole time walking out there, saying, "God, if you ever loved your child, please let me stop laughing, please." And I started singing, doing the background. And I couldn't . . . my shoulders were shaking because I was so tickled. Doris did that show like nothing had never happened. She could just make you think that everything was all right. Everything was all right. . . .

I mean, you're talking about a trouper. Doris is a trouper and she comes off very intelligent. She can always think of something to say. Sometimes she was so sick, it was almost like she couldn't go on. Shoot . . . that music started playing and Doris, she couldn't hold back. Walking on out there, I'd say, "Well, you just go ahead, girl." And it was always just insane. She was singing with it. And she might not say a whole lot of words when she gets offstage, but she'd be smiling. You never knew what she was feeling if you didn't know her. You know what I'm saying?

AUTHORS' NOTE: Doris Coley Kenner Jackson died from breast cancer on February 4, 2000. She was fifty-eight years old.

Florence Greenberg, The Shirelles' mother figure and manager, died from complications of a stroke on November 2, 1995, at the age of eighty-two.

In 2008, The Shirelles' hometown of Passaic, New Jersey, renamed their school auditorium and a street near their high school after the group. Shirley, Beverly, the families of Doris and Micki, and their old friend Mary Jane Greenberg, who watched them perform on the auditorium stage back in 1958, were all present to be honored by the city they loved.

JOEY DEE, Joey Dee and the Starliters: Passaic really honored us—The Shirelles and me. They were awarded the name of the high school auditorium, "The Shirelles Auditorium." And I got the second-highest award, Lincoln Middle School's auditorium is named after Joey Dee and the Starliters. It was just a marvelous situation.

SHIRLEY ALSTON REEVES, The Shirelles: You don't take things for granted. I was never like, "Oh, I can do this, I can do that, because I'm a Shirelle." I'm just another person trying to make it. I'm fortunate that I've had a nice little career. I was happy doing it. I didn't get rich from it—could have, but didn't. Things were beyond my control. At the same time, I've been everywhere in the world I wanted to be. Everything was good, all good since 1958. I did it with people that I love. We were real friends and we had the time of our lives.

BEVERLY LEE, The Shirelles: We've had a history, so if she ever needs me, I'll be there. I believe God put the four of us together, because we came from single-parent homes. He wanted to take these four young teenagers and let them bloom and blossom. He gets the glory.

CHAPTER 46

Royalties

The Same Old Song and Dance

BEVERLY LEE, The Shirelles: We just finally got the publishing a couple years ago for "I Met Him on a Sunday." That was a big plus for us.

LILLIAN WALKER, The Exciters: We thought it was only *us* with the money issues. But then when we met all these other girls, they're telling us the same stories! Oh, it was . . . it was disgusting. Like, we never actually started getting royalties until *The Big Chill*, which was about 1985.

BILLY JOEL, musician: A lot of the groups probably didn't get paid the way they should have. A lot of them, I'm sure, were ripped off by the record industry, which is pretty larcenous, especially back in those days.

RICHARD DUBIN, musician: The degree to which this business is set out to exploit people as commodities is really, really misunderstood.

DEE DEE KENNIEBREW, The Crystals: When we took Phil Spector to court, we used our contracts, and we didn't get any money, so I didn't think much of it. We got nothing. Goodbye, zip—go home. This guy, Chuck Rubin, had a bunch of people sign with him, "I'll get your money for you from your record company." And he asked me in 1977 . . . he wanted The Crystals to take Phil back to court again.

EMMA POUGHT, The Bobbettes: They got so many people out here that are crooks, because I don't know whether you ever heard of Artists Rights? Have you ever heard of that? It's the worst. The man's name is Chuck Rubin. I was all right, because I was a *writer*, and as a writer your checks come separately.

DEE DEE KENNIEBREW, The Crystals: The guy has now died, a couple of years ago. His daughter has my original contract. I've asked her for it a number of times. She'll probably keep it or sell it.

EMMA POUGHT, The Bobbettes: Well, he's dead now, but can't get rid of him to this day—I've been trying.

JON "BOWZER" BAUMAN, Sha Na Na: You should be getting checks as a performer, which, you know, as recently as last year [2020] was still a subject of congressional hearings, and that's where someone like a Chuck Rubin can swoop in and say, "I can give myself a piece of it in perpetuity forever, because otherwise people have no chance."

EMMA POUGHT, The Bobbettes: We met him at Radio City. . . . They had a big R & B, doo-wop show there years ago. He went from room to room—every group—he was talking to them, "I know there's a lot of money. I can help you get that money, that money that's *owed* to you."

DEE DEE KENNIEBREW, The Crystals: There was a movie that was out, and they were using "Da Doo Ron Ron" and "Then He Kissed Me." He says, "I can get money for you from that movie, but I need to see your contract and see how it reads." So, sure enough, I took Chuck the contract.

BEVERLY LEE, The Shirelles: When *Dirty Dancing* came out, there was an influx of younger girls buying our music. They had been doing that all the while . . . but that did help a lot.

STEVE GUARNORI, author of *Scepter Wand Forever!*: Everyone was doing it, all the big record companies were going back and digging out oldies and rebranding them.

EMMA POUGHT, The Bobbettes: You never know when somebody's liable to pick up one of them songs and record it or put it in a commercial or put it in a movie. Even if you only hear so many bars of that song, you get paid if you own that song.

And now, shoot, if you get a record as big as "Mr. Lee," when *Stand by Me* came out . . . that's why we got the platinum record. I don't know to this day if you could ever get to calculate how much money they made off it. But every time I see *Stand by Me* come on—which was on the other night—I said, "Oh, I'm going to get a good check."

LILLIAN WALKER, The Exciters: They put our song "Tell Him" in *The Big Chill*. And that's how we got to get the money. Because somebody said, "You know what? You should—you're supposed to get money." So then they got the entertainment lawyer to look into it.

LOUISE MURRAY, The Hearts, The Jaynetts: I used to get little, small, little royalties from "Lonely Nights," and then I stopped getting that, and I tried to figure out why. *How come I'm not getting royalties?* Somebody's getting royalties! *I made the record. Who's getting paid?* I see Martin Scorsese really loved it. It was in all of his movies, almost. . . . Oh, it's really depressing. I didn't even look at this last movie that we were in, *The Irishman*. I didn't even look at it, I don't even want to see it. I don't want to see it. . . . I know I'm not going to get paid. I'm not. I'm just never going to get my worth.

DEE DEE KENNIEBREW, The Crystals: When I got the check from the movie, it was a check from Chuck Rubin. I never did see what the original check was for. It was so small, I think it was maybe five hundred and some dollars, or something like that. I thought he cheated us. Because he's not even giving us a copy of the original check that was received.

So, the next time he asked me to do something, for another movie, that one was called *Stripes*, I said, "No. I don't want anything." Rather than just let this guy just take me, I'd rather not have the money. I'm not just going to give him the authorization to go after the money for us, and then he keeps the most and gives us the small amount.

I wouldn't sign anything with him, because I didn't trust the guy at all, especially after that first ordeal. I just wouldn't give somebody

50 percent of my money to get it for me. I'm not doing it. That's what a lot of them signed—*You get 50 percent of the money that you recover for me?* I thought, *That's ridiculous*. I said no. I wouldn't do it.

JON "BOWZER" BAUMAN, Sha Na Na: I guess the simplest way to put Chuck Rubin is . . . don't you think 50 percent was kind of a lot?

EMMA POUGHT, The Bobbettes: He had a lot of the doo-wops because they were the ones that were extorted back in the day, and he would take 50 percent of their royalties.

FANITA JAMES, The Blossoms: Well, do you believe we were getting royalties now from a gentleman in New York named Chuck Rubin? He has an office in New York, and he died. His daughter took over . . . and I get money twice a year. They're a godsend. They helped me pay my property taxes in March and October, it's just a blessing.

Well, he told me what he was all about, how he was helping the singers of the fifties and sixties with royalties they didn't get. And you know I jumped on that. I said, "Oh yes," and I signed contracts and everything.

LOIS POWELL, The Chantels: So, we negotiated for a lower fee, but there are a lot of people who were still paying the 50 percent. And it doesn't say anywhere that I know of in the contract that says "in perpetuity," but people who have challenged it have lost the case, so they're still paying 50 percent.

EMMA POUGHT, The Bobbettes: But the thing is, it's retrieved money, it's not ongoing earnings. When we got with him, it was understood that he would take a portion of money that was *retrieved*, meaning money that was back there and we couldn't get it. And we didn't know how to go about getting it, you understand? So you got a percentage for finding it, but not *ongoing* earnings—you don't get ongoing. That money, once we started earning money, you're not entitled to that.

RICHARD DUBIN, musician: This whole idea of "lawyers are going to protect you," this is silliness. The lawyers are not working for *you*, they're working for "them." The idea that you have a lawyer was actually . . .

they're not going to stay in business for *you*—you're coming, you're going. In the entertainment business, there's a saying among what I call the representative class—lawyers, agents, managers—there's a saying among those people, "Clients come and go, the buyer is always there." So they're always serving the buyer while convincing "artists" that "we're in your corner."

EMMA POUGHT, The Bobbettes: Then we even got a lawyer. We got an entertainment lawyer. And he made a deal with the damn lawyer, and the next thing you know, the lawyer was collecting the money and transferring the papers to *him*. . . . He's a crook. He is a crook. I've even talked to some of the people that have him. I told them, I said, "You know what it is, he counts on the thing that most of these people don't have enough money to get a lawyer and take his ass to court." Excuse my language, but that's how I feel.

*

LILLIAN WALKER, The Exciters: Mary Wilson of The Supremes and Bowzer, they started rallying and protesting for help to get our back money. When I say us, I mean older entertainers from the fifties and sixties.

MARY WILSON, The Supremes: When many of us were inducted into the Vocal Group Hall of Fame, we all came together and had the same stories—they were stealing our names.

JON "BOWZER" BAUMAN, Sha Na Na: If you're an artist—if you're a performer—and you're not writing your own music, you know, ASCAP [American Society of Composers, Authors, and Publishers] and BMI [Broadcast Music, Inc.] at least kind of protects composers, but nobody's protecting the *artists*. The artists usually had to be protected from *their own* managers and agents. And that didn't happen. There was no one to protect them from their own managers and agents.

MARY WILSON, The Supremes: Many of us did not have record companies at the time, I should say. So, therefore, we had no one to fight for us.

JON "BOWZER" BAUMAN, Sha Na Na: In later years, what was left was live performance. And then this imposter group thing sprung up, and now that was gone too. Because all of a sudden there were all these people roaming around, claiming they're you and taking your money, taking your gig, your legacy, your applause—everything. So that just made me completely crazy. You know, these are pioneers in music, and it was just getting worse and worse and worse.

JAY SIEGEL, The Tokens: There were a lot of phony groups going out like *they* were The Marvelettes. There were three or four different groups of Marvelettes, and none were them. The same thing happened with the groups like The Drifters or The Coasters. People just get four guys together, and they'll be The Coasters. And the next day they'll change their outfits and they'll be The Drifters.

EMMA POUGHT, The Bobbettes: They had about five different Drifters, and I don't know how many Platters are out there.

JON "BOWZER" BAUMAN, Sha Na Na: The originals—the *actual* people—are sitting at home waiting to work.

MARY WILSON, The Supremes: Not just Black groups, it was everybody. People were just stealing all of the groups' names and using them as their own.

JON "BOWZER" BAUMAN, Sha Na Na: Okay, so here's another thing . . . which is the concept of "the real one." This was a construct of the other side of this, which is sometimes what the audience thinks is, *Oh, he must be the real one.* In other words, this was often done fairly artfully, in the sense that there'd be like three guys in their thirties, who, you're sitting there going, *Okay, those guys are too young, they could have never been in this group*, but then there's one guy who's like, *seventy*, right? A real seventy-year-old person, but not a real seventy-year-old person who had anything to do with The Drifters, The Coasters, The Platters, or The Marvelettes. So then the audience sits there and thinks, *Oh, those guys are too young, but she, she must be the real one. She's the real one . . .*

OTIS WILLIAMS, The Temptations: I asked not to work with them, until they cut my work off so bad that I had to bite my knuckles and say, "I have to eat and not have it affect my work."

JON "BOWZER" BAUMAN, Sha Na Na: After a point, they became very careful not to say things from the stage that also would be in violation of case law. You know, things like "I sang this song back in" or "When I recorded this song back in '63." They don't say stuff like that. Whereas, "When this song first came out" and "When The Marvelettes first did this song in 1960 . . ."

MARY WILSON, The Supremes: To them, I guess it's not important. But it *is* important when people can no longer even work, say, in Vegas because of fake groups working there and using their name. A lot of people didn't have money to pay lawyers to fight for them, but does that still mean that it's right? So that's why we need laws, we need laws to make things happen.

JON "BOWZER" BAUMAN, Sha Na Na: It made me totally crazy, most of them were *kids* making music, you know—they weren't businesspeople. And they usually got taken advantage of by businesspeople who then didn't protect the names very well, leaving the artists of that generation, when they got older, with nothing of their own legacy.

MARY WILSON, The Supremes: And that's when all of this came together as a plan to do something about it, and put together this bill. . . .

JON "BOWZER" BAUMAN, Sha Na Na: Truth in Music says you need to have somebody in the group on the stage that night who *actually* has the right to use the name, unless you are the holder of a valid, federally registered trademark for that name. . . . On the state level, we actually got it done.

MARY WILSON, The Supremes: So it has been passed now in over thirty states. I think someone said the last count was thirty-eight.

JON "BOWZER" BAUMAN, Sha Na Na: Larry Marshak is the person who mainly created the system for abusing the famous names, and I think it's fair to say The Marvelettes were among the most damaged and the most targeted.

KATHERINE ANDERSON, The Marvelettes: What Larry Marshak did was he ended up using our name. People say the name was lost in a poker game. All of that was a bunch of lies. He just took the name and began to use it. Then he had two or three different girl groups that could go out and sing as us.

MARY WILSON, The Supremes: People say, "Imitation is the best form of flattery," or something like that. And ours went beyond all of that because people were not only imitating us, but they were stealing our property.

KATHERINE ANDERSON, The Marvelettes: Oftentimes, girls will come up to me and say, "Well, I used to be a Marvelette." I say, "No, because I'm an original Marvelette, so how did you get to be a Marvelette and you're younger than me?" Most of them ended up being embarrassed and then walked away.

JON "BOWZER" BAUMAN, Sha Na Na: The Marvelettes situation actually had nothing to do with the Truth in Music. The Marvelettes is a cold fraudulent registration of a mark by somebody who didn't own the mark.

If you'd like me to make your head spin, I can do it. With The Marvelettes, it took me a little while to figure out. The simple answer is they never *lost* the rights to their name, but it wasn't registered. Larry Marshak went to the Patent and Trademark Office, discovering—and with The Shangri-Las it was the same thing—that the name wasn't registered.

So, what did Larry Marshak do? He put together a group of three girls, put them on a stage, got some promotional material, publicized the date, and called them The Marvelettes, thereby accruing some material evidence of use, right? Created a packet and sent it to the Patent and Trademark Office as evidence of his use of the unregistered name "The Marvelettes." An examiner at the Patent and Trademark Office looks at this stuff and goes, *Oh, I guess this looks okay*, and gives Larry Marshak the registration. From that time on, Larry Marshak tells every agent, every venue, every producer of shows, including me . . . it became common knowledge—Marshak owns the name "The Marvelettes."

GLADYS HORTON, The Marvelettes: Every time someone called me or spoke to me about [Marshak's] Marvelettes appearing somewhere, the news was like a stabbing.

JON "BOWZER" BAUMAN, Sha Na Na: So then it becomes, you know, this level of helplessness sets in. I had an early conversation with Gladys where she's going, "There's nothing I can do about this. This guy's got the name."

I don't think it took more than two or three years—the actual process—once we figured out what was going on, which was, okay, this is a fraudulently obtained trademark and a fraudulently obtained registration.

KATHERINE ANDERSON, The Marvelettes: Whenever we do anything now, I have to show the contract to show them who we are. The contract is with me—I own the name.

CHAPTER 47

The Blossoms, Darlene Love, and Ellie Greenwich

JEFF BARRY, songwriter: In 1966, when Phil signed Tina Turner, there was a chance to write a more spectacular, stagey, certainly rangier, melodically rangier song than the others.

DARLENE LOVE, The Blossoms: He gave me the record, he told me to go and learn it. I rehearsed with Phil to learn the song, and then we rehearsed with the background singers for *them* to learn the song. So when the day came for us to go into the studio to do the song, Tina was in the recording room. And I'm going, "Why is she here?" And that's when I knew "River Deep–Mountain High" was going to be a Tina Turner record.

JEFF BARRY, songwriter: Definitely "River Deep" was aimed at her and created for Tina to sing.

DARLENE LOVE, The Blossoms: So, you know, it just went from bad to worse after that. With "River Deep," that was about all I could take. I just never wanted to see Phil again.

JEFF BARRY, songwriter: Phil had insulted some DJ, which is not surprising. So all the DJs decided that they weren't going to play his next record "River Deep–Mountain High." And it was a hit everywhere in the world except here.

DARLENE LOVE, The Blossoms: Then he sold my contract to Philadelphia International. That was fine with me. We started doing this television show called *Shindig!* It took us away from doing a lot of the background because *Shindig!* was an international rock-and-roll show that they were getting off of their feet. And it was a four-day event in the recording studio.

FANITA JAMES, The Blossoms: Gloria went on to college and graduated and she was a social worker and she has a wonderful family.

GLORIA JONES, The Blossoms: I had two years of college left to get my bachelor's degree. I said, "I'm staying home. I'll do studio work." I wanted to be home with my kids—they were little—and I said I just wanted to raise my own children, so I finished college.

FANITA JAMES, The Blossoms: When they called us to do *Shindig!*, we had Gracia Nitzsche, a white girl, singing with us. She sang soprano. But when they hired us, *Shindig!* did not want a white girl. So we had to find a Black girl, Jean King.

DARLENE LOVE, The Blossoms: We were on twice a week. So a lot of people got to see us in that two and a half years.

FANITA JAMES, The Blossoms: When *Shindig!* went off, we were able to get back to our background. In '68, Tom Jones came over and asked us to sing with him, and we did the Elvis Presley movies *Change of Habit* and his '68 *Comeback Special.*

DARLENE LOVE, The Blossoms: And during that time, I still was not looking to be a solo artist. I was happy doing background music, doing backup for other singers on the road. I was on the road with Tom Jones, Dionne Warwick, Elvis; I was on the road, you name it—Nancy Sinatra, Frank Sinatra. We were all in Vegas for years singing.

FANITA JAMES, The Blossoms: We were at Caesars Palace with Tom Jones. Then we waited on Elvis, because he wanted us to tour with *him*, but he took so long we went with Tom Jones. One night at Caesars Palace, he walked out onstage while we were performing—and while Tom was singing, he yelled at Tom, "Man, you took my girls and you took my tight pants." [*laughing*]

DARLENE LOVE, The Blossoms: Gamble and Huff got in touch with me. My contract had run out with Phil Spector, and I always wanted to be with them. I had been there for about four or five days going over different material—we were going to go into the studio as soon as we found some material that I wanted to do, but then I was called into the office by Gamble and Huff, they were both there. For lack of a long story, they had signed my contract back over to Phil Spector.

ANDREW LOOG OLDHAM, manager, the Rolling Stones: Phil was an artist first and businessman first and a businessman mainly, because he liked to win and for others to lose.

DARLENE LOVE, The Blossoms: I was in a state of shock. I called my manager, who was in California, I told him what happened. He called Gamble and Huff, who told him that their lawyer and Phil Spector's lawyer was the same lawyer. They just signed my contract back to Phil Spector. Phil Spector now had me on contract for seven years. I had been gone from Phil for a couple of years before I signed with them—I hadn't even *seen* Phil Spector.

I went into the studio with Phil . . . I guess about seven, eight months after I resigned with him. Did one song—a song called "Lord, If You're a Woman," which I hated. It was not a very pleasant thing.

I'd waited all those years to be away from him, and then went back. I did the one song, got sick of the games Phil was playing in the recording studio while we were recording that song, and just picked up my coat and my hat and gloves, my car keys, went and got in my car, and went home. I never heard from Phil again.

I said, "Listen, if this is what I have to go through to be a recording artist, I won't be a recording artist." That was the end of my life with Phil Spector, and with my recording career. I just wanted to get out of the recording business, I had just had it.

GLORIA JONES, The Blossoms: What was she doing? Just working in a cleaners and doing . . . Darlene had a gift. She used to always tell me, "I'm going to get a job in a factory. I'm going to clean me houses." I said, "You know what? You a fool. God gave you all this natural talent." The girl had natural talent. I said, "No, you're not." I was supposed to be Darlene's manager. I didn't know any more than Darlene did.

DARLENE LOVE, The Blossoms: That's when I decided, "Okay, let's pull this solo career out the bag that everybody's been talking about." I didn't really start my solo career until I was forty years old. Most people don't know that.

GLORIA JONES, The Blossoms: I said, "You know I like to write. I bet you I'm going to get you some jobs." I said, "You watch, I'm going to get you some jobs. . . . You watch." I would write these cruise ships and all these kinds of things.

DARLENE LOVE, The Blossoms: I decided to start on this journey at the Roxy in Los Angeles. Lou Adler, who was a big record producer that The Blossoms had worked for—that was his club. And I asked him if I could do a show there. He said, "Yeah, when you want to use it?" And I told him, "Anytime you got a vacancy over here."

Then I asked Lou, "Will you help me to get some people in here to see me?" I didn't know how to even go about trying to get people to fill up that room to have a concert. But he said, no problem. In the audience that night was Stevie Van Zandt and Bruce Springsteen. I knew Bruce Springsteen by the name of "Boss." I didn't even know his name was Bruce Springsteen. Stevie said, "You need to move to New York." I said, "Sorry, I can't move to no New York. I don't know nobody in New York." He said, "Well, if I get you a job, will you come?" And I said, "Yes, you get me a job in New York, I'll come and do the job." So he got me a job at the Peppermint Lounge and the Bottom Line.

GLORIA JONES, The Blossoms: Steve Van Zandt told me about the Bottom Line, so I wrote to them.

DARLENE LOVE, The Blossoms: I came to New York, Bottom Line, in '81, '82 just to do a Darlene Love show.

GLORIA JONES, The Blossoms: To this day, I can't figure out how we got to New York. I have no idea . . . we talked about this, I said, "Darlene, how did we fly to New York and nobody had money?" [*laughing*] We stayed at my cousin's house in Harlem. That bed was so broken-down—she would be on one side of the bed, I'd be on the other. The hole was so big in the middle of a mattress, we'd roll into each other.

DARLENE LOVE, The Blossoms: That's how my solo career actually started.

GLORIA JONES, The Blossoms: We did the Bottom Line. We met Ula Hedwig there. Ula and I did backgrounds with her. Somebody got a band together for us. Now, we are doing all this and don't have a dime, but Allan Pepper—that was his club—so maybe he paid for it? I know we didn't. If we did, I don't know where we got it from. Did we rob a bank? [*laughing*] I don't remember.

DARLENE LOVE, The Blossoms: It was hard at first, but with determination, and now I figured out this is really something I want to do, and I'm going to start this. And I'm the type of person, when I start something, I jump into it—I don't go halfway into it. *Whatever it takes, I'm going to start my solo career.*

GLORIA JONES, The Blossoms: And Darlene knocked those people out. They wanted her to stay. She stayed and we both just cried when I left. Darlene cried because she said, "What am I going to do without you?" I said, "You're going to make some money."

ALLAN PEPPER, nightclub owner: I was looking for concepts to pitch to have some stuff done at the club. And I got this book on my desk, somebody just sent it to me. It was a book called *Girl Groups: The Story of a Sound*, and it was written by Alan Betrock. I read the thing and I said, "Holy shit, there's like . . . there could be a show here about girl groups."

But the name that ran through the book was Ellie's. And I started to think maybe there was a show here around Ellie—it wasn't about girl groups—it was about Ellie, the songwriter, it was about her career.

MELANIE MINTZ, writer: Ellie didn't want to do it. She was a very reclusive person after all that stuff. She was looking for a reason not to do it, even though she was intrigued. But she didn't want to come out for something that would be a dud, basically.

SUSAN COLLINS, singer: I think it was a combination of many things. I think Ellie had her—God bless her—Ellie had her own struggles, psychologically, and they really got her. You know?

ELLIE GREENWICH, songwriter: I opened up a jingle production company and was doing fairly well with jingles. That can be healthy money, when you are writing jingles and singing on them. The residuals can be kinda nice. I thought, *Let me get away from records, and start a whole new thing*. I did that for a while, but towards the end of '72, into '73, I fell apart.

SUSAN COLLINS, singer: You know, I went to her mother's wake. . . . I got my lawyer manager to come because it was Ellie's lawyer, and we all went out there. And when driving home, I said to Richard, "I think she's gonna have a breakdown." And after that, things really fell apart for her, really fell apart, and Ellie really struggled.

ELLIE GREENWICH, songwriter: I guess you could say I had a nervous breakdown.

SUSAN COLLINS, singer: I was at her house several times when the phone rings, and, here's an example: it would be Elton John, or it would be Bob Dylan's office—"They want to write with you, okay?" And then the morning of the appointment, she would call and say, "I have a cold. I can't do it. . . . I have my period. . . ." There was always something that prevented her from moving forward.

ELLIE GREENWICH, songwriter: I left the business for a little over two years. When I came back into the industry, I thought, let me get back into background singing, I'm so happy on the microphone. I could pretend I was in a girl group, get a couple of other girls, have a good time. I inched my way back into the things I wanted to do. Then I started writing again. I had some records with Ellen Foley, then got involved with Cyndi Lauper. Slowly, I found my way in.

JAY SIEGEL, The Tokens: She had a jingle company called Hook, Line & Singer, and we did a whole bunch of TV and radio commercials.

ALLAN PEPPER, nightclub owner: Ellie did jingles. She was making a living in the studio, too, doing sessions.

SUSAN COLLINS, singer: We sang on "Evil Woman," ELO [Electric Light Orchestra]. Well, what happened was Jeff Lynne, the lead and producer and writer of the Electric Light Orchestra, somehow got a demo of mine, I don't know how. His office called Ellie and said, "You know, we hear that you're connected with Susan Collins, blah, blah, blah. We're coming from New York. Would you sing on the record?" And Ellie said, "Of course." So we sang on "Evil Woman" together, which became a number one smash, and it still lasts.

ALLAN PEPPER, nightclub owner: She had asked Mel to really suss the whole thing, because Mel was one of her closest friends. We set up a meeting and it's me and the director sitting next to each other and Melanie across . . . and I said, "So I have this idea. It starts with a voice, you hear a voice on the tape and you hear, 'Ellie, we want to do a show about you at the Bottom Line about what got you into songwriting.' And then as Ellie starts to talk, the music comes up and we hear 'Will You Love Me Tomorrow.'" And Melanie listens and she looks at me and she says, "Why would you want to start a show about Ellie Greenwich with one of Carole King's biggest hits?"

MELANIE MINTZ, writer: He was very sincere, even though he had a stupid idea of how to open the show. He was very much enamored with Ellie's work and who she was. He didn't want to embarrass or make fun of her. He wanted to make something great.

PAUL SHAFFER, musician: Her records of course were important to me as a kid, especially "(Today I Met) The Boy I'm Gonna Marry." And when I got to New York, I sort of fell in with a lot of characters from this era. I made a TV pilot for Don Kirshner and met a lot of them through him . . . developed an impression of him that I used to do on *Saturday Night Live*. . . . And one day I met Ellie Greenwich at his office.

And Ellie had a sort of almost a salon in her apartment at that time. A lot of the singers like Cyndi Lauper would look to her as a sort of a godmother of rock and roll, and me too. I called her my godmother. She was a great friend.

MELANIE MINTZ, writer: I said, "Well, call Shaffer." So she dials the number and Paul answers and she says, "It's Ellie." And Paul is very reverential—of all of these people. And she says, "They're talking about doing a tribute," and before she finished the sentence, he said, "Can I do it?"

PAUL SHAFFER, musician: At the Bottom Line in its original, raw form, it was incredible. It didn't have a full book. It just had a few sketches in between songs in which I got to play Phil Spector. That's how I connected with Darlene. And Darlene was such a powerhouse. She held the whole show on her shoulders. The show sounded incredible. It sounded like the Wall of Sound.

DARLENE LOVE, The Blossoms: People couldn't even get in the show. It was around the block—people trying to get in. What Allan Pepper did, what they did, they put speakers outside.

ULA HEDWIG, background singer: I was good friends with Ellie Greenwich, and I played Ellie in *Leader of the Pack*. It was how she met Lieber and Stoller and how she met her husband, Jeff Barry.

LAURA WEINER, Ellie Greenwich's sister: I think my sister would have liked to have been more in front. I think she loved what she did, but she would have been a very good performer. She had a very good sense of humor, and she was passionate.

VICKI WICKHAM, manager, Labelle: It was a huge event in Ellie's life.

ULA HEDWIG, background singer: She came out to sing during the second act. Second act, we all got into our regular stage clothing and it was just a concert.

VICKI WICKHAM, manager, Labelle: They also had a lot of problems with Phil Spector in terms of licensing music. He wouldn't let them use certain songs. He was really a pain in the ass about that.

ULA HEDWIG, background singer: Bette Midler and Liza Minnelli came.

PAUL SHAFFER, musician: Mary Weiss came to see *Leader of the Pack*. That's when I got to meet her. She was hurt bad by her experience in The Shangri-Las. I think, for that reason, she is very . . . she doesn't want to revisit the days of it. She doesn't want to sing the old hits and stuff like that.

BROOKS ARTHUR, sound engineer: Mary prefers to be anonymous.

ULA HEDWIG, background singer: That was the first jukebox musical—*Leader of the Pack*. Everybody followed suit after that.

DARLENE LOVE, The Blossoms: Allan Pepper is a great man, him and his wife. And they were really true friends. And I started working at the Bottom Line regularly.

I said, "Listen, I got to go back home because I don't have nowhere to live here." And they invited me, told me, "You can come stay with me." I lived with them for about six months until my career really got going.

PAUL SHAFFER, musician: I was doing this show after taping the *Letterman* show, then going down to the Bottom Line. And I invited Letterman down one night to see the show, and he was killed—knocked down by Darlene Love, *especially* when she did the Christmas song in *Leader of the Pack*. And she came on Letterman to do the Christmas song, and it just became a yearly, you know . . . next year he said, "Let's get her again," and he made it into a yearly tradition.

ULA HEDWIG, background singer: This is way past when she should've gotten recognized, but she finally got her due.

DARLENE LOVE, The Blossoms: Every year I was on his show, [*laughing*] "Christmas (Baby, Please Come Home)." That's what started my Christmas tours. I started doing them in the eighties, here I am, all these years later . . . and I have an unbelievable Christmas following because of the Bottom Line and because of the David Letterman show. People wanted to hear me sing that song, so I kept singing it and kept singing it. I started doing more television shows, doing more shows. So I ended up building my career off of "Christmas (Baby Please Come Home)," which is fine with me because I love that song.

ULA HEDWIG, background singer: Phil, every time we did "Christmas (Baby)," he would try to stop Darlene from doing it for some reason. It was a thing.

DARLENE LOVE, The Blossoms: You know, people have been very good to me. Because Phil Spector called the David Letterman show and told them I wasn't allowed to sing that song—if I sang it again, he was going to sue them. You know, just stupid stuff.

But there were other people more powerful than him. You know, like, the David Letterman show or NBC. You can't stop the person from their show, their livelihood, legally. You cannot stop them from doing that.

Once he went to prison, you know . . . then it was all . . . everything was open. He couldn't stop anything from happening. He needed all the money he could get to pay lawyers. That opened the door for a lot of us who were with Phil Spector. You know, we could go out now and do shows, he couldn't stop us. And now, all his artists were free to use all these songs without him bothering them.

AUTHORS' NOTE: In 2009, Phil Spector was sentenced to nineteen years in prison for murder in the second degree of Lana Clarkson.

Ellie Greenwich died of a heart attack August 26, 2009, at the age of sixty-eight.

LAURA WEINER, Ellie Greenwich's sister: I always hear her [on the radio]. I hear her and I love it because I can pick out her voice.

That was the best funeral of all, I must say—not to say that that was a good thing that she died, but we were at the graveside and the ceremony . . . the words and everything was done and everybody was going to start leaving, so we all sort of sang her songs. We just sang her songs. "Da Doo Ron Ron," "Going to the Chapel," any song that we could do, and we were just singing. . . .

We had to get a Reform rabbi to perform the ceremony, which really . . . he knew of my sister, and in fact he started singing with us. It was great . . . absolutely great.

In Jewish faith, you sit shiva, but we did not. We called it a celebration of life. My sister played the accordion when she was young—we had it at my sister's apartment and there was an accordion player there playing her songs. It was a wonderful celebration of my sister and I think that's what she would have wanted—I think she wanted to be celebrated.

CHAPTER 48

The Crystals

DEE DEE KENNIEBREW, The Crystals: We got back together in '71. I ran into Barbara again and she was doing some solo recording, and then the people who were recording her was saying, "Do you want to do backup for her and, if you can, call Mary," because Barbara and Mary were very close. And I thought, *Okay, great*, then the guy talked us into going out as The Crystals again.

BARBARA ALSTON, The Crystals: So once no one was working as The Crystals, we decided to start it back up with Dee Dee, Mary, and me.

LA LA BROOKS, The Crystals: Well, I got married. I got married at nineteen and I had my son. I just turned twenty, and I left the group. I just got married, and that was it.

DEE DEE KENNIEBREW, The Crystals: I just continued on because I didn't know how to do anything else, you know, and people started calling me for work. So I just got some of the girls and I started working as The Crystals.

LA LA BROOKS, The Crystals: Dee Dee was always trying to go back. She got into trouble with marriage as some of us do, and then she went back and got an all-brand-new image and had to work again because she was poor then. She needed the money and she called me. They asked me to go back to work with her. I said, "Dee Dee, I have the babies now." So I had these kids and I became Muslim and I was focused only on that.

DEE DEE KENNIEBREW, The Crystals: Another agent said, "We've got people calling you." It was Richard Nader. He wanted us to do a show at the Garden, Chuck Berry headlined. So we got together, the four originals without Patsy, and we did the show at Madison Square Garden. By then, La La Brooks had become a Muslim, and she only could wear dresses up to her neck and all the way down to the wrist and gowns all the way to the floor. So we got gowns—and so if you ever see that picture where she's in a different gown, that's the reason because she had become a Muslim, they couldn't show anything, but she did the one show with us. Anyway, we just became friendly again. But then her husband moved her.

LA LA BROOKS, The Crystals: I did *Hair* on Broadway. I did *Two Gentleman of Verona*, too, on Broadway, but I really stayed home.

DEE DEE KENNIEBREW, The Crystals: Well, he got on as a drummer for *Hair*, and then he had his wife come in as an understudy, which was La La. But then again, her husband's there, so it's okay.

LA LA BROOKS, The Crystals: So I just went in a different direction. Then I started traveling to different places, countries—India, Pakistan, Sudan, Saudi Arabia. I ended up leaving America and living in Austria for eight years and England for six years, six and a half years, whatever.

DEE DEE KENNIEBREW, The Crystals: But La La never did come back with The Crystals. . . . With girls it's very hard because, you know, when a girl starts having, or a lady starts having, children, it's hard on a child—for the mother to leave and go off on tour for five, six weeks, it really is. And that's one reason Barbara left the second time, her children were not happy. She had a little girl and a little boy, so she had to say, "Look, you've got to replace me," you know, so it was just difficult.

BARBARA ALSTON, The Crystals: I quit singing in 1976.

LA LA BROOKS, The Crystals: I stayed home twenty-five years, raised the kids until they were grown, then I got a nine-to-five job after.

DEE DEE KENNIEBREW, The Crystals: It's different if it's a dad, but when it's a mom, you have to, you know, you have to consider your children first. So, what can I say at that point . . . after that, I started back working with different girls because La La had her children. Barbara, by then, had two children. Mary had one.

Now I have a child to take care of—people are calling me for work, so I guess it's me. And so I just always made sure I had really strong people with me to, you know, work for me. And right now I still have two girls that are really strong. I guess it's either a blessing or a curse, but I didn't have any choice—that was my life. That's what I had to do for a living.

LA LA BROOKS, The Crystals: But the name is nothing without a song, you know what I'm saying? And the songs they would sell, a name won't sell if it doesn't have the song behind it.

MYRNA GIRAUD, The Crystals: I went to see the show and she made me come up onstage and blah, blah, blah, which I really wasn't prepared for, but it was very sweet of her.

DEE DEE KENNIEBREW, The Crystals: But, you know, it's just that it's been a career and I'd never thought when I started out at fifteen that this would be my life. So now at this point, it's like I do a few jobs here and there, but up until about a couple of years ago, I was pretty much gone, always traveling here, traveling there. And so I said, well, it's been a lifetime and I'm still here and I can't believe it because, I mean, I was never the lead person, but I was pushed out front because I knew nothing else to do.

CHAPTER 49

The Ronettes

RONNIE SPECTOR, The Ronettes: I never wanted to leave the stage. When I got married, I didn't think I was going to leave either, but evidently Phil didn't want me to go onstage.

NEDRA TALLEY-ROSS, The Ronettes: One day she said, just calling Phil not a very nice name, basically said, "That bastard promised me he would make me a single star and he locked me in the house instead." And that's exactly what he did.

DARLENE LOVE, The Blossoms: Ronnie was an unbelievable talent. She had the voice, she could sing, she had the body, she had the looks, she had all of that, and Phil took that away from her.

DIANNE LYNTON, singer: She used to tell me all those stories, you know, about Phil. Ronnie and I alone, talking in the bed or whatever.

RONNIE SPECTOR, The Ronettes: It was like two months after we got married, see, I didn't know anything about I wasn't gonna record anymore, I wasn't gonna go onstage and do performances. I thought that would continue—I mean, here is the man that owned the record company, wrote all my songs, and produced all my songs. How would I ever think he was gonna, like, just retire two months after we got married?

We moved into a twenty-three-room mansion and my first gift was a Rolls-Royce for my birthday. It was like I was taken away from everything, because I was brought up around family, people, liveliness, and then all of a sudden I got married, it was like [*stopping sound*] darkness.

DIANNE LYNTON, singer: He bought her a car, had one of the first car phones. She said, "I could drive around the property, but I could not go out. He would call me every fifteen minutes to make sure I was still in the car."

RONNIE SPECTOR, The Ronettes: Phil had to have everything dark in the house. I mean, there was no rock and roll. Everything was classical music played throughout the house. I wasn't allowed to, like, read *Cashbox* or *Record World*. I was cut off. I was no longer called Ronnie, I was . . . he called me Veronica, and the servants called me Mrs. Spector, so I believe he did that subconsciously so I wouldn't be thinking of The Ronettes. So, that's when he went into recluse. So, when he went into recluse, I went, you see.

NEDRA TALLEY-ROSS, The Ronettes: She was not married to Phil yet, and so then it just started off in '68 with him, you know, locking her in the house and not letting her out . . . frustrating her to the point of her going into a hospital in California. I said, "Ronnie, he's trying to put you in these hospitals so that at some point he's going to say, 'Look, she was in the hospital, she's crazy,' so he can control you legally."

DARLENE LOVE, The Blossoms: Nobody, no matter who they are, nobody has a right to take you away from your family if you don't want to go. If you ain't getting along with your family, that's the one thing, and y'all don't like one another. Well, that wasn't the case with her, but he took her and moved her from New York to California, where she knew nobody.

RONNIE SPECTOR, The Ronettes: He said, "If you leave, I'm gonna kill you." The gates were up, the barbed wire. I found myself in a prison. I couldn't get out.

DARLENE LOVE, The Blossoms: Her life was in New York. That's where Ronnie is from, that's where she was born. She knows people here. She knows nobody in California. And to take you from all of that, you know, to bring you to this mansion that looked like . . . it was a killer estate that Phil had . . . it was this huge place, way up in the mountains. I've been there a few times, and I wouldn't live there even if I was married to him, but unfortunately, you pay for all these things as you get older.

NEDRA TALLEY-ROSS, The Ronettes: You got to realize he was a millionaire, reportedly a millionaire. We were an uptown group. We had no millionaires in our family. So there were those who were like, "Ignore it," overlook—you know, Phil would help them with this and that—so they accepted it more. But he wasn't showing all of his cards back then either. He began to show his cards when they started to divorce, paying her off in nickels—spiteful, *spiteful* little man.

DARLENE LOVE, The Blossoms: She told me a lot of things I don't know if people know and I'm not getting ready to tell it, but it wasn't a real happy time for her, you know. She just thought . . . I think . . . sometimes she could lose her life.

RONNIE SPECTOR, The Ronettes: The last year of my marriage I didn't talk at all. Because if I said anything, he'd yell at me, so why say anything? I cried every night I was married.

NEDRA TALLEY-ROSS, The Ronettes: Ronnie wasn't telling everything. It's like somebody—any woman—who's getting abused by her husband, she doesn't go around talking about it too much, but when she leaves him, then she spills the beans—they just say it all. You know, it's crazy then.

JOEY DEE, Joey Dee and the Starliters: The stories she told me were just unbearable and disgusting—the way she was treated. Six or seven years of that, she endured that. He can make hit records, but that doesn't make him a good person, does it? He certainly created superstars. They were that good.

RONNIE SPECTOR, The Ronettes: I left Phil for good on June 12, 1972.

DIANNE LYNTON, singer: He didn't want her to wear shoes, because he knew she wouldn't go anywhere.

RONNIE SPECTOR, The Ronettes: My mother got me out of there. She said, "Honey, you're going to die here." She knew.

DIANNE LYNTON, singer: They sneaked out through the maid's room—she told me they snuck up to the maid's entrance, through the kitchen, and then through the back door. He thought she wasn't going to go anywhere with Ma Bennett—she had no shoes! So he thought it would be no problem. And she disappeared. Good heavens, what a crazy man, isn't he? I'm glad she got away.

*

NEDRA TALLEY-ROSS, The Ronettes: When Ronnie was going through rough times with her and Phil, my Aunt BeBe would call for Scott and myself to go to New York to be with her. That was a part that was good because Ronnie and I were getting to build that spiritual side. She loves Scotty—she calls him Scotty. Estelle, too, is, "How's Scotty?" He'll always be Scotty to them. But anyway, he says that it sounds like a dog, a Scottie dog.

SCOTT ROSS, Nedra Ross's husband: We had moved to Maryland after we left the city, after we got married. We went down there to spend some time with my mom. Then at the church that we had made that commitment to Christ at, I met a guy. He said, "Well, I'm going to go to a conference in Baltimore, if you want to go with me."

NEDRA TALLEY-ROSS, The Ronettes: Scott went to a gathering up in Washington where he met a very young, handsome young preacher named Pat Robertson. He was thirty-seven years old, so a young guy.

SCOTT ROSS, Nedra Ross's husband: I heard him speak and I was intrigued by some of the things he had to say and his appearance . . . he's a good-looking guy. He reminded me somewhat of John Kennedy. Afterwards, I went up and talked to him, and we hit it off.

NEDRA TALLEY-ROSS, The Ronettes: Scott was like, "I'm in radio, TV, done all these things." And Pat was like, "I've got a new fledgling TV station, it's Christian Broadcasting Network." There was only one station at that point. So we went to Virginia—we were there maybe for about eight months—and then Pat sent Scott and myself to upstate New York. We were given six radio stations from Albany to Buffalo.

SCOTT ROSS, Nedra Ross's husband: I said to Pat, "I've got an idea for a format." I explained to him—because back-to-back preachers, that's all you could hear about Christian stuff on the radio. I talked about playing music and a lot of rock-and-roll music—and there was no Christian music, no rock-and-roll Christian music at that time.

These radio stations were given to Pat, so, he said, "Go do it, be upstate, see what happens upstate." And it was based in Ithaca, but it was in Buffalo, Syracuse, and Albany.

NEDRA TALLEY-ROSS, The Ronettes: We started to work up there to hit young people *our* age. We saw that there was a movement going across the country—the West Coast and the East Coast—we were the ones from the East Coast, so we had a community of loving. People would go, "Well, why is that? Oh, everybody's free to love?" No, it was the love of Christ. We felt that movement there and we began to go places.

SCOTT ROSS, Nedra Ross's husband: We called it "Covenant Love Community," our church. There was a school, we had a gas company—we had huge companies—we had a record company; we were busy.

NEDRA TALLEY-ROSS, The Ronettes: It just went from that to starting up a school, a theater for the arts—we were very much into the arts—a record company, and concerts.

SCOTT ROSS, Nedra Ross's husband: We weren't completely divorced from showbiz because we still had a heart for a lot of people in it. We influenced a number of them. Obviously, Dion, he knew what I was doing and Eric Clapton and others . . . Bob Crewe, who produced the Four Seasons. We didn't impose anything. They just saw what had happened to Nedra and what had happened to me and it was deep. They would ask questions on that. We care about those people and we still do. We pray for them a lot and we're grateful for them.

NEDRA TALLEY-ROSS, The Ronettes: So we had a heart for young people like us. We saw the church as very stiff—you know, organ music. We brought rock and roll into the Word.

SCOTT ROSS, Nedra Ross's husband: Christians didn't like that very much because they didn't think that rock and roll and Jesus were compatible. I proved otherwise.

Later the Scott Ross show emerged out of some of these events in upstate New York. We syndicated it to rock-and-roll stations across the country. It won a number of awards for best syndicated show from *Billboard* magazine.

NEDRA TALLEY-ROSS, The Ronettes: And we helped build the vision of Christian Broadcasting Network, which today is, like, 265 stations around the world.

*

RONNIE SPECTOR, The Ronettes: The first year I missed it so much, and after that I went bananas. I love the stage. I would sing for nothing. Phil couldn't understand why I would want to sing when I had everything I could want—money, this, that. I said, "I like the stage. I get a charge out of being up there doing my thing."

BROOKS ARTHUR, sound engineer: Well, I'm going to take a guess and I'll add some knowledge to the guess. I would think it was probably the loneliest time of the year when you're not on the Top 10 or not on the radio anymore. It's an emptiness. It's like, "My dream didn't really come true. I'm only halfway there and I got my whole life to live." Then it was like some gloomy days, and somehow or other, the revival shows started popping around.

BILLY VERA, musician: So, the early seventies was really a windfall for a lot of these groups, most of whom hadn't worked since the fifties. And suddenly, they're able to make some decent money.

In the early seventies my career went down the tubes. There was a big oldies revival in New York, so we were able to be the house band at a bunch of shows at the Academy of Music on 14th Street, and we were working six, seven nights a week in local clubs. . . . Richard Nader was doing these oldies shows at Madison Square Garden. He managed to get Dion and the Belmonts to agree to perform together after years of not.

CHIP HURD, performer: And so Ronnie, I guess, was accepting the tour. But she didn't have her group because her sister and cousin weren't interested in going back out on the road. You know . . . older, married, children. They weren't planning on going back out.

BILLY VERA, musician: Her cousin Nedra didn't want to go into the group because she'd become a born-again Christian and she didn't want to do the sexy act anymore.

NEDRA TALLEY-ROSS, The Ronettes: You know, she'd call and we'd say this and that and I'd say, "Ronnie, you know, I have a family."

BILLY VERA, musician: But Estelle needed the money and Ronnie wouldn't have any of it, because she would've had to split the money evenly with Estelle. I tried, I tried to appeal to her sisterly love, but you know, with Ronnie it was . . . it was just all about Ronnie.

DIANNE LYNTON, singer: They didn't want to do it. That's what she told me—they did not want to do it anymore. She said she wanted to get everyone back together, but they didn't want to.

RONNIE SPECTOR, The Ronettes: I decided my only hope was to find two new Ronettes.

DIANNE LYNTON, singer: I was in this restaurant and by myself. A man comes over to me and says, "Hey, listen, would you like to be a Ronette?" I said, "Excuse me?" Would I like to be a Ronette?! I go, "Well, yes, who wouldn't like to be a Ronette?" "I'll bring Ronnie to your house tomorrow. Give me your phone number. Give me your address." And I'm thinking, *Yeah, right, sure. He's just trying to pick me up*. So I gave him the address, but I'm thinking the doorman would stop him if there was a problem. Next day the doorman says, "Dianne, Ronnie Spector here to see you." I'm thinking, *What?*

CHIP HURD, performer: So she auditioned, and I was sent down because I was a good alto and I could harmonize really well . . . and, you know, I pretty much got hired on the spot. And Ronnie and I got along real well in the audition. And I think her mother just thought I was a safe choice. I was one of those "good girls," so I guess she thought that it'd be good. Send her with some people that are going to, you know, keep her grounded.

DIANNE LYNTON, singer: Chip was like the "good girl" and we weren't. We were the two bad ones that used to sneak around to go to parties and stuff.

CHIP HURD, performer: But you can only ground people when you're around people. The problem is, you know, once we got off the stage, everybody went to their hotel rooms. So I didn't really see her.

DIANNE LYNTON, singer: We got along very well. I'm a mixed lady—I have a Ukrainian mother and my father is Apache, Cherokee, and Navajo. . . . So, you know, she used to say, "We understand each other."

BILLY VERA, musician: This was the first gig she did after she left Phil Spector. And so we had rehearsal and afterwards she said to me, "I'm looking to start doing some gigs again and I hear you're the best conductor in New York." I said, "Well, I'm pretty good." She said, "Would you work for me?" I said, "Well, I'm working for The Shirelles, but you know, I'll be happy to help you out when they're not working."

RONNIE SPECTOR, The Ronettes: Billy was good, and he was also a cute guy. He reminded me a little of Phil—he had the same dimple when he smiled, and the same receding hairline.

BILLY VERA, musician: So that developed into, uh . . . I became her first boyfriend after she broke up with Phil. And we did some dates, but she was . . . I guess as a result of living with this madman, she was like a virtual prisoner in this big mansion, you know, in Los Angeles before, and now she was back home and living with her mother, way up in Washington Heights.

JOEY DEE, Joey Dee and the Starliters: The reason I think oldies shows were successful was the beauty and messages of the songs. They were a time . . . There's a special time frame from the fifties, I'd say '56, '57 to about '62, that music—the doo-wop era, they call it—could never be replicated. So the people, as they got older and they graduated college and they got on . . . and they're listening now to different music. . . . Now you're listening to Woodstock, and don't get me started about Woodstock, okay? But that was another lifestyle, you know? The LSD and this and that. People were doing drugs. And see, we never—even as musicians, I knew a couple of kids that smoked pot in the early sixties, like, during my time, and that was it. But after the LSD and the coke and all the other stuff that can . . . the heroin, that can . . . I mean, when you want to try to go back to the era where life wasn't as complicated. So of course, people yearn for that.

JIGGS ALLBUT, The Angels: I think people may have wanted to just get happy and away from all the turmoil.

PEGGY SANTIGLIA, The Angels: We all got labeled. We sort of got cemented in a place with oldies shows, but I'm not complaining. I mean, they were fun, especially being with a lot of friends. Fans don't care that you're older. In fact, they *want* to hear the old songs more than the new ones. One of the times that we played Madison Square Garden was with Ricky Nelson. We're in the dressing room and we hear him getting booed—the poor guy was just trying to perform some of the newer songs that he recorded and that he wrote.

RONNIE SPECTOR, The Ronettes: I did an oldies show at Madison Square Garden.

CHIP HURD, performer: Phil Spector had threatened her and so there was this concern about us going onstage and whether he was going to have somebody bother her onstage or whatever.

RONNIE SPECTOR, The Ronettes: We were seventh to go on. It was awkward waiting for the six acts to go on.

CHIP HURD, performer: She came alive when she hit that stage. But she had such a unique voice that the *audience* came alive once they were hearing it again.

RONNIE SPECTOR, The Ronettes: Everybody had gotten the same reaction of "Good, good, good." And then we went on with the second song. They started lighting matches and lighters. We were in the middle, like at a boxing match, and trying to play to all the audience. I'd go on this side and turn around and there'd be all these lights. Before I knew it, the whole place was lit up.

CHIP HURD, performer: All the cigarette lighters start being lit up and waving in the air with such regard for her. It was emotional for me, just to see someone being loved like that. It was just an extraordinary moment that I'll never forget.

RONNIE SPECTOR, The Ronettes: At first, I thought maybe they didn't like us. But when I saw they were jumping up and down . . . I still sometimes think it was a dream.

CHIP HURD, performer: I was not there long enough to really have any memories of much of anything except the enormous love the audience had for her when we went to the Garden. We didn't have any behind-the-scenes issues with each other, everybody kind of loved each other. It was just Ronnie went back to some of her old bad habits, I guess, when she got offstage, or before she came onstage, and so you know, I'm not trying to do anything to her reputation. It's stuff that everybody knows, you know, the drinking and whatever drugs she was using.

DIANNE LYNTON, singer: Ronnie and I would wait till Chip goes to bed and we'd sneak out.

BILLY VERA, musician: And she was also drinking and she was on tranquilizers, which is a lethal combination. And I could tell when Ronnie had got her hands on some booze 'cause her face would get puffy—her eyes would get puffy.

DIANNE LYNTON, singer: I remember she was laughing on the floor and saying, "Oh! I love to laugh!" 'Cause she was almost—my goodness, take a breath. She couldn't breathe, like she was going to die. I'd have to give artificial respiration simply because she couldn't stop laughing, you know . . . being happy again—being free.

CHIP HURD, performer: I started noticing after a few shows that she was a little wobbly, and now not remembering her lyrics and stuff.

DIANNE LYNTON, singer: We went to Philadelphia, Billy was doing his thing, Chip and I come out first, you know, and then you start "Be My Baby"—*bom, bom-bom*—we are doing our little movements, and we're wondering, *Where's Ronnie?* . . . *Boom, boom-boom,* but nothing's happening. All of a sudden, Ronnie comes out kind of staggering and she says, [*slurring*] "Sing it, girls!" and Billy—Billy grabs with his foot to pull the electricity, the cord out of the wall—so it went dark, thank goodness. In the paper the very next day, it said, "Ronettes drunk onstage."

CHIP HURD, performer: She fell off the stage for Dick Clark, and he was pissed. I remember him saying, "You guys are gonna go home." And I told her, "That's it for me. I don't, I don't want this," so then I left the group.

BILLY VERA, musician: I mean, you could tell she suffered.

CHIP HURD, performer: I left the group after that, because I just didn't want to . . . you know—that was humiliating to see her fall off the stage.

BILLY VERA, musician: I remember one time we came home from a gig out in New Jersey. Everybody was hungry. There was a place up in Harlem called Wells Chicken and Waffles, and it was me, the bass player, the mother, the two fake Ronettes, and Ronnie. And she was a hometown girl—she was a Harlem girl, born and raised. And somehow, I think her little cousin who was sort of dedicated to taking care of her, she apparently snuck her some vodka and Coke and I saw the eyes rolling around her head and I saw her face get puffy and next thing I know her face was in her food.

DIANNE LYNTON, singer: I was always sneaking the drinks to her. . . . You know, putting supposed to be only cola, but there was rum in the cola. Ma Bennett told us, "Do not give her any alcohol." She was a nice lady—she was stern with Ronnie, but she knew more than we did. She used to say, "My mother is too strict." I was also this young girl, I was thinking, *Yeah, I understand that, you know—mothers*. We were so bad . . . it was terrible—but I didn't realize that she had a problem with alcohol.

BILLY VERA, musician: And so, I sort of picked her up by the back of her clothes, sat her up, and I said to everybody, I said, "All right, here's some money. Go pay the check." I said, "We're all going to get her out of here quietly," because if we don't, you know, Harlem is like a little gossipy small town. And I said the next morning everybody in Harlem would know that she fell facedown in her chicken and waffles. So I managed to get her out of there without anybody knowing what had happened. But that was the kind of thing I had to deal with with her. . . . It was really tough.

RONNIE SPECTOR, The Ronettes: After a few months, Billy Vera got tired of looking after me and he just gave up.

BILLY VERA, musician: I said, "You're on your own now." I said, "I can't deal with this girl anymore," and eventually she got into the Alcoholics Anonymous, and as far as I know, she's turned her life around, thank God. But it was rough going there with her.

RONNIE SPECTOR, The Ronettes: Looking back, I can see that he really had no choice. He couldn't stand by and watch me hurt myself, but there was nothing he could do to stop my drinking and he knew it.

BILLY VERA, musician: I mean, having been around show-business people all my life, I didn't have a word for it, but I knew what narcissism was, and she was one of the most extreme examples of it. And, listen, out here in Hollywood, I mean narcissism lives out here. But, you know, I felt sorry for her, in a way, because she had gone through all that stuff. So, she was convinced that Phil was having us followed and she was very paranoid about that.

NEDRA TALLEY-ROSS, The Ronettes: Estelle was sick by then.

BILLY VERA, musician: She's an extreme narcissist. You know, [*posh accent*] "Mother, draw my bath." You know, as if she's . . . I mean, literally . . . I said, "Bitch," I said, "that's your mother. You don't talk to your mother like that." I said, "You better show a little respect. This woman bore you, raised you. You don't treat your mother like that." I said, "It's bad enough you wouldn't let your sister in the group," because her sister came to me one day and said, "Hey, you think you could talk Ronnie into letting me in the group again?"

NEDRA TALLEY-ROSS, The Ronettes: Estelle was a whole different story.

TOYIN DONG, Estelle Bennett's daughter: No, Estelle is not Ronnie, no Estelle is not Diana Ross, but Estelle Bennett lived through hell and tragedy with a smile.

NEDRA TALLEY-ROSS, The Ronettes: Estelle hated The Ronettes ending, but I couldn't help. I couldn't do anything. I couldn't. I felt like, *I know you want it. But I don't. . . . It's not what I want.*

TOYIN DONG, Estelle Bennett's daughter: I lived with my mom until I was twelve years old. At this point in my life, I draw so much strength from that little girl. I need to honor her. I need to honor my mother. Because their spirits are strong—resilient—in ways that a lot of people will never know. So, yes, that little girl lived in the mystery of Estelle Bennett. Estelle Bennett, the Ronette—that is *not* who I grew up with.

NEDRA TALLEY-ROSS, The Ronettes: Estelle began to get sick, mentally. We didn't know it, because it was in the Ronette days where she would not eat like we ate. And then they did put her in the hospital . . . and she was bones. She just could *not* eat, she *wouldn't* eat. So we knew that there was mental illness that had come, but we didn't know where it . . . we sort of knew where it came from.

TOYIN DONG, Estelle Bennett's daughter: I've just been taught that after The Ronettes, my mother's mental illness started to take a stronger and stronger hold. So it was slowly progressing, you know. It could be the straw that broke the camel's back . . . different speculations.

LA LA BROOKS, The Crystals: I lived on 82nd, between Amsterdam and Columbus, and there was a nice store on Broadway. I went there. Just by coincidence, Estelle was there, and I hadn't seen her for a while, because I had gotten married, had the baby, my son was about one, I had him in a stroller, and I walk in there, and I see Estelle. I said, "Oh, Estelle." I said, "How have you been?" She said, "Hey, La La." She was just fabulous, you know? Very trendy. I was saying, "What's going on?" And this time she looked so sad. That's when the group was breaking up.

She said to me, "Ronnie doesn't want to work with us anymore, she's with Phil." Her face was so . . . I'll never forget . . . because I was going through, she was pushing clothes from the rack and her expression, and you could tell it was a letdown for her.

NEDRA TALLEY-ROSS, The Ronettes: Joey and Estelle got pregnant with Toyin, and Joe was very opinionated and strong. He saw Estelle as being weaker, and . . . she was. So his control—to a group of controlling Black women—wasn't going over too good. . . .

So when she had Toyin, Joe said, "Oh, I'm taking the baby." They were like, "We don't give away our children." Estelle was going, "It's okay if he takes the baby." And they were going, "*No, it's not.*" Mother was like, "We can fight for the child, and who is *he*? Who is he, anyway? We don't know his family, and you're gonna let the baby go with him?" Aunt BeBe was like, "We'll help you with the baby," like Toyin could get to be with all the aunts and uncles.

TOYIN DONG, Estelle Bennett's daughter: My father kept trying to take, get custody of me or something. . . . And then finally, my mother, father, and I moved to Midwood Street in Brooklyn, a one-bedroom apartment, and my mom slept in the living room.

NEDRA TALLEY-ROSS, The Ronettes: Estelle came up and stayed with me and put the baby in the crib. And when the baby cried, she didn't respond. So I knew something was really wrong there. If your baby's crying and you can sleep through it . . . mothers just wake up, you know?

TOYIN DONG, Estelle Bennett's daughter: And I was right next to her, but my mother . . . it didn't faze her at all. So Nedra had to calm me down, and that was the first signal that something was wrong.

NEDRA TALLEY-ROSS, The Ronettes: I wonder if . . . I think a lot of women . . . the sort of flow of hormones that happen when you give birth a lot of times trigger something that's already in there, you know? Like postpartum depression.

When I would go to New York and see her, and I would listen to her voice, I heard her going, [*whispering*] "How's Scotty? And what about the children?" And she just became so soft, Estelle was always soft-spoken, but then it became almost childlike quiet—so quiet that we're going, "Speak louder, we can't hear you," ya know . . . and her voice just went out.

TOYIN DONG, Estelle Bennett's daughter: It was just me and my mother at 11 Midwood Street, Apartment 4B. It was like a hole in another time, outside of this physicality—it's crazy, that's the thing about being an only child—without my memory, it doesn't exist.

NEDRA TALLEY-ROSS, The Ronettes: I think it was that space, Estelle had a space in her brain. So it wasn't like she was always focused in on you and looking you in your eyes.

TOYIN DONG, Estelle Bennett's daughter: She was always in the bed, drinking tea. She would always sing a song called "Yesterday." When I listen to the song now, it's heart-wrenching, because it's really . . . I remember her singing, "Yesterday . . . all my troubles seemed so far away . . ." She'd always be sipping tea, just like Lipton hot tea.

My father didn't live with us. I remember him being a hustler. He's driving cabs, working at a luncheonette, security guard, whatever he could do to get money. And then, he would always come in the morning to take care of me, take me to school. And then my mother would pick me up. But I would tell people she was my babysitter, because she always had a wig on.

My father would always be, like, cursing her out, telling her to take off the wig. I remember them tussling, and he'd be grabbing the wig off of her and cursing her out, she'd be on the floor just like, "Stop! Stop, Joey, stop!" So I grew up . . . I was groomed to have disdain for the wig. Plus disdain for my mother. So I just remember telling people, "She's my babysitter."

My father—it's a very complicated relationship I have with my father. As my father relates to my mother, I have no memory of him other than being abusive towards her—but my father is the reason I'm here today.

NEDRA TALLEY-ROSS, The Ronettes: I lived in upstate New York. Estelle never came to me and said . . . of course, I would've got cousins on him.

TOYIN DONG, Estelle Bennett's daughter: My grandma was the only person who would come to visit us and it was really nice. I do have, like, in my memory, this feeling, you know, *She's coming to see me and my mother!*

"TOY-in!" [*imitating BeBe's voice*] And she would always go in her bra and give me money.

NEDRA TALLEY-ROSS, The Ronettes: Aunt BeBe loved her. Aunt BeBe really loved her.

TOYIN DONG, Estelle Bennett's daughter: I was very close to my grandmother, as close as can be.

NEDRA TALLEY-ROSS, The Ronettes: But Estelle needed care because of the mental illness.

TOYIN DONG, Estelle Bennett's daughter: I had this therapist. And I just asked him one day, because my mom, she wouldn't take her medicine—I know that—and she was definitely afraid of doctors . . .

I don't know why . . . maybe she had a bad experience. . . . And so I asked Dr. Curtis to come with us. I just said he was my friend, so that he could kind of, like, provide some kind of analysis. And he said she was schizophrenic, but that's such a wide . . .

NEDRA TALLEY-ROSS, The Ronettes: She would sometimes have her own place, and then at times stay with Aunt BeBe. But then she would sit out the door, like she was waiting for someone.

TOYIN DONG, Estelle Bennett's daughter: Eventually, we got evicted. I went to live with my paternal grandparents full-time. And my mother, she went to live with my grandmother. That's what I remember . . . a woman with a wig . . . and then she just got worse and worse.

When I lived with my grandparents in middle school, my mother would just kind of show up at their house. My grandparents never talked about it, but they were Chinese and the first generation here, so English is their second language. I don't know . . . we weren't equipped, whether it's lost in translation, or just a cultural thing.

And then when I moved to my aunt and uncle's, she would always be there on the corner, right in front of the building, just standing there. Now I'm high school—she looks like a bag lady. She has a beard, long hairs—she always tied these plastic, like, the handles of plastic bags, around her wrist. And was, she just would always be showing up . . . and of course now I understand—I was her daughter.

NEDRA TALLEY-ROSS, The Ronettes: Aunt BeBe took care of Estelle and her daughter. Ronnie—as her sister—was shitty. Now, that's the truth.

TOYIN DONG, Estelle Bennett's daughter: She called me every day. Every day. She found a way to call me. I always gave her my phone number. She said the same thing every time she called, the same thing: "Excuse me. Hello. This is Estelle, is Toyin there, please?" Not "This is Mom." "This is Estelle."

I would give her gifts, give her new coats, give her new wigs. . . . I remember when I had my son—I'm still living in Brooklyn—I had him in the baby carrier in front of me and I went to meet her at Junior's. She didn't even see him—as if he was invisible. And she was giving me little girls' toys, still—crayons, little girl's underwear—she just saw me as a little girl.

NEDRA TALLEY-ROSS, The Ronettes: And so she went into her own head quietly. She would be okay being by herself. She would be out at night by herself and, I mean, I would be afraid that somebody's going to grab me. And we were like, "Come in, come into the house, come to go to your mother's," and stuff like that . . . and she wouldn't want to go.

TOYIN DONG, Estelle Bennett's daughter: You know, if you bring her somewhere and she doesn't want to stay, she can't be forced. It's just very complicated. Growing up, I was just like, *What the heck, they just left my mother?* But now I see, it's very complicated, especially if you're . . . if you're on your own . . . then forget about it. . . . She lived with my grandmother, so then it's like when that's gone, you're left to the city.

AUTHORS' NOTE: BeBe Bennett died in 1998. After this date, Estelle's whereabouts are difficult to pin down. Along with her struggles with anorexia nervosa and schizophrenia, after BeBe Bennett's passing, Estelle was intermittently homeless, staying sometimes with family, in boardinghouses, and on the street.

*

AUTHORS' NOTE: In 2007, The Ronettes were inducted into the Rock and Roll Hall of Fame by longtime friend Keith Richards.

TOYIN DONG, Estelle Bennett's daughter: They called me when I was in California, and they wanted me to accept the award on her behalf. I don't know how the words came out of my mouth, but I was like, "No, she can accept her own award." Goes against everything I knew in my brain.

NEDRA TALLEY-ROSS, The Ronettes: I had mixed feelings because I wanted to protect her. Why expose somebody in their mental illness stages? And you'd hate for them to get up there and have a traumatic experience.

AUTHORS' NOTE: All three Ronettes were in attendance and accepted the award. It was the first time they were together in twenty years.

TOYIN DONG, Estelle Bennett's daughter: And that was the first time ever that I got a glimpse of Estelle Bennett the "Ronette." It's the first time I saw it. When I walked with her through this, whatever you call that, taking pictures and stuff, she paused at every camera, [*imitating paparazzi*] "Estelle! Estelle!" She paused, posed, she paused and posed. I was like, *Whoa, what?*

NEDRA TALLEY-ROSS, The Ronettes: They had coached her to just say, "I'm Estelle Bennett of The Ronettes." And she did *exactly* that. It was a very, *very* sweet moment.

TOYIN DONG, Estelle Bennett's daughter: It was really unbelievable. I really, still to this day, I'm in awe . . . how she was posing—and just automatically went to the camera when they were calling her name. I was just there to witness.

NEDRA TALLEY-ROSS, The Ronettes: We were backstage and Ronnie said, "I haven't seen my sister in twenty years." I was like, *Are you bragging or complaining right now?* And then she did like she was gonna cry, like she was so excited. That's bullshit. . . . Ronnie should have cried a bucket.

TOYIN DONG, Estelle Bennett's daughter: She had that moment. She really enjoyed herself—she snapped right into it. Swear to God. Never. That was, that's the first time I saw Estelle Bennett, the Ronette. She loved it.

NEDRA TALLEY-ROSS, The Ronettes: Estelle went to stay with my dad in New York and my dad was saying, "She's not eating, she won't eat anything." And I said, "Well, don't yell at her to eat. If she can't eat, she can't eat, but something's wrong." And I said to Estelle, "Get your medical records and you come to Virginia. I have a very good Jewish doctor. He's very attentive, he loves me, we love him. He'll find out what's the matter."

She said, "Okay." I got the schedule for the bus because she wouldn't want to fly, but she can take the bus because she could get around the subway system—she's a New Yorker.

So I said, "You're going to get an express to Virginia—don't get off. They will have a bathroom on there." I said, "Don't get off even if anything happens, you just stay on that bus, because I'm going to be at the door."

When the bus came and the door opened, everybody came out, but Estelle didn't come out. So I went in, I looked for her—she wasn't there, she didn't get on. So they said, "Well, maybe she missed it and she'll get the next bus a few hours later." And I came back for that bus, but she didn't get off that one either.

About two days later, Toyin called and said that her mother was dead. I was screaming. I realized how much we had lived our lives . . . [*crying*] so much together. You slept together, you ate together, you dressed together, you did your shows *together*—all these things and you don't think that someone . . . it wasn't the mental sickness, it was just the sickness in her body which turned out to be cancer.

TOYIN DONG, Estelle Bennett's daughter: The crazy thing is, the ironic thing—her church—the pastor came to talk at my mother's funeral and said the most amazing things about her. I thought she was just *going* to the soup kitchen there, but she was also *serving* at this soup kitchen, which is crazy, because I just knew she needed the food there. But she was, like, always there and he said that she was always coming to volunteer. I was like, *Wait, what? How could she be volunteering?* Testament.

NEDRA TALLEY-ROSS, The Ronettes: Had she not been sick, it had been a whole 'nother outcome for her. And when I'd speak to Toyin about it, I said, "Your mother got mental illness later, but she . . . she stood out in a way that even Ronnie and I didn't stand out."

TOYIN DONG, Estelle Bennett's daughter: She lost everything, including her only daughter. That's why I get to tell her story—because she deserves to be respected on so many levels. She survived and she lived in the streets. Who knows what happened to her.

People, they love The Ronettes. They don't know.

AUTHORS' NOTE: Ronnie Spector passed away on January 12, 2022, after a short battle with cancer, at the age of seventy-eight, at her home in Danbury, Connecticut. Despite attempts by Phil Spector to stop her from performing The Ronettes' material, she revived her career and as recently as January 2022, The Ronettes' hit "Sleigh Ride" appeared in Billboard's Top 10.

NEDRA TALLEY-ROSS, The Ronettes: You know, when Ronnie died this time—it's not that she died before; I caught myself [*laughing*]—I was putting makeup—lipstick—on today in the bathroom and had a thought, *This is the first time that I am putting my lipstick on alone*—that *Estelle and Ronnie are both gone, and not on earth, here, anymore with me*. Because the reality is, I only saw the three of us, all the time. We put our makeup on, we sat next to each other, we didn't even, like, smoke individually—because that many cigarettes, it would make the dressing room too smoky. So we would share a cigarette—take a puff, take a puff, put it back on the ashtray. In my memory, it's just the three of us. I could not breathe when I woke up in the morning after Ronnie died, thinking, *She's dead—no more for this earth*. And then I remembered—we were baptized together. So you know, we'll be okay, and I won't need to bring anything up in heaven.

Acknowledgments

We would like to thank first and foremost the women of the girl groups for sharing their stories. We are honored to have spoken to every person interviewed for this book and are humbled by the time each person took to teach us about their lives. Thank you to *each* and *every one* of you: Barbara "Bibs" Allbut, Phyllis "Jiggs" Allbut, Katherine Anderson, Joshie Jo Armstead, Brooks Arthur, Rosalind Ashford, Bertha Barbee, Norma Barbee, Jeff Barry, Jon "Bowzer" Bauman, Annette Beard, Peter Benjaminson, Ginger Bianco, Jerry Blavat, Jean Bouldin, Janie Bradford, La La Brooks, Artie Butler, Susan Collins, Dawn Craig, Judy Craig, Ron Dante, Joey Dee, Louvain Demps, Toyin Dong, Richard Dubin, Barbara English, Bob Feldman, Bob George, Cal Gill, Millie Gill, Myrna Giraud, Whoopi Goldberg, Linda Goldner-Perry, Sonia Goring Wilson, Richard Gottehrer, Stanley Greenberg, Steve Guarnori, Sylvia Hammond, Barbara Harris, Barbara Ann Hawkins, Rosa Lee Hawkins, Ula Hedwig, Jackie Hicks, Brian Holland, Chip Hurd, Fanita James, Bobby Jay, Billy Joel, David Johansen, Gloria Jones, Artie Kaplan, Dee Dee Kenniebrew, Margie Latzko, Beverly Lee, Nanette Licari, Sandy Linzer, Darlene Love, Dianne Lynton, Phil Margo, Ernie Martinelli, Johnny Mathis, Trudy McCartney, Melanie Mintz, June Monteiro, Louise Murray, Andrew Loog Oldham, Renee Pappas, Allan Pepper, Emma Pought, Lois Powell, Tony Powers, Denny Randell, Genya Ravan, Martha Reeves, Brenda Reid, Artie Ripp, Barbara Rose, Margaret Ross, Scott Ross, Peggy Santiglia, Marvin Schlachter, Neil Sedaka, Paul Shaffer, Jay Siegel, Mickey Stevenson, Mike Stoller, Nedra Talley-Ross, Charlie Thomas, Steve Tyrell, Billy Vera, Lillian Walker-Moss, Beverly Warren, Laura

Weiner, Vicki Wickham, Otis Williams, Sylvia Williams, Mary Wilson, and Toni Wine.

Thank you to our agent Alex Kane at WME and our editor Ben Schafer and the whole team at Hachette Books, who helped bring this book to fruition.

A special thank-you must be said to La La Brooks of The Crystals. Without having met La La Brooks, we would never have understood how little the women of the girl groups have been recognized by greater music culture at large. Thank you, La La Brooks, for your inimitable voice and spirit.

This book would not exist without the generosity of these friends of the project—we are forever in your debt. Thank you for sharing expertise, connecting us with subjects, lending interviews, and believing in this project from start to finish: Eric Adolfsen, Fran Agnone, Mariah Balaban, Lynn Grossman and Bob Balaban, John Clemente, Sam Cullman, Krista Delosreyes, Carrie Dessertine, Jim DiGiovanni, Carlton DeWoody, Cheryl Duncan, Alan Felsenthal, Susan English, Paul Errante, Alison Fensterstock, Jordan Galland, Elon Green, Cory Henson and Saul Choza, Carrie Imberman, Dana Jaasund, Fatima Jones, Austin Kilham, London King, Bella Klein, Kate and Carol Klenfner, Sarah Kohn, Erin Katzen Leslie, Madeline Mackenzie, Jon Mallow, Mirabelle Marden, Camille Moitoret, Denyse Montegut, Anne Marie Mustafa, Dan Novak, Janet Oseroff, Renee Pappas, Allan Pepper, Adrienne Raphael, Doug Richter, Barbara Rose, Ryan Ross, Kristen Spielkamp, Jill Sternheimer, Hillary, Carlyn, and Dr. Timothy Tandrow, Marc Taylor, Amber and Jamie Vanderbilt, Adam Voith, Marguerite Wade, Freya Wallace, Jenny Wallack, David Wasserman and Joshua Woltermann.

The deepest gratitude to our families for their unwavering support and love of both us and the book: Bonnie Burnham and Jack Flam, Ninh Doan, Ben Liebowitz and Erin Diers, and Samuel, Gail, and William Grossman.

Since we began this project in 2019, we have lost many friends and want to especially honor them; thank you all for the music: Bibs Allbut, Brooks Arthur, Jerry Blavat, Bertha Barbee, Sarah Dash, Lamont Dozier, Rosa Lee Hawkins, Phil Margo, Ronnie Spector, Charlie Thomas, Lillian Walker-Moss, Mary Wilson, and Wanda Young-Rogers.

And lastly, we would like to thank Sara, Rebekah, and Philip Maysles for introducing us.

Bibliography

Because many of the figures in this book passed away before the project was undertaken, we are especially grateful to those who gave us permission to use their texts in our book: the Apollo's Education Programs, Peter Benjaminson, Steve Bergsman, Hermione Hoby, Richard Podolsky, Sheila Weller, and Stephanie Bennett and Christian John Wikane.

Alston, Barbara Ann. 2007. *There's No Other*. Frederick, MD: America Star Books.

"Apollo Live Wire: She's a Rebel: A Tribute to the Girl Groups of the 50s, 60s, and 70s." 2019. Moderated by Christian John Wikane. Produced by Apollo Education, November 14, 2019. https://issuu.com/apolloeducation/docs/program_she_s_a_rebel_book_order_updated_2.

Ballard, Maxine "Precious." 2007. *The True Story of Florence Ballard*. Detroit: Precious4Max, Inc.

Benjaminson, Peter. 1979. *The Story of Motown*. New York: Random House.

———. 2007. *The Lost Supreme: The Life of Dreamgirl Florence Ballard*. Chicago: Chicago Review Press.

Betrock, Alan. 1982. *Girl Groups: The Story of a Sound*. New York: Delilah Books/Putnam Publishing.

Clemente, John. 2013. *Girl Groups: Fabulous Females Who Rocked the World*. Bloomington, IN: AuthorHouse.

Cohn, Nik. 1970. *Awopbopaloobop Alopbamboom: The Golden Age of Rock*. Glasgow: HarperCollins.

Cosgrove, Stuart. 2016. *Detroit 67: The Year That Changed Soul*. Edinburgh: Polygon.

Emerson, Ken. 2006. *Always Magic in the Air: The Bomp and Brilliance of the Brill Building Era*. New York: Penguin Books.

Fletcher, Tony. 2009. *All Hopped Up and Ready to Go: Music from the Streets of New York 1927–77*. New York: W. W. Norton.

George, Nelson. 2007. *Where Did Our Love Go?: The Rise and Fall of the Motown Sound*. Champaign: University of Illinois Press.

Girl Groups: Story of a Sound. MGM/UA home video presentation of 1983 Delilah Films production. [VHS tape.]

Goffin, Louise, and Paul Zollo. 2019. "Episode 21. Carole King, Part 1." *Great Song Adventure* (podcast). http://thegreatsongadventure.com/episode-21-carole-king-part-1/.

Gordy, Berry. 1994. *To Be Loved: Music, the Magic, the Memories of Motown*. New York: Warner Books.

Greene, Andy. 2009. "Neil Diamond Remembers Songwriter Ellie Greenwich." *Rolling Stone*, August 31, 2009. https://www.rollingstone.com/music/music-news/neil-diamond-remembers-songwriter-ellie-greenwich-243543/.

Greenwich, Ellie. n.d. Interview by Charlotte Greig. Spectropop. https://spectropop.com/EllieGreenwich2/.

Gross, Terry. 1986. "Writing Pop Hits for 60s Stars." *Fresh Air*, WHYY, June 10, 1986. https://freshairarchive.org/segments/writing-pop-hits-60s-stars.

———. 2017. "Singer Ronnie Spector." *Fresh Air*, WHYY, February 17, 2017. https://freshairarchive.org/segments/singer-ronnie-spector.

Grow, Kory. 2016. "Ronnie Spector on Keith Richards, David Bowie and Life After Phil." *Rolling Stone*, April 14, 2016. https://www.rollingstone.com/music/music-news/ronnie-spector-on-keith-richards-david-bowie-and-life-after-phil-181599/.

Guarnori, Stephen. 2016. *Scepter Wand Forever!* Haywards Heath, UK: Stephen Guarnori.

Haig, Diana. 1992. *Capricorn Records Presents: The Scepter Records Story*. [Liner notes.] Nashville, TN: Capricorn Records.

Harvey, Chris. 2022. "Ronnie Spector in 2019: 'MeToo Is Now, but I've Been Living It My Whole Life.'" *Sunday Telegraph* (London), January 13, 2022. https://www.telegraph.co.uk/music/artists/ronnie-spector-interview-metoo-now-living-whole-life/.

Hawkins, Rosa, and Steve Bergsman. 2021. *Chapel of Love: The Story of New Orleans Girl Group the Dixie Cups*. Jackson: University Press of Mississippi.

Hitmakers: The Teens Who Stole Pop Music. Directed by Morgan Neville. Produced by Peter Jones. Aired July 29, 2004, A&E's *Biography*.

Hoby, Hermione. 2014. "Ronnie Spector Interview: 'The More Phil Tried to Destroy Me, the Stronger I Got.'" *Sunday Telegraph* (London), March

6, 2014. https://www.telegraph.co.uk/culture/music/rockandpopfeatures/10676805/Ronnie-Spector-interview-The-more-Phil-tried-to-destroy-me-the-stronger-I-got.html.

Holland, Eddie, Brian Holland, and Dave Thompson. 2021. *Come and Get These Memories: The Genius of Holland–Dozier–Holland, Motown's Incomparable Songwriters*. London: Omnibus Press.

Horner, Charlie, Val Shively, and Pamela Horner. 2016. "The Musical Legacy of Richard Barrett." *Echoes of the Past*. http://classicurbanharmony.net/wp-content/uploads/2016/02/Richard-Barretts-Musical-Legacy-Part-1-The-Valentines.pdf.

"Interview: Rex Garvin." 2011. Othersounds.com. January 31, 2011. http://othersounds.com/interview-rex-garvin/. [Site is no longer functioning.]

Jackson, John A. 1999. *American Bandstand: Dick Clark and the Making of a Rock 'n' Roll Empire*. New York: Oxford University Press.

King, Carole. 2020. *A Natural Woman: A Memoir*. New York: Grand Central Publishing.

LaBelle, Patti. 1997. *Don't Block the Blessings: Revelations of a Lifetime*. Boston: Little, Brown.

Leiber, Jerry, and Mike Stoller. 2009. *Hound Dog: The Leiber and Stoller Autobiography*. New York: Simon & Schuster.

Linna, Miriam. 2006. "Good-Bad, but Not Evil." Norton Records. https://web.archive.org/web/20110617083155/http://www.nortonrecords.com/maryweiss/index.php.

Love, Darlene. 2013. *My Name Is Love*. New York: William Morrow & Company.

Marcus, Greil. 1975. "Girl Groups: How the Other Half Lived." *Village Voice*, September 8, 1975. https://www.villagevoice.com/2020/11/17/girl-groups-how-the-other-half-lived.

Martin, Michael. 2007. "The Leader of the Pack Is Back." *New York Magazine*, February 22, 2007. https://nymag.com/arts/popmusic/profiles/28500/.

Mayer, Ira. 1974. "Ronnie Spector Returns." *Record World*, May 18, 1974.

NJ Hall of Fame. 2014. "The Shirelles—7th Annual NJ Hall of Fame Induction Ceremony." YouTube video, 6:01, November 13, 2014. https://www.youtube.com/watch?v=VBfwqzdTVi0.

"Nona Hendryx Talks to Randall Pinkston." 2015. Aljazeera.com, October 30, 2015. http://america.aljazeera.com/watch/shows/talk-to-al-jazeera/articles/2015/10/30/nona-hendryx-talks-to-randall-pinkston.html.

Oldham, Andrew Loog. 2014. *Stone Free*. Vancouver, BC: Because Entertainment.

Podolsky, Rich. 2012. *Don Kirshner: The Man with the Golden Ear—How He Changed the Face of Rock and Roll*. Milwaukee: Hal Leonard.

Ponderosa Stomp. 2022. "Ronnie Spector Oral History at the 2010 Ponderosa Stomp Music History Conference." YouTube video, 40:34, January 12, 2022. https://www.youtube.com/watch?v=6HRx8jcunCc.

Punkcast. 2009. "Tony Fletcher & Arlene Smith—All Hopped Up and Ready to Go." YouTube video, 1:15:38, November 13, 2009, published December 2, 2009. https://www.youtube.com/watch?v=1EFaQo3icqs.

Reeves, Martha, and Mark Bego. 1995. *Dancing in the Street: Confessions of a Motown Diva*. New York: Hyperion.

Ribowsky, Mark. 1989. *He's a Rebel: Phil Spector—Rock and Roll's Legendary Producer*. New York: Cooper Square Press.

Richards, Keith. 2011. *Life*. Oxford: Weidenfeld & Nicolson.

Robinson, Smokey. 1989. *Smokey: Inside My Life*. New York: McGraw-Hill.

Ross, Diana. 1993. *Secrets of a Sparrow*. New York: Villard Books.

Ross, Scott, with John Sherrill and Elizabeth Sherrill. 1976. *Scott Free*. Grand Rapids, MI: Chosen Books.

Selvin, Joel. 2015. *Here Comes the Night: The Dark Soul of Bert Berns and the Dirty Business of Rhythm and Blues*. Berkeley, CA: Counterpoint.

Simpson, Dave. 2015. "How We Made the Ronettes' Be My Baby." *The Guardian*, November 17, 2015. https://www.theguardian.com/culture/2015/nov/17/how-we-made-the-ronettes-be-my-baby-ronnie-spector-phil.

Smith, Joe. 1988. *Off the Record: An Oral History of Popular Music*. New York: Warner Books.

Spector, Ronnie. 1990. *Be My Baby: How I Survived Mascara, Miniskirts, and Madness, or My Life as a Fabulous Ronette*. New York: Harmony.

Sullivan, Caroline. 2014. "Ronnie Spector: 'When I Hear Applause, It's like I'm Having an Orgasm.'" *The Guardian*, April 17, 2014. https://www.theguardian.com/culture/2014/apr/17/ronnie-spector-ronettes-applause-orgasm-interview.

Taylor, Marc. 2004. *The Original Marvelettes: Motown's Mystery Girl Group*. Jamaica, NY: Aloiv Publishing Company.

———. 2008. "Simply Supreme: Cindy Birdsong." *A Touch of Classic Soul* 2(4).

———. 2009. "Martha & The Vandellas' Betty Kelley." *A Touch of Classic Soul* 4(3).

———. 2009. "The Shirelles: Baby It's You." *A Touch of Classic Soul* 4(5).

Turner, Reather Dixon. n.d. "Memories of The Bobbettes." Marv Goldberg's Yesterday's Memories Rhythm & Blues Party (blog). https://www.uncamarvy.com/Bobbettes/bobbettes2.html.

Ward, Ed. 2017. *The History of Rock & Roll, Volume 1: 1920–1963*. New York: St. Martin's Press.

Weller, Sheila. 2009. *Girls Like Us: Carole King, Joni Mitchell, Carly Simon—and the Journey of a Generation*. London: Ebury Press.

Whitall, Susan. 1999. *Women of Motown: An Oral History*. Edited by Dave Marsh. New York: Avon Books.

White, Renée Minus. 2016. *Maybe: My Memoir (an Original Member of the Chantels)*. Pittsburgh, PA: Rosedog Books.

Wikane, Christian John. 2020. "Cosmic Dust and Interstellar Grooves: An Interview with Nona Hendryx." PopMatters, May 1, 2020. https://www.popmatters.com/nona-hendryx-2020-interview-2645881559.html.

Wilson, Mary, and Patricia Romanowski. 1987. *Dreamgirl: My Life as a Supreme*. New York: St. Martin's Press.

Wright, Vickie, Louvain Demps, and Marlene Barrow-Tate. 2007. *Motown from the Background*. New Romney, UK: Bank House Books.

Index